To Desire Differently

SANDY FLITTERMAN-LEWIS

To Desire Differently

Feminism and the French Cinema

University of Illinois Press
Urbana and Chicago

For my parents,
Anita and Phil Weisbaum
and to the memory of my Dad,
David Flitterman (1917–88)

Society for Cinema Studies annual dissertation award winner.

Publication of this work was supported in part by
a grant from the Andrew W. Mellon Foundation.

Illini Books edition, 1990

Cover photo: *La Maternelle* (Marie Epstein and Jean Benoit-Levy,
1933). Chapters 7 and 10 are revised versions of articles published
in *Enclitic*, 5:2/6:1 (Fall 1981/Spring 1982) and 7:2 (Fall 1983)
respectively. Portions of Chapter 4 appeared in somewhat different
form in *Wide Angle* vol. 6, no. 3 (1984) and in " 'Poetry of the
Unconscious': Circuits of Desire in Two Films by Germaine Dulac,"
in *French Film: Texts and Contexts* (London: Routledge, Chapman and
Hall, 1990).

Library of Congress Cataloging-in-Publication Data

Flitterman-Lewis, Sandy, 1946-
    To desire differently : feminism and the French cinema / Sandy
Flitterman-Lewis
        p. cm.
    Originally presented as the author's thesis (Ph.D.—University of
California, Berkeley).
    Bibliography: p.
    Includes index.
    ISBN 0-252-01654-8 (cloth : alk. paper). ISBN 0-252-06086-5 (paper : alk.
paper).
    1. Feminism and motion pictures. 2. Motion pictures—France.
I. Title.
PN1995.6.W6F6 1990
791.43'082—dc20   89-31664
                                                                       CIP

Contents

Acknowledgments

IN ORDER TO SITUATE this project historically, let me first trace a short personal history. My interests in feminism and film theory coincided with my graduate studies at a time when feminist approaches to both film and literature were in the process of being formulated. In fact, my interest in feminist analysis of cultural forms grew out of my graduate work in comparative literature at the University of California at Berkeley. As fascinating and compelling to me as the study of the traditional literary canon was, I began to realize that there were other modes of inquiry, other textual voices that spoke profoundly of (for want of a better term) "women's experience." At the same time, I became actively involved in editing two journals that saw as their project the feminist analysis of the cinema. In 1973, I was an associate editor of *Women and Film*, the first magazine devoted specifically and entirely to the concerns of its title. It was there that I published my first article of feminist film criticism, a biographical portrait of Germaine Dulac. In 1974, I, along with three other women, founded *Camera Obscura: A Journal of Feminism and Film Theory*, and I worked with the journal until 1978. We conceived of our activity as a theoretical intervention in an area that had somewhat complacently assumed that the simple conjunction of the words *women* and *film* would automatically imply a feminist field of inquiry. It was the aim of *Camera Obscura* to provide a critical investigation and theoretical reflection on the construction and representation of gender, not only in the cinema, but in other cultural forms as well. As I stated in the inaugural editorial, "It is important to know where to locate ideology and patriarchy within the mode of representation in order to intervene and transform society, to define a praxis for change. Crucial to the feminist struggle is an awareness that any theory of how to change consciousness requires a notion of how consciousness is formed, of what change is, and how it occurs." This is a concern that has guided all of my writing on the cinema, and one which suggests the profound social implications of any feminist-theoretical enterprise.

The original form of this book was as a Ph.D. dissertation for the Department of Comparative Literature at the University of California at Berkeley. It received the first dissertation award given by the Society for Cinema Studies, and I am deeply grateful to the members of the committee—E. Ann Kaplan, Douglas Gomery, and Brian Henderson—for selecting me for the prize and for their helpful comments regarding revisions. Because part of the award was a contract with the University of Illinois Press, the problem of revision from thesis to book immediately emerged; three relatively separate monographs needed to be joined into an internally coherent argument about feminine authorship. The first step, a title, came easily, for when I thought of *To Desire Differently* in early 1985, it seemed to suggest exactly how the connections could be made between the work of Germaine Dulac, Marie Epstein, and Agnès Varda. The rest, as time suggests, was a little more difficult, and the process of revision was complicated by the appearance of significant new material (in the case of Dulac), access to more films (in the case of Epstein), and continued productivity which forced me to revise my earlier conclusions (in the case of Varda).

I am indebted to my dissertation director, Bertrand Augst, not only for his energy and originality, which have been a constant inspiration to me, but also for his sustained attention to my project both in its thesis stage, and more recently, as a book. When I was working on the thesis, a Regents' Fellowship from the University of California Regents partially funded my work. I was also extremely fortunate to have the opportunity to do part of my research while at the Centre Universitaire Américain du Cinéma et de la Critique à Paris, where the environment for film scholarship is unusually productive and rewarding, and where I was able to take courses with Christian Metz, Raymond Bellour, and Jacques Aumont, among others. Also during the dissertation stage, several people made archival and research materials available to me: Bernard Eisenschitz, Jonathan Rosenbaum, Richard Abel, Ester Carla de Miro, Reynold Humphries, Dugald Williamson, and Carlos Clarens. I am also grateful to Charles Silver of the Museum of Modern Art and Ann Harris of the Cinema Studies Department at New York University, both of whom were especially helpful in numerous ways.

Carol Pippolo also provided invaluable assistance at the dissertation stage.

The beginning of the transposition process from dissertation to book was greatly eased by the insightful and useful comments provided by several readers of the manuscript: Richard Abel, Dudley Andrew, Alan Williams, Ernest Callenbach, and Michael Silverman. Financial assistance came in the form of a Rutgers University Research Council Summer Fellowship, and time for writing was also provided by Rutgers through a Faculty Academic Study Program leave; I am extremely grateful to Rutgers for both. To Stephanie Holm (of International Film Exchange, Ltd.), Albert Gabriel Nigrin, and Patricia Santoro I am thankful for assistance with research materials, and to Philip Lewis I owe a special thanks. When it came to illustrations, a number of people were extremely helpful: Cathy Holter and Ann Harris of the NYU Cinema Studies Department, Julio Fierro of Ben-Ness Photo Studio, David Speer of the International Center for Photography, Bertrand Augst, Ron and Howard Mandelbaum of Photofest, Mary Corliss and Terry Geesken of the Museum of Modern Art, Stephanie Holm of International Film Exchange and Varda's production company, Ciné-Tamaris.

Deborah Linderman, Elissa Greenwald, and Lynn Joyrich gave me considerable and much-appreciated help on portions of the manuscript through their incisive comments, suggestions, and critiques. Throughout all of this, Joan Copjec has been an inspiring source of intellectual and emotional support, and I am truly grateful for our many working conversations. I am grateful, too, to my colleague, Miriam Hansen, whose generous and perceptive reading of the entire manuscript provided me with not only suggestive critical commentary but with the benefit of her excellent scholarship as well. There are a number of friends who, through encouragement and interest in this project, helped me focus my thinking and shape my arguments: Andrea Slane, Kathryn Kalinak, Maria Marewski, Susan Ellis Wolf, John McClure, Ibex and Emo Bumpas, David King and Sharon Flitterman-King.

Of course the opportunity to interview both Marie Epstein and Agnès Varda has been invaluable, not only for the obvious material reasons, but also for the enduring energy and inspiration that each one of them generates. Marie Epstein was exceedingly helpful and gracious, and her shrewd observations about a wide range of topics have continued to be a source of great interest to me. Agnès Varda generously provided me with extensive documentation of her work, and with illustrations as well, and her enthusiastic support of my project (in both its dissertation and its book form) has been a great encouragement.

At the University of Illinois Press, Lawrence Malley combined patience with enthusiasm and sustained a supportive interest in the project that was essential to its completion. Mary Giles provided valuable assistance in copyediting and Lyall Bush deserves thanks as well. Linda McKenna's contribution is immeasurable, for she confidently managed the word-processing for an author still unable to confront a computer and thus to enter the modern age; at times she did the impossible under pressure.

There are ways too numerous to mention in which my husband, Joel Lewis, provided help, not the least of which was having the foresight to buy an air-conditioner for the summer of '88. His contribution to this work is inestimable, for which I owe him endless thanks.

ONE

Introduction

[T]he cinematic apparatus, as a social technology that transcends the work of individual directors, was and is fully compromised in the ideology of vision and sexual difference founded on woman as image, spectacle, object and *locus* of sexuality.
—Teresa De Lauretis, *Alice Doesn't*

The American cinema is entirely dependent, as is psychoanalysis, on a system of representation in which the woman occupies a central place only to the extent that it's a place assigned to her by the logic of masculine desire.
—Raymond Bellour, *Camera Obscura* 3/4

AN ASTONISHINGLY BEAUTIFUL YOUNG WOMAN sits in a projection room, gazing in rapt fascination at her first performance in a film. As she smiles, bobbed hair framing her luminous face like a dark helmet, she listens to the words of her song: "If they say I'm Venus, I'm flattered . . . but don't be jealous. I have only one love, that's you." Sitting in the next seat, her male companion and agent shares her delighted absorption in the image. Outside in the hallway, her estranged husband clutches a gun, making his way slowly toward the door. When he reaches the room, he enters and shoots her as we—the viewers of *this* scene—see only the startled expression in her eyes. Then, one powerfully emblematic shot condenses the woman's face (frozen in profile close-up in the foreground) and her projected image (alive on the screen in the background), as her singing continues in the film-within-a-film and on the soundtrack.

This is the astounding final sequence of *Prix de beauté,* an early French sound film made in 1930 and directed by Augusto Genina.[1] Essentially a film about Louise Brooks's face, it offers a striking concretization of the critical intersection of representation and desire in the woman's screen-image. Ever since Laura Mulvey's landmark article of feminist film theory,[2] the image of the woman in mainstream commercial cinema has been understood as a contradictory textual disturbance which each film must work to resolve. The female figure, always and inevitably defined in terms of sexuality, is seen as the structural mainspring—the very site of desire—of conventional cinematic narrative. According to the lines traced out by Mulvey, the resolution of this crisis evoked by the woman's image is most often achieved in one of two ways—ways that outline the available representations for the woman in dominant cinema: The female figure is either fetishized in the luminous isolation of an objectifying image, or made subject to the abusive mastery of some form of sadistic domination through the narrative. The ending of *Prix de beauté* achieves a kind of apotheosis of the woman's cinematic image, then, by condensing these two traditional options into a single, fantasmatic, representation.

But is our fate as women—our representations in the dominant cultural institution of our time—so completely bound to such structures of desire? What of the question of *feminist* cinema, an alternative cinematic practice which speaks (of) *our* desire? Are there other conceptions of desire, ways of formulating different terms? The work of film theory[3] has shown that Hollywood cinema produces and reproduces a particular logic of desire, a logic which is masculine, for it is always the hero who stabilizes his desire in relation to the (image of the) woman. Can a voice which speaks through an apparatus so fundamentally structured according to this masculine logic say anything of—and in—the feminine? And, given that psychoanalysis describes the production of a subjectivity which is irrefutably male, what kinds of psychoanalytic models can we apply when it is precisely *female* desire that feminist films turn on, articulate? Do the films that form the body of "feminist cinema" say something different, speak a different desire, desire in difference? In short, does feminist cinema posit a way *to desire differently?*

As the title of this book implies, in feminist cinema there is already a way of desiring—in difference—that is "spoken" in feminist films. It is not simply a matter of "learning" to speak a new language, nor of deploying new cinematic strategies, but of a desiring process itself that emerges from a locus of difference. "Desiring differently" posits another logic (logic of an Other?) whose terms and positions are precisely—feminine. For the woman critic, the definition of this "feminine" is at the core of the critical enterprise. In defining an "alternative language of desire" in women's cinema, we must account for the specific and pervasive operations of the dominant apparatus of Hollywood. It is only by understanding how "femininity" is constructed and represented in patriarchy that we can avoid the pitfalls of a traditional feminist criticism which seeks to discover a preexisting "feminine sensibility" as the specific essential property of women. Likewise, it is only through a reexamination of the prescriptive categories of "female experience" and "identity," with their problematic criteria of authenticity, that we can understand how notions of lived experience are themselves socially constructed and fully implicated in structures of desire. Only then can we define resistance in *textual* terms and begin to delimit the parameters of a truly alternative practice of feminist cinema.

Thus a feminist cinema must necessarily conceive its challenge textually, and this implies an understanding of the entire cinematic apparatus—its operations, its functioning, and its specific determinations for figuring female sexuality. This apparatus is designed to produce and maintain a fascinating hold on its spectator by mobilizing pleasure—the unconscious desire of the subject—through interlocking systems of narrativity, continuity, point of view, and identification. But this is not simply an individualized and self-contained process. In emphasizing the *social* inscription of the cinema as an institution, Christian Metz has described what he calls the "dual kinship" between the psychic life of the spectator and the financial or industrial mechanisms of the cinema.

> The cinematic institution is not just the cinema industry (which works to fill cinemas, not to empty them). It is also the mental machinery—another industry—which spectators 'accustomed to the cinema' have internalized historically, and which has adapted them to the consumption of films. (The institution is outside us and inside us, indistinctly collective and intimate, sociological and psychoanalytic, just as the general prohibition of incest has as its individual corollary the Oedipus complex . . . or perhaps . . . different psychical configurations which . . . *imprint* the institution in us in their own way.) The second machine, ie, the social regulation of the spectator's metapsychology, like the first, has as its function to set up good object relations with films . . . the cinema is attended out of desire, not reluctance . . . [T]he institution as a whole has filmic pleasure alone as its aim.[4]

The cinema's immediate and encompassing establishment as a powerful social institution is thus linked to the manner in which every film inscribes—in a pleasurable form that demands repeated reenactment—very deep and globally structuring processes of the human psyche. But because these processes emphatically hinge on sexual difference (for the power of psychoanalysis lies precisely in its ability to describe how the small human being comes to establish a *gendered* position and identity within the network of social relations that constitutes culture), such a psychoanalytic notion of the cinematic apparatus cannot be without important consequences for feminists. For if all cinema is seen as a fantasmatic production which mobilizes primary processes in the circulation of desire, and if film-viewing itself is posited as an erotic, voyeuristic activity, then it is always the woman-image— existing precisely to be looked at and to be desired—which is perpetually offered to the male spectator-consumer who possesses the gaze. The cinematic apparatus structures and constructs its spectator's relationship to the screen image along the psychoanalytic modalities of fantasy, the scopic drive, fetishism, narcissism and identification, while the image of the woman is continually evoked as the impossible fantasm through which the spectator's desire is activated and constantly condensed, displaced, and transformed onto new objects. The theory of the apparatus itself is therefore bound to gender hierarchies and to a sexual economy of vision that both produces and maintains specific definitions and conventions of female sexuality.

Yet, even at the very inception of the Hollywood machine—and the mode of narrative fiction film that it implies—alternative models were being conceived by European and women filmmakers alike. This effort to develop a counter-discourse, either at the margins or from within the center of the structure itself, transcends distinctions of period and genre, and characterizes the very earliest efforts by French filmmakers to conceive of challenges to dominant cinematic representations from abroad. *Prix de beauté* is highly emblematic of the male-dominated cinema as it evolved, and as such it represents the contradictions of feminine representation inherent in the cinema as an apparatus and as an institution. The work of altering and reversing that frozen image was begun very early in France in the 1920s (particularly by Germaine Dulac), carried through the 1930s (and exemplified by Marie Epstein), and continued in contemporary filmmaking (most significantly by Agnès Varda). All of these attempts to originate a different representation of the woman—to evolve a feminine cinematic discourse—are best understood against the background of a theoretical elaboration of the cinematic institution. The following discussion of feminist film theory is therefore intended as a preamble to the analyses of Dulac, Epstein, and Varda that comprise the major portion of this book.

Femininity and Spectatorship

In order to gain insight into the particular cultural function of the female image, feminism has looked to contemporary theories of film spectatorship and the cinematic apparatus. The impact of Mulvey's founding article (which subsequent rereadings have extended and clarified) on the way that feminists have conceptualized the issue of spectatorship cannot be overestimated. Mulvey was the first to posit the fact of sexual differentiation in systems of cinematic fascination and visual pleasure. While film theory had already established that film spectatorship itself was a textual construction—that cinema viewers, engaged in relations of pleasure and meaning, were both constructed and produced as subjects in the very process of watching a film— this was not, prior to 1975, articulated specifically in terms of sexual difference. Mulvey's analysis suggests that visual pleasure in narrative cinema in fact hinges on the representation of the figure of the woman; she thus posits a "dominant polarity of vision"[5] in which the dichotomy of subject and object is conceived along the axis of gender. Her critique of the patriarchal system of representation is based on the fact that the division between active/looking, passive/looked-at is always delineated in terms of masculine and feminine positions: masculinity confers the power of the gaze and control over narrative events, while femininity inevitably consigns the woman to a position as object of desire. The subject of both narrative and spectacle, then, is male, while the object of both is always defined as female. For Mulvey, cinematic modes of looking and narrative structure invariably "create a gaze, a world, and an object; thereby producing an illusion cut to the measure of desire";[6] cinema, that is, creates its illusions in accordance with an assumed notion of masculine passion.

When she turns to identification, Mulvey asserts that "the look" in traditional cinema is structured in such a way that the spectator is made to identify with the male protagonist in the narrative. A relay of three articulated trajectories of vision (from the camera to the pro-filmic event, between characters within the diegesis, and from spectator to screen) makes the male character's control over the female object on the screen coincide with the spectator's power of vision over the images displayed. As such, Mulvey maintains that in dominant narrative cinema there is always "a 'masculinization' of the spectator position regardless of the actual sex (or possible deviance) of any real live movie-goer."[7] Modes of cinematic identification inevitably impose a masculine point of view on the spectator, while the powerful erotic impact of the highly coded woman's image always connotes, to use Mulvey's descriptive but awkward phrase, "to-be-looked-at-ness." Doubly empowered by the patriarchal logic of the cinema, then, the position of spectatorship privileges the male as both viewer of the woman-spectacle and as controller of the narrative events.

Yet while Mulvey's critique of patriarchal modes of vision made the issue of sexual difference central to any discussion of spectatorship, her argument in fact reinforces a repressive binarism, one which is locked into conventional associations of masculinity with activity, femininity with passivity. Therefore, where this conception implies the undeniable coincidence of looking with masculine control and mastery, some feminists have urged a more nuanced model of spectatorship which emphasizes flexibility, instability, and heterogeneity, or one that, based on the psychoanalytic concept of fantasy, suggests multiple positions of identification that shift according to variable scenarios of desire. Mulvey herself, in a subsequent article that appeared six years later ("Afterthoughts on 'Visual Pleasure and Narrative Cinema' Inspired by *Duel in the Sun*"), felt the need to consider the problematic possibilities for the female viewer, having implied what is in essence the *impossibility* of female spectatorship in dominant cinema. Her conclusion—that the feminine position of viewing necessarily involves identification with an alien masculine gaze, a psychic borrowing of "transvestite clothes"—perhaps reinforces the dichotomy more than it helps redefine its parameters. Substituting an aesthetics of simple inversion for a viable articulation of feminine subjectivity and vision, Mulvey maintains that the female spectator "temporarily accepts 'masculinization' in memory of her 'active' phase."[8] This, however, should not detract from Mulvey's important contribution: What can be derived from this analysis is a new emphasis on the variability of spectatorial positions in classical cinema, and the absolute necessity of conceptualizing the visual field in terms of gender.

Other attempts to come to terms with female desire and point of view, to complicate the notion of spectatorship with considerations of feminine sexuality, have followed Mulvey's important initial formulations. In her highly interesting and influential work on the female viewing subject, Mary Ann Doane agrees with Mulvey's contention that in classical cinema the woman's point of view—the position of her desire—is regulated and confined by the imperatives of the male psyche. But she argues that Mulvey's model for looking and identification, which constructs an active male maker of meaning and a passive female bearer of meaning, is too limited. For Doane, the female spectator is not outside of subjective or signifying processes at all; rather, she argues, the "woman's film," conceived institutionally for a female audience, implies a contradictory pressure on the psychical mechanisms of voyeurism and fetishism traditionally related to the male viewer. Within Mulvey's framework of masculine address, Doane finds two options for the female viewer: narcissistic identification with the female, object of the spectacle, or "transvestite" identification with the male hero, subject of the action. But it is "precisely this oscillation that demonstrates the *instability* of the woman's position as spectator," a movement which "functions in a rather complex way to deny the woman the space of a reading."[9] For Doane, the immobilized, impossible position of female viewing, emphasized by reiterated scenarios of masochism in the "woman's film," is symptomatic of the ideological crisis instigated by the shift to a form of female address in a cinema which depends so heavily on masculine structures of seeing. However pessimistic this conclusion might be, this exploration into the unstable, problematic constitution of female spectatorship in the cinema—indicative of that same contradiction in the patriarchal construction of the feminine psyche—reveals much that is necessary in rethinking dominant representations toward the formulation of feminist alternatives.

In "Film and the Masquerade: Theorising the Female Spectator,"[10] Doane further explores the possibilities available to the female spectator who finds herself either too close (absorbed in her own image as the object of narcissistic desire) or too far (assuming the alienated distance necessary to identification with the male voyeur) in relation to the classical text. Either position involves the emperilment of female subjectivity—for the woman, a perpetual loss of sexual identity in the act of viewing. But although Doane must conclude that in dominant cinema the woman possesses a gaze which does not see, she stops short of asserting the total impossibility of woman as subject of the gaze. There are still pleasures available to the female viewer—pleasures, for example, in the masquerade's "potential to manufacture a distance from the image which is manipulable, producible, and readable by the woman,"[11] pleasures to be gotten from a liberating dislocation of the feminine gaze. For, as Doane asserts, female spectatorship itself is never *entirely* foreclosed, repressed, or irretrievable; even in its negation it is produced—as is femininity itself—as a position, a position empowered (by the very activity that produces it) to suggest a radical challenge to dominant modes of vision.

From another perspective, Teresa DeLauretis emphasizes the

heterogeneity implicit in the female spectator's position. Finding
limitations with both Mulvey's "masculinization" and Doane's ultimately suggested masochism, she posits a process by which the
woman might identify as both subject *and* object of the Oedipal
scenario continually restaged by dominant cinema. An identification
"with both the subject and the space of the narrative movement,
with the figure of movement and the figure of its closure . . . would
uphold both positionalities of desire, both active and passive aims:
desire for the other, and desire to be desired by the other."[12]
DeLauretis calls for a type of cinema which would engage a play
of tensions between subject and object, narrative and image, disrupting a strict male-female polarity to establish "other positionalities of
desire" that would "address the spectator from an elsewhere of
vision."[13] Thus that very reciprocal subjective process that comes
into effect in film-viewing could potentially provide a variability in
gender definitions, a displacement, reworking, or destabilization of
the Oedipal configuration which structures our relations of meaning
both within and outside of the cinema. Ironically, Mulvey's arguments have led to what can be considered an abandonment of
the notion of sexual *difference*—for this is what is implied by
an overwhelming emphasis on the hegemony of the masculine.
DeLauretis reintroduces sexual difference into the theory of spectatorship by pointing to a cinema that engages "an interruption, a
disalignment of the triple track by which meaning, pleasure, and
narrative are constructed from [Oedipus'] point of view,"[14] and thus
disturbs the fixed sexual dichotomy implied by this structure.

The question, then, invariably comes back to one of pleasure: if
cinematic fascination turns on the mobilization of unconscious desires, what are the possibilities for spectatorial pleasure for women?
Mulvey calls for a break with conventional modes of looking altogether—a disruption of the patriarchal logic of vision might provide
alternative visions, other desires for the feminist text to engage. She
suggests a filmmaking practice which will "free the look of the
camera into its materiality in time and space and the look of the
audience into dialectics, passionate detachment."[15] By providing
textual distancing, moments which foreground the viewing process
and point to the constructed nature of the cinematic world, radical
filmmaking might highlight and therefore problematize the voyeuristic and fetishistic mechanisms involved in film viewing. Doane's
suggestive analyses take up the problematic representation of the
female body itself, the complex relations of body to psyche, positing
a feminist cinema that "speaks" the female body differently, displac-

ing the gaze in an effort which consists "of reworking, rearticulating the specular imaging of woman."[16] Thus the look at the female body would incorporate, in every instance, women's different relation to language and the unconscious—a differential relation existing at the very moment constitutive of femininity. This look of difference would redefine voyeuristic pleasure and fascination in the cinema while still maintaining the importance of the psychoanalytic model. DeLauretis emphasizes the *social* nature of subjectivity: for her, a new feminist cinema implies a new articulation of female subjectivity itself. She maintains that "the project of feminist cinema is not 'to make visible the invisible' . . . or to destroy vision altogether, as it is to construct another (object of) vision and the conditions of visibility for a different social subject."[17] It is in the *relations* of female subjectivity to representation, a reconceptualization of the position of female viewing and femininity itself, that, for her, a truly alternative feminist cinema can be found.

However, it is absolutely crucial for feminist film scholarship to recognize the distinction between the actual *experience* of film-viewing and the *positionality* of film-spectatorship elaborated by film theory. While the former is accessible through sociological methods of study and relies on the empirical evidence of felt impressions (what Freud would call the pre-conscious or subconscious), the latter is a theoretical construct involving unconscious processes—not available to the immediacy of conscious perception—which transcend the particularity of specific individuals. In a debate around precisely this issue of defining the female spectator, E. Ann Kaplan points out the necessity of distinguishing between the historical spectator (the actual person in the audience at the time of the film's release), the hypothetical spectator (the "subject" constructed by the film's textual strategies, its modes of address and its activation of psychoanalytic processes such as scopophilia and identification), and the contemporary female spectator (whose reading of the film might be inflected by a feminist consciousness that suggests alternate interpretations, meanings "against the grain").[18] The related issues of experience and response still remain obstacles to the theorization of feminine viewing subjectivity, for while the psychic and the social are intimately connected in a conception of the unconscious as a social fact, the sociological approach can function quite well without acknowledging psychoanalysis at all. In fact, empirical acts of viewing, in which spectators are equipped to discuss their cognitive reactions to films, have only a contingent relation to those psychic and signifying processes crucial to the cinematic apparatus and central to the textual construction of positions of identification and desire.

One might have an analysis of a character, and even have recourse to an interpretation based on psychoanalytic constructs, but without a *theoretical* conception of the cinema's operations as a global institution this will remain on the level of interpretation alone. It will not elucidate the complex psychic processes whereby we, as viewers, are engaged in relations of desire with the images on the screen. As Teresa DeLauretis notes,

> Film spectators enter the movie theater as either men or women, . . . each person goes to the movies with a semiotic history, personal and social, a series of previous identifications, by which she or he has been somehow engendered.
> And because she and he are historical subjects, continuously engaged in a multiplicity of signifying practices which, like narrative and cinema, rest on and perpetuate the founding distinction of culture— sexual difference— the film's images for them are not neutral objects of a pure perception, but already "significant images."[19]

This conception of spectatorship incorporates elements of the psychic, the semiotic, and the social and thus goes beyond any simple notion of a perceiving individual. Feminist thinking about film must therefore find a way to mediate between the social audience of a film (in which distinctions of class, race, and gender come into play) and the textual subject-positions constructed by it (in which relations of sexuality, subjectivity, and desire are mobilized)—a way to mediate between the social construction of feminine identity and the textual construction of "female" viewing positions. It must emphasize the dynamic process of subject production over the fixed identity of actual viewers, while still maintaining a balance between textual and contextual analyses.[20] Interpretation and spectator-positioning are two very different things. Although an alternative reading might offer "multiple points of view" regarding a particular film, this is not the same as offering a "variety of different subject-positions"; the level of interpretation should not be conflated with that of psychic processes.

In positing the irreducible discontinuity of psychic life signified by the unconscious, Jacqueline Rose further illuminates this important distinction between individual female viewers and textually constructed spectators.[21] Born in division, the formation of the unconscious implies a perpetually disordered subjectivity in which psychic meaning always exceeds conscious understanding and continually frustrates the coherence of a fixed self, a stable sexual identity. Because the human psyche is irremediably split (between conscious and unconscious), the identity of the speaking subject—fully self-present and in command of its meanings—is a fictional, or fantasmatic, construct. The dynamic unconscious is thus the site of an incessantly active play of forces of desire inaccessible to rational discourse, and, as such, acts as a challenge to any form of empiricism based on observation. It is wrong to assume an unproblematic causal relation between psychic life and social reality, or between either of these and their textual representations in film, for this denies the very complexity at the level of psychic conflicts that defines the unconscious as a site of desire.

For this reason, resistance to patriarchal representations is not exactly synonymous with alternative readings, and this is what makes the notion of the unconscious so central to any attempt to theorize the relations of women and the cinema. Without a theory of representation which can account for the construction of sexuality as it is lived in patriarchal culture, a theory capable of describing the unconscious organization of sexuality that preexists—and to a certain extent produces—individual subjects and specific definitions of "masculine" and "feminine," we can have no understanding of how sexual difference itself comes about, of how the inscription of feminine desire in a text is achieved, or indeed, of what the definitions of this "feminine desire" might be. As Elisabeth Cowie has cogently maintained, we must be able "to see 'woman' not as a given, biologically or psychologically, but as a category produced in signifying practices . . . or through signification at the level of the unconscious."[22] The cinema does not simply reflect or reproduce already constituted or given definitions of woman, it is itself a point of production of those definitions. There is thus a reciprocal process of production—of woman as a category and of femininity within a signifying system—that is continually activated by the conjunction "women and the cinema."

The Enunciative Apparatus

Following from the preceding discussion, it is the figure of the woman—woman *as* image—that holds a crucial position in the functioning of the cinema as an institution, for within the context of psychoanalytic film theory, the woman is the pivotal figure which allows the entire machine to operate. According to this theory, film-viewing is structured on a system of voyeuristic pleasure, the viewer's erotic contemplation of the spectacle working in tandem with the desire of the filmmaker as it is figured in the film. Questions of gender, the apparatus, and textual processes crystallize around the concept of enunciation, for it is this concept that defines the spectator as a "construction" of the cinematic machine, and productively demonstrates how the erotic power of "the look" is built into the apparatus itself. For an understanding of precisely how the film-text constructs its spectator (in some sense) independent of the actual viewing experience, feminists have looked to the theory of the cinematic apparatus, since it is this notion of the spectator-text relationship which posits the film as part of a reciprocal, fantasmatic process involving the viewer as desiring subject. This arguably implies a much more subtle notion of the film-text than one that considers it simply as a discrete art object on the screen, for the emphasis is on a dynamic process of desire that circulates between author/filmmaker, screen, and viewer. The conception/production of the film, the viewing-state, and the film-text itself are all seen, in some way, as mobilizing structures of unconscious fantasy.[23] The notion of fantasy is something that permeates all theoretical reflection on the cinema, for fantasy—in its definition as a hallucinatory, wish-fulfilling staging of desire—is at the base of all "stories told in images," in essence, all films and all dreams. French post-Freudians Jean Laplanche and J.-B. Pontalis describe the fantasmatic process thus: "[U]nconscious ideas are organized into phantasies or imaginary scenarios to which the instinct becomes fixated and which may be conceived of as true *mises-en-scène* [performances] of desire."[24] Within this framework, desire is understood not as a relation to a real object, independent of a subject and capable of being satisfied, but as a relation to a representation or unconscious scenario, a relation of the subject which is mobile, variable, and defined by its circulation in an infinite process.

In a sense, then, *both* the viewer (as "producer" of the text) and the film-text itself can be understood as fantasmatic productions of desire. The psychoanalytic conditions of reception that give the cinema its affinities with the dream (the totalizing "fiction-effect," the regime of belief, the state of artificial regression, primary identification with that which engenders vision, secondary identification with fictive positionalities, and the status of hallucinatory perception) all allow the film viewer to have the impression of dreaming the images and situations (the "ideational representatives" of the Freudian dream-work) that appear on the screen. In this way, cinematic discourse can be considered among other fantasy structures in the psychoanalytic field, for the subject in all fantasmatic productions is invariably present, even in those "primal scene" fantasies (or perhaps here most of all) where the subject may be only a perceiving eye, an illicit observer, a hidden voyeur. But while all fantasies originate from the subject who produces them, the cinema necessarily involves a complicated process of slippage between the unconscious desire of the filmmaker activated on the screen and that of the viewer who is made susceptible to having his or her own fantasies interact with those generated by the film. As a consequence of this, the concept of cinematic enunciation emerged as a way to describe both the textual articulation of the filmmaker's desire across the visual field and the spectator's desire as it is engaged by this articulation.

What follows is a brief explanatory digression to outline the operative terminology for the model of cinematic enunciation. Enunciation is a concept, rooted in authorship, which combines linguistics and psychoanalysis in an effort to account for the production of "texts"— literary, cinematic, or fantasmatic. It is conceived as a "productive instance" related to, but not reducible to, the author and the text. Borrowed from structural linguistics, the term *enunciation* is used to emphasize the social inscription of the discursive situation, for, as Emile Benveniste notes, "What characterizes enunciation in general is the emphasis on the discursive relationship with a partner, whether it be real or imagined, individual or collective."[25] In every verbal exchange there is both the *énoncé* (the utterance, the statement itself) and the *énonciation* (the process of production, the position from which the statement proceeds). Consideration of enunciation as a *process* thus involves extralinguistic determinations—social, psychological, unconscious—as well as the specific linguistic features of the language system mobilized by the speaker. As such, it points to the fundamental importance of the extralinguistic in any act of communication, and therefore emphasizes subjectivity—the subject's place in language—as constitutive of the production of all utterances, of all human discursive exchange.

When it is applied to film studies, enunciation refers not to verbal statements and their production, but to the entire cinematic process, comprising *both* "author" and "spectator" in the desiring production of the text. For his model of the cinematic apparatus, Christian Metz transforms the linguistic emphasis into a concept of the enunciator as "producer of the fiction," indicating that process by which every filmmaker organizes the image flow, appropriating and designating the series of images, the diverse views that comprise the relay between the one who looks (the camera, the filmmaker—the subject of enunciation) and what is being looked at (the scene of the action—the site/representation of desire).[26] This implies various narrative strategies and editing techniques used to enhance the cinematic illusion as well as the development and articulation of point-of-view structures designed to encourage fictive identifications. Enunciation thus involves a logic of both actions and views, structuring principles of coherence and vision which allow the audience to make sense of cinematic fictions. Each filmmaker appropriates and then designates "the look" in a specific way, and this is what characterizes a particular director's system of enunciation—the way vision is organized in the construction of the cinematic discourse.

But cinematic enunciation is a reciprocal process; in order for the cinematic fiction to produce and maintain its fascinating hold on the spectator, to reinforce the regime of the fantasm, it must appear as if the screen images are the expressions of the spectator's own desire. Or rather, as Bertrand Augst concisely describes it, "The subject-producer must disappear so that the subject-spectator can take his place in the production of the filmic discourse."[27] Metz describes exactly how this space of cinematic enunciation becomes the position of cinematic viewing by connecting the enunciative process to cinematic voyeurism, the libidinal aspect of pleasurable looking that founds the cinema: "If the traditional film tends to suppress all the marks of the subject of enunciation, this is in order that the viewer may have the impression of being that subject himself, but an empty, absent subject, a pure capacity for seeing."[28]

This slippage is thus achieved via the suppression of the marks of enunciation, signifying elements which indicate that the filmic discourse has emanated from a source other than the site of viewing. Metz maintains that one of the primary operations of the classical narrative film (what distinguishes it as "classical" in fact) is precisely this effacement of the enunciative indicators. The work of cinematic production is thus concealed in a variety of operations which disguise the *discourse* (in which an enunciative source is present, its reference point is the present tense, and the discursive relation is foregrounded by the engagement of the pronouns "I" and "you") so that the film might present itself as *history* [*story*] (in which the source of enunciation—that absent term, either camera or author, which controls the discourse and organizes the narrative logic—is suppressed, the verb tense is an indefinite past of already completed events, and the more distant, impersonal pronouns of "he," "she," and "it" are engaged). Given these terms of cinematic production and address, in order for the spectator to assume the position of filmic enunciation, as punctual generator of textual desire (as *ciné-subject,* in short), it must appear as if the fiction on the screen emerges from nowhere. The enunciative slide can accomplish this "since history . . . is always (by definition) a story told from nowhere, told by nobody, but received by someone (without which it would not exist). It is therefore, in a sense, the receiver (or rather the receptacle) who tells it. . . . "[29] The effective functioning of the cinema as an apparatus is only possible on the basis of this concealment of its operations; through the invisible conversion from discourse to history a "pseudo-viewer" is created which every spectator can appropriate at will, and in this way the enunciative apparatus, as articulated through the look, structures its very specific unconscious relation of spectator to screen.

For Raymond Bellour, this model of the cinematic apparatus is marked by the insistent inscription of sexual difference, for although he theorizes the place of cinematic enunciation as a *position*—not to be confused with the specific individual filmmaker—his most illuminating analyses are based on the work of that consummate auteur and exemplar of patriarchal power, Alfred Hitchcock. Bellour defines the source of cinematic enunciation as a "subject endowed with a kind of infinite power, constituted as the place from which the set of representations are ordered and organized, and toward which they are channelled back," a subject "who sustains the very possibility of any representation."[30] However, he anchors this process ("which defines and structures a certain subject of desire") in a conception in which the female figure is irrefutably inscribed and represented in the fiction according to a masculine logic—for this subject of desire "is always, first and last, a masculine subject."[31] Ironically, then, in exchange for a liberating conception of authorship not grounded in a restrictive notion of individual personality—and productively engaging the psychoanalytic force of the unconscious (Bellour remarks how, in Hitchcock's films, the viewer can easily move, through the visual trajectories of the characters, "to a central point from which all these different visions emanate: the place, at once productive and empty, of the subject-director.")[32]—he ends by asserting the power of the patriarchy to limit, define, and circumscribe the feminine both socially and cinematically. In locating the power of the cinematic gaze—the image-generating function—within the realm of masculine subjectivity, Bellour effectively links cinematic enunciation to the dominant psychoanalytic model of masculine sexuality: the female figure, in both, occupies a symbolic position as object of desire, a position that corresponds to the central place accorded the woman by all Western cultural representations.[33]

Bellour's work on the production and generation of textual systems (for which he takes the classical Hollywood cinema as paradigm) examines how the figure of the woman has a critical determining role in the ensemble of representations organized by the film; he connects this to the central role of sexual difference in the unconscious structuration of the subject in patriarchy. In terms of narrative sequencing, his analyses demonstrate the way in which traditional narrative films present a scenarization of psychic conflicts that is "organized around a very insistent and very strong representation of the feminine figure."[34] Using extremely precise analyses of, in particular, *The Birds, North by Northwest,* and *Psycho,*[35] and linking the fictive logic of narrative events to woman's symbolic value as erotic object, Bellour shows how a highly systematized movement of substitutions and relations allows the hero (necessarily defined as male), through the course of the film's action, to stabilize his desire in relation to the female figure. He demonstrates in minute detail how this process of resolution and containment, a process he links to the psychic articulation of the Oedipal scenario, even works at the micro-level of the relations between sequences and those between shots. All of classical film, for Bellour, works toward homogeneity and closure, and it is the very definition of textual systematicity that it produces fissures and contradictions precisely in order to smooth them over.

For Bellour, the question of female desire is thereby assimilated to—and represented in terms of—the masculine Oedipal standard. In this sense, features of the cinematic apparatus combine with those of narrative elaboration to negotiate the organization of textual desire according to a cultural and psychic logic that privileges the male. In these examples from Hitchcock's films, sexual difference is at the heart of this narrative process, for its inaugurating and resolving functions (the introduction of conflict and the establishment of the legitimized heterosexuality of the couple) define the limits of the story that the text has to tell. In all of these analyses, Bellour's focus on the masculine Oedipal trajectory is designed to demonstrate the extent to which the symbolic pressure of patriarchy, in its inscription of sexual difference, exerts its force at the most basic level of operation in the cinematic text.

These latter analyses demonstrate the woman's function as sexual signifier in terms of the organization of the narrative; Bellour deals as well with the function of the woman as visual spectacle. It is in his article, "Hitchcock: The Enunciator," that he uses an analysis of *Marnie* to show how the Hitchcockian system of enunciation "crystallizes around the desire for the woman,"[36] illustrating by this example how Hitchcock's films are repeatedly structured on an economy of pleasure that defines a specific position for the female as image-object of the look. It is also here that Bellour coins the terms *camera-*

wish and *film-wish* to designate the way in which Hitchcock uses his privileged position to represent his own desire, and to indicate how the "logical unfolding of the phantasy originat[es] in the conditions of enunciation."[37] In so doing, Bellour locates his discussion of authorship within the context of unconscious sexuality, and thus accords a (textually demonstrable) central importance to the structural and symbolic role of the woman. As image and as female character, Marnie is in fact constituted by a look. From the outset Bellour makes an equation between the body of the woman and the film body, asserting that the camera's look (its "pure image-power") implies possession of the screen object. Just as Hitchcock's power to make the image—to give Marnie concrete existence through the look—enables his "film-wish" to be articulated visually, so does his power to delegate that look to the male characters, his fictional surrogates, inscribe them onto the "trajectory of virtual possession of the object."[38]

Bellour's analysis is further inflected by cultural definitions of femininity when he discusses the possibilities of identification available to the viewer. He suggests that Marnie's answer to the sexual aggression wrought on her by Hitchcock and his substitutes is, ironically, theft and shifting identities, a perverse and deceptive change of "image" with its own sexual provocation: "All she can offer is the surface of an image and this is precisely what is attractive in her."[39] In one crucial moment of the film, as she is transforming herself into yet another persona, Marnie looks into a mirror and thus, for Bellour, constitutes herself as an image of desire, desired because she is an image, and desired by both camera/filmmaker and viewer, "whose" image she has become. Yet even more important is the fact that she is also desired by herself, thus constituting herself, finally, as an image of *her own* desire. This complicates what Bellour maintains are the two processes of identification that conventionally transfix the spectator—(primary) identification with the camera, and (secondary) identification with the object (in Bellour's terms, the male character) on the screen—identification with both seeing *and* seen thus lining up on the side of the male. When Marnie appropriates the look in order to "see herself seeing," she reverses the traditional process whereby identification for the male is with the act of seeing while identification for the female is only with being seen. Or, to put it another way, this is a privileged and unusual textual moment because it condenses not only the three looks (of camera, viewer, and character), but also the *female* object of the looks who happens, in this specific instance, to be looking herself. As such, it illustrates the fact that the woman can only be the subject of vision insofar as she is also its object; her possession of vision is predicated on her objectification—in a way that seldom happens for the male character. Because her vision is so circumscribed by masculine structures, this moment in the film dramatizes the precise limitations on the woman's gaze dictated by the classical cinema. Bellour resolves the contradiction implied in this moment of Marnie's gaze by concluding that "her absorption in her desire for her own image . . . extends to the male spectator (the camera held by Hitchcock, Mark, Strutt) the deferred orgasm of desire for an object; for any woman spectator, who, for all practical purposes is alienated by this structure, she stimulates an identificatory desire [to be that object]."[40]

As Janet Bergstrom points out,[41] Bellour thus limits his consideration of sexual difference and identification to fixed poles of masculinity and femininity (male and female spectators, the latter confined to either masochism or sadistic reversal), positing both stable definitions of masculine and feminine sexuality and an immutable—"masculine"—position for the spectator. His conclusions are thus open to a deterministic reading, for he does in fact acknowledge that those parallel apparatuses, psychoanalysis and the cinema, imply specific definitions of the female—the irreducible difference of the "dark continent" for the former, the "extreme condensation of sexuality in the woman's body-image"[42] for the latter. And within this context, he must concede that both the cinema and psychoanalysis construct feminine sexuality in masculine terms, as either object of desire or as narcissistic reduplication in a mirror-reversal of the masculine (a disturbing symmetry).

Yet the force of Bellour's analysis suggests more complicated models, for what is implied by his focus on textual operations and their articulation with unconscious processes, in fact, are constant points of oscillation and variation between object-choice and identificatory desire, between activity and passivity, and between their traditional counterparts of masculinity and femininity. Rather than a spectatorial positioning rigidly aligned to either biological or social constructions of the masculine and the feminine, Bellour's conception of the textual system in terms of desire and enunciation—in terms of fantasmatic production—suggests the very possibility of blurring those sexual boundaries, the possibility for spectators "to take up multiple identificatory positions, whether successively or simultaneously."[43] If the delegation of the look implied in the theory of enunciation makes a splitting of vision possible (makes it, in fact, the very condition of its possibility), then what also becomes available to the viewer is a whole array of unconscious positions and roles within the fantasy structure itself. It is within this context, then, that Bellour's highly refined model for the unconscious articulation of vision and desire in the classical cinema yields productive insights for feminists interested in understanding the terms and processes of cinematic fascination and seduction, and, importantly, our position as women within those structures.

Femininity and Authorship

All of this becomes extremely complicated when we apply the enunciative model of authorship to women's work—when we attempt, in fact, to consider this theoretical apparatus in terms of the feminine—for the consideration of films made by women adds another, absolutely crucial, dimension to these discussions. An important paradox arises when we think of feminist filmmakers, because although the effort to define the terms of a feminist counter-tradition must, of necessity, focus on the work of women, the power of the theories heretofore elaborated shifts the discussion of authorship away from actual individuals and toward relations of unconscious desire generated by the text. Yet this does not mean that cinematic production is somehow gender-neutral; indeed to ignore sexuality in considerations of authorship is to, in essence, support the masculine status quo. As Stephen Heath observes, "[A]ny discourse which fails to take account of the problem of sexual difference in its enunciation and address will be, within a patriarchal order, precisely indifferent, a reflection of male domination."[44] This raises a number of complex questions, each suggesting a different level of analysis: How can we define a "desiring look" when the position of looking is feminine? What are the parameters and articulations of a "female discourse" as it traverses a particular text? And how can we conceptualize a "woman's desire" from the triple standpoint of the author, text, and viewer?

To consider female authorship within these theoretical parameters is to pose the problem of sexual difference across the field of cinematic enunciation. Enunciative positioning must be conceived in a *different* way when the female is taken into account, but specific definitions of female enunciation are currently only in the process of being elaborated, and much work still remains to be done. While a feminist cinema must necessarily posit its enunciative position as feminine, this does not simply mean that there is a feminine "content" or "expression" that emanates directly from the woman's place. Rather, the notion of authorship/enunciation in the feminine raises the question of female *desire,* indicating a terrain of representation from which various new positions can be engaged, scopic modalities which imply alternative conceptions of female subjectivity and desire. These supersede either individual filmmakers or particular fictional characters. Within this context, a film made by a woman (even one with strong female models) might still organize its vision according to masculine structures. This is because, regardless of a film's content, it is always taken up in the unconscious processes of desire which negotiate the cinematic text. Feminist analyses of the cinema must work at this level of complexity because it is here that the cultural (unconscious) and the representational (cinematic) intersect, and it is only in these terms that the impasses of biology and of content analysis can be avoided. However, defining the "I" who speaks cinematically—as a woman—is a deceptive and difficult task.

Another complication that sexual difference suggests concerns the theoretical assumption that the enunciative apparatus itself is masculine. Yet while Bellour's work on Hitchcock and enunciation does focus on the way that *male* desire is articulated, the debated "masculinity" of enunciation refers more to the kind of analysis in which Freud defined the libido itself as "masculine" than to the presumed sex of the enunciator. In fact, there is often a confusion between actual men (male filmmakers) and the global system of enunciation, in which the circulation of desire is interpreted and examined in terms of the psychoanalytic category of masculinity. More important for feminists, however, is the fact that Bellour defines *the place* of the enunciator as that which monitors the different types of scopic relation to the object, classifying the relative positions of the camera-look in relation to what is represented. It is a splitting of vision which inscribes the enunciation of a film's textual system, and the delegation of "the look" is what makes this splitting of vision possible. Therefore, although a masculine standard might be implied by the theoretical construct (its elaboration, in fact, having come about precisely in terms of the generation of masculine desire), the question of enunciation *in the feminine* recasts the very terms and relations of sexuality, vision, authorship, and text. This suggests a number of possibilities for female enunciation: a problematization of the enunciating subject itself and the indication of alternative positions, a denaturalization of the gaze structured according to phallic logic, a shift of emphasis in the quality and intensity of the controlling look—as well as in its object, a new recognition of what Chantal Akerman calls "*la jouissance du voir*" (the erotics of vision unhampered by the strictures of voyeuristic definition), and, at the level of the diegesis, differing structures of point-of-view and identification as well as the creation of new possibilities for destabilizing the inevitability and homogeneity of the patriarchal narrative.

A closer look at the paradox of authorship reveals some productive contradictions. On the one hand, theory's dissolution of the concept of authorship into questions of enunciation and subjectivity means an end to the idea of the author as source and guarantee of meaning— a refusal to see the film as the manifestation of the personal vision of a unique artist—in favor of a notion of the text which implies both signifying and psychic operations in its construction. On the other hand, the study of any specific individual filmmaker will take into account *history* (the historical moment when the filmmaker lived and worked) and *biography* (the specific personal history, including the gender of the filmmaker, particularly—and emphatically—if a woman). A film's preoccupations, interests, and stylistics will be shaped by the individual *and* her time, and will indicate what we might consider a feminine voice. A theoretical position must incorporate this—it is a political necessity for feminists—and cannot obviate it altogether in a general theory of the apparatus. The problem, specifically for this book, becomes one of critically discussing the work of particular female authors while remaining within the context of enunciative theory. If the author is no longer understood as an expressive, fully self-present individual whose conscious intentions are manifested in film, still feminism necessitates that films and filmmakers be looked at in terms of how they treat the feminist problematic, how they (and we) define a "female perspective," "feminine desire," "feminist discourse," the "woman's film"—in short, how they pose the *difference* of women's filmmaking. However, the border between those definitions and authorial intentionality becomes quite thin, while it is that very intentionality which the theory seeks to displace.

At least three solutions to the contradiction between the textual instance of enunciation and the "author as individual" present themselves. Although both history (culture) and biography (gender) crystallize in the latter notion, these important elements must be inserted into a theoretical context which denies such individuality. The resolution of the paradoxical emphases of authorship is achieved by combining both tendencies to produce "authorship" as a tripartite structure, comprising 1) authorship as a historical phenomenon, suggesting the cultural context; 2) authorship as a desiring position, involving determinants of sexuality and gender; and 3) authorship as a textual moment, incorporating the specific stylistics and preoccupations of the filmmaker. At the same time, each of these components of authorship implies the other two, for they exist in a perpetually dynamic relation.

Following from this, if one recognizes that the textual author—understood as an enunciative source—is a feminist filmmaker, then her function as controller of the discourse (the one who organizes the narrative logic, negotiates the disparate visions) can be seen as one which attempts to originate the representation of her own (female) desire. Janet Bergstrom offers a series of questions posed from this perspective, questions that suggest a feminist reformulation of authorship in enunciative terms: "Who 'speaks' beneath the deceptively neutral and objective voice of the 'third person' narration? According to what logic(s) does the film make sense? In whose interest are the images and sounds recorded and ordered in a specific way, as one particular system? Who controls the look, and with it, the diegesis, and what kind of spectator does this presuppose?"[45]

The third avenue out of the paradox involves making a link between the historical discourse (which contextualizes a particular filmmaker's work in terms of production and aesthetics) and the discourse of textual analysis (which focuses on processes of desire) in such a way as to maintain the integrity of each while emphasizing the necessity of their interrelation. Thus the construction of a history—a usable tradition of alternative feminist film practice—would be possible in terms of forms of textual resistance to the dominant cinematic model. Feminist cinema would be defined, then, not according to the biological gender of the filmmaker, but according to specific textual and enunciative processes that posit the work as alternative cinema. In this way, an articulation of both forms of authorship—individual and textual—could be forged.

Given the conditions imposed by formulating cinematic production in terms of enunciation, then, what are the possibilities for an alternative feminist cinematic practice? What happens when a female enunciating subject is posed, when the desiring look articulates a different economy of vision? If we accept the theory's founding premise—that meaning is located not in the film-text itself, but in the relationship between author, spectator, and text, or more specifically in the enunciating instance of the text—how can we then specify precisely what is "feminine" (or feminist, in fact) about a particular film? How can we articulate the terms of feminine desire and female specificity both within a text and at its enunciative source? For one thing, a feminist cinema will attempt to restore the marks of cinematic enunciation so carefully elided by the concealing operations of patriarchal cinema, or at least it will work to undermine them. In any case, it will foreground sexual difference in the enunciative relay, focusing on the status and nature of the representation of the woman—her desire, her images, her fantasms. In so doing, a counter-cinema will attempt to reinsert the subject—a sexed subject—into the process of meaning-production, thereby allowing its structures to subvert, rework, or offer alternatives to the pervasive logic of masculine desire articulated by dominant cinema. As a consequence, new spectator-text relationships—ones which render problematic the pleasures of cinematic voyeurism— might be generated, new subjective structures obtained. For it is never a question of films having been made by individual men or women, or of a specific content speaking to the needs of a particular sex. Rather, as Stephen Heath maintains, "What one has is always a structure of representation in and from the terms of which positions, enunciations can be engaged, specified as 'masculine,' 'feminine,' with the possibility of reappropriating the latter as site of resistance to the domination, the definitions, the assignments of the former."[46]

The French Cinema: An Example

Nevertheless, the elaboration and definition of a feminist counter-cinema requires that the very possibility of an alternative be situated *both* theoretically and historically. While feminist critic Silvia Boven-schen has noted that there is always an element of resistance—even if passive—in women's art,[47] this gets quite complicated when the discussion turns to film, for here the problem becomes one of specifying precisely what is being resisted, and of analyzing exactly what forms that resistance takes. The emergence of what has come to be called the "dominant Hollywood model" is useful as a frame of reference because, as a rule, the very notion of an alternative cinema has consistently developed as a deviation from the specific type of textual system and mode of narrative organization that culminated in the late 1920s and has dominated Hollywood film production ever since. The cinema's stabilization as a powerful social institution and the formation of its massive public worked in a mutually determinant way with the establishment of this narrative model. Therefore, it is not accidental that, historically, the formulation of alternative cinematic practices has emerged as a response to the all-pervasive cinematic machine perfected in Hollywood.

The question of an oppositional filmmaking practice intersects with notions of both art cinema and national cinema. It is art cinema—in which there is a theoretical reflection on the specific properties of cinema as a signifying system and, as a consequence, experimentation on what can be understood as its language, its mode of organizing meanings—that has traditionally provided a context for the development of alternatives to the normal commercial mode. At the same time, because Hollywood has continued to dominate the world film market since the end of World War I, cinematic resistance on a global level has tended to crystallize around the establishment of various national cinemas in relation to this dominance. Work on cinematic language by filmmakers marginalized by industrial concerns has thus coincided historically with efforts to develop a national cinematic identity that could effectively resist the hegemony of the American film industry. By definition, then, a link between art cinema and national cinema has emerged in terms of both the economic reconstruction of an indigenous film industry and the emphasis on national cultural and cinematic traditions, and national cinema has come to be defined in terms of the development of a specific alternative aesthetic.

From this perspective, national cinema is no longer defined in geographical or sociological terms, nor is it designated by a body of films that demonstrate either a typical national style or a pervasive cultural ethos. Rather, as in the case of art cinema, the emphasis of analysis is shifted from the manifest content of particular film texts to the productive mechanisms which generate those texts. This means that possibilities for opposition can be conceived in terms of the type of subject constructed by a particular (national *or* art) cinema and by the alternative enunciative positions it suggests. It is this reformulation of national cinema and of art cinema along theoretical lines that connects both of them to the project of a feminist counter-cinema, for all three work at the margins of mainstream commercial production in an effort not only to subvert and undermine the structures of dominance, but also, and perhaps more importantly, to generate new textual forms. In this way, all three types of cinema define resistance as a struggle within representation and, because of this, assert the *political* necessity of conceptualizing new aesthetic models.

The present study is an effort to contribute to a theorization of sexual difference in the cinema through an analysis of the work of three French women directors: Germaine Dulac (and the First Avant-Garde of the 1920s), Marie Epstein (and the Poetic Realism of the 1930s), and Agnès Varda (and the New Wave of the 1960s). The focus on a national cinema, and on films made by women within that, provides a situation of double rupture, for (as I have noted) the question of an alternative cinematic practice is doubly formulated from these borders. That is, within the context of resistance to Hollywood represented by virtually all of the major French directors of these periods, the women filmmakers differed (yet again) from their male counterparts. Historically, the work of these filmmakers represents three critical moments in the evolution of the French cinema, for all three periods were times in which sharp economic crises intensified the interest in the development of both a national cinema and a specific alternative aesthetic. Each period proposed different solutions to the problem, and, from the standpoint of the enunciative apparatus of cinema, each solution implied different relations of spectator, text, and filmmaker. The cinema of the First Avant-Garde in the 1920s was clearly defined as an "art-house" cinema; many of the filmmakers were also involved in developing alternative distribution and exhibition systems that would ensure an audience apprised of the issues and enthusiastically receptive to aesthetic innovation. In contrast, the Poetic Realists created a popular cinema that had both commercial appeal for French audiences and a precisely defined national character, evidenced in their films by an interest in populist subjects and the creation of a texture of the quotidian. Broadly speaking, the cinema of the New Wave combined an interest in the evolution of a new cinematic discourse and a new form of expression with the kind of commercial attraction of French film in the thirties, thereby succeeding in revitalizing French filmmaking without being confined to an aestheticizing marginality. The French cinema is a particularly good example because all of these periods were characterized by an atmosphere of cultural ferment, an atmosphere in which a combination of political inspiration, formal experiment, and avant-garde activity was proven to be artistically productive. And at each of these times the main participants were unified in their self-perception as opponents to Hollywood dominance.

Within this specific historical context, each of the filmmakers I deal with (beyond having chosen subject matter of singular relevance to women) can be seen to have made a particular contribution to the development of film language, and it is through the analysis of their individual films that I assess these contributions with an eye toward establishing a viable feminist tradition for an alternative cinematic practice. A set of common themes and concerns—a group of problems pertinent specifically to women filmmakers—unites the work of these three directors, for all three (with varying degrees of self-consciousness or intentionality) attempt to formulate and resolve the questions of a feminine discourse, to conceive new possibilities for the expression and representation of female desire. While my approach is, at first glance, both chronological and biographical, it is, finally and most importantly, textual.

The aim of the study is threefold: To discuss the careers of three women filmmakers, and in so doing to make available, or reevaluate, their work; to situate this work within a historical, economic, and aesthetic context; and to locate, through detailed analyses of specific texts, the theoretical issues surrounding the representation of women and the cinematic apparatus. Therefore, although my preliminary focus is on three women filmmakers as *individuals*—their lives, their art, and their times—it is with the analysis of the films themselves that the main feminist interest lies. Because of that, this study does not attempt to construct a teleology of feminist filmmaking that would posit an evolution from so-called "primitive" early efforts to deal with women's issues and themes to a culmination in explicitly agitational films. Nor is it an attempt to identify films as "more" or "less" feminist, depending on how they portray the struggles of women or where the filmmakers' sympathies lie. It does assert, however, that there is a difference in women's filmmaking—a different construction of the object, a different mode of organizing meaning, a different language of desire—and that this can only be understood by means of a theoretical grasp of the production of both "femininity" and its representations.

Germaine Dulac and the First Avant-Garde

In France, the first attempts to subvert the Hollywood model and develop an alternative system were undertaken by what is known as the "First Avant-Garde." Germaine Dulac, whose theoretical writings were consistently formulated in terms of an effort to deconstruct this dominant cinema, was a feminist and a polemicist for a formal counter-cinema. Along with Louis Delluc, Marcel L'Herbier, Jean Epstein, and Abel Gance, she worked for the formation of a specifically French cinema which was posited in a relation of ambivalence to the mainstream American cinema, for it simultaneously resisted and benefitted from the standard practices of Hollywood. Some of these filmmakers viewed their work as antinarrative (i.e., anticommercial), and all of them experimented with ways of defining and achieving cinematic specificity, arguing for artistic liberation from literary and theatrical models. Dulac agitated for the creation of a "pure cinema" whose resources and forms of expression would be specifically cinematic. She called for a visual poetics which emphasized the materiality of the cinematic signifier as against the conventions of narrative causality and visual continuity of the traditional commercial cinema. Toward this end, her desire to free the cinema from the constraints of its literary and theatrical antecedents placed her at the center of a debate over the constitutive elements of the medium, in short, over the specific features of "cinematic language." For Dulac, this resulted in calling for a cinematic equivalent to music (she referred to Gance's *La Roue* as a "symphonic poem based on images"). In addition, Dulac's active concern with feminist issues and her prolific film-theoretical writings provide one of the earliest examples of an attempt to conceptualize a feminist cinema in formal terms.

Two of her films, *La Souriante Mme Beudet* (*The Smiling Mme Beudet,* 1923) and *La Coquille et le clergyman* (*The Seashell and the Clergyman,* 1927), both readily available in the United States, are central to the analysis of her work, for they clearly define both the parameters and the progression of her inquiry into alternative modes of cinematic expression. The first film, perhaps her best known, is a powerful example of Dulac's incorporation of a subjective dimension into a traditional narrative structure and of her experiments with the cinematic rendering of interiority. In it she attempts to both explore and convey female subjectivity—the dreams, fantasies, and desires of her heroine—through specifically cinematic means. The second film's focus on the unmediated depiction of unconscious forces, and thereby, necessarily, on processes of cinematic meaning-production, can be understood as a logical step toward Dulac's eventual works of "pure cinema." Her experimentation with the nonreferentiality of the cinematic image (through technical variations such as superimpositions, dissolves, and unusual camera techniques) and with the structures of narrative (through manipulations of duration, alternation, and repetition) provide examples of one possible form of resistance to the dominance of the traditional narrative cinema. It is within the context of experimentation provided by these two films that the terms in which Germaine Dulac has been understood as a feminist filmmaker can be reformulated.

Marie Epstein and Poetic Realism/Populist Cinema

In *L'Age ingrat du cinéma,* the French critic and film historian Léon Moussinac points out that in 1914, 90 percent of the films shown throughout the world were French; by 1928, 85 percent of them were American.[48] In 1929, French film production, which had been the most considerable in the world, fell to fifty full-length films per year. Louis Delluc's maxim of the twenties, which called for both national and cinematic specificity ("The French cinema must be *cinema;* the French cinema must be *French*"), had become all but submerged as the massive machinery of the Hollywood system wrought financial chaos in the French film industry. The construction of giant American and German film factories near Paris and the exorbitant costs of installing sound equipment virtually induced the collapse of the French film industry in 1934. As a consequence, the galvanizing spirit of French film production in the twenties emerged once again a decade later: there arose in the thirties the economic, political and aesthetic need to create something French—a national industry that could produce films expressive of a national character. Thus despite this economic chaos, or more correctly, perhaps, because of this desire, the period between 1934 and 1940 has come to be called the "Golden Age" of French cinema, a period that produced major works by such filmmakers as Jean Renoir, Jacques Feyder, Julien Duvivier, Marcel Carné, René Clair, Jean Grémillon, and Marcel Pagnol.

I have situated my discussion of Marie Epstein against this background of a developing cinema that was both specifically French and freely experimental (in terms of sound production and alternative solutions to Hollywood). Epstein's work as a filmmaker can be seen to span several critical periods in the development of French cinema, and her output during the thirties—this French cinematic renaissance—is considerable. It is difficult to convey the incredible paradox of her situation: having participated in all three of the major phases of cinematic production (scenarist, director, editor) and having played a central role in making important theoretical work available (although she takes no credit for compiling and publishing the seminal writings of her brother Jean), as well as having been the nerve center of the Cinémathèque Française until her retirement in 1977—she is almost totally unknown to dominant film history. Between 1927 and 1939, Marie Epstein co-directed eleven feature films with Jean Benoît-Lévy. Although she speaks of her absolute egalitarian relationship with him, and although, in fact, the directorial credit is shared on the credits of the films themselves, all references in film histories credit the films to Jean Benoît-Lévy alone. This represents a considerable difficulty for the feminist theorist and critic seeking to establish a tradition of women's cinema, for in these circumstances the question of authorial intentionality is rendered extremely complex, due to both a self-effacing partner in a collaborative effort and to a culture that automatically constructs a position of marginality for women's activities.

Nonetheless, the work of collaboration itself is important within the context of the French film industry at the time. Production was unstable, fragmented, and faced with heavy competition; cooperation among scriptwriters, directors, and technicians can be seen as a response to this. Collaborative activity was thus a historical fact of French film production of the thirties, and as such inflects discussions of authorship of the period. In addition, this notion of collaboration is useful from the standpoint of an alternative feminist filmmaking practice because it shifts the emphasis from the product of a unique subjectivity, some form of purely personal expression, to a production process involving various contributions and distinct elements. Therefore, my discussion of Epstein's work concentrates less on discerning the actual contributions of each participant and more on the textual processes of the films themselves.

Although I discuss all of the films of Marie Epstein (and Jean Benoît-Lévy), my analytical focus is on *La Maternelle* (*The Nursery School,* 1933), by far their most important film, and the only one available for rental in this country. *La Maternelle* provides a powerful example of what I consider a characteristic attempt by the French cinema to subvert the dominant Hollywood model. In addition, the film represents one of the most interesting options for the creation of an alternative feminist cinema. French film production was varied at the time of *La Maternelle*. In addition to the burlesques and social comedies of manners and the filmed theater of major commercial production, there were the films made at Paramount's "European Hollywood." Although Paramount, too, had gone bankrupt in 1934, these Joinville studios had established a successful formula for mass-producing films for wide consumption, already thus setting the tone for a systematic mode of production: overall scenarios where details of dialogue were unimportant; interchangeable casts of different nationalities; cheap and easily constructed sets; and cosmopolitan subjects to appeal to a generalized international audience. Against this machine, French films began to develop alternative methods and forms—both of production techniques and of cinematic devices and narrative conventions. *La Maternelle* is a striking example of the assimilation of the experimental techniques of the First Avant-Garde of the twenties with the feeling for ambience, the populist milieu, and location shooting of the thirties. The term *Poetic Realism* given to these films—and definitions of the term vary widely—can be said to describe the way in which they combine the lyricism and formal interest in visual style of the twenties with the populism of subject and setting characteristic of the nineteenth-century Realist novel.

Jacques Feyder's formula for filmmaking—"A setting, an atmosphere, and a popular plot with a little melodrama in it"—could be one way of describing how this form of filmmaking used environment as a way of telling a story. A new form of narrative organization, one that relied more on the articulation of visual figures and the rhythms of montage, can be seen as a response to the system of linear narrative progression of the Hollywood model. This can also be seen in the articulation of point of view (reminiscent of the subjectivization of the camera in the twenties) and the spatial organization used to dramatize it (arbitrary camera movements and change of angles rather than spatial construction in the service of unfolding "action"). In addition, the techniques of sound production (the use of direct sound, of rhythmic articulation of silence and noise, and the structural use of music) provide another means of resistance to the dominant model. It is within this context that the specifically feminist import of Marie Epstein's work will be considered, for *La Maternelle*, in particular, combines this populist aesthetic with a subject matter more relevant to women's lives, and, more importantly, with a highly suggestive alternative structure for the organization of point-of-view, perhaps the central mechanism of the narrative fiction film.

Agnès Varda and the New Wave

The third "period of resistance" to the domination of Hollywood extends roughly from 1956 to 1963 and is associated with the films of the French New Wave. The name *nouvelle vague* has been used to link a very diverse group of filmmakers with certain tendencies toward formal innovation and experimentation, an emphasis on personal style, social or political commitment, and new techniques and procedures of shooting. It is neither a genre nor a school, nor does nouvelle vague designate a group of filmmakers with a shared set of beliefs. But the term has been useful as a kind of generalized rubric for a whole new generation of filmmakers who literally erupted onto the cultural scene. Between 1958 and 1961, more than one hundred filmmakers made their debut—a sudden resurgence of film production that contrasted with the period of stability (Georges Sadoul calls it stagnation) that had preceded it in the 1950s.

In the late fifties, French producers began to realize that the ambitious productions and costly literary adaptations of directors like Claude Autant-Lara and René Clément were not profitable, and they started investing in low-budget features. In 1948, the government had introduced a quality film award, the *Loi d'Aide*, in an attempt to revive a moribund film industry besieged by inflation and foreign competition. This prize, redefined in 1955 and again in 1959, provided a financial incentive for independent filmmakers, encouraging artistic quality in both features and shorts. (Because of its low budget and limited format, the short was an ideal form for filmmakers interested in experimenting with new cinematic ideas.) Thus an economic climate that fostered experimentation and innovation enabled a generation of young film enthusiasts and critics to make films of their own. Although some New Wave filmmakers went on to make more generally commercial films later in their careers, at the outset the New Wave provided an exciting and vibrant context for both theoretical work and original cinematic production. Included in this grouping were filmmakers François Truffaut, Jean-Luc Godard, Claude Chabrol, Eric Rohmer, Jacques Rivette, Agnès Varda, Alain Resnais, and Chris Marker; some critics consider the latter three as a subgroup, the "Left Bank" directors.

It is, in fact, Agnès Varda who is credited with inaugurating the New Wave with her film *La Pointe-Courte* (1954, the English title is the same), which Georges Sadoul has called "genuinely the first film of the French *Nouvelle Vague*."[49] And all of Varda's work can be seen to embody characteristics traditionally associated with these filmmakers: independence and originality, a highly personal vision, a continuing research into the language and syntax of film, and a sustained attention to forms of narrative organization. It is important, however, to understand the work of the New Wave directors from the perspective of the dominant Hollywood narrative model, for the dual imperatives of Louis Delluc's maxim regain their force in this third moment of national cinematic identity. It is in this sense that the films of the New Wave can be seen as continued attempts both to establish the main codes of classical American cinema and to subvert, undermine, and rework them.

Throughout her career, Varda has experimented with different processes of narrativity in an ongoing effort to explore all of the parameters of cinematic storytelling. From her first film onward, she has worked on both thematic and structural levels with parallelism and contrast/alternation and juxtaposition, examining and reevaluating the (ideological) categories of documentary and fiction along the way. There are several conclusions to be drawn. First, these experiments with alternation work at the core of what constitutes the major narrative articulation of the dominant cinema, and can thus be interpreted as a means of contesting the traditional cinema's mode of organizing its meanings. Second, this integration of "documentary" material into fictional structures suggests new uses for improvisation and new functions for the written scenario. While traditional criticism has seen this departure from the strict confines of the script (typical of the New Wave) as a sign of openness and freedom of the individual artistic vision, the context of resistance to the dominant model that Varda's work suggests implies something else—an effort to delimit and define the specific processes of cinematic meaning-production. Third, Varda's experimentation with ways of telling a story and with the integration of an almost sociological analysis demands a new role for the viewer, and it is this, in fact, which can be seen as a reactivation of that crucial space between spectator and screen so central to contemporary film theory.

Most important from the standpoint of this book, however, is Varda's continual preoccupation with constructions of "the feminine"— and for her this has been increasingly posed in terms of a problematics of vision. Two of Varda's most significant films, *Cléo de 5 à 7* (*Cleo From 5 to 7*, 1962) and what I call its "remake," *Sans toit ni loi* (*Vagabond*, 1985), deal directly with this by focusing, within different contexts, on a deconstruction and examination of the production of the woman's image. Varda was well-prepared to articulate resistance to dominant images of femininity, for in the very same year that *La Pointe-Courte* was released, Roger Vadim's *Et Dieu créa la femme* (*And God Created Woman*) launched a scandalous new type of sexual iconography with Brigitte Bardot. Characterized by the French press as a "*monstre sacré*," the pouting Bardot inaugurated a new mechanics of representation for mythifying female sexuality and forged the relation of woman and image into an equivalence. This period also saw the fetishization of female stars like Jeanne Moreau (feminine mystery incarnate in François Truffaut's *Jules et Jim* and Jacques Demy's *Baie des Anges*) and Catherine Deneuve (whose glacial, swanlike beauty was exploited in a variety of ways). Throughout her work, but most particularly in *Cleo From 5 to 7* and *Vagabond*, Varda deals with precisely this form of sexual exploitation of the woman's image by consistently examining the ways in which this image is both a social and a cinematic production. These two films provide a textual focus for the highly significant feminist issues raised in and by all of Varda's work.

To Desire Differently

Germaine Dulac, Marie Epstein, Agnès Varda: A sustained look at the work of these directors can give us productive insights into the varied ways of conceptualizing the difference of women's filmmaking, for while each works at a different textual level, the films of all three suggest a number of possibilities for an alternative cinematic practice. It goes without saying that the very notion of a feminist appropriation of the cinematic gaze will imply new forms of representation, new narrative structures, and new terms of address. The particular textual elaboration of these exemplified by Dulac, Epstein, and Varda can be seen to represent three different options for a feminist practice of the cinema, three directions that feminist filmmaking might take. There is, however, no *direct* relation between the avowed feminism of the filmmakers themselves and the feminist import of their work, for this relation is extremely complex, and one that only the perspective of theory—of enunciation, sexual difference, and the cinematic apparatus—can elucidate. Germaine Dulac was both a militant feminist and an ardent film theorist, but only rarely did these two commitments coincide in her work. Marie Epstein has never openly subscribed to a political position and is clearly uncomfortable with the "feminist" designation. And while Agnès Varda directly agitates for feminist issues, her more avowedly feminist films have not always been the most productive theoretically; her films of a less overt feminist conception have had more useful implications for feminist analysis.

Looking at the work of Dulac, Epstein, and Varda, then, from the standpoint of the theoretical framework presented earlier in this introduction, there is a suggestive correspondence between each woman's films and some of the forms of resistance to the dominant cinema which that theoretical framework implies. In their attempts to both challenge prevalent cinematic norms and to redefine filmmaking from a female perspective, these filmmakers' strategies of subversion can be categorized, in a very general way, as follows: Dulac can be associated with work on the representation of unconscious processes, Epstein with reworking modes and structures of cinematic address, and Varda with the use of particular narrative, discursive, and textual strategies. Germaine Dulac was one of the earliest filmmakers to focus on issues of (a specifically female) subjectivity by experimenting with new cinematic forms. Within the aesthetic context of her time—a period of definition of the "Seventh Art" in terms of the specific properties of its "language"—Dulac utilized nonnarrative and poetic means to achieve the representation of female consciousness, to accomplish a different representation of the woman conceived in terms of subjective, internal, and unconscious processes. Marie Epstein shifts the focus of her narratives from the traditional masculine trajectory of Oedipal desire to desiring relations of the feminine (relations between mothers and daughters in particular) and in so doing, realigns point-of-view structures to emphasize both the *child*'s vision in the primal scene and the unconscious structure of fantasy. Agnès Varda examines the social and psychic constructions of femininity by adopting specific distancing devices to produce a critical, reflective spectator. This, too, is within the context of her time, for all New Wave filmmaking that defined itself as political worked with self-conscious techniques of narrative disruption and fragmentation, the interweaving of different types of discourse, and the refusal of traditional notions of character and plot.

Thus while all three filmmakers are concerned, on the level of content, with questions of feminine identity (not only the central character, but the central problematic is of—and in—women's lives, treating issues of woman's self-image, of motherhood, marriage, sexuality, and friendship between women), they can be constructively differentiated at the level of form (signifying processes) through an analysis of Dulac's exploration of cinematic parameters, Epstein's emphasis on structures of fantasy and point-of-view, and Varda's interest in narrative and discursive practices. If classical cinema can be said to give a determining role to the woman's image—as the pivotal center around which the masculine subject organizes his desire—we can say that the work of these women directors maintains the centrality of the female, but, importantly, inverts the terms and priorities. Psychic conflicts are staged, to be sure, but precisely from the perspective of feminine desire, and it is this inversion that constitutes their challenge to dominant cinema.

As noted earlier, Dulac's early exploitation of the creative possibilities of the cinema in an explicit effort to portray both female subjectivity and unconscious processes led her to make what are considered to be two classics, *The Smiling Mme Beudet* (an acknowledged model of feminist cinema) and *The Seashell and the Clergyman* (Surrealism's first film). In the former film (in which a frustrated bourgeois housewife seeks liberation through imagination and fantasy), Dulac uses a fairly traditional narrative sequence as an armature for a whole range of dazzling cinematic techniques that evoke the inner world of her heroine. *Seashell,* on the other hand, borders on abstraction because it disrupts both narrative causality and logical character development in an effort to portray the unmediated associations of unconscious thought. Although the two films are often contrasted precisely because of the consequent use of narrative and its antithesis, from the standpoint of Dulac's own preoccupation with what constitutes an alternative language of desire "in the feminine," the films demonstrate a consistent evolution. Dulac shifts her interest from the representation of fantasy, through the rendering of Madame Beudet's intensely active mental world, to the actual *generation* of the fantasmatic process, through the depiction of a generalized unconscious "scene." Thus, regardless of any superficial contrast, at the heart of both films is an interest in psychical mechanisms, an exploration of subjective reality which—whether determined by the specific confines of fictional characterization or liberated by the arbitrary play of the logic of dreams—

reveals not only productive insights into processes of unconscious desire, but also the manner in which these might be cinematically conveyed.

The coherence of Dulac's triple project—experimentation with cinematic language and its constructions of the spectator, exploration of the structures of unconscious fantasy, and research into the possibilities for representing (female) desire—can be discussed in another way. Dulac begins her work in *Beudet* by inscribing her female character as the locus of subjectivity, using plot only as a pretext for the exploration of the feminine psyche. She thus posits a notion of female desire by constructing a parody of the action genre film (a gun is loaded, a murder will ensue) in which everything leading up to this crime is "told" from a woman's subjective point of view. The life of the unconscious is thus figured in terms of the fantasy productions of the female protagonist. But in *Seashell*, Dulac eliminates the conventional notion of character altogether, thereby extending her experimentation so that the cinematic techniques become the narrative itself. It is these techniques, in fact, which provide the actual textual generation of the cinematic "fiction." This shift from diegetic character as subject of the fantasy to cinematic spectator as subject of the fantasmatic process entails a transformation in the figuration of femininity as well, for in *Seashell* the woman (no longer a character in the traditional sense) comes to *represent* prevalent notions of "the feminine" in the process of the filmic writing. Her protean, evanescent form corresponds to a concrete visualization of unconscious desire as it circulates from representation to representation. In a film whose very textuality entails the cinematic actualization of unconscious mechanisms, the equivalence of woman and desire yields much of consequence for an understanding of the mutually determining forces of sexuality and representation, and the place of the feminine within the fantasmatic structure. What is accomplished in a close analysis of these two films is the recognition that Dulac's continued interest in the very sources of cinematic expression, and her effort to link the filmic rendering of subjectivity to a specifically feminine consciousness, comprise a productive formulation of aesthetic resistance in terms of cinematic language.

It is at the deeper enunciative level of the cinematic apparatus that the strategy of resistance represented by Marie Epstein's work can be found; in *La Maternelle*, her dual focus on the primary emotive relationship of mother and child and, more important, on the relations of vision and desire in the structure of fantasy, leads her to fundamentally alter the central mechanism of viewer identification, the articulation of point-of-view. However, to state it in this way ascribes too much intentionality to the filmmaker herself; rather, it is from the perspective of the theory of enunciation that this challenge to the dominant model must be understood. Thus at the level of textual processes, over and above the implementation of a new content that reworks patriarchal definitions of the maternal, the film resituates the viewer as producer of the fantasm not in terms of Oedipal desire, but of the female child's longing for the mother, and it does this through repeated scenarios of the primal scene. Because of this, the subject of enunciation no longer coincides with the masculine hero, but becomes reformulated as a desiring position of vision, a position organized in terms of female desire. In this the film constitutes a double transgression, for the posing of a female subjectivity and a child's fantasy—both at the margins of the stabilization of the male psyche—suggests an alternative emphasis to the dominant textual machine.

In *La Maternelle*, a little girl named Marie is abandoned by her mother, a prostitute; she subsequently recovers this loss by establishing an intense friendship with Rose, a maid at the nursery school. When this new maternal relationship is threatened by a marriage proposal witnessed by the child, Marie attempts suicide as she envisions couples—actual, remembered, and fantasized—before throwing herself into the river. The film's resolution involves her reconciliation with Rose, a reunion predicated on her acceptance of Rose's fiancé, and hence of the parental couple.

In this we find a central structure of classical cinema derailed, for while it is traditionally the project of the Hollywood film to pattern itself in terms of the constitution of the couple, here such a unity can function as resolution only to the extent that it is the *child* who accepts it. The scenarization of psychic conflicts that the film represents, then, is articulated in terms of the female child's recognition of the heterosexual duality rather than the masculine hero's achievement of it (a conclusion which implies very different structures of spectatorial identification than its Hollywood counterpart requires). The logic of masculine desire central to the classical narrative film is thus destabilized, displaced, rearticulated from another source.

Beyond this, in order to understand how the film is able to rework traditional patterns of viewer-identification, we must look to the psychoanalytic notion of fantasy and its particular articulation in the primal scene, for it is here that some of the most significant feminist challenges to the cinematic apparatus are engaged.[50] In one sense, the staging of the primal scene for the spectator is crucial to the apparatus, for it is one of the dominant modes of channelling spectatorial identification. As was noted earlier in this introduction, the fantasy structure can be posited as an alternate mode of spectator involvement, offering multiple positions and interchangeable roles to the singularity suggested by the primacy of the male Oedipal scenario. *La Maternelle* substitutes reiterated scenes of vision for the teleology of the narrative, and in so doing makes the story act as mere support for the articulation of visual figures. But more important, it makes the condensation of these repeated moments (of the mise-en-scène of desire) its organizing principle; it is thus fantasy, rather than the Oedipal trajectory, which structures the film. In *La Maternelle*, the primal scene is not only the central trauma of the film, it is staged in a manner which critically inverts the terms of masculine desire. The desire here is that of the child for the mother, and the witnessed scene is traumatic only because the spectator is meant to identify with the child. In this the primal scene is radically restructured, redefining the notion of trauma in the film. For if this vision is traumatic, it is decisively and repeatedly the vision of the child, cast in terms of the love for the mother and worked throughout the film as female desire.

It is this reformulation of so central a structure in terms which are pre-Oedipal (or at least structured according to a different logic) that makes the film so unique. This is a primal scene enunciated from another source of desire, another enunciation. These elements—the child's point of view, the reworking of the fantasy of the primal scene, the female's desire for the maternal object—are what allow *La Maternelle* to posit another vision within the dominant apparatus. Something of an alternative is gained by rearticulating these fundamental structures, but it is a subtle kind of subversion. Rather than dismantling the apparatus entirely, *La Maternelle* works at the margins of the established system, not abandoning but, instead, transforming its central enunciative structures.

Much of Agnès Varda's work is also concerned with the attempt to redefine "looking" in the cinema, but for her, this is at the level of specific textual strategies. She often uses an essayistic structure composed of fragmented, juxtaposed "episodes" to engage the viewer in an activity of critical reflection and evaluation. Conceived, perhaps, in a more directly political fashion, Varda's films exemplify the type of feminist cinema called for in an early formulation by feminist theorist Claire Johnston: "Any revolutionary strategy must challenge the depiction of reality; it is not enough to discuss the oppression of women within the text of the film; the language of the cinema/the depiction of reality must also be interrogated, so that a break between ideology and the text is effected. . . . The 'truth' of (women's) oppression cannot be 'captured' on celluloid with the 'innocence' of the camera: it has to be constructed/manufactured. New meanings have to be created by disrupting the fabric of the male bourgeois cinema within the text of the film."[51]

What Johnston argues for is a "counter-cinema" defined by a two-pronged attack on the cultural representations of women and on the language of those representations. Varda, in fact, exemplifies this challenge by her consistent refusal to take cinematic language for granted. Through a variety of strategies she contests its traditional status as transparent reflection of an already constituted "reality" by foregrounding the meaning-production process, and in so doing she achieves both a restructuration of the language of film and a critical investigation into the nature and the function of gender images.

Cleo From 5 to 7 traces the two-hour odyssey of a vain pop singer who, while anxiously awaiting the results of a medical test, begins to realize the importance of an intrinsic social connectedness. By focusing on a character who makes the transition from object to subject of the gaze, Varda combines an explicit feminist intent with an interrogation of textual processes, for while there is a conscious effort on her part to explore the woman's image as a social construction, at the same time, the film-text produces a crisis in representation, as the heroine struggles for authorship of her own image. *Cleo From 5 to 7* problematizes the representation of the feminine by examining how the female image is constructed and read. Woman's work, pleasure, sexuality, and personal relationships are all viewed through the theorization of the woman-as-image; feminine existence is formulated as an ontology of the gaze. The film's episodic structure and its emphatic division into chapters posit each instance of growing self-awareness as a dramatization of the visual. Varda examines the commercial cinema's focus on the female star and the fetishization of her screen image by means of an analysis of those areas of female image (and self-image) traditionally objectified in dominant cinema, those points of idealization which, in fact, constitute the textual prominence of the woman's figure as linchpin of the classical cinema. By combining the quasi-documentary depiction of Parisian daily life with a foregrounding of the iconography of femininity, she thereby produces an acknowledgment of representational issues as part of the larger social fabric. Thus in *Cleo*, a feminist perspective is embedded not only in the film's subject matter, but also in the very means of representation itself.

Varda extends this exploration some twenty-three years later in *Vagabond*, where the intersecting issues of feminism and representation are articulated through a double deconstruction of the myths of romantic freedom and the enigmatic woman. The film begins with the cryptic discovery of a young woman's corpse in a ditch and then proceeds to recount the last weeks in the life of this fierce and solitary vagrant named Mona. The French title, *Sans toit ni loi* (*Without Roof nor Law*) implies at once Mona's strident rejection of any attachment, and the cultural geography that the film's probing gaze maps out, the material and social structures that regulate and define our lives. Mona is described by the variety of people who encountered her as she strode defiantly across the frozen vineyards of the Languedoc; these include workers, peasants, hippies, professionals—a spectrum as diverse as French society itself. As these "characters" (both actors and nonprofessionals) remember their impressions, the complex plurality of discourses—documentary, direct testimonial, fictional construct—creates what Varda calls an "impossible portrait" of Mona as decidedly as their interweaving constructs a social vision. These accumulated descriptions maintain us in a position outside the character, allowing Varda to scrupulously avoid both the empathy required by traditional narrative and the moralizing feminism of an explicit manifesto. This wanderer, a hieroglyph of rebellion, offers no positive model of resistance, for she espouses no cause, values no ideal. Rather, Varda's exploratory and unsentimental mise-en-scène presents her viewers with a series of questions that engage their analytical capacities about issues as varied as feminine existence, personal liberation, and cinematic representation.

Vagabond represents the most significant accomplishment of what Varda calls *"cinécriture,"* a notion of "cinematic writing" that involves a total visual/aural conception of the film as textual process. In placing her interest in "how a story is told" (the discourse) over the narrative events themselves (the story), she exemplifies one of the primary deconstructive strategies of a feminist counter-cinema: Against the invisible, naturalizing movement of the classical cinema's fictions she poses a discursive process which emphasizes contradiction. An episodic narration disrupts and fragments linear causality; temporal dislocations replace teleology with simultaneity, circularity, and repetition; the integration of narrative implausibilities interrogates the notion of cinematic "truth"; the alternation of fictional and documentary sequences dialecticizes the definition of each; the interweaving of multiple textual voices fractures the singular enunciative source; and an emphasis on visual surfaces foregrounds the materiality of the text.

This is a contemplative film of "psychic wandering"—of the character, for the viewer. One feature of Varda's *"cinécriture"* is the long tracking shot that stops, rests on an object for punctuation, and provides a moment of reflection. A very visual film (in the trademark punctuating shots as well as the seductive beauty of its cinematography), it is a *process of vision* rather than a story. If Cleo "sees herself" too much (and finally learns to see herself through others in a prism of the social), Mona lacks such vision altogether. It is precisely her failure to make a social connection—which is linked with her inability to both "see herself" and see others—that leads to her destruction. By refusing a traditional character with psychological depth, Varda forces the viewer to reflect on the social inscription of vision and in so doing discovers a new language, a new type of discourse which permits her to write/film *in the feminine.*

Perhaps this is seen most forcefully in her rearticulation of the gaze, for in denying traditional modes of looking at the female body in favor of a camera that is both analytic and direct, Varda redefines pleasurable looking as something independent of sex. The camera projects a sustained flatness over the stunningly desolate landscapes, a look that forestalls voyeurism in the traditional sense, suggesting instead an erotics of vision based on process over content. There is no fiction of the visual, no hidden position of seeing, but an acknowledgment of the spectator's desiring look manifested in an uncompromising and frontal way. Through these self-conscious strategies of resistance Varda is able to achieve a profoundly engaging cinematic reflection on the related problematics of feminism and representation.

As mentioned before, film theory posits a hypothetical spectator who is constructed, in the process of film viewing, by a triple articulation: 1) by the activation of unconscious processes at work in all productions of desire; 2) by the appeal to the viewer's subjectivity through various terms of enunciation and modes of address; and 3) by the textual strategies at work in the particular film being viewed. These three areas, of course, intersect, so that each impinges on and, to some extent, determines the others. For example, strategies of address can involve unconscious processes of identification, and these can be influenced by the specific choice of textual device. It follows that challenges to the dominant system will have to be formulated in terms of this extremely complex organization of vision and desire, this *production,* in fact, of a viewing subjectivity. From the preceding summaries of the work of Dulac, Epstein, and Varda, it is possible to frame their confrontations with patriarchal cinema on these lines, for each can be seen to address the textual construction of the spectator along one of these intersecting routes. Dulac's interest in unconscious mechanisms aligns her with the first, Epstein's emphasis on fantasy as an alternative structure of enunciation corresponds to the second, and Varda's use of deconstructive textual mechanisms coincides with the third.

However—and it cannot be emphasized enough—these three processes are interrelated in a highly complex way; a discussion about one of them is more often than not a discussion of all three simultaneously. Enunciation's appeal to viewer subjectivity is not so easily abstracted from the activation of unconscious processes and the engagement of textual strategies: Enunciation is, in fact, the activation of unconscious processes through a specific mode of textuality. In relying perhaps too much on the explanatory value of a schematic breakdown, I might have overstated my case. Separating the three intersecting routes and attributing each to a single filmmaker is a necessary methodological reduction for a very specific purpose: defining the particular strategies and methods of a feminist counter-cinema. Yet while I want to assert that each filmmaker's work is characterized by (and characteristic of) one of these approaches, it is important to avoid reification of the categories. Such a schematization is meant merely to suggest an emphasis, an inflection on the part of each filmmaker's texts; in the final analysis, any one of these texts involves a complex articulation of all three processes.

But the cinematic spectator is constructed historically as well, and while the establishment of an implied female viewer can be understood from this theoretical perspective, the problem of contemporary women viewers for each of these films remains. Little is known of the contemporary female audience for Dulac's work, if in fact an art-house audience can be studied in terms of gender. It is precisely the rereading of her films by modern feminists that has been responsible for the interest in her work. It is equally difficult to determine the gender-specific audience contemporary to Epstein, yet the point made about Dulac can be made for Epstein as well—it is recent feminist interest which led to her "discovery." Varda enjoys a somewhat different situation, although a similar temporality exists. Her early New Wave work was not acknowledged at all, yet Varda has been able to benefit from a more recent reading of her films from a feminist perspective, in an activity that newly recognizes what was always there. In a sense, then, this study allows all three directors to be re-seen from the standpoint of feminist theory, a productive context that was lacking at the time the films were released.

Earlier I discussed several postulations of feminist film theory that suggested ways of thinking the difference of women's cinema. For Mary Ann Doane, a feminist cinema will be concerned with posing the complex relations between the female body and psychic/signifying processes. This is precisely where the force of Germaine Dulac's film-making lies, for her two most important films strategically locate work on unconscious signification within images of the feminine. Her later works of "pure cinema" posit a plurality of meanings, multiple positions of subjectivity which foreground relations of language and desire. For Teresa DeLauretis, the conceptualization of a new female social subject implies a different articulation of female subjectivity itself. It is here that the films of Marie Epstein are most applicable, for her reformulation of fantasy and the reciprocity of female desire implies a feminine figure constituted as another (object of) vision, one other than that of the dominant cinema. Laura Mulvey's call for a break with conventional modes of cinematic discourse involves both a liberation of the look from its voyeuristic/fetishistic structures and a destabilization of the rigorous Oedipal narrative. Agnès Varda's continual preoccupation with the problematics of vision and with narrative dislocation—particularly as these relate to the representation of the feminine and the redefinition of visual pleasure—situate her clearly within the province of the radically self-conscious feminist cinema posited by Mulvey.

At the same time, each of these filmmakers works at the other levels as well; they do not fit so resolutely into fixed categories as this description at first might seem to imply. Rather, a reconsideration of female authorship in enunciative terms suggests different desiring constructions of both filmmaker and viewer, positions which are engaged and actualized textually. All three areas are joined in feminist cinema in its attempt to express and address that "other" of patriarchal culture which constitutes the feminine. While each of these filmmakers might have a more direct relation to one of the options, the notion of a female enunciating subject encompasses all three. The theorization of a feminist cinema can be posed as a series of problems, with each director representing a particular solution: The work of Germaine Dulac suggests some answers to the questions involved in conceptualizing a woman's desire; Marie Epstein, perhaps, can suggest responses to the definition of a feminine gaze; and Agnès Varda comes to mind when the parameters of a female discourse are explored. Yet the related constructions of sexuality, vision, authorship, and text—and their triple articulation in terms of female subjectivity, the cinematic apparatus, and textual processes—form the problematic of feminist filmmaking itself. It is through an examination of these filmmakers and their work, as each engages with the issues of figuring the feminine and representing her own (different) desire, that some understanding of a truly alternative practice of the cinema can come about.

NOTES

1. It was actually René Clair who was to make the film from a silent script that he had written, with the intent of using Louise Brooks. When he reworked the scenario for sound, the German-French production company, Sofar, was displeased and so removed him from the project, which was then given to Genina, a prolific Italian director. As Clair recalls, "They cut everything I wrote, except the last scene." This visually and aurally astounding ending I've described, then, is actually the work of René Clair, and one can only speculate as to what the entire film might have been like had he been able to direct it.

2. Laura Mulvey, "Visual Pleasure and Narrative Cinema," *Screen* 16:3 (Autumn 1975): 6–18.

3. See especially Janet Bergstrom, "Alternation, Segmentation, Hypnosis: Interview with Raymond Bellour," *Camera Obscura*, nos. 3/4 (1979): 70–103, for a complete discussion of Bellour's work, as well as a bibliography of his articles (pp. 133–34). Bellour's "Hitchcock: The Enunciator" (*Camera Obscura*, no. 2 [1978]: 66–91) is particularly important to the points I am discussing here, as is my own discussion of Bellour's article, "Woman, Desire, and the Look: Feminism and the Enunciative Apparatus in Cinema," in *Theories of Authorship*, ed. John Caughie (London: Routledge and Kegan Paul, 1981), pp. 242–50.

4. Christian Metz, "The Imaginary Signifier," in *The Imaginary Signifier: Psychoanalysis and the Cinema*, trans. Celia Britton et al. (Bloomington: Indiana University Press, 1982), p. 7.

5. See Miriam Hansen's "Pleasure, Ambivalence, Identification: Valentino and Female Spectatorship," *Cinema Journal* 25:4 (Summer 1986): 6–32, for a cogent summary of the arguments concerning the female viewer.

6. Mulvey, "Visual Pleasure," p. 17.

7. Laura Mulvey, "Afterthoughts on 'Visual Pleasure and Narrative Cinema' Inspired by *Duel in the Sun*," *Framework*, nos. 15–17 (1981): 12–15, here, p. 12. A subsequent article by Mulvey, "Changes," in *Discourse*, no. 7 (1985): 11–30, discusses feminist filmmaking from the standpoint of both spectatorship and her own position as filmmaker.

8. Mulvey, "Afterthoughts," p. 15.

9. Mary Ann Doane, "The 'Woman's Film': Possession and Address," in *Re-Vision: Essays in Feminist Film Criticism*, ed. Mary Ann Doane, Patricia Mellencamp, and Linda Williams (Frederick, Md.: University Publications of America and the American Film Institute, 1984), pp. 67–80; cited here, pp. 79–80, emphasis added. This is a continuation of work in which Doane demonstrates, through extremely lucid textual analyses, that films that attempt to trace female subjectivity and desire do so in terms of fantasies traditionally associated with the feminine —masochism, hysteria, paranoia:

"*Caught* and *Rebecca:* The Inscription of Femininity as Absence," *enclitic* 5:2/ 6:1 (Fall 1981-Spring 1982): 75–89. Since my writing of the present chapter, Doane's book, *The Desire to Desire* (Bloomington: Indiana University Press, 1987), in which she reworks and expands some of her arguments, has been published.

10. Mary Ann Doane, "Film and the Masquerade: Theorising the Female Spectator," *Screen* 23:3–4 (September–October 1982): 74–87.

11. Doane, "Film and the Masquerade," p. 87.

12. Teresa DeLauretis, *Alice Doesn't: Feminism, Semiotics, Cinema* (Bloomington: Indiana University Press, 1984), p. 143.

13. DeLauretis, *Alice Doesn't*, p. 83.

14. Teresa DeLauretis, "Oedipus Interruptus," *Wide Angle* 7:1–2 (1985): 34–40, here, p. 40.

15. Mulvey, "Visual Pleasure," p. 18.

16. Mary Ann Doane, "Woman's Stake: Filming the Female Body," *October,* no. 17 (Summer 1981): 23–36, here, p. 36.

17. DeLauretis, "Oedipus Interruptus," p. 38.

18. This is suggested in E. Ann Kaplan's reply (*Cinema Journal* 24:2 [Winter 1985]: 40–43) to Linda Williams's " 'Something Else Besides a Mother': *Stella Dallas* and the Maternal Melodrama," *Cinema Journal* 24:1 (Fall 1984): 2–27, which responds, in part, to Kaplan's "The Case of the Missing Mother: Maternal Issues in Vidor's *Stella Dallas*," *Heresies,* no. 16 (1983): 81–85. In a section of "Pleasure, Ambivalence" Miriam Hansen also takes up these issues, with more emphasis on the social factors that impinge on the first and third notions of the spectator. Kaplan's *Women and Film: Both Sides of the Camera* (New York: Methuen, 1983) goes into detail regarding the "male gaze" and provides a useful overview of the basic arguments. And all of the essays in *Re-Vision,* ed. Doane, Mellencamp, and Williams, in one way or another touch on the notion of spectatorship in the feminine.

19. DeLauretis, "Oedipus Interruptus," p. 36.

20. Annette Kuhn explores the relationship of social audience and textual spectator in film and television in "Women's Genres: Melodrama, Soap Opera, and Theory," *Screen* 25:1 (January–February 1984): 18–28.

21. Jacqueline Rose, "Femininity and Its Discontents," in *Sexuality in the Field of Vision* (London: Verso, 1986), pp. 82–103.

22. Elisabeth Cowie, "Woman as Sign," *m/f,* no. 1 (1978): 49–63, here, p. 60.

23. See my chapter, "Psychoanalysis, Film, and Television" in *Channels of Discourse: Television and Contemporary Criticism,* ed. Robert C. Allen (Chapel Hill: University of North Carolina Press, 1987), pp. 172–210, for a detailed introductory discussion of these concepts.

24. J. Laplanche and J.-B. Pontalis, *The Language of Psychoanalysis* (New York: W. W. Norton, 1973), p. 475.

25. Emile Benveniste, "L'Appareil formel de d'énonciation," *Problèmes de linguistique générale* (Paris: Editions du Seuil, 1974), p. 85. For illuminating

discussions of psychoanalytic and semiotic film theories, as well as theories of enunciation and sexual difference, see Kaja Silverman's *The Subject of Semiotics* (New York: Oxford University Press, 1983).

26. Metz, *The Imaginary Signifier.* This discussion refers to the chapter entitled "Story/Discourse: A Note on Two Kinds of Voyeurism." Another translation, as it was originally delivered, appears in *Theories of Authorship*, pp. 225–31, and it is to this version that I will refer.

27. Bertrand Augst, "The Order of [Cinematographic] Discourse," *Discourse*, no. 1 (Fall 1979): 51.

28. Metz, "Story/Discourse," p. 230.

29. Ibid.

30. Bellour in Bergstrom, "Alternation, Segmentation, Hypnosis," p. 98.

31. Ibid., p. 94.

32. Ibid., p. 98.

33. See my article, "To See and Not to Be: Female Subjectivity and the Law in Alfred Hitchcock's *Notorious*," *Literature and Psychology* 33:3–4 (1987): 1–17, for an extensive analysis of femininity and enunciation in the Hitchcock text. For a very different reading of Hitchcock's films, see the articles of Tania Modleski, collected and expanded in her book, *The Women Who Knew Too Much* (New York: Methuen, 1988).

34. Bellour in Bergstrom, "Alternation, Segmentation, Hypnosis," p. 90.

35. These articles are included in Bellour's book, *L'Analyse du film* (Paris: Editions Albatros, 1979), for which an English translation is forthcoming. The article on *The Birds*, "*Les Oiseaux: Système d'un fragment*," is available from the British Film Institute Educational Advisory Service in mimeo translation; "Le blocage symbolique" (on *North by Northwest*) is summarized by Kari Hanet in *Edinburgh 76 Magazine* (1976): 43–49; "Psychose, névrose, perversion" (on *Psycho*) is translated in *Camera Obscura*, nos. 3/4 (1979): 104–32.

36. Bellour, "Hitchcock: The Enunciator," p. 85.

37. Ibid., p. 73.

38. Ibid., p. 72.

39. Ibid., p. 79.

40. Ibid., p. 81.

41. Janet Bergstrom, "Enunciation and Sexual Difference," *Camera Obscura*, nos. 3/4 (1979): 32–69.

42. Bellour, "Hitchcock: The Enunciator," p. 86.

43. Bergstrom, "Enunciation and Sexual Difference," p. 58.

44. Stephen Heath, "Difference," *Screen* 19:3 (Autumn 1978): 50–127; here p. 53.

45. Janet Bergstrom, "The Avant-Garde: Histories and Theories," *Screen* 19:3 (Autumn 1978): 119–27; here p. 125.

46. Heath, "Difference," p. 103.

47. Silvia Bovenschen, "Is There a Feminine Aesthetic?" *New German Critique*, no. 10 (Winter 1977): 111–37.

48. Léon Moussinac, *L'Age ingrât du cinéma* (Paris: Les Editeurs Français

Réunis, 1967), p. 238. This is a collection of Moussinac's writings on the cinema; the citation is taken from *Panoramique du cinéma*, which originally appeared in 1929. Although these figures have since been shown to be inaccurate, Moussinac's figures are typical of the thinking of the time: The *perception* of American dominance was widespread. I am grateful to Richard Abel for pointing this out.

49. Georges Sadoul, *Dictionnaire des films* (Paris: Editions du Seuil, 1965), p. 196.

50. See in particular, Elisabeth Cowie, "Fantasia," *m/f*, no. 9 (1984): 71–105, and Elisabeth Lyon, "The Cinema of Lol V. Stein," *Camera Obscura*, no. 6 (1980): 7–41, and my own "Nursery/Rhymes: Primal Scenes in *La Maternelle*," *enclitic* 5:2/6:1 (Fall 1981-Spring 1982): 98–110, revised in this book as chapter 7.

51. Claire Johnston, "Women's Cinema as Counter-Cinema," from the pamphlet *Notes on Women's Cinema* (London: Society for Education in Film and Television, 1973), reprinted in *Sexual Stratagems: The World of Women in Film*, ed. Patricia Erens (New York: Horizon Press, 1979, pp. 133–43); my citation is taken from p. 140. Johnston's essay has been extremely influential in establishing the premises of feminist cinema. Ironically, it is in this article that she is highly critical of Varda. My interpretation of Varda contradicts this position; I find her films to be precisely the paradigm of the type of cinema that Johnston calls for.

TWO

Germaine Dulac:
First Feminist of the Avant-Garde

THE FILM CAREER OF GERMAINE DULAC is a good place to begin a feminist analysis of the cinema, for as a feminist and a polemicist dedicated to the emerging cinematic art, Dulac made both commercial and experimental films, wrote a wide range of theoretical articles, and lectured extensively. She enthusiastically agitated for the creation of a "pure cinema" which owed nothing to its literary and theatrical antecedents, a type of filmmaking that would illustrate, in its very processes, the famous "cinematic specificity" that preoccupied all those concerned with film in the twenties. She theorized a visual poetics which foregrounded the materiality of the cinematic signifier, concentrating on the rhythmic play of light, movement, and form over the content-based conventions of narrative causality and visual continuity of the traditional commercial cinema. This meant, among other things—and in both her narrative and experimental films—exploring the possibilities of nonreferentiality by attempting to divorce the diegetic content of the films (their narrative meanings) from their formal structures (the way those meanings are organized). As a filmmaker, a film theorist, and a film activist, then, Dulac was continually concerned with the specific nature of the film medium, and she analyzed this from the point of view of both the artist's impulse (the source of textual production) and the audience's perception (the site of spectatorial engagement).

Dulac's enthusiasm for the expressive possibilities of the new medium led her to discuss cinematic form in terms of a musical analogy. "The pure film we all dream of making is a visual symphony, composed of rhythmic images which the artist's feelings alone organize and project on the screen."[1] This postulation of a "visual music" was not without a prior critical tradition, and it held a prominent position in the aesthetic theories of the time, for numerous filmmakers sought to engage, in both their writing and their films, with the suggestive correlation between cinema and music. But what makes Germaine Dulac's writing about it unique is her effort to make this coincide with a specifically feminine aesthetic. Or, from a slightly different perspective, what makes this writing unique is what Dulac's conceptualization *implies* for feminist theory. Although her language might suggest an idealist notion of individual creativity, a harmonious aesthetic realm beyond social contradiction, it is important to consider Dulac's argument for cinematic composition as an effort to lay the foundation for discussing feminist cinema in formal terms. Her work thus resituates feminist debate within the areas of formal experimentation and the production of meaning, conceptualizing alternatives to the prevalent forms in terms of a gendered position of resistance. Dulac is important for feminists precisely because she did not view feminist filmmaking simply as the suffusion of available forms with "feminist" content. Rather, for Dulac, feminist filmmaking meant working at the very sources of cinematic expression, through the manipulation of formal elements, in order to provide an alternative to the dominant film practice, to speak in *another* voice. Her formal preoccupations were thus indivisible from her feminist politics.

Germaine Dulac was born on November 17, 1882, into a cultured, haute bourgeois environment; her father was a cavalry officer, her mother a sophisticated and intelligent woman with a lively appreciation of the arts.[2] Early in her life Dulac experienced a passionate love for music; she said that from the age of five, certain passages of *Tannhauser* overwhelmed her,[3] and she studied music, especially Wagner, in her teens. When her parents died she moved to Paris and combined her interests in socialism and feminism with a career in journalism. From 1909 to 1913, she worked on the staff of one of France's first feminist publications, *La Française* (founded in 1906), where she interviewed accomplished women artists, actresses, and writers and wrote drama criticism. She also worked on the editorial staff of *La Fronde,* a radical feminist journal of the time, which had the improvement of the situation of women as a practical political goal. Apparent in these early articles is an ideal of female creativity linked in some way with the social liberation of women. Thus even before her filmmaking career

Sandy Flitterman-Lewis

began, Dulac was interested in the articulation of formal problems with feminist concerns.

During this time Dulac also pursued her interest in still photography, an interest that preceded by some amount of time her actual entry into cinema in 1910. As she recounts it, she was already convinced of the evocative power of the art, of its capability to do much more than simply reproduce objective reality. "My first childhood savings were consecrated to the purchase of a camera which I can still see in M. Gaumont's store on the rue Saint-Roch. Little by little the camera was perfected, the lenses were made more precise, and soon, by my own reflection, I arrived at this observation: It isn't enough to simply capture reality in order to express it in its totality; something else is necessary in order to respect it entirely, to surround it in its atmosphere and to make its moral meaning perceptible through the care taken with angles and framing."[4]

Although tempered with a romanticism that, problematically, runs through much of Dulac's thinking, this early recognition of the transforming power of the lens points to something absolutely central to Dulac's theory of the cinema. Much of her filmmaking career is marked by this effort to pry the cinema from its assumed ability for simple photographic reproduction in order to engage its capacity for evocation. At the same time, the recognition that material signifying factors (such as angle and composition) can shape meaning is at the base of even her earliest formulations of the visual image.

Although she originally preferred the music that accompanied the cinema over the films themselves, and was initially overwhelmed by the frenetic activity of the production studio, Dulac began to be interested in moving images "not for what they were at the time, but with the intuition of what they could become."[5] In 1914, she traveled to Rome (where film production was said to be the best) to assist her friend Stacia de Napierkowska on the filming of *Caligula;* this experience convinced her even more that the film medium offered possibilities that had only begun to be explored for artistic expression. Late in 1915, along with the writer Irene Hillel-Erlanger (her first scenarist) and her then-husband Albert Dulac, she founded a film production company, D.E.L.I.A. Films.

Between 1915 and 1916, this company made three films, all scripted by Hillel-Erlanger and directed by Germaine Dulac: *Les soeurs ennemies, Géo le mystérieux,* and *Vénus victrix (Dans l'ouragan de la vie).*[6] Although at least one critic commends these early films for their attention to detail in costuming and decor,[7] Dulac criticizes them for their primitive—and theatrical—notion of action as a simple accumulation of events. This emphasis on external facts made these films "little dramatic or charming stories which hardly held more interest than those films before which I closed my eyes in order to listen to the music."[8]

In 1918, Dulac directed *Ames de fous,* a four-hour film divided into six episodes, for which she had written the scenario. The film seeks to reconcile two contradictory modes of thought, and, not coincidentally, two conflicting images of woman. The romantic image of the woman associated with the past must give way to the active woman of the future, one who affirms herself in her work and predicts a new age of autonomy. As Henri Fescourt describes it, the film gives "the impression of a subtle juncture of two epochs: the one coming to an end . . . and the era of the future, with its indications of contemporary dynamism."[9]

Structurally similar to the commercially successful serials of the time, *Ames de fous* already employed cinematic techniques such as backlighting, silhouettes and shadows in order to evoke an atmosphere—thereby creating an "art of spiritual nuances" in the service of expressing the "interior movements of the soul"[10] which was to become the hallmark of Dulac's cinematic production. Continuing the early recognition of the evocative power of specifically cinematic techniques, Dulac discussed the film's popularity in terms that suggest a nascent theory of film as codicity, that is, as an interplay of different systems which carry meaning.

This film, which permitted me to organize my thoughts, was understood in terms of its dramatic action, but not in terms of its technique. Nevertheless, I wonder if its success was not due to its suggestive methods which extended the action, methods which I used but which took hold of the public without their being aware of it . . . [Ames de fous] made me understand that beyond precise facts and events, atmosphere is an element of emotion, that the emotional value of a film lies less in the action than in the subtleties it exudes, and that if the expression of an actor is obviously of value in itself, it can only attain its fullest intensity by a complementary play of images coming in reaction to it. Lighting, camera placement and editing all appeared to me as more essential elements than the production of a scene uniquely played according to dramatic laws.[11]

Dulac takes as her starting point the film's effect on the audience, making a distinction between the viewer's conscious responses to the dramatic action and the more subtle signifying work of film technique that can be seen to operate at an unconscious level. It is this division which allows her to develop a thesis of filmic signification as a systematic process that works in tandem with the more obvious or accessible narrative meanings. This dualism persists throughout Dulac's career, allowing her to conceptualize a cinema of atmosphere and evocative emotion (derived from fundamental cinematic mechanisms), and laying the groundwork for her later interest in unconscious processes. It is not the particular dramatic value of the image itself—consciously apprehended—that generates meaning, but rather its placement in a complex relation with other images through editing, an articulation of formal elements of lighting, composition, and rhythm. Beyond that, Dulac's thinking about Ames de fous is significant for another reason, one highly relevant to the project of a feminist cinema, for the film's central character and organizing image is a woman. It would seem, from accounts of the film, that Ames de fous posits a reciprocity between two notions of "the feminine"—between "woman" as a metaphor (for the past, for the future) and "woman" as a social construction, composed of varied social discourses on femininity. It is this kind of reflection, suggested here in a popular serial film, that will be most fully achieved in the two films that take explorations of femininity as their central concern, The Smiling Mme Beudet and The Seashell and the Clergyman.

Eve Francis, a major actress of the twenties who starred in many of the important "Impressionist" films of the period, played the lead in

Ames de fous. She introduced Dulac to Louis Delluc, her (Francis's) husband and perhaps the most important figure in French film of the twenties ("he was truly the leader, the prophet that cinema was awaiting").[12] It was Delluc who first formulated the call for a national cinematic identity by inscribing the motto—"The French cinema must be *cinema;* the French cinema must be *French*"—at the top of his journal *Cinéa.* The struggle then took place on two fronts: 1) experimentation and formal innovation with the specific properties of the cinematic medium; and 2) an effort to elaborate a truly national art form rooted in French cultural traditions and life.

Delluc, who, in addition to documenting the cinema's history and sources, attempting to discover the specific nature of cinema through his theory of *photogénie,* and militating for the creation of film societies to inspire public interest in the new medium, was also one of the first people in France to make explicit reference to Freud in his writing. There is perhaps some connection between Delluc's interest in Freud and his emphasis on narration in cinema; he insisted on the importance of a strong scenario in filmmaking. A great lover of the Westerns of Thomas Ince, he felt that French filmmakers should study American films in order to become more professional. Most important of all was the necessity to understand how to tell stories cinematically, how to visually organize a film. This meant, above all, integrating film technique with narrative concerns, rather than allowing cinema to remain subservient to literature.

Delluc wrote the scenario (his first) for *La Fête espagnole,* the next film that Dulac directed after finishing work on *Le Bonheur des autres* (1918). Starring Eve Francis as a beautiful woman around whom a vicious rivalry revolves, the film attempted to convey some of the ambience of American Westerns. It was praised by some critics (who called Dulac's direction "remarkable" and "first rate") and harshly attacked by others. Because, due to finances, the film could not be shot in Spain (it was done in the South of France), Dulac avoided general shots that would disclose too much of the landscape, and concentrated on details like walls and isolated benches under trees for the creation of atmosphere. Most notable in the film is the fiesta sequence, which was shot in a quasi-documentary style.

Henri Langlois elaborates on the film's capacity to make these descriptive passages the fundamental part of the film's action: "*La Fête espagnole* is quite simply a long description achieved by little touches."[13] The landscape, rather than functioning as a background for the action, became the action itself (this already incorporating the major lesson learned in the twenties from the Swedish films of Sjostrom and Stiller).

Langlois says that the film owes much to Germaine Dulac's comprehension of the musical aspects of montage. This film without intertitles built its ambience and rhythm through a rapid cadencing of images (in themselves relatively straightforward, devoid of unusual camera angles or focal lengths), leitmotifs that circulated through the film to envelop characters with landscape, bullfight, and dancing couples in order to create a charged emotional atmosphere. The climactic dancing scene (portions of which survive in the fragment at the Cinémathèque) is particularly exemplary in its use of rapid montage to convey the accelerated experience and subjective impression of dancing itself.

Importantly, this intensely sensual and exciting atmosphere circulates around the pivotal figure of the femme fatale, Soledad, whose intoxicated dancing is intercut with the knife fight between the two men. The alternation of sexual passion and violence that results in the death of the two suitors and Soledad's flight with a third lover suggests something more than the poetic evocation of an exotic milieu: It would seem that the film was constructed around an attempt to portray a certain cultural myth of the woman and to convey, in as powerful a way as possible, the effect of the unconscious association of femininity and sexuality. As Philippe Soupault attests, "The great passion which hovers over the clouds and which leaves an odor of blood in its wake, rests for an instant on a woman's shoulder. . . . With a gesture, a glance, Eve Francis knows how to evoke anger, hatred, joy, love. . . . We cannot forget this smile, distant like smoke."[14]

In the period between *La Fête espagnole* and *The Smiling Mme Beudet* (1923), Dulac made a number of films in which she continued to explore cinematic methods for the rendering of characters' psychologies, techniques that would allow her to portray subjectivity on the screen.

> With *La Cigarette* (1918), I began to make psychological films, a genre which I was not to leave until *La Folie des vaillants,* which marks another evolution.
> Psychology with *La Cigarette,* impressionism with *La Fête espagnole* (1919), more and more I was considering the cinema not as something to be used in order to describe a dramatic action or to create interest through a story, but to reflect this infinity of impressions of which the "fact" is purely and simply a result. . . . I moved farther and farther away from a theatrical conception in order to approach the art of rhythm.[15]

Already *La Cigarette* (based on her own scenario) achieves something that approaches abstraction by creating an atmosphere that "undulated like the smoke of a fine tobacco . . . with a finesse unknown in the cinema."[16]

As character psychology in film became more and more a question of subtle impressions and the visualization of feelings for Dulac, she began to realize "that movement in the cinema could reside in a sort of immobility of character, surrounded by mobile and changing impressions."[17] It was in this context that she made the independently produced *Malencontre* (1920) and *La Belle dame sans merci* (1920). The latter, based on a scenario by Hillel-Erlanger, achieved what Louis Delluc described as "the touch, the sensitivity, the sense of distillation, a sort of style which makes you think of Manet at his best."[18] Dulac calls it a transitional film in which she focussed on the subtleties of characterization in a minute and detailed way, arriving, through this suggestive method, at the creation of certain character types.[19]

La Mort du soleil (1922), based on a scenario by André Legrand, gave Dulac the opportunity to expand her technical repertoire in the service of character development. "During this film I began to utilize what I call 'technical acrobatics,' considering that certain methods, such as fade-outs, dissolves, superimpositions, masks (mattes), irises, etc. had a suggestive value which was equivalent to musical signs. The public was not yet accustomed to these methods and a few passages, which now seem quite simple, had to be cut from the film."[20] For example, when the film's protagonist regains consciousness after a stroke, Dulac inserted what she called "an emotional commentary" ("*un commentaire sensitif*") into the key scene in order to elaborate on his psychological state. In a manner reminiscent of her comments on *Ames de fous,* she articulated the facial close-ups with shots of his arms, of objects, of the play of light and shadow, "giving these elements a visual value equal in intensity and cadence to the physical and moral state of the character. . . . Suggestion thus worked to prolong the action, creating a much wider emotional domain since it was no longer contained within the confines of precise facts."[21]

In addition, Dulac attempted to convey the character's state of consciousness by placing gauze in front of the camera lens to evoke his subjective impression of things. The audience merely assumed that the image was out of focus. Even more disturbing to the public was the effort to symbolize the thought processes of this character, now paralyzed and obsessed with the impossibility of happiness. The appearance of a ship, first sharply in focus and then hazy, "evocative of the long voyages henceforth impossible," and the image of a young woman, "symbol of love now forever inaccessible,"[22] interrupted the linear flow of the action and frustrated the viewers' desire for verisimilitude.

Richard Abel points out an even further confusion responsible for the suppression of these sequences, and one that is significant to Dulac's particular project within the general context of the exploration of subjectivity. In *La Mort du soleil* Dulac focusses not only on the inner conflict of Dr. Lucien Faivre as he combats tuberculosis, but also on the emotional struggle of Marthe Voisin, equally committed to both the doctor's research and her own family. In a sequence of shared delirium, Dulac attempts to render the passion, the torment, and the eventual mutual dedication to scientific research through the evocation of mental or psychological images for both of the characters. Because the film only exists in fragmentary form, one can only speculate, but it is possible that this film represents an early attempt on Dulac's part not only to depict emotional states of feeling, but to differentiate between a masculine and a feminine consciousness, and in this it anticipates *The Smiling Mme Beudet*'s focus on a specifically female subjectivity.

In addition to these four films, Dulac worked on several projects that were never completed: two films based on novels (*The Sorrows of Young Werther* and *Manon Lescaut*), a short film inspired by "Le Lac" by Lamartine, and one based on "Le Cachet rouge," a novella by Vigny.[23] Dulac's early interest in Romanticism, in the suggestive power of the cinematic image, and in the elaboration of a visual poetics can be discerned from the subjects alone of these unrealized treatments.

La Souriante Mme Beudet (*The Smiling Mme Beudet*), perhaps Dulac's most well-known film, was made during 1921 and released in Paris in November of 1923. Applauded by feminists from the time it was first shown, the film concerns a latter-day Madame Bovary, a provincial housewife who escapes the torments of her boorish husband by means of imaginative flights into an extraordinarily rich fantasy world. Eventually, suffocated by the overwhelming vulgarity of this fabric merchant who thinks only of his business, and who has contempt for her love of poetry and music, she tries to kill him. The accident is averted, and the couple returns to its monotonous provincial rut.

Through stylistic experimentation with an abundance of technical devices ranging from dissolves, punctuating fades, soft focus, double exposures and superimpositions, to both fast and slow motion, accelerated montage, dramatic lighting effects, masks, distorting lenses, and camera manipulations, Dulac creates a highly charged visual atmosphere to convey Madame Beudet's imaginative world. This time, however, suggestive methods were not put entirely in the service of character development; they became the very elaboration of the film's poetic texture itself. Dulac was thus moving away from a notion of cinema tied to narrative causality, and toward a more abstract notion of film that dealt with the essence of the medium and its specificity. And, it is not accidental that this particular research finds its expression in the consciousness of a female character. In speaking of her work on *Beudet,* Dulac says, "I realized that the cinema was finding its way, more and more, in the rhythmic opposition of images, more, even, than in the play of the actors, because the art of acting became, with these new methods, the art of expressing oneself in immobility."[24] Implicit in this formulation, then, is an emphasis on editing in the production of meaning, for Dulac here comes to recognize the significance resulting from the relations between the shots.

Thus the importance of the shot as the fundamental unit of filmic construction, an element of composition, emerged as a result of Dulac's thinking about *Beudet.* During a lecture at the Musée Galliera in which she projected, among other things, the opening sequences of *Beudet,* Dulac discussed this in detail.

> The shot is the image in its isolated, expressive value, emphasized by the framing of the lens. . . . The shot is place, action, and thought at the same time. Each distinct image which is juxtaposed is called: shot. The shot is the parcelling out of the drama, a nuance which converges/combines to form the conclusion. It is the keyboard on which we play. It is the only means we have with which to create, in a single movement, a bit of interior life. . . . Interior life rendered perceptible through images, combined with movement—this is the whole art of the cinema. Movement, interior life, these two terms are not incompatible. What is more active than the life of the psyche, with its reactions, its multiple impressions, its swells, its dreams, its memories?[25]

And, after a similar projection, she said simply, "I wanted to show you that movement and its diverse combinations could evoke emotions without the arrangement of facts or dramatic complications and I wanted to shout: Keep cinema on its own (to itself): Movement, without literature."[26]

In constructing an equivalence between a primary cinematic element, movement, and the inner life of the psyche, Dulac formulates what will become the cornerstone of her theory and what makes it so critical in terms of contemporary feminist issues. Thus for Dulac, it is never simply a question of technique, a formalist discourse on the virtues of montage; rather, her concern with unconscious processes and the cinematic articulation of desiring subjectivity makes these explorations both a signifying and a social fact. While many of Dulac's contemporaries, too, were involved in theorizing the reciprocity between cinematic and mental processes, it is the precise inflection of Dulac's interest that differentiates her work from the pervasive modernism of the era. For Dulac's preoccupation with "interior life" was never far from the consideration of a distinctly feminine voice, although it is in the films themselves, rather than in her writing, that this becomes apparent. To contemporize her discourse is to understand the varied and "multiple impressions" of the psyche as another language of desire, a discourse in the feminine which suggests alternatives to the dominant fictions of reality.

In 1921, Dulac went to New York, where she met D. W. Griffith; she was greatly impressed by the combination of technical efficiency and artistic skill in his American studios. She described her visit for the journal *Cinéa* in an article entitled "Chez D. W. Griffith." At the time, French audiences were enthusiastically seeing Griffith's *True Heart Susie, Broken Blossoms,* and *Way Down East; The Birth of a Nation* and *Intolerance* had already confirmed Griffith's status as a major director. In her article, Dulac took the opportunity to elaborate on two themes that traverse much of her writing: 1) autonomy for the cinema as an independent artform free from the influences of painting and literature; and 2) the importance of the filmmaker as an individual artistic and creative force. "In vain you'd seek the large industrial factory. You are in the *atelier* of an artist. . . . Research which is personal and constant. . . . To disengage the cinema from the other artforms, reveal its own distinct path, its own greatness and its own personality—in these efforts the direction of Griffith has been greatly innovative."[27]

In 1922, hoping to appeal to a more general audience, Dulac went to work for the Société des Cinéromans, which produced the six episodes of her *Gossette* (1922-23), a commercially successful serial film. Interspersed with the popular intrigues of the conventional adventure story were sequences that revealed Dulac's continuing concern with poetic evocation through technical means. Henri Fescourt discusses the film in these terms: "I remember a succession of close-ups (scythes cutting wheat, shafts bending [in the wind], fluttering leaves, wheelbarrows on dirt paths, etc.) which constituted, by themselves, a complete visual poem, a rustic evocation at once beautiful and restrained."[28]

Gossette was another film that Dulac was fond of projecting in conjunction with her public lectures. The fragment she showed illustrated how "the movement of 'an emotional state of mind' could be realized not simply by a succession of images, but by the double movement of the images and their juxtaposition."[29] Dulac was particularly pleased with this example because *Gossette* was a serial film—a genre critically discredited but widely liked by the public. In order to portray the subjectivity of the young heroine who had been kidnapped and

drugged, Dulac combined images of roadways shot through deform-
ing lenses, elongated trees, multiple close-ups of heads, and fantastic
impressions in a rhythmic relay that emphasized movement within
movement: "Movement, and only movement, was the basis of my
psychological technique."[30] Thus in attempting to translate an emotional state into cinematic terms, Dulac was able to illustrate her ideal
of visual music. "Poetry and symphony with Abel Gance, psychology
with *Gossette,* a song of the soul, hearts beating, interior rhythms,
movements. . . . Theme of the action: a sensation . . . not a single story,
and yet, an impression."[31]

Le Diable dans la ville (1925), a film about religious fanaticism in the
Middle Ages, represents an early attempt of Dulac's to materialize the
fantastic, something she fully achieved later with *The Seashell and the
Clergyman* (1927). Based on a scenario by Jean-Louis Bouquet, the film
deals with a contagious fear—which general superstition attributes to
the devil—that spreads through a village. In fact, a band of smugglers
is responsible for the bizarre occurrences in the town. While Bouquet's
version was set in a fictive village of 1840, Dulac was forced by her
producers, Cinéromans, to choose the quasi-medieval tone of the fifteenth century and was thus obliged to shoot the entire film on studio
sets. An even more unfortunate consequence of this change of setting
was the fact that the scenario's disturbing confusion of fantasy and
reality was now legitimized by a fifteenth century belief in witchcraft.
While working on the film, Dulac gave an interview to J. A. de Munto
in which she said: "[It] will be my first film in which movement plays
a major role. It is a film of crowds, a bit satirical, with a slight tendency
toward caricature. The soul which stirs about in my film is that of a
small town in the Middle Ages. And its activity will necessarily be an
activity of the masses, with all its elements: the leaders, the figurehead
authorities, the peaceful flock, the discontented flock."[32]

Henri Fescourt finds this desire to film movement, or to make
movement itself a major subject, a shortcoming of the film. For him,
Dulac sacrificed expressive atmosphere for the quasi-abstract play of
moving forms and the film suffered from this sort of transfer. "In the
terror of the petit bourgeois shopkeepers, the grocers, the sextons,
and the religious folk, she saw above all the element of movement, of
flight, of running about, and not the comedy which emanated from
these bizarre characters and incidents . . . a certain nocturnal poetry
was lacking as well."[33]

Fescourt asserts, however, that Dulac was too talented a director not
to have created some form of ambience, and "the film was exquisite
to look at." What he seems to have missed in this commentary is the

place experimentation with internal rhythms held in Dulac's general movement toward cinematic abstraction, an emphasis on rhythmic, musical composition that was to culminate in her later, nonnarrative, films. *Le Diable dans la ville* managed, however, to combine its nascent abstraction with nuances of satire and social criticism—enough so that the Soviets purchased a copy of the film[34]—but the artificiality of the sets and costumes considerably undermined the level of critique.

Dulac became an independent director again and her next feature, *Ame d'artiste* (1925), was produced by a Franco-German company, Ciné-France-Westi, with French, German, and Russian emigre financing. This film was a great commercial success; a costume spectacle, made in collaboration with the Russian director Alexander Volkoff and based on a play by the Danish playwright Christian Molbeck, it benefitted from the elegant costuming, elaborate sets, spectacular scenes, international cast, and cultural cross-references particular to this type of film. Because of its high production values, the film was able to compete with similar American productions popular in France at the time, and thereby set the standard for the commercial studio spectacular.

Set in the London theater world (reconstructed in the studios at Billancourt),[35] the film integrates a fairly sentimentalized notion of artistic creation with the traditional material of melodrama, a love triangle. An aspiring playwright named Herbert Campbell is loved by two women, his wife Edith and a famous stage actress, Helen Taylor. Confrontations typical of the genre (as when Herbert asks for a divorce, or when the two women meet) abound, but it seems that Dulac was able to "introduce some absolute manipulations of pure film processes"[36] within the confines of the commercial formula in order to create visual effects that were absent from the stage version. Some critics compared the film's powerful opening sequence—a violent quarrel with an imminent stabbing—to the rapidly edited portions of Griffith's *Broken Blossoms,* finding that the "alternation of different actions attained a simultaneity heretofore unknown in the cinema."[37] The film's climax involves a complex alternation between Helen performing Herbert's play (*Ame d'artiste*), Edith watching in the audience, and Herbert attempting suicide in a seedy hotel room. This conclusion, too, seems reminiscent of Griffith, as Edith's last-minute rescue of Herbert is deferred and intensified through cross-cutting. What distinctly marks Dulac's film, however, is the characteristic subjective orchestration of Herbert's mental confusion with the unwitting activities of the two women rivals, suggesting a psychological complexity that adds a new dimension to the narrative simultaneity. However, the conventional ending, which leaves only Herbert satisfied in love and career, attests to the powerful commercial constraints placed on a director so intensely involved in the exploration of female subjectivity.

Nonetheless, the opportunity to work with Volkoff gave Dulac the occasion to continue her cinematic experimentation with modes of subjectivity, and her comments on one of his films illustrate how much she appreciated the chance to work with the Russian director. His *Kean* (1924) was another film that she projected during her public lectures about cinema art. She chose a passage which, appropriately, illustrated the subjective impressions of a character who had gotten drunk. Pointing to the psychological effect that was translated by movement alone—by the musical rhythm of the images themselves— she exclaimed, "A whole drama is played out in this short passage, a whole interior drama. . . . Cinema is movement, I constantly repeat, and this movement is more internal then external."[38] Emphasizing an aspect of film viewing that was to recur throughout her public talks and theoretical writings, Dulac pointed out that one did not need to know anything at all about the character in order to experience the sensations conveyed by this passage.

Dulac was particularly fond of her next film, which she financed herself, *La Folie des vaillants* (1925). Based on a short story by Maxim Gorky, it was her most abstract film to date, illustrating, through its poetic structure, Dulac's increasing emphasis on the kinship between cinema and music, and requiring specific musical accompaniment. Editing the film through a technique similar to musical composition, Dulac intended for spectators to experience something akin to the experience of listening to a symphony. Set in a gypsy milieu on the Black Sea, this tragic story of a violinist's love for a beautiful woman was told through the rhythmic interplay of images, often superimposed, of fields of flowers, roadways, clouds, the violin, and the young woman.

In spite of its distribution throughout the world, including such places as Roumania and Argentina at the time of its release,[39] there is no extant print of the film. We do, however, have Dulac's comments on the film, as well as a fragment of six images used to illustrate one of her theoretical texts.[40] "Above all, what I sought in *La folie des vaillants,* was the expression of a spiritual life cadenced by the rhythm of the images, their duration, their dramatic or emotional intensity, following the sweetness or violence which emerged from the souls of my characters."[41] In other words, the ideal film for Dulac would use character merely as a starting point; at its best, the real material of the film was to be "pure sensation": "I was unable to totally achieve what I had in mind. The visual symphony which I dream of creating someday—a day very far off, alas—will use fewer characters; it will go further in terms of the play of light, the clash or the union of objects and fleeting expressions. It will escape all literary logic in order to work, as a musician does, only with feelings."[42]

In the article that uses *La Folie des vaillants* as an illustration, Dulac further clarifies her position by stating that as the art of cinema evolved, the emphasis on narrative storytelling and the actors' performances gave way to a more studied concern with the images themselves and their juxtaposition. Like the musician who works with the sonorities of the musical phrase, the filmmaker must consider the formal rhythms of the images over their objective content. In this way the "emotive value" of the images can carry the expressive weight, doing away with the need for interpretative intertitles. "This was the ideal I had in mind when I *composed* [my italics] *La folie des vaillants;* I avoided the acted scene in order to concentrate solely on the powerful song of the images, the song of feelings. . . . "[43]

The six images illustrating the text are an example of this "song": A close-medium-shot of the violinist, a close-up of the violin taken from another angle, trees seen from a very low angle, a cloudy sky, a calm sea, a close-up of the woman, listening, fields of flowers, and rippling water. The caption reads: "The violin's song: A young woman transforming the melody into a personal dream. An example of suggestion replacing action."[44]

With *Antoinette Sabrier* (1926), Dulac returned to commercial filmmaking and to the Société des Cinéromans (*La Folie des vaillants* had had its premiere at the art house Théâtre du Colisée during a special Amis du Cinéma presentation).[45] The film was another theatrical adaptation, based on a play by Romain Coolus that had been a vaudeville success at the turn of the century. Although superficially similar to *The Smiling Mme Beudet*—both films deal with unsatisfactory bourgeois marriages—the technical innovation and visual brilliance of *Beudet* are absent from this later film. One possible reason for this is the fact that *Beudet* concentrates on the interiority and subjective reveries of its female protagonist, whereas *Antoinette Sabrier* focusses more on the milieu of high finance of its main male character, and on his internal conflict over whom to love—his wife or a younger woman. Charles Ford comments on its "intelligent utilization of classical procedures," but points out that this might be why certain critics reproached it as "too cold and academic, almost '*Comédie-Française*.' "[46] It would appear, in fact, that Dulac's heart was simply not in the project.

After this, in a desire to pursue her own interests, which were continuing to evolve in the forefront of the cinematic avant-garde,

Dulac broke once again with commercial production. In 1927, she made *La Coquille et le clergyman* (*The Seashell and the Clergyman*), based on a screenplay by Antonin Artaud; the film was an attempt to give concrete, objective form to human thought processes and fantasms through a studied organization of images which evolved their own logic—a logic unconstrained by the conventions of narrative coherence and free to explore the evocative powers of the image. This scenario was inspired by an article entitled "La Valeur psychologique de l'image," written by Artaud's close friend, a psychiatrist named Dr. René Allendy, which appeared in the journal *L'Art cinématographique*, the same journal that had published Dulac's "Les Esthétiques, les entraves: La Cinégraphie intégrale" in 1926.[47] The American critic Harry Alan Potamkin called the film "the only visual-motor film of a mental obsession," pointing out that its technical brilliance was its greatest achievement: "It does not concern us whether the images are exact from a psychoanalytic point of view, they are justified by their aesthetic, cinematic structure. The film does not ask for the oneirocritic [Apollinaire's term], but for the ciné-critic."[48]

Too much has been made of Artaud's dissatisfaction with Dulac's cinematic execution of his scenario. The famous "Madame Dulac is a cow" episode, which occurred during the film's premiere at the Studio des Ursulines on February 9, 1928,[49] seems to be a rather quixotic myth that grew up around the incident itself, partly out of a confusion of memories, partly out of an inability to deal with the film's revolutionary poetics, partly out of a largely misconstrued clash of personalities. Georges Sadoul's about-face regarding the film is indicative of this ambiguity. His vehement participation in the riot turned out to be mistaken; some thirty-five years later he admitted to Alain Virmaux that he had thought the protest was directed against Artaud rather than Dulac. It seems, as well, that Dali and Buñuel's *Un Chien Andalou* narrowly missed being shouted down in a similar manner two years later.[50] Perhaps more important is the shift in Sadoul's critical evaluation of the film. Having discredited the film for a long time on the basis of the "Ursulines riot," he was forced to reverse his judgment upon seeing the film in 1962: "The *mise en scène* was certainly not that dreamed of by Artaud, but the film has aged quite well, has acquired power with the passage of time, and deserves its place among the classics of Surrealist cinema."[51]

His fulsome praise notwithstanding, Sadoul's assessment of the accuracy of Dulac's transcription appears to labor under the same misconceptions as his earlier participation in the riot. A careful study of the film reveals that it is extremely close to Artaud's scenario; even the visual "tricks" of which Artaud is said to have later complained are suggested in his screenplay. Alain and Odette Virmaux even go so far as to call the film the work of a "good student," in which "Dulac limited herself to transcribing, or rather illustrating Artaud's text. It was an illustration which was careful, assiduous, a bit scholarly."[52] By his own admission, Artaud wanted to create a film that emphasized the visual: "It is a film of pure images. The meaning must emerge from the very impact [*rayonnement*] of these images. There is no psychoanalytical, metaphysical, or even human meaning underlying them. The film describes true states of mind without any attempt at clarification or demonstration."[53] From Dulac's own comments to Marie-Anne Colson-Malleville about the film, it is clear that she remained faithful to this conception: "[The film] is an effort to capture the human ineffable [*l'invisible humain*], that is, the instincts which do not find their impression in a series of facts constituting a story, but which spread out in a succession of images, attempting to symbolize them in their abstraction: images which sometimes appear incoherent, evocative of the disparate and unforeseen impressions lying below the course of coherent events which structure our lives. . . . "[54]

A further complication in the legacy of this film stems from a simplistic reading of Artaud's "sexism" and an equally reductive notion of Dulac's "feminism." One view bases its conclusions on criticism of the film (as having "feminized" the script) misattributed to Artaud and written some five years after his death. Another argument is grounded in an incorrectly edited version of the film that was widely distributed in the United States. Nonetheless, these conflicting arguments suggest something extremely important in determining the parameters of a feminist cinema: Assumptions about a "female aesthetic" must be considered along more theoretical lines than those implied by the biological gender of the filmmaker. The possibilities for the expression of a female voice evoked by *Seashell*'s articulation of unconscious desiring processes go far beyond an easy application of authorial stance. The complicated issues involving several levels of debate around this film will be explored more fully in chapter 4.

Shortly before working on *The Seashell and the Clergyman*, Dulac finished *L'Invitation au voyage* (1927). Based on her own scenario and freely inspired by the Baudelaire poem of the same title, the film attempted to create a cinematic equivalent to Symbolist poetry through its suggestive methods and associative play of images. Dulac's early interest in evoking the "interior life" of her characters is here advanced a step further in the direction of abstraction; the minimal plot almost serves as a pretext for the creation of atmosphere and the rendering of emotional states.

A short film (about thirty minutes) that consists primarily of "a visual orchestration of looks, gestures, and objects, in relatively close shots, with few intertitles,"[55] *L'Invitation au voyage* uses the first three lines of the poem as its starting point:[56]

Mon enfant, ma soeur,	[My child, my sister
Songe à la douceur,	Dream of the gentleness
D'aller là-bas vivre ensemble.	Of going off to live there together.]

But as Henri Fescourt notes, Dulac did not claim to illustrate the poem; rather, she intended the film "to be saturated with the poem as with a vague perfume."[57] This is one of Baudelaire's most melodious poems; in it, his research into the science of rhythms and harmonic effects evokes a seductive atmosphere of calm beauty. Its slow, rich, ordered tones give it the quality of an incantation, as opposed, for example, to the heavy, sensuous languor of a poem like *La Chevelure*. More important, it is a concretization of Stéphane Mallarmé's Symbolist formulation—"Describe not the thing, but the effect it produces"—because its evocative power consists in eliciting a desire for escape rather than in describing a particular locale.

This desire for evasion is the subtext which structures the minimal narrative of Dulac's film. A married woman, whose situation bears some resemblance to that of the frustrated Madame Beudet, meets a young officer in a smoky bistro, and, after dancing with him and hearing of his tropical voyages, experiences an intense desire to go off with him. As he speaks, she "already imagines herself sailing off toward distant countries,"[58] as a dream sequence alternates her gaze between a miniature ship on an imaginary sea and the shoddy surroundings of the cabaret. Richard Abel suggests that the rather mundane quality of the fantasy sequences, harshly criticized at the time, might have been Dulac's incisive satire of conventional visions of escape.[59]

In "Le Poème du haschisch," Baudelaire speaks of the poet's work as "evocative witchcraft" which strives to create "the mysterious and temporary state of mind in which the depth of life, jostled by its multiple problems, is revealed in its totality in the spectacle, no matter how natural or trivial it may be, that is taking place before your eyes—where the first object that strikes your eye becomes a speaking symbol."[60] For both Dulac and Baudelaire, artistic work—whether poetry or film—was a way of creating a subjective reality. The concrete image was seen as the bridge between everyday life and poetic experience, intensifying the quotidian with an aura of the marvelous. In *L'Invitation au voyage*, Dulac allowed images of blurred sails, pounding surf, and clouds to become her "speaking symbols." It has been suggested that Baudelaire saw poetry itself as a kind of "invitation to a voyage." It does not seem improbable that Dulac, given her theories of cinematic evocation, regarded this film as a similar invitation to the spectator—an invitation to participate vicariously in the flights of fantasy and dream as she conceived them, especially if one considers Dulac's emphasis on the quality of emotional transport ascribed to both cinema and music. From this perspective, the longing that she wished to convey in this film, the profound desire to escape to a sensuous elsewhere, might have easily been intended to leave, quite quickly, that sketchy female character from whence it had originated.

It was during this time that Dulac produced her most ambitious writing project; she conceived and edited the journal *Schémas*, whose single issue bears the publication date of February 1927.[61] Through it she continued her pursuit of "pure cinema" by working on the theoretical front; each article that she chose deals with the problems and aesthetics of a cinema from a slightly different perspective. Dulac herself wrote one piece, and produced a running editorial commentary to unify the separate discussions. Articles were contributed by filmmakers, artists, theorists, historians, and critics. A brief listing of its contents indicates the journal's scope and intentions: Miklos N. Bandi on *La Symphonie diagonale* by Vicking Eggeling; Hans Richter's discussion of "Mouvement"; Dulac's own article, "Du Sentiment à la ligne"; Henri Fescourt on "L'Esprit moderne"; Fernand Divoire on "Danse et cinéma"; Jean-Louis Bouquet on "Action"; plus the following articles: "Vers la conquête d'un nouvel univers" by Hubert Revol; "De l'incohérence onïrique à la cohérence cinématographique" by Dr. Paul Ramain; "Le Tableau du cinéma" by Alberto Cavalcanti; "Les possibilités artistiques de la cinématographie" by the biologist Dr. Comandon; and a "Proposition" by Jules Romains.

These articles and their interspersed commentary reiterate the main postulations of the "pure cinema" movement associated with the French avant-garde of the twenties: Cinema was an artistic creation whose rhythmic organization of shots into a kind of visual music—an organization that emphasized the orchestration of images through the pure play of light and form—would have a direct appeal to the sensibility and emotions of the audience. The foreword to the journal states, in the optimism typical of this kind of enterprise, that *Schémas* is not a review in the ordinary sense. Its dedication to the future possibilities of cinematic art would lead it to publish monographs and special issues whenever something relevant or important appeared: "We have the right and the responsibility to prepare the future. . . . [I]t will enable us to perfect our art."[62] But it warns against keeping debates on the cinema confined to an ivory tower; the journal was thus posited as a locus for the collective burgeoning of creative energy with the aim of keeping lively debate accessible to many.

In her own article,[63] Dulac attempts to answer the question, "Why is [movement] an art, rather than simply the scientific research of physicists?" She had begun to answer this question in 1925 when she described the essence of cinema in the following way: "For the cinema—which is moving, changing, interrelated light—only light, genuine and mobile light, can be its true decor."[64] In *Schemas*, she defines movement as the fundamental element of cinematic art, but goes beyond simple mathematical combinations to identify "an 'emotional and suggestive' inspiration, analogous to musical thought," which composes and organizes this movement. At the basis of this is the belief that pure movement has the power, through its rhythm alone, to excite the feelings of the spectator.

However, Dulac is careful to clarify her position by noting that "pure cinema" is only one form of filmic production. "I don't mean to say that 'integral cinema,' whose expression is composed of visual rhythms materializing in forms refined of all literal meaning, should be the 'only cinema' but merely that 'integral cinema' is *the very essence of cinema* considered in its general sense, its inner reason for being, its direct manifestation, seen as independent of the dialectics and plasticity of the other arts."[65] She concludes the essay with a passage that has become fairly popular as a quotation because its succinct formulation and energetic prose are among the best illustrations of both the aesthetic principles and the artist.

> *Because movement and rhythm remain, in any case, even in a more material and meaningful embodiment, the unique and intimate essence of cinematic expression.* I'm evoking a dancer! A woman? No. A line leaping about to harmonious rhythms. I'm evoking a luminous projection! Precise matter? No. Fluid rhythms. . . . Harmony of lines. Harmony of light. Lines, surfaces, volumes, evolving directly, without artificial devices, in the logic of their forms, stripped of all meaning that is too human, in order to aspire more successfully toward abstraction and give more space to feelings and to dreams: total cinema (*le cinéma intégral*).[66]

Between 1928 and 1929, Dulac put these theories into practice by making a number of "visual symphonies," short quasi-abstract films in which the organizing structure of a narrative was rejected in favor of emotional or musical inspiration. Dulac had said,

> A musician's writing is not always inspired by a story, most often it is through the inspiration of a feeling. *Jardin sous la pluie* [which is what Mme Beudet plays on the piano] by Debussy or *Prélude de la goutte d'eau* by Chopin for example, are the expressions of a soul's outpouring, a soul reacting. The only story is that of a soul that experiences and thinks, and yet we are moved by it. The heart of a musician sings in notes which, perceived in turn by those who hear them, give birth to an emotion. In the same way, the sensitivity of the filmmaker can be expressed through the superimposition of light and movement, the vision of which will move the soul of the spectator.[67]

Throughout all this work, Dulac never left her commitment to the emotional directness of the cinema, nor, in fact, did she give up the optimism in which it is based. The titles of these films indicate the extent to which Dulac sought to materialize these words: *Disque 927* (1929), *Thème et variations* (1929), and *Arabesque* (or *Etude cinématographique sur une arabesque*—1928).

Through the synaesthetic principle fundamental to Symbolist poetry—in which one type of stimulation evokes the sensation of another—Dulac attempted to find the visual equivalent of music by structuring her films around actual musical compositions. For example, *Disque 927* is subtitled "Germaine Dulac's Visual Impressions While Listening to the Fourth and Sixth Preludes of Frederic Chopin." *Arabesque* consists of a performance of Debussy's piece by the same name, which intersperses shots of hands at a keyboard with images intended to evoke the metaphoric associations of the music (images of rippling water, lily pads, feet on gravel paths, chairs in a park, scarves blowing, and water sprays) in an astonishingly beautiful rhythmic play of form. This is already at work in embryonic form in *The Smiling Mme Beudet*, which utilizes one or two similar images of rippling water to illustrate the fact that the dreamy Madame Beudet is playing Debussy on the piano.

Freddy Chevalley's account of a screening of experimental films at the Ciné-Club de Génève in March of 1930 offers a description of two of these films.

> Germaine Dulac has composed a moving *Arabesques* using extremely diverse materials, and succeeds in holding our attention with a generally pleasing succession of sights: a fan-shaped spray from a fountain, taken from both front and profile, tree branches converging in a luminous archway, a trail of smoke stretching out before a filter of clouds, a snail's shell, a spider's

web, flowers bursting suddenly out of rocky terrain, luminous parallel
reflections curving over an agitated background. *Disque 927* is somewhat
less successful. Germaine Dulac intended to visually recreate the motifs of
Chopin's *Prelude in B Flat,* which was inspired, according to Georges Sand,
by a gray, rainy day at La Grande Chartreuse [described in her *Winter in
Mallorca* as the melodious sound of the rain hitting the tile roof]. A turning
record appears, divides . . . then fades into luminous sprays rushing forth
precipitously, which finally give way to natural signs of musically-inspired
emotion: the monotonous oscillation of a clock pendulum which alternates
with details of the exterior atmosphere: water trickling on windowpanes,
the regular tumbling of raindrops into a puddle surrounded with foliage,
sad and rain-soaked walkways.[68]

One can readily determine the kind of problem that emerges with
too literal an equation of cinema and music: These films might seem
like hardly more than visual illustrations of the musical works that
"inspire" them. As Ian Christie formulates the problem: "[T]his raises
the question as to whether we are intended to 'hear' or imagine the
music. If so, the result would be redundant (and a denial of *musical*
specificity); if not, then there is nothing to structure the image sequence except the images themselves, which would render the musical
reference pointless. So, unless the *specificity* of the cinematic is to be
abandoned, how can cinema aspire to the condition of visual music?
The problem is perhaps that of establishing what exactly the cinematic
material is and what are its modalities. . . . "[69]
Likewise, the fundamentally Romantic notion of the artist as inspired "seer" can be challenged for its essentially idealist foundations.
However, as examples of "pure cinema," these films stand out as
lyrical rejections of the dominance of narrative logic and causality so
prevalent in the mainstream commercial cinema. Something else has
been used to structure the sequence of shots. Thus when Christie says
"there is nothing to structure the image sequence except the images
themselves," he is touching on a major point, albeit from the opposite
direction. The musical analogy was often invoked by Dulac not in order
to claim that cinema should be like music, but rather to emphasize
the nonreferential factors important in the organization of cinematic
images. In other words, the "visual harmonies" evoked by montage
were to be articulated in terms of formal properties rather than in
terms of cognitive essences. With these films Dulac was able to achieve
that "visual orchestration" about which she spoke so frequently, and
which, possibly, can be seen as a way of bypassing the pervasive patriarchal logic of Western thought. Perhaps the most aphoristic expression
of this idea can be found in her comment on Abel Gance's *La Chanson*

du rail (a short film that comprised the veritable core of *La Roue,* combining accelerated montage with modern painting's fascination for machines in movement): "Play of lights, play of forms, play of perspectives. An intense emotion derived from a simple vision of something felt sensitively."[70]

During this time Dulac also made a short "scientific" film, *Germination d'un haricot* (1928), which documented, through time-lapse photography and slow motion, the germination and growth of a lima bean. To call the film "scientific" is a bit misleading; the film was as lyrical and poetic as her other visually symphonic short films. In fact, Dulac often used this film (or one about the germination of a grain of wheat) as a striking example of her thesis that the "visual drama" in cinema was dependent on the development and rhythm of the movement of the shots (both within the frame and in the formal interrelations of images). In describing the "pure movement which unfolds according to the continuous logic of its dynamic force" as the tendrils and stalk proceed along their course, Dulac noted: "Roots and stem create harmonies. The movement and its rhythms, already refined in their form, determine the emotion, *the purely visual emotion.*"[71]

Dulac also made use of this film, and others like it when defining her concept of "pure cinema" (*la cinégraphie intégrale*), or what might be considered as an early formulation of "cinematic writing." In her article entitled "Aesthetics and Obstacles of Pure Cinema" ("*Les Esthétiques. Les Entraves: La Cinégraphie intégrale*"), she calls the germination of a grain of wheat a "joyful hymn," whose harmonized movement of light and forms produces "an exclusively cinematographic drama." Six shots from a Pathé film about crystallization illustrate this portion of the text; the caption reads "Phenomena of crystallization: Play of volumes, lines, and light. Progress toward the visual symphony."[72] Dulac demonstrated particular eloquence in articulating the poetic potentials of these scientific films in her comments about a film on the birth of sea urchins: "A purely visual emotion, in its embryonic state, a physical rather than a cerebral emotion, equal to that which an isolated sound can produce. An artist's care can unify diverse rhythms in a single image, then juxtapose them in a succession of images. Imagine several forms in movement, and we will succeed in conceiving 'pure cinema.' "[73]

From these short films of 1928 and 1929, a precise definition of Dulac's film aesthetic emerges. As a filmmaker dedicated to the liberation of cinematic images from all literary, dramatic, or philosophical expression, Dulac sought to create for the spectator a "cinegraphic sensation" that could be achieved through the contemplation of pure forms in movement—the melodic arrangement of luminous reflections, the rhythmic ordering of successive shots. Cinema was meant to delight the senses by the formal play of its moving images in much the same way that a musical fugue might provoke joy by its harmonics. Thus the referential content of the filmic shot was deemphasized in favor of plastic and rhythmic composition, elements of which were valorized in terms of the kind of spectatorial participation they evoked. The decisive modernism of a "drama" conceived not in terms of a realist ruse, but from the mechanisms of cinema itself, that is, the intersection of unconscious processes of desire with the harmony of forms on the screen, is everywhere apparent, and the implications for feminism are no less obvious.

La Princesse Mandane (1928) was Dulac's last major commercial film. Very loosely adapted from a novel by Pierre Benoît entitled L'Oublie (Forgetfulness), it combined the adventure-tale quality of the original with a spirit of fantasy and humor. Dulac described her film in the following way: "In my film, Benoît's hero becomes a victim of the cinema [my italics]. His obsession with all the glorious adventures on the screen forces him to abandon his peaceful life and roam the world. He becomes transported into a country full of wonders, a marvelous kingdom ruled by a fairy princess. A moral ends this story: After many adventures, my hero prefers to find happiness in simplicity."[74] Charles Ford sees this film as a lightly parodic glance at the film medium itself, speculating that Dulac had "enveloped this whimsical tale in a fine mesh of humor, woven with the constant care to adorn dream in the appearance of reality and to confer on its lightheartedness the gravity of drama."[75] And indeed, if one takes Dulac's own words about the film as any indication, there is a happily ironic delight in the cinema's power to captivate and enthrall. It is almost as if Dulac's own words about the powerful effect of cinema on the spectator, offered in the seriousness of her theoretical writings, were now designed for a commercial audience and presented in the form of a conventional, if fanciful, narrative.

It would seem that the advent of sound, or at any rate its exacerbation of the conflict between "art cinema" (aesthetic imperatives) and "commercial cinema" (industry demands)—a conflict which Dulac worked tirelessly to harmonize—put an end, for all intents and purposes, to one aspect of Dulac's filmmaking career. She felt that the exciting potentials of the sound film could not be fully explored so long as the emphasis remained on the verbal text and sound remained simply a means to accrue greater realism to the image. Dulac made an important distinction, saying that she was not opposed to the sound film, but only to the *talking* film. In fact, sound offered a new dimension for cinematic art in that a film could play with aural harmonies as it had played with the orchestration of visual forms. "Passionately fond of music and film, I use the sound film to realize my conception: to make a synchronous orchestration of sounds and images and not a bastardized and banal recording of music. I'm afraid we may be ignoring exceptional artistic achievements which would within the next few years come to fruition."[76]

But while Dulac seemed to abandon the cinema of artistic experimentation, she turned to another type of filmmaking, one that embraced her interests in the social and historical aspects of cinema. In 1932, Dulac had founded a subsidiary group of Gaumont to produce a "magazine of filmed news events." These consisted of the most representative items of the week's news presented "in a lively and interesting manner."[77] The newsreels became extremely popular in France within one year after they were initiated. It was toward these weekly newsmagazines that Dulac directed her efforts. In her work on newsreels in the years between 1930 and 1940 for Pathé Journal and France-Actualités Gaumont, she tried to incorporate some of the principles of rhythmic montage and formal composition so prominent in her prior cinematic work.

Although these newsreels were neither avant-garde art films nor commercial narratives, and it seems possible that the urgency of events eclipsed theoretical investigation into the specific properties of the medium, two longer films from this period stand out. *Le Cinéma au service de l'histoire* (1936) was a compilation film that combined newsreel footage and archival material in a montage construction that Dulac herself designed. And *Les Marchands de canons* (also made in 1936) was an antiwar documentary that unfortunately has disappeared.[78] Dulac brought her characteristic enthusiasm to these projects as well as to the weekly newsreels, as evidenced by her statement: "The news item is the history of an epoch which the filmmaker and his [or her] camera trace from day to day. The news item is a lived and irrefutable document which one year bequeaths to the next, transmits to the next."[79]

Dulac was a tireless advocate of the cinema and considered her activity of lecturing and writing to encourage love and understanding of the new medium as important as her filmmaking. She played a major role in founding ciné-clubs (film societies) in France and worked to encourage discussion on a wide range of issues concerning film art. In 1922, she was elected secretary-general of the Ciné-Clubs de France and was instrumental in making quality foreign films (such as films from Sweden, Soviet Russia, and Germany) available to French audiences. The regional ciné-clubs proliferated, and Dulac later became president of the Fédération des ciné-clubs. She encouraged and presented the work of new young filmmakers (Joris Ivens and Jean Vigo are two examples). She traveled extensively and gave lectures, illustrated by projections of portions of films, throughout Europe, discussing her theories and inspiring interest in film as an artistic medium: "Germaine Dulac carried the torch."[80]

In addition to this, Dulac taught film courses at the Ecole Technique de Photographie et de Cinématographie on the rue de Vaugirard. According to one biographer, she was an inspiring teacher who was able to generate enthusiasm in her students and make even the dullest subjects interesting.[81] Henri Fescourt, a close friend of Dulac's at the time, says that she was caring and affectionate with her students; he describes how even those who were skeptical about the medium "became taken with the charm of her tender and assured words" when they heard her lecture.[82] In appreciation of the energy and devotion that seem so characteristic of Dulac he said, "If those who go to the movies today are not simply enlightened professionals, curious amateurs or snobs, it is because Germaine Dulac prepared the way."[83]

This seems a fitting epitaph for a woman whose death in 1942, after a long illness that left her paralyzed in one leg, was to be adequately marked by the film community only after the end of the war. In his biography of Dulac, Charles Ford makes note of the difficulty that the French press had in printing her obituary—a single article in *La Revue de l'écran* (printed in unoccupied Marseilles) had to have Vichy authorization: "Bothered by Dulac's non-conformist ideas, disturbed by her impure origins, the censors had refused the article which, only after a vigorous protest by the editor-in-chief of the magazine, appeared three weeks late. Even dead, Germaine Dulac still seemed dangerous. . . . "[84]

Germaine Dulac, as both a feminist and filmmaker, is a central figure in understanding and theorizing the development of a feminist cinema. Her continued dedication to the cinematic art, her spirit and enthusiasm as a polemicist for the avant-garde, and her healthy sense of struggle on a multitude of fronts—both social and aesthetic—make her an important example for anyone attempting to formulate a feminist film aesthetic. In concluding, a final quote from Dulac seems appropriate: it exemplifies the energy and the positive spirit of resistance that characterize all of her efforts in the cinematic domain. It is from an article written for *Le Film,* a journal marked by a fierce sense of national pride so important to the cinema's emergence as an art form in France. It is possible to see a double meaning in this quote, which has value for both film theory and feminism, for it can be read as a call for cinematic specificity as well as for an alternative artistic practice, a call for—and in—"another voice."

> We may lack faith in ourselves, and that's the cause of our trouble. Our so-called inferiority in cinematic art has given us this unfortunate critical obsession which leads us to seek perfection through the correction of our faults rather than through the development of our good qualities. We believe less in the latter than in the former. Instead of seeking inside ourselves, having lost confidence, we look to the accomplishments of others, over in America, and try to conform to their standards. The time has come, I believe, to listen in silence to our own song, to try to express our own personal vision, to define our own sensibility, to make our own way. Let us learn to look, let us learn to see, let us learn to feel.[85]

NOTES

1. Germaine Dulac, "L'Essence du cinéma: L'Idée visuelle," *Les Cahiers du mois,* nos. 16/17 (1925): 64. All translations of French texts are my own unless otherwise noted. Another translation of this article, by Robert Lamberton, can be found *The Avant-Garde Film: A Reader of Theory and Criticism,* ed. P. Adams Sitney (New York: New York University Press, 1978), pp. 36–42.

2. Parts of this biographical notation are derived from Charles Ford's *Germaine Dulac* in *Anthologie du cinéma* 31 (January 1968), and from my own "Heart of the Avant-Garde: Some Biographical Notes on Germaine Dulac," *Women and Film,* nos. 5/6 (1974).

3. Mentioned by Henri Fescourt in *La Foi et les montagnes (ou le septième art au passé)* (Paris: Paul Montel, 1959), p. 295.

4. Unpublished manuscript; texts collected by Marie-Anne Colson-Malleville, who was Dulac's close friend and assistant from the time of Dulac's divorce in 1920 on. After Dulac's death she maintained the filmmaker's estate and dedicated herself to preserving her memory. This manuscript is from the Georges Sadoul archive, courtesy of Bernard Eisenschitz. This passage is from chapter 14, "Germaine Dulac et son oeuvre de cinéaste," p. 2. Further references to this manuscript will be designated as "Colson-Malleville text."

5. Colson-Malleville text, chapter 14, p. 2.

6. Unfortunately, many of Dulac's films are no longer in existence, although some can be found in fragmentary form at the Cinémathèque Française. Only two of her films, *The Smiling Mme Beudet* and *The Seashell and the Clergyman,* are in distribution in the United States, but these are by far the most important, and arguably the most interesting.

7. Fescourt, *La Foi et les montagnes,* p. 296.

8. Colson-Malleville text, chapter 14, p. 3.

9. Fescourt, *La Foi et les montagnes,* p. 296.

10. Germaine Dulac, "L'Art des nuances spirituelles," *Cinéa-Ciné-pour- tous,*

no. 28 (January 1, 1925); reprinted in *L'Art du cinéma*, ed. Pierre Lherminier (Paris: Editions Seghers, 1960), pp. 559–60.

11. Colson-Malleville text, chapter 14, p. 3.

12. Henri Langlois, "L'Avant-garde française," *Cahiers du cinéma*, no. 202 (June–July 1968): 10.

13. Langlois, "L'Avant-garde," p. 14. For a brief description of this short (only two reels) film, see Ford, *Germaine Dulac*, p. 9, and Richard Abel's comprehensive and highly readable *French Cinema: The First Wave, 1915–1929* (Princeton: Princeton University Press, 1984). Abel has much useful and interesting information on Dulac, as well as detailed discussions of her films. Only a small fragment of this film, about ten minutes, remains at the Cinémathèque Française in Paris. However, the scenario is available in Louis Delluc, *Drames du cinéma* (Paris: Aux Editions du Monde Nouveau, 1923).

14. Cited by Eve Francis in her autobiography, *Temps héroïques* (Paris: Denoël, 1949).

15. Colson-Malleville text, chapter 14, p. 4.

16. Fescourt, *La Foi et les montagnes*, p. 296.

17. Colson-Malleville text, chapter 14, p. 5.

18. In *Cinéa*, May 20, 1921.

19. Colson-Malleville text, chapter 14, p. 5.

20. Ibid.

21. Germaine Dulac, "Les Esthétiques. Les Entraves: La Cinégraphie intégrale," *L'Art cinématographique*, vol. 2 (Paris: Alcan, 1927); reprinted in French in *The Literature of the Cinema* (New York: Arno Press, 1970), pp. 41–42, and translated by Stuart Liebman as "The Aesthetics, the Obstacles: Integral Cinegraphie" in *Framework*, no. 19 (1982): 6–9.

22. Colson-Malleville text, chapter 14, p. 5.

23. Ford, *Germaine Dulac*, p. 14.

24. Colson-Malleville text, chapter 14, p. 6.

25. Germaine Dulac, "Les procédés expressifs du cinématographe," *Cinémagazine*, no. 28 (July 11, 1924): 67–68. This was a talk given on June 17, 1924, at the Musée Galliera. *Cinémagazine* reprinted the text of the talk over a number of issues. *Cinémagazine* kept no volume numbers until 1930, and thus each year's issues were numbered by the week. This can lead to some confusion, as issues can bear the same number while having widely varied dates. Therefore, for purposes of bibliography, the date of each issue of *Cinémagazine* is more important than the number.

26. Germaine Dulac, "Conférence de Mme Germaine Dulac," *Cinémagazine*, no. 51 (December 19, 1924): 518. Reprinted in *L'Art du Cinéma*, ed. Lherminier, p. 66. This was a talk given at a meeting of Les Amis du Cinéma, on December 7, 1924, at the Salle du Colisée.

27. "Chez D. W. Griffith," *Cinéa*, no. 7 (June 17, 1921): 11–12.

28. Fescourt, *La Foi et les montagnes*, p. 298.

29. Dulac, "Conférence," p. 518. This passage does not appear in the Lherminier edition.

30. Ibid.

31. Ibid.

32. "Madame Germaine Dulac nous parle du *Diable dans la ville*," *Cinémagazine*, no. 19 (May 9, 1924): 246.

33. Fescourt, *La Foi et les montagnes*, p. 299.

34. Ibid.

35. Ester Carla DeMiro, "Personale di Germaine Dulac," *Giornate Internazionali di Cinema d'Artista* [Florence] (December 1979): 12. The following comments are based on Abel's discussion of the film in *French Cinema*, pp. 210–12.

36. Harry Alan Potamkin, "The Woman as Film Director," in *The Compound Cinema* (New York: Teachers College Press: 1977), p. 140.

37. Ford, *Germaine Dulac*, p. 27.

38. Dulac, "Conférence," p. 518. This passage does not appear in the Lherminier edition.

39. DeMiro, "Personale," p. 12.

40. Dulac, "Les Esthétiques," p. 45.

41. Colson-Malleville text, chapter 14, p. 7.

42. Ibid., p. 6. An evaluation of the conceptualization of cinematic art in this way will appear further in the chapter.

43. Dulac, "Les Esthétiques," p. 45.

44. Ibid., plate 5.

45. Ford, *Germaine Dulac*, p. 28.

46. Ibid., p. 31.

47. In *The Literature of the Cinema*, pp. 75–103. This was pointed out by DeMiro in "Personale," p. 14.

48. Harry Alan Potamkin, "Phases of Cinema Unity: I," in *The Compound Cinema*, p. 18.

49. The story of the incident, recounted in numerous texts on Surrealism and the cinema, is available only through eyewitness accounts, which are contradictory. A loud exchange interrupted the projection of the film: "Who made this film?" "Madame Germaine Dulac." "What is Madame Dulac?" "She is a cow." A journalist who was present claims that Artaud led the disruption; others say that Artaud was not there. However, certain Surrealists (including Robert Desnos and Louis Aragon) participated in the riot, yelling obscenities and throwing objects at the screen. Armand Tallier, director of the theater, demanded an apology and got insults instead; in the ensuing scuffle, some mirrors were broken as the troublemakers were ushered out of the theater. The incident was described in *Le Charivari*, February 18, 1928, and reprinted in *Les Oeuvres complètes d'Antonin Artaud*, vol. 3 (Paris: Editions Gallimard, 1978), pp. 326–27.

50. Alain Virmaux, "Artaud and Film," *Tulane Drama Review* 11:1 (Fall 1966): 156.

51. Georges Sadoul, "Souvenirs d'un témoin," *Etudes cinématographiques* 38/39 (1965): 19.

52. Alain and Odette Virmaux, *Les Surréalistes et le cinéma* (Paris: Editions Seghers, 1976), p. 47.

53. Letter to Germaine Dulac, September 25, 1927, in *Oeuvres complètes*,

vol. 3, pp. 128–29. Also cited by Virmaux, "Artaud and Film," p. 157, trans. Simone Sanzenbach.

54. Colson-Malleville text, chapter 14, p. 6.

55. Abel, *French Cinema*, p. 414. Produced independently between commercial assignments, the film was distributed by Dulac and Anne-Marie Colson-Malleville to commercial exhibitors who had the option of screening it with their regular program.

56. See Ford, *Germaine Dulac*, p. 34.

57. Fescourt, *La Foi et les montagnes*, p. 301.

58. Ford, *Germaine Dulac*, p. 34.

59. Abel, *French Cinema*, p. 415.

60. Charles Baudelaire, "Le Poème du haschisch," in *Les Paradis artificiels* (Paris: Flammarion, 1966), p. 59. This translation is from Anna Balakian, *The Symbolist Movement* (New York: Random House, 1967), pp. 40–41.

61. *Germaine Dulac présente: Schémas* (Paris: Imprimateur Gutenberg, 1927). A photocopy of the entire February 1927 issue can be found at the library of the Anthology Film Archives, courtesy of Wendy Dozoretz.

62. *Schémas*, p. 6.

63. Germaine Dulac, "Du sentiment à la ligne," in *Schémas*, pp. 26–31.

64. Dulac, "L'Essence du cinéma," p. 61.

65. Dulac, "Du sentiment à la ligne," p. 27. This translation, by Felicity Sparrow and Claudine Nicolson, appears on p. 128 of *Film as Film: Formal Experiment in Film 1910–1975* (London: Arts Council of Great Britain, 1979).

66. Dulac, "Du sentiment à la ligne," pp. 30–31. Emphasis in the original.

67. Dulac, "L'Essence du cinéma," p. 65.

68. Freddy Chevalley, "Ciné-Club de Génève," *Close Up* 6:5 (May 1930): 409–10.

69. Ian Christie, "French Avant-Garde Film in the 20's: From 'Specificity' to Surrealism," in *Film as Film*, p. 39.

70. Dulac, "Conférence," p. 517; page 65 in the Lherminier edition.

71. Dulac, "Du sentiment à la ligne," p. 29; trans. Sparrow-Nicolson, p. 129. Emphasis in the original.

72. Dulac, "Les Esthétiques," plate 6.

73. Ibid., p. 47.

74. Quoted by Ford, *Germaine Dulac*, p. 36.

75. Ibid.

76. Germaine Dulac, "Jouer avec les bruits," *Cinéa-Ciné-pour-tous*, August 15, 1929, p. 250 in Lherminier, where this text is anthologized.

77. Fescourt, *La Foi et les montagnes*, p. 302.

78. DeMiro, "Personale," p. 20.

79. Colson-Malleville text, chapter 11, "Le cinéma au service de l'histoire," p. 1.

80. Fescourt, *La Foi et les montagnes*, p. 303.

81. Ford, *Germaine Dulac*, p. 38.

82. Fescourt, *La Foi et les montagnes*, p. 303.

83. Ibid.

84. Ford, *Germaine Dulac,* p. 41.

85. Germaine Dulac, "Ayons la foi," *Le Film,* no. 164 (October 15, 1919): 46.

THREE

Dulac in Context:
French Film Production in the Twenties

IN ORDER TO APPRECIATE the specifically feminist import of Germaine Dulac's work—to understand what distinguishes that work from the filmmaking of her contemporaries—it is useful to look at the economic and aesthetic contexts of French film production in the twenties. French filmmaking of that period is traced with the ambiguous and contradictory legacy of both its own pioneers and the richly innovative work of the Americans. In the search for "cinematic specificity" that preoccupied not only Dulac, but the other major directors (Louis Delluc, Jean Epstein, Marcel L'Herbier, and Abel Gance) as well, there is a simultaneous rejection of the theatrical and literary emphases of the traditional commercial cinema along with an appreciation of both the technical achievements and the purely visual conception of this same cinema. Out of this contradiction emerged some of the first attempts to subvert what came to be called the dominant "Hollywood model" and to develop the systematic alternatives associated with this first cinematic avant-garde.

French filmmakers found themselves in an ambivalent situation regarding the hegemony of American production during the twenties. On the one hand, they resented the massive importation of American films that dominated the market and absorbed the film-viewing audience. Before World War I, the French film industry had led the world in film production; after the war, which concurrently saw the industry's collapse, film production suffered from the diversion of capital to the reconstructed areas of northern France. During the war the two major French film companies, Pathé and Gaumont, which also controlled the exhibition circuits, started projecting great numbers of American films in order to draw audiences. The result was that by 1924, 85 percent of the feature-length films shown in France were American-made.[1]

At the same time, French filmmakers were fascinated by the technical innovations and artistic achievements of the American cinema. Notably, Cecil B. DeMille's 1915 film *The Cheat,* shown in France in late summer of 1916, was seen as something of a cinematic revelation: Dulac said simply, "*The Cheat* represents the beginning of human feelings in the cinema."[2] The films of D. W. Griffith and Thomas Ince, actors like Pearl White, Douglas Fairbanks, and Sessue Hayakawa, and the comedies of Buster Keaton, Charlie Chaplin, and Mack Sennett were received enthusiastically. It was American films that marked the transition from enthusiastic viewing to actual filmmaking, and in a short time these films provided emerging filmmakers not only with inspiration, but also with cinematic models to analyze and emulate.[3]

Paradoxically, the attention paid to the American cinema led French filmmakers toward a national cinema grounded in experimentation, one that turned away from the commercial imperatives of the Hollywood product toward new areas of cinematic expressivity and specifically filmic construction. In addition, attempts to challenge the dominant cinema were characterized by a situation of double rupture in relation to commercial cinema in France. At the time, the so-called "mainstream" cinema consisted of filmmakers like Louis Feuillade and Henri Pouctal, among others, whose popular serials concentrated on an economy of action and narrative motivation, leaving little room for stylistic elaboration or technical virtuosity. In very general terms, filmmakers like Gance and L'Herbier attempted to create a quality French art cinema within the context of this popular commercial cinema by utilizing influences from literature, painting, and music in films with wide popular appeal. At the same time, Dulac, along with Delluc and Epstein, concerned herself with defining the essence of cinema, concentrating on the plastic rhythms of montage. It is in this sense that all five of these filmmakers have been called the First Avant-Garde, particularly when their work is seen in relation to the films of the Dadaists and the Surrealists (René Clair and Luis Buñuel, for example), as well as to films by those filmmakers interested in more purely formal or graphic concerns, such as Hans Richter, Vicking Eggeling, and Henri Chomette.

In his highly interesting, if idiosyncratic history of the French cinematic avant-garde, *En marge du cinéma français,*[4] Jacques B. Brunius begins his discussion with a clarification of terminology. Brunius feels that a general confusion of the terms *experimental, abstract, pure, total* (*intégral*), and *avant-garde* has allowed them to be used interchangeably while they all describe very particular—if in some sense similar—approaches to the cinema. All of these types of production, of course, are seen in a position of marginality in relation to the dominant commercial cinema.

Experimental cinema, a term used particularly in the United States and England, refers to everything outside of ordinary commercial production and is characterized by an orientation toward research and experimentation. Brunius points out that once this kind of cinematic research is successful, it runs the risk of becoming standard fare, stereotyped and imitated by those who lack the spirit of exploration. He also specifies that this type of experimentation is primarily for those interested in it for the sake of experiment. On the other hand, *pure cinema* emphasizes the rhythmic possibilities of the cinema, abandoning representational forms, actors, and decors for the pure play of light and movement. Henri Chomette's *Jeux des reflets et de la vitesse* (which worked with moving light reflected on a crystal, and images of the Metro and Bâteau-Mouches in negative and accelerated motion) and *Cinq minutes de cinéma pur* are cited as examples. It is this type of filmmaking that Dulac's later "symphonic poems" represent as well. Eggeling's *Symphonie diagonale* and Ruttmann's *Les Quatre études* exemplify the work of abstract cinema by taking the interest in nonrepresentation even farther in the realm of graphics.

Brunius is harshest on the loose usage of the term *avant-garde*, which he dismisses as so many "ill-bred pedants" who populate "avant-garde boutiques." For him, the avant-garde must abandon a fascination with gratuitous novelty and the style of the day in order to seek new methods for expressing truly original thoughts. In this—almost in spite of himself—he is quite close to Dulac's formulation in her 1932 article "Le Cinéma d'avant-garde." She sees the term *avant-garde* as applying to any film that strives to "*renew* the expressive possibilities of image and sound, breaking with established tradition in order to search out, in the domain which is strictly visual and auditory, new emotional chords."[5] For Dulac then, the avant-garde cinema does not simply attempt to appeal to large audiences through clever artificial tricks and devices, for, in the double movement characteristic of her thinking, this cinema is at once profoundly personal (internal) and significantly social (external). It is, in her words, both more egotistical and more altruistic than films of superficial innovation: "Egotistical because it is the personal manifestation of a pure thought; altruistic because it is only interested in progress."[6] Beneath the sometimes inaccessible surface of a truly avant-garde film are the seeds of discoveries that suggest the cinematic form of the future. It is in this sense that the avant-garde both critiques the present and anticipates the future. As such, avant-garde cinema, in Dulac's formulation, becomes undeniably political in its suggestion of new cinematic forms to describe a new social reality. The feminist implications of this kind of thinking are far-reaching, for in positing alternative structures of seeing, Dulac implies the necessity of social transformation as well. Her "new emotional chords," then, can be understood as another discourse of desire, a way of conceptualizing "otherwise," for it is thus at the level of cinematic language that true social change can be conceived.

Regardless of the shades of difference in the terminology used to describe various aspects of the cinematic avant-garde, the intellectual and artistic ferment of France in the twenties created a situation in which polemics about film and its modernist context thrived. This produced Impressionist, Dadaist, Cubist, and Surrealist experiments, all of which conceived of film as an art whose specific nature was visual, and all of which took various positions in relation to the narrative, fictional component of the art. This led to an emphasis on the visual image, on mise-en-scène, on montage, and on technical devices of lighting and camerawork as opposed to what was conceived of as the narrative linearity of the literary or theatrical commercial cinema. The cinematic avant-garde thus self-consciously defined itself in opposition to mainstream narrative cinema.

It is often the case that the formation of an art cinema (that is, film production-distribution-exhibition circuits on the margins of dominant commercial cinema, usually characterized by a high degree of experimentation, and often surrounded by polemics on the specific nature of the medium) coincides with the development of national cinemas. Traditionally, this convergence has come about in terms of a mutual response to the domination of domestic markets by foreign—primarily American—films. This is particularly true of French cinema of the twenties, whose rallying cry, as has already been noted, crystallized on the masthead of Delluc's journal *Cinéa:* "The French cinema must be *cinema;* the French cinema must be *French.*" In very general terms, French film production of the twenties can be identified by an emphasis on visual style (which can be seen to highlight a personal artistic vision in reaction to the more homogenized institutional spectacle), an exploration of subjective or internal elements of character elaboration (as opposed to the emphasis on dramatic action), and a concern with the spectator-screen relationship conceived in philosophical or aesthetic terms (as opposed to a spectator-screen relationship understood simply in terms of consumption). Thus, although none of these characteristics might be recognized as specifically nationalistic, a field of artistic endeavor generated in opposition to the foreign model unites both national and artistic claims of this cinema.

The First Avant-Garde thus functioned in the manner of any political opposition force—it assumed a role of critical negation. Activity crystallized around three major areas of endeavor: the creation of a field of critical inquiry and appraisal through the development of film criticism in magazines and specialized journals; the establishment of widespread viewing availability and the creation of an audience interested in cinematic experimentation through the founding of art theaters, ciné-clubs, and noncommercial distribution circuits; and the development of a cinematic avant-garde through increased filmmaking and theoretical activity, this often accompanied by researches in style and technique and by open forums for the theoretical elaboration of these researches.

Film Journals

Although there were many industry trade journals throughout the twenties, the period saw the emergence of a new kind of film journal in France, one geared to nonprofessional audiences and committed to the exploration and elaboration of the cinema's artistic possibilities. Dulac, who along with Ricciotto Canudo, Jean Tedesco, and Louis Delluc, was a major figure in the film journal movement, appraised such critical activity: "In the current state of cinematography, the work of criticism, analysis, and polemical exchange has as much productive value as the films themselves. I would even go so far as to say they have more value. . . . They direct the cinema toward a specific goal, revealing its ideal form, an image of its perfection. . . . "[7]

With a few important exceptions, such as Ricciotto Canudo's "Manifesto des sept arts," published in Paris in March of 1911,[8] Abel Gance's "Qu'est-ce que le cinématographe? Un sixième art," appearing in the trade magazine *Ciné-journal* in 1912,[9] film reviews by Maurice Raynal in the avant-garde monthly *Les Soirées de Paris,* and a few enthusiastic commentaries on the cinema by Guillaume Apollinaire, there was relatively little of what could be called actual film criticism before World War I. However, slowly during the course of the war, and then finally at its end, the situation changed quite radically. A body of "film criticism" in the form of columns in daily newspapers (for example, *L'Oeuvre, Le Journal, Paris-Midi, L'Intransigeant*) or articles written by such figures in the literary world as Guillaume Apollinaire, Blaise Cendrars, Robert Desnos, Louis Aragon, Max Jacob, Colette, Jean

Cocteau, and Philippe Soupault began to develop. At the same time, specialized journals emerged that were concerned with theoretical and aesthetic issues.

The weekly journal *Le Film*, founded in February of 1914 by its publisher Henri Diamant-Berger, was the first large magazine devoted entirely to the cinema. When Louis Delluc was appointed as editor-in-chief in 1917, he began the work of establishing an indigenous French film culture, informing his articles on the cinema with appraisals of its aesthetic potential, encouraging polemics around the specific nature and possibilities of the medium, and supporting the work of young filmmakers like Dulac, Gance, and L'Herbier. Delluc changed the format of the magazine and began soliciting articles from scriptwriters and directors (Dulac, Gance, and L'Herbier all had articles in *Le Film*) along with the work of artists and poets. Apollinaire's "Avant le cinéma," as well as Aragon's first published poem, "Charlot sentimental," and his seminal article asserting that film was the art of modern life, "Du Décor," all appeared in *Le Film*.

The same ambivalent relation toward American film that characterized the general cultural scene in France—wild enthusiasm tempered by resistance to its dominance—was present in *Le Film*. Delluc's first piece for *Le Film* was an enthusiastic review of Thomas Ince's 1916 film *Home*, which contained references to all of Ince's other films seen in France, along with William S. Hart's *The Aryan*. What impressed Delluc most about the American films was their sense of vitality, naturalness, and spontaneity. Next to the stiffness of acting and gesture of the contemporary Film d'Art productions, for example, American films virtually radiated with life, generating a surplus of realism when placed against the stale artificiality of the commercial French product.

At the same time, *Le Film* was militantly nationalistic, encouraging the work of new French filmmakers in the face of what was recognized as the massive threat of foreign competition. In the editorial commentary that prefaced an article by Dulac entitled "Mise en scène,"[10] Delluc notes that in France there are a handful of new directors whose work is "animated with a new vitality," concluding, in reference to Dulac's *Ames de fous*, that "we can expect quite a bit from French talents, when they are French in this way." In the article itself Dulac argues that the cinema can take its place among "the superior forms of artistic expression" once it is seen on its own terms and not as a poor relation of the theater. Exclaiming "Oh! The Americans have shaken us up a bit!" she confidently predicts, "When we've understood that the cinema is an artform, a French artform, . . . which can expand and affirm the great reputation of our literature in the world, reestablish the uncontested superiority of our taste, and *defend our culture,* we'll have achieved our real goal." Although perhaps a little excessive in its chauvinism, Dulac's formulation is nonetheless significant of the association of aesthetics and nationalism characteristic of film activity of the time.

In 1920, Delluc and another young film critic, Léon Moussinac, started *Le Journal du ciné-club* as an organ of information serving the burgeoning French film culture. In addition to listings, film reviews, and articles on other forms of popular entertainment such as vaudeville and the music hall, it contained historical and biographical information, as well as articles by film stars and directors. Also during this time (starting in 1918) Delluc wrote film criticism for the daily *Paris-Midi.*

In May of 1921, Delluc founded *Cinéa* (he had left *Le Journal du ciné-club* after sixteen issues), a major weekly film journal that he edited until December 1922. It was on the masthead of issue number 45 (March 17, 1922) that Delluc placed his famous slogan calling for national and cinematic specificity. In the interests of extending theoretical and aesthetic debate around French film by removing it from its more commercial context and reinforcing the artistic and intellectual components of film writing, Delluc included articles and interviews with those whom he felt were pointing the way for French cinema of the future—actors Jacque Catelain, Ivan Mosjoukine, Eve Francis, and of course the filmmakers Dulac, Gance, L'Herbier, and Epstein. Attention was also paid to avant-garde activities in the other arts in France in the form of articles discussing such things as Cocteau's *Les Mariés de la Tour Eiffel* and the Ballet Suédois production of Canudo's *Skating Rink.*

While *Ciné-pour-tous* (1919) came out bimonthly, *Cinémagazine* (begun in 1921) published complete transcripts of lectures given at the specialized theaters and ciné-clubs (in particular, Germaine Dulac's series of talks around *The Smiling Mme Beudet,* and her "workshops" illustrated with short fragments from individual films), and also conducted polls and inquiries with filmmakers and critics. In November 1923, *Cinéa* and *Ciné-pour-tous* merged to form a new bimonthly film journal under the editorship of Jean Tedesco. *Cinéa-Ciné-pour-tous* then carried the banner of sophisticated and intellectual film studies through the remainder of the twenties. It aimed at a more cultured audience than either of its predecessors, focusing on such aesthetic debates as the question of a cinematic avant-garde, the issues surrounding the adequacy of the musical analogy and the necessity of intertitles, and the polemic raised by the notion of "pure cinema." This latter raged in a series of articles throughout 1926, which included such titles as Pierre Porte's "Une sensation nouvelle" (number 64, July 1) and "Le Cinéma, art objectif ou subjectif?" (number 69, September 15), Henri Fescourt and Jean-Louis Bouquet's "Sensations ou senti-ments?" (number 66, July 31), Jacques Brunius' "Musique ou cinéma?" (number 68, September 1), Henri Chomette's "Cinéma pur, art nais-sant," and Paul Ramain's "A La Recherche de l'émotion vraie" (both number 71, October 15). It was a debate that carried over into the single issue of Dulac's journal *Schémas*, where many of the same authors contributed articles that further elaborated their positions.

Cinéa-Ciné-pour-tous also included articles by the French filmmakers whom Delluc had championed at the outset of their careers, now firmly established as the innovators of the French cinematic avant-garde. Several important texts of Impressionist film theory by its practitioners thus appeared in this journal, among them: Dulac's "Le Cinéma, art des nuances spirituelles" (number 28, January 1, 1925), Gance's "Le Cinéma, c'est la musique de la lumière" (number 3, December 15, 1923), Epstein's "Pour une avant-garde nouvelle" (number 29, January 15, 1925) and "L'Objectif lui-même" (number 53, January 15, 1926), and two minor articles by L'Herbier. In an interview some forty years after this period, L'Herbier commented on the crucial nature of the activity of critical writing undertaken by these filmmakers: "Dulac, Epstein, Delluc, myself—we did not at all share the same aesthetic positions. But there was a point of communion between us: the search for that famous 'specificity.' On that point we all agreed, without any possible dissent. Another point in common was the fact that we all wrote a great deal, in magazines and journals, what we thought about the cinema: we needed to clarify, on paper, the ways in which we conceived cinematic art."[11]

To balance this heavy emphasis on theory and aesthetics, *Cinéa-Ciné-pour-tous* published detailed weekly listings of new films, including specific production information, as well as articles explaining cinematic procedures for amateurs, and a series entitled "Les Cinéastes," which examined the work of filmmakers both foreign and domestic. The journal also ran an extensive interview with Gance after the release of *La Roue*, and seven production articles on *Napoléon*.

Thus by the end of the decade, a significant body of film writing had been developed, to the extent that by 1929, *Le Tout cinéma* could estimate that there were thirty-eight specialized film journals, counting trade publications, in Paris.[12] In addition, regular film review columns had become widespread in French daily newspapers. Therefore, a context for writing seriously and critically about the cinema had been created; an ongoing awareness of contemporary film culture was established and the formulation of a specifically cinematic aesthetic was encouraged. Dulac's prolific film-writing activity is due in no small part to this productive cultural context, and the reciprocity between theory and practice so important to feminist thinking finds its specific historical roots in this critical milieu as well.

Film Culture

In addition to the development of a critical practice of writing about the cinema, the establishment of a serious film culture in France was also due to the creation of ciné-clubs and specialized theaters. These alternative, noncommercial viewing situations stimulated an independent film production and exhibition sector distinct from the mainstream commercial cinema. This enabled the diffusion of new ideas to a wider audience, an audience often open to experimentation and energetically interested in aesthetic issues. The ciné-clubs [film societies] promoted the same French, German, Swedish, and American films as did the journals, but they added something—they provided the element of active participation from the audience by stimulating discussions, organizing debates and forums, and coordinating lecture series. They also provided the opportunity for short, noncommercial films of an experimental nature to be viewed by an audience flexible enough to appreciate their experimental status. As previously noted, Germaine Dulac was a key figure in the ciné-club movement, in part because she felt that these film societies provided the audience most receptive to experimentation. In the educating tone characteristic of her film lectures, she used these opportunities to increase appreciation of avant-garde films: "An experimental film [film d'essai] is not necessarily a good film. Realized with haphazard means, it is often less perfect than films shown on the regular circuits, but it always contains some new principle and spirited researches worthy of being encouraged and retained."[13]

Louis Delluc initiated the idea of ciné-clubs with his publication of the Journal du ciné-club (it was also he who coined the term cinéaste), but Ricciotto Canudo, along with Henri Fescourt and Bernard Deschamps, actually founded the first regularly functioning group of this kind. The Club des Amis du Septième Art (C.A.S.A.) had its first official meeting on April 22, 1921. Dulac describes the alternative status of ciné-clubs in her precise definition: "A ciné-club is a group of spectators who, without scorning those classic or popular works offered by the official circuits in commercial theaters, are interested in learning about and encouraging the technical and artistic progress of avant-garde films and films of quality, by means of special screenings at irregular intervals. . . . In contrast to the audience of commercial theaters, which is careful to expect the pleasure of known quantities each evening, the audience of *ciné-clubs*, constantly on the watch, encourages and commends new endeavors. . . . "[14]

Dulac sees the ciné-club's function of encouraging critical reception of filmmakers' work as highly important, both to the evolution of the art of the cinema, and to the development of a sophisticated audience. However, she is careful to deny an elitist conception of this audience, noting the cinema's peculiar combination of aesthetic sophistication and mass popular appeal. If the ciné-club functions to proselytize and educate about the cinema, it must also be aware of the needs of the audience it seeks to "convert." "Certainly we must not divide the cinema into an exceptional class and a commercial class. A popular art [the cinema] must reach both the general public and the elite."[15]

Starting in the mid-twenties, specialized theaters represented another form of alternative film exhibition, and in some cases they provided an alternative financial base for experimental film production as well. Before 1924, Paris did not have a single theater exclusively showing films of special artistic interest; this was the area taken up by the independent ciné-clubs and individual special screenings. On November 14, 1924, Jean Tedesco opened the Vieux-Colombier in order to show French and foreign films of precisely this kind. Dulac points out that Tedesco was the first major exhibitor to envision the need for a specialized distribution sector in order to show films that either could not obtain commercial distribution or were not commercial enough to maintain mainstream audiences.[16]

Between 1913 and 1924 Jacques Copeau had made the Vieux-Colombier one of the most famous showcases in Paris for dramatic avant-garde theatrical productions. When Tedesco took it over for film exhibition, he carried this interest in the artistic avant-garde over to film (both production and exhibition). He premiered Dmitri Kirsanov's *Ménilmontant* (made entirely free of studio economics) and Jean Renoir's *La Petite marchande d'allumettes* (commissioned and partially directed by Tedesco, with interiors shot in the theater's attic). Screenings of independent films, often shorter than regular features because of the smaller amount of money invested in their production, included all of Dulac's later short "visual poems" and Jean Epstein's *Photogénies*—short cinematic "documents" commissioned by Tedesco and dismantled after the screening. In addition, in 1925 the theater cosponsored a series of conferences with Le Ciné-Club de France and the important literary journal *Les Cahiers du mois,* at which filmmakers and critics gave lectures accompanied by screenings. Dulac's "Les Esthé-tiques, les entraves: La Cinégraphie intégrale" is the text of one such lecture; Epstein's "Pour une avant-garde nouvelle" is another.

On January 21, 1926, Armand Tallier and Mlle L. Myrga opened the Studio des Ursulines with the following statement of purpose: "We propose to recruit our public from among the best writers, artists, and intellectuals of the Latin Quarter, and from among the growing number of people who have been driven away from the movie theaters due to the poverty of existing films. Our program will be composed of French and foreign films of quality which represent diverse tendencies and schools: everything which represents originality, value, *effort* will find a place on our screen."[17] Some of the films shown at this theater, which had also previously served the theatrical avant-garde (Charles Dullin's "atelier" ensemble was based there), are evidence of the Ursu-lines' eclectic programming, which included both commercial Ameri-can and foreign films with works of the cinematic avant-garde: James Cruze's *Jazz,* Howard Hawks's *A Girl in Every Port* (with Louise Brooks), Stroheim's *Greed,* German classics such as *The Joyless Street* and *The Blue Angel,* Man Ray's *Emak Bakia* and *L'Etoile de mer,* Epstein's *La Glace à trois faces,* Cavalcanti's *Rien que les heures,* and of course, Dulac's and Artaud's *The Seashell and the Clergyman.*

There was a constant effort, especially on the part of Dulac, to integrate this particularized audience into the larger context of the general cinema-viewing public. Continually maintaining that the goal of the avant-garde was to seek out new modes of expression that could expand the parameters of cinematic thought, she worked consistently to bring the audience into a relation of discovery compatible with her own excitement for the possibilities of the cinema. Avant-garde film work thus had a dual aim: to enrich the visual language and style of the cinema while at the same time educating mass tastes. Dulac therefore insisted on the educational function of agitational work: "To bring together those works of the screen possessing an intrinsic cinemato-graphic value, in order to study them and to make them appreciated by the general public which ordinarily might scorn them through lack of comprehension."[18] In her emphasis on the educational function of certain types of film exhibition, then, Dulac introduces a conception of cultural production which contrasts with the notion of film as aesthetic object. Avant-garde activity is seen in a social context rather than as the product of ivory-tower experimentation, and it is in this sense that the ciné-club and alternative screening activities intersect with the works themselves in a reciprocal meshwork which can be understood as the "text" of culture.

Film Practice

The creation of a film culture in France in the twenties, attuned to aesthetic issues and enthusiastically receptive to experimentation, provided a fertile context for the theoretical and practical explorations of Dulac and her contemporaries, Gance, L'Herbier, Delluc, and Epstein. These filmmakers are often designated as Impressionists because of their common interest in the cinematic rendering of subjectivity through the exploitation of the expressive possibilities of film. While serious debate about the accuracy of such a title continues, it is nonetheless true that there exist between these filmmakers certain similarities in their work and aesthetic formulations. In addition, they all conceived of their work as being in opposition to established film practice of the time, and all were mutually supportive in encouraging the aesthetic advancement of the cinema as an autonomous art form.

Dulac employs the term and provides a description in an essay written for *L'Art cinématographique* in 1927; she repeats her definition, in slightly modified form, five years later in "Le Cinéma d'avant-garde."

> Then came the period of the psychological and impressionist film. It seemed frivolous to place a character in a given situation without penetrating the secret domain of his [or her] interior life, and the actor's playing became complemented by the play of his [or her] thoughts, of visualized feelings.[19] Once the description of the multiple and contradictory interior impressions (which occur in the course of an action) was joined to the specific facts of the drama—the facts no longer existing in themselves, but becoming the consequence of a moral state—a duality imperceptibly intervened which, in order to remain harmonious, adapted itself to the rhythmic cadence, to the dynamism, and to the tempo of the images.[20]

Toward this end of cinematically rendering the life of the mind and psychological states of the characters, the Impressionist filmmakers employed a wide variety of cinematic devices. From camera techniques (prisms, distorting lenses, masks, unusual camera angles and focal lengths), through technical devices (dissolves, punctuating fades, soft-focus, multiple superimpositions, and double exposures), to experiments with rhythm and motion (both fast and slow motion, accelerated montage, and multiple repetitions) and the exploitation of other parameters in film (large grain film stocks, dramatic lighting effects, and new techniques of make-up and gesture), a battery of experimental techniques was devised that became the stylistic hallmark of Impressionist filmmaking.

The "duality" that was "adapted . . . to the rhythmic cadence . . . of the image" enables Dulac to see this work as a prelude to abstract filmmaking, a practice of cinema which rejects referentiality (and the potential surplus realism of the filmed image) in favor of the more cinematically "pure" properites of light, rhythm, and movement. "Imperceptibly, narrative storytelling and the actor's performance lost their isolated value in favor of a broad orchestration of shots, rhythms, framings, angles, lighting, proportions, contrasts and harmonies of the images."[21] She expands on this by means of the musical analogy, equating the filmmaker and composer in their artistic efforts: "Just as the musician works with the rhythm and sonorities of the musical phrase, the *cinéaste* began to work with the rhythm and sonorities of the image."[22] In this formulation, cinematic images take on an "emotive value" in some way related to their plastic composition and the rhythmic relations between them; meaning is generated by the properties of the images themselves, "without the aid of the [written] text."

For Dulac, however, this cinematic abstraction does not necessarily mean the total denial of humanistic concerns. Rather, in a pre-semiotic grasp of the interrelations of form and signification, she posits an early formulation of the cinematic signifier. "In sum, the avant-garde has provided the abstract research and manifestation of pure thought and technique later applied to more clearly human films. It not only posited the foundations of screen dramaturgy, but discovered and disseminated all of the expressive possibilities contained within the camera lens."[23]

In other words, Dulac sees all of the work of experimentation in the cinema—from the films of the Impressionists to the more abstract work of the adherents of "pure cinema"—as having a signifying function. Insisting on the aesthetic qualities inherent in the cinema at a time when the new medium was obliged to assert its difference from other forms of popular entertainment, she concludes: "Whether partisans of lyrical, poetic, psychological or pure cinema, all of these schools are valid. Cinematographic expression is not single, but multiple. Will it not be the conjunction of all these diversities of its form, carried to their extreme degree, which will make the cinema a very great art?"[24]

It is critical that the work of the five Impressionists, this first cinematic avant-garde, be understood as much more than stylistic renovation or technical advancement of the medium. As the film scholar

Bernard Eisenschitz points out, each film that they made was conceived as "a struggle to define a new artistic practice"[25]—a struggle that was fundamentally in opposition to the dominant commercial cinema, both French and American, of the time. In their effort to put cinema on the same level as the other arts, these filmmakers were also agitating for its status as a specific, autonomous practice with its own history, evolution, conventions, and procedures. The keynote of the dominant cinema as it emerged in Hollywood is found in the particular kind of effect produced in the cinema spectator. The impression of a continuous and homogeneous spatial unity, the centrality of the perceiving subject, and the reinforcement of the reality of depicted events all contribute to the production of this effect, which makes the spectator a credulous participant in the cinematic fiction. The research into cinematic signification carried on by the Impressionist filmmakers—whether this was on the level of the intrinsic properties of the filmic image itself or on the level of types of narrative organization through rhythmic montage constructions—represents one of the earliest attempts to develop an alternative type of meaning-production in the cinema.

In these researches, the reproduction of an illusory world, irreducibly tied to its referent, ceased being of prime importance, while the status of filmic images as signs and their organization into a discursive structure became foregrounded. Eisenschitz formulates this in similar terms when he describes the work of Epstein (*L'Auberge rouge, La Glace à trois faces*), Gance (*J'Accuse, Napoléon, La Roue*), and L'Herbier (*L'Argent*): "One already finds in their work the destruction of the taboo of the image as a transparent, total, and inviolable reflection of the world and a construction of a filmic space-time dimension (*un espace-temps du film*)."[26] In this light, the proliferation of visual experiments associated with Impressionist filmmaking—and often used as evidence of an aestheticizing sensibility—stands among the first serious theoretical reflections on the cinema in its history.

Cast in ideological terms, this construction of a "filmic space-time dimension" indicated the way toward a radical disruption of the spatial and temporal cohesion offered by the dominant cinema. Conventionally, it is this cohesion which provides the viewer with the illusion of a unified fictional space which can be penetrated and "experienced." Absolutely necessary for the production of this illusion is the strongest possible coincidence between narrative (diegetic) motivation for shot changes and their formal or rhythmic potentialities. Any attempt to highlight the fragmentary and *constructed* nature of the cinema by exploiting the plastic and rhythmic elements of composition can be seen as an effort to disrupt the work of narrative unity and spatial coherence. This can operate on many different levels, and the Impressionist filmmakers, in differing ways, explored every formal permutation. In all of their experiments with camera distance and angle, with rhythmic editing, and with technical devices, it is possible to see a wedge being driven between narrative referentiality and the discursive organization of the film. Thus a new signifying dimension became part of filmic discourse, the plastic emphasis on film's fragmentary nature suggesting a multiplicity of effects instead of a single expressive meaning. Therefore, although one might interpret the Impressionists' efforts to increase the viewer's participation in the film as the imposition of a univocal meaning, the fact remains that their films have an undeniable formal and material dynamism, an explosion of signification fundamental to establishing the specificity of cinematic language.

Thus in the work of the First Avant-Garde can be found an early form of cinematic writing, what Dulac refers to as "*cinégraphie*" and contemporary theory calls the meaning-production process of the film-text. Henri Langlois says as much in his critical assessment: "They were already writing films with the camera; they had already achieved a form of cinematic language. Through their research with the contrasts of black and white, through the meaning they conferred on each image according to their choice of camera angle, through their intertwining of surfaces, volumes, and temporal variations by means of montage, through an ever-increasing fragmentation of shots and their simplification, our avant-garde was leading directly to the cinematographic hieroglyph, to this ideographic language on which Eisenstein would base his work."[27]

Dulac is only slightly more concrete when, in an introduction to one of her illustrated lectures at the Musée Galliera, she refers to "the expressive procedures of the cinema—the role of different types of shots and angles, the fade-out, the dissolve, the superimposition, soft-focus, distortions—in sum, the entire syntax of the film."[28] Problems with the linguistic metaphor aside, this early formulation of the signifying possibilities of formal structures is basic to the conception of filmic writing. Going on to discuss the arrangement of individual shots through editing she says, "You will understand . . . the emotion that a logical succession of images can provoke . . . the work moves us, therefore, by means of a purely cinematographic technique."[29] To the extent, then, that the filmmakers of the First Avant-Garde realized that the cinema was a "language," they began to tell stories by a sequence of images alone, an organization without recourse to verbal intertitles or literary elaboration.

The Impressionist propensity for intimate psychological narratives which permitted the exploration of the life of the mind led to an effusion of cinematic devices and techniques capable of portraying memories, flashbacks, dreams, fantasies, and mental states. For all of the Impressionists, then, the cinema was thus put not in the service of the "realistic" reproduction of dramatic characters, but rather in the service of the expression, suggestion, translation, and representation of emotions, thoughts, and feelings. As Jean Mitry puts it, "The descriptive image, in some sense, became 'subjectivized.' "[30]

In addition to Dulac, both Jean Epstein and Abel Gance are credited with adding rhythmic editing to the repertoire of subjective techniques. Gance's *La Roue* emerged on the scene in 1923; an exciting crystallization of all of the experimental techniques that had preceded it, it demonstrated an expressive lyricism that became a hallmark of French film of the twenties. As Dulac notes, it marked a decisive turning point in the evolution of cinematographic art. Its use of accelerated montage techniques to establish a rhythmic, methodically organized structure paved the way for future experiments and further definitions of cinematic specificity as movement and rhythm. By basing his rhythmic editing of *La Roue* entirely on the metric relations between the shots, Gance was able to achieve a creation of "pure visual rhythm" whose "meaning was established on the value of the *duration* of the images."[31] In other words, the filmed image's referentiality ceased to have primary importance, while other meanings, more related to the plasticity of montage, emerged.

The rapidity of tempo due to shots that became increasingly shorter, for example, created the sensation of an emotional crescendo. Dulac's description of this process is fairly precise and wildly enthusiastic:

> Abel Gance's *La Roue* marked a great step forward. In this film, psychology, gestures, drama all became dependent on a cadence. The characters were no longer the only important factors in the work, but objects, machines, the length of the shots, their composition, their contrast, their framing, their harmony all play a role. Rails, locomotive, boiler wheels, pressure-gauge, smoke, tunnels functioned—through images—along with the characters. A new drama emerged composed of feelings, of raw movements, of unfolding lines. The conception of the art of movement and of rhythmically organized images came into its own, as did the expression of "things," magnificently achieving the visual poem composed of human life-instincts, playing with both the material and the ineffable. A symphonic poem in which feeling explodes not in facts, not in acts, but in visual sonorities.[32]

It is easy to see how this exciting evidence of the expressive possibilities of movement and form could lead to the theories of pure cinema, so dear to Dulac, based on rhythmic structures capable of signifying by themselves. The visual orchestration of signs achieved through the rapid alternation of shots thus produced a dynamic theory of cinematic articulation. Rhythmic patterns based on internal (within the shot) and external (between shots) relations became the foundation of cinematic composition.

In one way or another, all of the Impressionist filmmakers took up researches into the rhythmic potentials of accelerated montage and the aesthetics of pure movement. But it was Dulac who was to follow this more consistently toward its logical conclusion of nonreferential signification. She used a fragment of *La Roue* (considered the core of the film, it was entitled *La Chanson du rail*) for her illustrated talks, thereby removing it from extraneous narrative and diegetic material in order to concentrate on the purely aesthetic properties of its accelerated montage structure. "One can be moved without characters, therefore without theatrical means: Look at the song of the train-tracks and wheels. A theme, but no dramatic action. . . . The train-track, a railway of rigid steel, intertwined, the train-track, far removed from human life, a poem whose rhymes are moving lines, simple, then multiplied. . . . Then the wheels, a rhythm, a speed . . . a connecting-rod whose mechanical movement follows the rhythm of a heartbeat."[33]

Dulac used this fragment as evidence of the signifying capacity of pure form. A profoundly emotional sense of rhythm proved capable of evoking feelings, thoughts, experiences, without recourse to "the petty little stories with which the audience too often satisfies itself."[34] Through this kind of formulation, Dulac was positing the *metaphoric* elaboration of the fragment as a form of resistance to the powerful drive of narrativity associated with dominant cinema. She was thus paving the way for the consideration of the cinema as a sign system in its own right. Arguing for the artistic autonomy of the cinema she declared: "A real film should not be capable of simply being 'told,' since it draws its active and emotive principle uniquely from visual vibrations. Can one 'narrate' a painting? Can one 'narrate' a sculpture? Certainly not!"[35]

This raises the issue of assessing the filmmaking practice of the First Avant-Garde. While the title "Impressionist" is perhaps reductive, linking the five filmmakers in a relationship based too much on a strict interpretation of the content of their films ("subjectivity," "interior life"), no single name covers the magnitude of their collective contribution to the history of cinematic language. Differing fundamentally from what preceded them, they endowed the cinema with a "marvellous power of formal renovation, which was linked, as well, to a very specific conception of their material."[36] This involved a major recasting of narrative conceptions—a new formulation of the film's subject matter conceived visually, in terms of plastic or formal organization. What emerged was a fundamentally cinematic method of constructing films.

This meant, among other things, that a film could move not by a linear concatenation of events, as in its literary predecessor, the novel, but by a "vertical" (to use L'Herbier's term) structure more akin to poetics. This latter could deploy all of the signifying possibilities of the cinematic image and its relations, giving filmic discourse a productive new dimension. The work of the First Avant-Garde thus situated itself in the space between narrative referentiality and discursive organization, thereby emphasizing cinema's systematicity—its particular way of producing meaning through a constant dialectical interaction between diegetic content and formal structure. No longer considering formal elements as mere stylistic devices tacked on in the service of narrative imperatives, the filmmakers of the First Avant-Garde advanced the understanding of cinematic language, whose fundamental dialectic of continuity (which bridges the transitions between shots) and discontinuity (which introduces ruptures at another, formal, level) is at the core of its meaning-production.

What are the *feminist* implications of Dulac's contribution to film language, then, given the general aesthetic context of her time and its widespread cinematic exploration of subjectivity? Or, to put it another way, what is the resisting status of her films within a cinematic practice that had already conceived of itself as oppositional? To arrive at the precise feminist inflection of Dulac's concern with unconscious signification, it is necessary to consider her work from the perspective of feminist theory. It is possible to understand Dulac's move toward abstraction and the nonreferentiality of the image—her theorization of "pure cinema"—as an attempt to conceptualize a form of "feminine cinematic writing" in which the oppressive logic of patriarchal structures of thought would be bypassed for the more suggestive, multiple, and varied forms of signification on the connotative level. Dulac's particular emotional emphasis, her enduring belief in the evocative power of cinematic technique and the proliferation of meanings implied, suggests that against the tyranny of hierarchical meaning the filmic image could counterpose a celebration of flux. Moreover, Dulac's most incisive researches into processes of signification are cinematically worked out precisely in terms of figuring "the feminine" and the specificity of female desire. These issues will be explored in the following chapter.

NOTES

1. Carlton J. H. Hayes, *France: A Nation of Patriots* (New York: Columbia University Press, 1930), p. 186. It seems probable that Hayes's (inaccurate) figure comes from Léon Moussinac, *Panoramique du cinéma* (Paris: Au Sans Pareil, 1929), p. 17. Again, Richard Abel's exhaustive and comprehensive study of the period, *French Cinema: The First Wave, 1915–1929* (Princeton: Princeton University Press, 1984) provides a detailed background. David Bordwell's *French Impressionist Cinema: Film Culture, Film Theory, and Film Style* (New York: Arno Press, 1980), is also useful.

2. Germaine Dulac in Colson-Malleville text (unpublished manuscript of Dulac's collected writings), chapter 2, "Historique du cinéma: Evolution vers le cinéma pur," p. 8. All translation from the French are my own unless otherwise noted.

3. For a highly useful discussion of the Parisian excitement around American films, see Richard Abel's "The Contribution of the French Literary Avant-Garde to Film Theory and Criticism (1907–1924)," *Cinema Journal* 14:3 (Spring 1975): 18–40, and his more recent article, "On the Threshold of French Film Theory and Criticism, 1915–1919," *Cinema Journal* 25:1 (Fall 1985): 12–33.

4. Jacques B. Brunius, *En marge du cinéma français* (Paris: Editions Arcanes, Collection Ombres Blanches, 1954).

5. Germaine Dulac, "Le Cinéma d'avant-garde," in *Le Cinéma des origines à nos jours,* ed. Henri Fescourt (Paris: Editions du Cygne, 1932), p. 357. An alternative translation of this article, by Robert Lamberton, can be found in *The Avant-Garde Film: A Reader of Theory and Criticism,* ed. P. Adams Sitney (New York: New York University Press, 1978), pp. 43–48.

6. Dulac, "Le Cinema d'avant-garde."

7. Germaine Dulac, quoted in Pierre Leprohon, *Histoire du cinéma* (Paris: Editions du Cerf, 1961), p. 64.

8. Reprinted in Ricciotto Canudo, *L'Usine aux images* (Geneva: Office Centrale d'Edition, 1927), pp. 5–8.

9. Reprinted in Marcel L'Herbier, ed., *L'Intelligence du cinématographe,* (Paris: Editions Corréa, 1946), pp. 91–92.

10. Germaine Dulac, "Mise en scène," *Le Film,* no. 87 (November 12, 1917): 7–9.

11. Marcel L'Herbier, "Autour du cinématographe: Entretien avec Marcel L'Herbier par Jean-André Fieschi," *Les Cahiers du cinéma,* no. 202 (June–July 1968): 29.

12. Cited by Bordwell, *French Impressionist Cinema,* p. 62.

13. Colson-Malleville text, chapter 10, "Les ciné-clubs," p. 3.

14. Colson-Malleville text, chapter 10, pp. 1, 2.

15. Ibid., p. 2.

16. Dulac, "Le Cinéma d'avant-garde," p. 362.

17. Quoted by Dulac in "Le Cinéma d'avant-garde," p. 362.

18. Colson-Malleville text, chapter 10, p. 1.

19. Germaine Dulac, "Les Esthétiques. Les entraves: La Cinégraphie intégrale," in *L'Art cinématographique*, vol. 2 (Paris: Alcan, 1927); reprinted in French in *The Literature of the Cinema* (New York: Arno Press, 1970), p. 41, and translated by Stuart Liebman as "The Aesthetics, the Obstacles: Integral Cinegraphie" in *Framework*, no. 19 (1982): 6–9.

20. Dulac, "Le Cinéma d'avant-garde," p. 359.

21. Ibid., p. 360. A similar, but less precise, statement can be found in "Les Esthétiques," p. 45, where Dulac simply refers to "the study of images and their juxtaposition."

22. Dulac, "Les Esthétiques," p. 45.

23. Dulac, "Le Cinéma d'avant-garde," p. 364.

24. Colson-Malleville text, chapter 10, p. 3.

25. Bernard Eisenschitz, "Histoires de l'histoire (Deux périodes du cinéma français: le muet—la génération de 58)," *Défense du cinéma français*, January 8–March 16, 1975, Maison de la Culture de la Seine Saint-Denis, p. 28.

26. Eisenschitz, "Histoires," p. 28.

27. Henri Langlois, "L'Avant-garde français," *Les Cahiers du cinéma*, no. 202 (June–July 1968): 17.

28. Germaine Dulac, "Les procédés expressifs du cinématographe," *Ciné-magazine*, no. 27 (July 4, 1924): 15.

29. Dulac, "Les Procédés," p. 15.

30. Jean Mitry, *Le Cinéma expérimental (Histoire et perspectives)* (Paris: Editions Seghers, 1974), p. 67.

31. Mitry, *Le Cinéma expérimental*, p. 69.

32. Dulac, "Le Cinéma d'avant-garde," p. 360. This passage is similar, though not identical, to what appears in "Les Esthétiques" on page 43.

33. Germaine Dulac, "Conférence de Mme Germaine Dulac" *Cinémagazine*, no. 51 (December 19, 1924): 517. This also appears in *L'Art du cinéma*, ed. Pierre Lherminier (Paris: Editions Seghers, 1960), p. 65.

34. Ibid.

35. Germaine Dulac, "Films visuels et anti-visuels," *Le Rouge et le noir* (July 1928): 39. This can also be found in Lherminier, *L'Art du cinéma*, p. 70. An alternate translation, by Stuart Lamberton, can be found in *The Avant-Garde Film*, ed. Sitney.

36. Noel Burch and Jean-André Fieschi, "La Première vague," *Les Cahiers du cinéma*, no. 202 (June–July 1968): 24.

FOUR

From Fantasy to Structure of the Fantasm: *The Smiling Mme Beudet* and *The Seashell and the Clergyman*

[U]nconscious ideas are organized into phantasies or imaginary scenarios to which the instinct becomes fixated and which may be conceived of as true *mises en scène* of desire.[1]

The cinema is marvellously equipped to express the manifestations of our thought, of our hearts, of our memories.[2]

DISCUSSIONS OF DULAC'S FILMS tend to contrast what are perceived as the two poles of her work, to compare two conflicting—and consecutive—cinematic practices. The first is represented by *La Souriante Mme Beudet* (*The Smiling Mme Beudet,* 1923), frequently cited as an outstanding example of feminist filmmaking because of its exploration of what would constitute a feminine imaginary. In it, a fairly traditional narrative sequence is amplified by a whole range of suggestive poetic and cinematic techniques used to evoke the inner world of the main character, rendering her fantasies and desires through the cinematic depiction of mental processes. The other tendency, exemplified by the violent clash between the sexes depicted through a kind of antinarrative experimentation bordering on abstraction, is seen in Surrealism's first film, *La Coquille et le clergyman* (*The Seashell and the Clergyman,* 1927).[3] Based on a scenario by Antonin Artaud, the film demonstrates an astonishing originality in its structure, exploding all myths of character and plot in an effort to generate the fantasmatic process of dreaming itself. This use of narrative and its antithesis would seem to suggest contradictory conceptions of the cinema. However, from the standpoint of Dulac's own preoccupation with what constitutes an alternative language of desire "in the feminine," a remarkable consistency strongly connects such superficially divergent projects.

Another level of debate contrasts the overt and easily interpreted feminism of *Beudet* with what is perceived as the stridently masculine Surrealist aesthetic of *Seashell*. For example, in a rather serious instance of misattribution, an article that pits Dulac-the-feminist against Artaud-the-misogynist bases its argument on the claim that Artaud had objected to the film on the grounds that Dulac has used optical tricks and had "feminized" the script.[4] In fact, Artaud never actually made either assertion. More specifically, both criticisms were made some twenty-five years after the release of the film, and five years after Artaud's death. It was Jacques B. Brunius, in his 1954 book *En marge du cinéma français*, who criticized Dulac's film for having "drowned [the scenario] under a debauch of technical tricks"[5]—a criticism which, it has been established, was first launched not by Artaud himself, but by Yvonne Allendy. For the second, infinitely more offensive, criticism, Ado Kyrou must take credit. In a 1953 assessment of the film that borders on the hysterical, he states: "The script is very beautiful; filled with eroticism and fury, it could have been a film in the same class as Buñuel's *L'Age d'or*, but Germaine Dulac betrayed the spirit of Artaud and made a FEMININE film."[6]

This misunderstanding about the nature of the debate surrounding *Seashell* illustrates, in a fairly graphic way, the pitfalls of a form of feminist criticism that too readily employs unexamined assumptions and notions of a "feminist aesthetic." An analysis which shifts its emphasis from a superficial reading of the content of the films to a more nuanced understanding of the place of the woman within the mechanisms of fantasy and desire in the cinema suggests a way to overcome this problem. Seen from this latter perspective, Dulac's shift in interest from the representation of fantasy (through the portrayal of the intensely active mental world of her heroine in *Beudet*) to the actual generation of the fantasmatic process (through the seemingly arbitrary and irrational depiction of those processes themselves in *Seashell*) can be understood as an entirely consistent evolution in her search for a new cinematic language capable of expressing female desire. Dulac's two films can thus be seen to crystallize certain positions within her ongoing theoretical research into cinematic language, from the more explicitly feminist content of *Beudet* (the dissatisfied housewife brutalized by an obnoxious husband and a repressive bourgeois system) to a concentration on the processes of cinematic meaning-production in *Seashell* (the cinema's capacity to materially reproduce the structure and logic of dreams and the unconscious), and eventually to her concern with pure cinema. At the heart of *both* films is an interest in the psychical mechanisms of the unconscious, an exploration of subjective reality which—whether determined by the specific confines of fictional characterization or liberated by the unmediated play of the logic of dreams—is capable of revealing not only productive insights into our deepest longings, but the structure and function of "femininity" in its social, psychic, and cinematic contexts, as well.

The Smiling Mme Beudet

The Smiling Mme Beudet depicts the imaginative life of its main character with a psychological precision previously unseen in the cinema at the time of its release in 1923. In fact, its slim plot, which concerns an aborted murder—misread as a suicide attempt—by an unhappy middle-class housewife, serves merely as a pretext for the visual orchestration of thoughts, memories, dreams, hallucinations, and fantasies that constitute Madame Beudet's internal world. The film's unsmiling protagonist, whose revolt against the stifling constraints of her bourgeois marriage is demonstrated by a desire for liberation through fantasy, provides the point of focus for both narrative articulation and spectator identification. The plot involves two days in the life of this cultured and sensitive provincial housewife (Germaine Dermoz) and her oppressively vulgar fabric merchant husband (Arquillière). One evening, having found her piano locked by Monsieur Beudet, who is at a performance of *Faust*, Madame Beudet loads the gun that her husband—in a jokingly sadistic parody of suicide—often puts to his head. The next morning, overcome by guilt, fear, and remorse, she unsuccessfully tries to empty the chamber before the habitual joke's repetition, but before she can do so Beudet impulsively aims the gun at his wife instead. The film climaxes and resolves ironically, as the egotistical husband mistakenly interprets the loaded gun as his wife's suicide attempt, and his renewed appreciation of her is matched by Madame Beudet's disbelieving resignation—and the implied closing off of any future possibilities for her fertile imaginative world.

Yet it is the very interiority of this world that comprises the majority of the film's forty minutes. Dulac uses a whole range of experimental cinematic techniques in order to represent Madame Beudet's dreams and desires, to render female subjectivity filmically through the metaphoric figuration of her character's fantasies. Through a battery of technical devices ranging from dissolves, punctuating fades and irises, soft-focus and superimpositions to both slowed-down and accelerated motion, distorting lenses, camera manipulations, high-contrast distortions, and unusual angles, Dulac creates a highly charged visual atmosphere for these mini-scenarios of the fantasmatic. The actual narrative action of the film, as I've noted, is relatively sparse; it is in the visual orchestration of Madame Beudet's inner world that Dulac's prime interest in cinematic experimentation can be found. In her desire to eliminate those constraints on expression implied by the logic of narrative causality and of character development through action, Dulac turned to music as a model for cinematic composition. For her, the unmediated directness of the visual image could best be conveyed through a musical form: "Shouldn't the cinema—an art of vision, as music is an art of hearing—lead us . . . toward the visual idea, made of movement and of life, toward a conception of an art of the eye composed of emotional inspiration, evolving in its continuity and attaining, just as music does, our thoughts and feelings?"[7]

Thus for *Beudet*, Dulac relied upon such musical inspiration in order to organize the flow of images constituting Madame Beudet's solitary reveries, her flights of fantasy, and her perceptions of the emotional prison that enclosed her. Images chosen for their evocative power—for their ability to suggest a state of mind or feeling—were thus filmed using technical devices meant to enhance this power or interpret its effects. These images in turn were organized according to a psychical and subjective logic rather than one based on dramatic or causal requirements of the narrative.

This emphasis on feeling led Dulac to call the close-up the "psychological shot" because of its peculiar ability to materialize "the very thoughts, souls, emotions, and desires of the characters projected on the screen."[8] Dulac felt that in this way she was able to bypass the logical structure of verbal language in order to more profoundly move and directly touch the spectator by means of a filmic structure based on visual rhythm.

In a 1928 article entitled "La Musique du silence," Dulac affirmed the importance of correctly assessing the cinema's fundamental capacity to visualize feelings. She saw a danger in the traditional cinema's reliance on precise dramatic action for its structure: "Two actors are speaking to each other in the course of a scene. A mistake. Only the silent expressions on their faces will be visual. Alas, in ordinary dramatic cinema, facts count more than expressions."[9] Dulac felt that traditional cinema was too literary because, following in the footsteps of its predecessor, the novel, it developed its action uniquely through a succession of dramatic situations. For her, the cinema was most consistent with its expressive and aesthetic potential when it was able to "develop emotively through the image alone. . . . The cinema can certainly tell a story, but one mustn't forget that the story is nothing. The story is a surface. The seventh art, the art of the screen, is the palpable rendering of the depth which extends beneath this surface: the musical ineffable (*l'insaisissable musical*)."[10]

Yet, although a universalist assumption of consciousness might be inferred from these formulations, it is not simply a generalized notion of fantasy that interests Dulac here; clearly, in *Beudet,* she is concerned to articulate what might be called a feminine "imaginary," as she makes the exploration of *female* subjectivity the very core of her film. For this reason, the fantasy sequences—organized in each instance by a relay of mental associations—are anchored in the particulars of the woman character she creates, a frustrated, imprisoned housewife who longs for some sort of romantic evasion. Thus a focus on the content of the representation of fantasy is necessary as Dulac finds metaphoric equivalents and subjective distortions for each of Madame Beudet's imaginings. The most complete realization of this filmic rendering of unconscious processes is found in what can be called the "fantasy-solitude" sequence of the film, a series of seven segments in which Madame Beudet's fantasies take hold and overpower her in the moments preceding her decision to load her husband's gun. However, although this sequence is virtually the longest in the entire film (comprising roughly one-fifth of its total shots) Dulac is careful to prepare this cinematic explosion of perception, fantasy, and desire by a number of shorter subjective sequences, momentary indications of the power of Madame Beudet's imaginative capacities.

This "prologue" to the fantasy sequence has a trajectory of its own, for it moves from a purely mental representation of Madame Beudet's thoughts through a metaphoric image signifying her wish for escape, to an imagined scenario of desire in which a fantasm of her creation actually interacts with the space of the room in which the Beudets sit. This gradation in the type of mental or unconscious operation is matched by an increase in duration, as each of the three sequences furthers the demonstration of Dulac's interest in combining the experimental techniques of the First Avant-Garde with a cinematic elaboration of female desire. There is in this progression a movement from a more conventionally accepted icon of feminine resistance, through a momentary display of the power of the female imagination, to a situation which locates the productive capacity to dream (and thereby enact the possibility of liberation) within the female psyche itself. In this way the prologue prepares the more extensively developed fantasy sequence, whose conclusion to the complex visual chain of associations results in the ultimate act of resistance, a fantasy of murder.

The first of these "preparatory" sequences is a simple exchange of two pairs of shots, each representing the Beudets' part in a conversation. Monsieur Beudet tries to convince his wife to see *Faust,* and she replies with a polite shake of her head. A close-up of Beudet singing (fade to black) is followed by a shot of the opera chorus, while Madame Beudet's close-up (again, a fade to black) leads into a glowering Mephistopheles, large in the left foreground, and a resisting Marguerite, arm stretched out to fend off his intrusion. Although the first of these has been attributed to Dulac's attempt to give some small measure of subjectivity to other characters,[11] I maintain, instead, that Dulac's chief interest is in the subjective experience of her female character and the possibilities it represents for expressing feminine desire. From this standpoint, Beudet's shot simply illustrates what he is saying (a silent film convention), while Madame Beudet's shot—a representation of her thoughts—is a first indication of the interiority that will control our identification with her throughout the film.

This is an appropriate preparation for the sequence that follows, the first demonstration of Madame Beudet's ability to imaginatively call up an image of something longed-for, and thus a mark of the shift from a mental image to the representation of a wish. The five shots of this sequence cluster around a subjective inversion of the reverse-shot structure, a cinematic figure conventionally used to indicate perceptual point-of-view. Instead of the traditional alternation of character seeing/object seen, Dulac gives us a sequence of object-seen/character seeing/object-fantasized—and thus a transformation from *perception* to *imagination* as a close-up of a car advertisement (for a Sizaire-Berwick) in a magazine dissolves to a profile close-up of Madame Beudet reading, and its fade to black then opens on a shot of the miniature car gliding across a background of clouds. The sequence ends on an extreme close-up of Madame Beudet's eyes (reminiscent of a subsequent use of this ethereal and haunting shot in *Seashell,* to which I will return), as the frame is filled with eyes that close—in resignation or in satisfaction. This momentary insertion of two antinaturalistic shots within the context of the narrative development connects Dulac's interest in mental processes with her related belief in the close-up as a powerfully evocative expressive tool. But more important, this first indication of Madame Beudet's fantasmatic capacity to escape what she cannot leave in reality reflects Dulac's own desire to represent cinematically the psychic force of the human mind, as well as her uncanny ability to designate such subtle distinctions as those between thought, imagination, and, ultimately, unconscious fantasy.

The last preparatory sequence depicts precisely that latter process of the unconscious, for in it Madame Beudet advances from a picture that she imagines to a fantasmatic scenario that she directs. Having succeeded in mentally projecting an image of a vehicle for escape (if only for an instant), she is now able to envision a little mise-en-scène of action in the form of a confrontation between an imaginary lover and the oppressive husband who sits across from her. In no fewer than twenty-four shots the sequence depicts a phantom tennis player (come to life from the pages of the magazine by means of a superimposition) who waltzes over to Beudet's desk, lifts him bodily, and carries him off. To Madame Beudet's spontaneous—and exceptional—eruption of laughter, Beudet responds in mimicked glee, taking the gun from the drawer as a title explains: "A stupid and oft-repeated joke, dear to Monsieur Beudet: The suicide-parody." A subjective shot of the blanched and contorted face of Beudet in large close-up (Dulac's cinematic distortion to suggest Madame Beudet's emotional attitude toward her husband) is matched by a profile shot of Madame Beudet wincing. The return to a more "realistic" shot of Beudet as he places the gun back in the desk and shrugs is followed by a close-up of the back of Madame Beudet's head and a subsequent alternation of similar shots and shrugs.

This sequence is notable for a number of reasons. First, it is the introduction of the suicide joke that will generate the central dramatic action of the film. But, and this is the second point, this joke is not presented in the form of a simple narrative event. Rather, it is prefaced by the first example of Madame Beudet's mental ability to "create" a character of her own who performs in a fantasmatic scene enacted within the actual space of her life, a fictive character capable of representing through action her desire to rebel against her despotic husband. And so powerful is this imaginary scene that it can accomplish what nothing else in her oppressive existence can do—it makes her laugh. A smile that explodes in one single moment of the film thus gives renewed ironic substance to its title, for it is not simply that Madame Beudet never smiles; she is, in fact, quite capable of smiling—even laughing—but only as a result of the power of her own fantasmatic capability.

Third, the conclusion of the sequence is a foreshadowing of the film's ending. The two shots of the back of Madame Beudet's head function in direct contrast to her interaction with the fantasy tennis player. In the moment when we see her face, we observe her as the sole member of an audience reacting to a scenario of her own creation, and are thus given access to her interiority. But when the back of her head is depicted, there is a sealing off of this capacity to fictively interact, and of our capacity to identify as well. Therefore, just as these last shots of the sequence represent a temporary cessation of Madame Beudet's imaginative activity, the final images of the film itself signify a similar—and this time permanent—closure. The film's ending shot depicts Monsieur and Madame Beudet in American-shot (depicting characters to the hip, that is, three quarters of the body), seen from the back, as they continue down the provincial cobblestone street toward the vanishing point of the frame. Madame Beudet's resignation to the suffocating trap of bourgeois marriage is signified by the narrative action; the impossibility of future flights of fantasy is equally emphasized by the symbolic "closed door" of the back of the head. To return to the sequence under analysis, then, the hostile sarcasm of the exchange between the couple that concludes this fantasized scene of the tennis player's triumph is a forceful indication of just how powerfully Madame Beudet's painful reality can limit and confine her imagination's play.

Having thus prepared the view with these glimpses into the visual richness of Madame Beudet's interior world, Dulac now turns to her most sustained exploration of processes of the psyche (to date) by creating a situation in which fantasy emerges from enforced solitude. Having been left alone by the boorish husband—off at the opera with two of his provincial peers—and discovering that he has locked the piano—her one objective source of pleasure—Madame Beudet paces aimlessly through the darkened parlor as her thoughts and reveries fill the screen. The very minimal situation of a woman at home alone thus becomes the simple dramatic framework (the surface) that permits the purely visual elaboration of subjectivity (its depth).

For purposes of analysis, this sequence will be called the "fantasy-solitude sequence." Madame Beudet's subjective vision is constructed through a series of montage units, seven smaller segments which each evoke a different emotion, and which collectively combine to create a generalized atmosphere that both objectifies her state of mind and articulates her desire. In this cinematic texture of perception, thought, and fantasy, each sub-segment portrays a different type of subjective relation of Madame Beudet to the external world. In order to render this, each smaller segment is structured by a different type of technical device, alternating montage pattern, or cinematic punctuation, allowing the full range of expressive possibilities of the cinema to come into play.

I have identified the seven segments by titles that denote their content: 1) "Initial Solitude" (two shots); 2) "The Poem" (fourteen shots); 3) "The Maid" (eight shots); 4) "Imprisonment" (eighteen shots); 5) "Fantasy of the Phantom Lover" (thirteen shots); 6) "Monsieur Beudet's Haunting Appearances" (nineteen shots); and 7) "The Resolution" (three shots). In each segment, an alternation that interposes shots of Madame Beudet with different types of subjective image renders the emotional and mental atmosphere of her psyche. Thus Madame Beudet "sees" optically subjective images (shots which convey her perceptual viewpoint), semi-subjective images (shots which suggest her emotional attitude toward an object), and purely mental images (memories, thoughts, and fantasies).[12] Each of these segments is thus organized on the basis of an alternation of seeing and seen, implying that Madame Beudet's vision, both perceptual and imaginary, articulates the shot-changes that compose the sequence. In this way, Madame Beudet is continually determined as the central focus of spectator-identification and Dulac is able to achieve her stated intention: "If the opposition and succession of images are capable of creating movement, they can also perfectly depict the state of mind of a character, enabling us to enter his [or her] thoughts more readily than words can do."[13]

Initial Solitude

The first segment ("Initial Solitude") simply uses its two shots to establish the situation: Madame Beudet, alone in the study, turns off the desk lamp and discovers that the piano has been locked. The soft chiaroscuro created by her first gesture can be seen to initiate the sequence, marking the transition from the brutal reality of the Beudets' marriage to the imaginative realm of the subsequent flow of images. This short segment is matched in its simplicity (and lack of technical effects) by the three shots at the end of the sequence ("The Resolution"): Madame Beudet goes over to the desk, takes out the revolver, and reaches into the drawer for the bullets. The repetitions (Madame Beudet in American-shot, the desk, the window) reinforce the framing effect of these two segments that enclose the sequence, a sequence that effectively demonstrates "the multiple and contradictory interior impressions" which characterize "the secret domain of [Madame Beudet's] inner life."[14]

As such, the entire sequence can be read as a microcosm of the film, for within its limits—precisely defined by the "realistic" representation of Madame Beudet in the study—the whole interplay of fantasy and desire is rendered through a visual equivalent of stream-of-consciousness narration. In the context of the film itself, Madame Beudet's imaginary reveries are her only means of escape from her suffocating bourgeois marriage. Thus the film's introductory title, "In the provinces. . . . " is repeated at its end, with the additional commentary "In the quiet streets, without horizon, under the heavy sky. . . . Joined together by habit." The same dismal images of Chartres ("Notations of sadness, the empty streets, the mundane, colorless people. . . . ")[15] occur after both opening and closing titles, with the important addition of the Beudet couple, firmly ensconced in the provincial environment of the film's final image, and this provincial environment now equally ensconced in the narrative legibility required by cinematic illusionism. But while the end of the "fantasy-solitude" sequence is marked by Madame Beudet's resolve to liberate herself from the tyrannical husband—an active solution that involves loading his revolver—the end of the film, as noted before, confirms her powerlessness, enclosing her extraordinarily rich fantasy world within the immutable shape of "reality," and closing off the film's expressive psychological depth with an image of stark realism.

The Poem

Throughout her writing, Dulac stressed the importance of conceiving a film visually, of working from a "visual idea" or a "visual theme" that she equated with feelings, emotions, or sensations. In accordance with this, the "fantasy-solitude" sequence originates with a state of mind— despair, loneliness, frustration—and evokes this by means of suggestion rather than through precise definition. The interplay of images thus takes the place of what might have been the free indirect discourse of verbal intertitles ("Madame Beudet longed to be transported by a fiery, romantic lover . . . ," for example). The spectator is appealed to directly, without recourse to rational processes of the intellect, by means of a visual language which functions, paradoxically, by indirectness. This is a process of "suggestive magic" actualized in cinematic images—the Symbolist poem visualized.

Therefore, it seems quite natural that in this sequence, Madame Beudet first seeks escape through Symbolist poetry, Baudelaire's "La Mort des amants," to be precise. The fourteen shots of the next subsegment are thus patterned on an alternation that shifts between images of Madame Beudet reading and thinking, intertitles of lines from the poem, and corresponding shots of objects around the house. The implication of this logic of montage, the cinema's discursive process, is that Madame Beudet is trying to imagine the poetic images as she reads by calling to mind objects of her quotidian reality.

The result, of course, is undeniably ironic, as the banality of the objects only reinforces her dissatisfaction with a loveless marriage. The

Baudelaire poem is in fact about a perfect union of two lovers (lines not quoted in the film): "Our two hearts will be two immense torches,/ Which will reflect their double lights/In our two minds, these twin mirrors" ["Nos deux coeurs seront deux vastes flambeaux,/Qui ré-fléchiront leurs doubles lumières/Dans nos deux esprits, ces miroirs jumeaux"]. But what Madame Beudet "sees" in her mind's eye—each image prefaced by a fade-in and closed by a fade-to-black—are the Beudets' empty bed, their neatly stacked pillows, and the vase of flowers that has become a symbol of their confrontation. In response to the poem's invocation of spiritual doubling, then, images of her alienated life emphasize Madame Beudet's sense of isolation. The punctuating fades signify her thoughts as she tries to conjure, from her own experiences, images of "beds wafted with light scents" ["des lits pleins d'odeurs légères"], "couches deep as tombs" ["des divans profonds comme des tombeaux"], and "strange flowers" ["d'étranges fleurs"]. But the vague perfume, the suggested swoon, the exoticism of the poem are lost in the bland reality of her life's objects. She throws the book down in disgust. Thus the spectator's first entry into Madame Beudet's feelings is guided by the character's own cognitive powers of imagination and the ensuing frustration when these efforts fail.

The Maid

The spectator goes deeper into Madame Beudet's unconscious mind— but only for an instant—in the next sub-segment. In a conventional exchange of the reverse-shot structure, the maid enters and asks if she may go out with her fiance (the question is rendered in an intertitle). The only two shots of Madame Beudet in this segment (indicating her reply by a sad nod of the head) surround the first truly imaginary apparition of the sequence. In a single close-up of the maid, the fiance is made to appear, kiss her cheek, then disappear through a superimposition that dissolves in and out. Framed as it is by identical images of Madame Beudet in American-shot, this sequence of shots implies her own mental projection of a loving relationship. This image of desire is thus a foreshadowing of things to come: Madame Beudet will only experience the love she longs for through an imaginary scenario of her own creation.

Imprisonment

The sub-segment treating Madame Beudet's sensation of entrapment is marked by signifiers of imprisonment and chronological time. Clocks, associated with calculated and measurable time, and thus with the mercantile mentality of Monsieur Beudet, first seem to harass her by appearing everywhere she turns. Thus a strict alternation of close-ups ("psychological shots" of Madame Beudet back-lit in a shadowy halo effect, then various clock faces and clanging bells) terminates with a close-up, accentuated by a hazy iris, of Madame Beudet's eyes, another image in a paradigm of shots of this kind. In this way, the experimental flow of the subjective time of consciousness (perhaps emphasized by the "luminous halo" that surrounds Madame Beudet, and calling to mind Virginia Woolf's definition of life as "a luminous halo, a semi-transparent envelope surrounding us from the beginning of consciousness to the end")[16] is cinematically contrasted with metonymies of the implacable and ordered movement of chronological time. This contrast is then condensed into one striking, emblematic image that is repeated in various avatars for three shots. Madame Beudet, in medium-close-up, stands before a mantelpiece mirror and rests her head on a glass clock cover. Where the signifying function of editing had contrasted the two types of temporality across the cut, the temporal registers are now juxtaposed by a form of internal montage that relates elements within the frame among themselves.

Madame Beudet's sensation of temporal oppression is matched with one of spatial entrapment in the remaining shots of the segment. Once again, this is provided by a metonymy, this time of physical imprisonment: a penitentiary. After an intertitle that announces (a bit too literally), "Always the same horizons. . . . " close-ups of Madame Beudet in profile looking out the window enclose shots of a dreary provincial doorway and its facade that reads "House of Detention and Corrections." There is perhaps a problem with this notion of an objective correlative that relies too heavily on the content of the image to convey a state of mind. Images of clocks and prisons remain too anchored in their referents to fully achieve the suggestive evocation of the Symbolists. It is conceivable that at this point Dulac would have been more successful if she had adopted a pattern of accelerated montage, for example, which might have allowed the spectator to experience the feeling of suffocation more readily. Nonetheless, in terms of the overall structure of the sequence, this segment largely functions as preparation for the more viable imaginary production, Madame Beudet's "Fantasy of the Phantom Lover," and thus successfully contrasts an overt referentiality with what is ultimately the most fantasmatic sequence of the film.

Fantasy of the Phantom Lover

Here "fantasy" refers to the fulfillment of a wish by means of the production of an imaginary scene in which the subject (in this case, the character Madame Beudet) is the protagonist. It is distinguished from the world of imaginative activity in general by its profound and systematic relations of desire: "[T]he primary function of phantasy [is] namely the *mise-en-scène* of desire—a *mise-en-scène* in which what is *prohibited* (*l'interdit*) is always present in the actual formation of the wish."[17] Thus in terms of the film, Madame Beudet has engaged in imaginative activity of a conscious or subliminal kind up until this point in the sequence. Now, in order to convey the transition into the "dream-state" which makes imaginary production of a fantasmatic sort possible, Dulac has recourse to the figure of the "double."

First, in American-shot, Madame Beudet slumps into a chair, recalling the habitual gesture of Emma Bovary that characteristically precedes her transports of vague desire ("She sank down into an armchair"). The next shot—an axis-match close-up of Madame Beudet which dissolves into and then fills the frame—provides us with her double, the character who will act as protagonist in her ensuing fantasy. *This* Madame Beudet turns her head and looks off toward left frame as the image fades to black. Suddenly, the apparition, the phantasm, the phantom lover appears in a doorway—a blurred, superimposed image, advancing on air, arms outstretched. The corresponding close-up discloses Madame Beudet's hands in a gesture of response. The following shot, rendered hazy by a sort of reverse-iris effect which frames Madame Beudet's face in a halo of light, reveals her ecstatic smile—her only genuine smile in the entire film.

Whereas Madame Beudet's laughter, discussed earlier with the action of the tennis-player, had the effect of an unexpected eruption, here her smile emphatically retains something of an enigmatic quality. It is a smile of *jouissance,* of orgasmic ecstasy, of an expressiveness not seen on Madame Beudet's face before or since. This has the effect of suggesting a kind of condensation of woman's sexuality, of undecipherability, and of pleasure in a momentary image that is as uncertain as it is fleeting. And it is in this sense that the earlier laughter (related to an imagined vision) prepares this moment, a moment which is particularly significant in that it is linked precisely to the "representation" of the fantasmatic object of desire. For this reason, it is *this* smile which carries the weight of the film's title. Completely enclosed in an imaginary, subjective realm which has been prepared by the entire sequence, it is this smile to which all of the action returns, this smile that signifies at the same time the desire of the character, the filmmaker, and the spectator herself.

But the signifier of contradiction appears in an intertitle ("But. . . . "). A close-up of Madame Beudet's eyes, framed in an iris and now looking toward the right of the frame, prepares the way for the following shot—a high-contrast, distorted image of Monsieur Beudet's grinning face. As if to oppose the harsh reality of the marriage evoked by this image with the possible excitement and suggestive sexuality offered by the fantasy, the shot of the phantom lover is repeated. Subsequent shots reveal Madame Beudet tossing her wedding ring until the segment's final shot irises on her hand, the ring firmly back in place.

Throughout this sub-segment, then, Madame Beudet's fantasmatic projection is rendered through an alternation of shots: her "double" seeing, the imagined representations seen. Her hallucination of the phantom lover confronts the memory of her oppressive husband in a scenario that subsumes desire to the law. The figure of the double, indicating the dream-state necessary to the production of this fantasm, also functions to induce the spectator's participation in this production. It is by virtue of this double that Madame Beudet becomes a character in her own fiction. Likewise, the viewer twice removed (watching Madame Beudet watching her fantasm), becomes a credulous participant in the hallucination, spectator to the fantasy-within-a-fantasy offered by the film, and equal participant in her desire.

Monsieur Beudet's Haunting Appearances

The penultimate sub-segment of the "fantasy-solitude" sequence elaborates on the horrific appearance of Monsieur Beudet, as subsequent shots render him capable, even in his absence, of preventing Madame Beudet's fantasy of escape. This is the longest sub-segment in the sequence, and as such demonstrates his power, both narratively and textually, to foreclose his wife's desire. The segment opens as Madame Beudet, still seated in the armchair, jumps up, startled. The image of Monsieur Beudet, made even more grotesque through a variety of technical procedures from bizarre camera angles and distorting lenses to both fast and slow motion, appears in nine of the segment's nineteen shots, alternating (in general) with close-ups of a terrorized Madame Beudet.

The effect is such that he seems to surge up wherever Madame Beudet, in increasing panic, turns. First he bounds over the balcony in slow motion. This apparition differs from that of the phantom lover in that while the latter, an imaginary creation of Madame Beudet, appeared from an imagined doorway in a barely distinguishable soft-focus haze, Monsieur Beudet, a remembered figure, climbs through the window of the Beudet apartment and has some degree of corporeality. He grimaces, grins, and laughs in subsequent images, chasing her in accelerated motion, pushing the flowers to the center of the table in slow motion, demanding that she adjust his collar. These last three are characteristic gestures, memories of Monsieur Beudet's behavior that now haunt Madame Beudet as she sees him before her eyes. The image of her fear thus concretized, these gestures culminate in a repetition of Monsieur Beudet's parodic suicide joke. And as he disappears from the frame in this final haunting image, leaving the empty desk, Madame Beudet's "resolution" to load the gun seems the logical conclusion.

The Seashell and the Clergyman

> *A dream on the screen*—The most recent psychological research has established that the dream, far from being a formless and chaotic mass of images, always tends to organize itself according to precisely defined rules, and thus has its own—affective and symbolic—logic. Consequently, someone else's dream (if we were able to see it) would be capable of moving us as effectively as any other spectacle, by addressing not our logic and our intellectual comprehension, but this obscure and unconscious sensibility which elaborates our own dreams for us. Such is the bold attempt of poet Antonin Artaud, who has proposed a scenario made of a dream: *The Seashell and the Clergyman.* Madame Germaine Dulac has just finished making this film . . . and we can expect that [she] has surpassed herself in this effort of the avant-garde. It concerns a dream which is not enclosed in any kind of story and which each spectator will have to understand, or better, experience uniquely according to the resources of his own personal sensibility.[18]

With *The Seashell and the Clergyman,* Dulac extends her concern with the mechanisms of the unconscious by shifting her focus from a fantasy of which a fictional character is the subject to the fantasmatic process itself. Thus, while her interest in the processes of the psyche remains constant, one of the things that marks the difference between the two films is a modification in the type of spectatorial involvement required by each text. Whereas in *Beudet,* as we have seen, the spectator is made to identify with a specific character whose thoughts, dreams, and fantasies are represented within the confines of a fiction, what *Seashell* elicits is the spectator's actual participation, as the subject of the fantasm, in the experience of those psychic processes themselves. And it is here that the consequences for the exploration and expression of desire, and of feminine desire in particular, are most provocative. In *Beudet,* Dulac had conceived of her female character's unconscious desires as specific objects capable of being rendered on the screen through formal means: here, in *Seashell,* she uses the female figure

The Smiling Mme Beudet (The Phantom Hero)

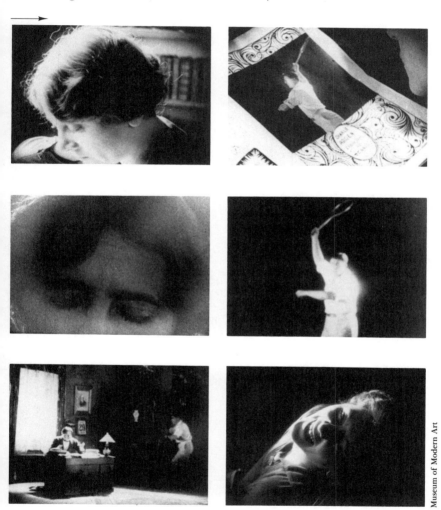

The Smiling Mme Beudet (Fantasy-Solitude: Alone)

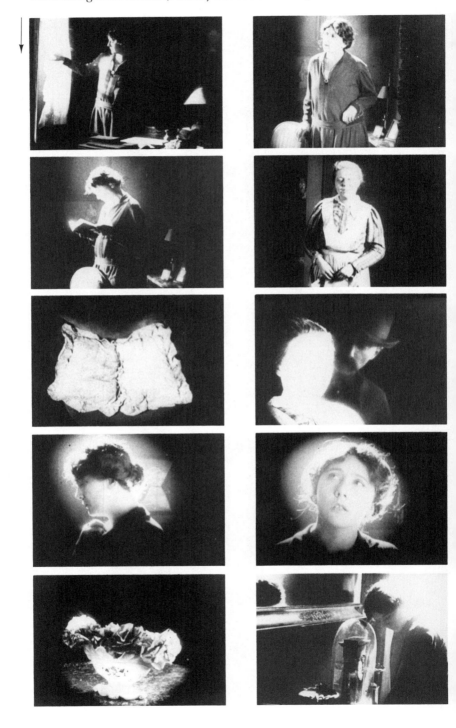

The Smiling Mme Beudet (Fantasy-Solitude: The Lover)

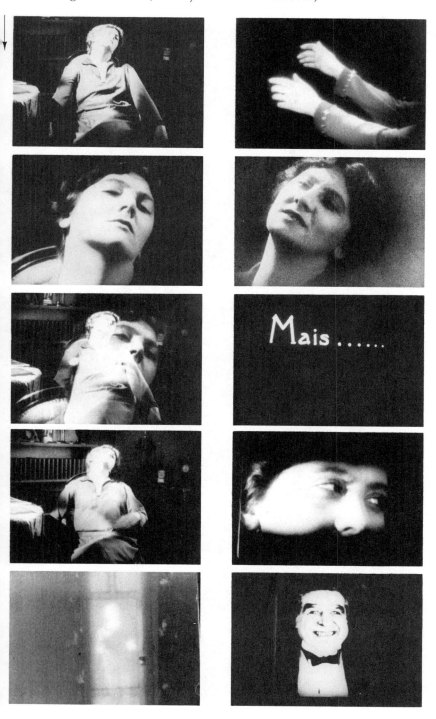

The Smiling Mme Beudet (Fantasy-Solitude: The Resolution)

precisely *as* a representation, thematizing woman as a force of desire within the production of the filmic writing itself.

In order to have a better understanding of the radical feminist potential of a film like *Seashell,* it is first necessary to grasp the distinction between the mobilization of spectator identification through a fictional construct and the production of a liberated and active viewing subjectivity—a distinction that characterizes the specific procedures of the two films. As discussed earlier in relation to the entire cinematic apparatus, contemporary film theory posits that the film spectator is in some sense "constructed" in and by the viewing experience, and that fictive participation in the film's events has its roots in fantasy. As is evident from the analysis of Madame Beudet's imaginings, "Even where they can be summed up in a single sentence, phantasies are still scripts . . . of organized scenes which are capable of dramatization— usually in a visual form."[19] Within this framework of a wishfulfilling staging of desire, all fantasmatic production is conceived as a relation to a representation, a relation of the subject born of loss and marked by the perpetual impossibility of satisfaction. The desiring process, then, is one of infinite circulation, of endless displacement from representation to representation. And it is the intersection of film and unconscious fantasy around a concept of "dramatization" that accounts for the mobilization of the spectator's desire in the viewing situation.

It is this dramatization which connects *Seashell* to *Beudet* in terms of Dulac's feminist project. Certain formulations of the Surrealist film conceived it as a textual space in which various psychic forces were made to interact—in short, they posited a notion of film as textual process. Alain and Odette Virmaux's definition of the Surrealist film as "a means of exploring the profound life of consciousness, obsessions, and fantasms in their spontaneous and irrational eruption"[20] foregrounds this staging of psychic processes at the base of the Surrealist film's textuality. It can be successfully argued that *Seashell,* undeniably acknowledged as the first example of Surrealist cinema (both chronologically and aesthetically), represents the earliest attempt to cinematically render these unconscious forces in a way that engages the viewer in a process of identification with the film-text itself, rather than with any specific fictional construct. Once liberated from the constraints of both character and plot, these forces are thus free to circulate on the screen with all the energy of unconscious drives themselves. A film like *Seashell,* then, facilitates the spectator's own—and unique—participation in the meaning-production process without recourse to the traditional mechanisms of identification.

As noted earlier, Dulac's film is based on a script by the revolutionary poet and dramatist Antonin Artaud. This double authorship has been the source of much critical confusion, for the riot that accompanied the film's inaugural screening on February 9, 1928, has led to extensive debates concerning artistic theory, intentionality, and cinematic transcription from verbal to visual text.[21] What interests me here, however, is the way that *Seashell*'s articulation of hallucinatory dream-images is consistent with Dulac's exploration of unconscious processes throughout her career and how, in fact, this suggests possibilities for the conceptualization and representation of feminine desire. My concern is with how a concept of "femininity" is produced in the text of *Seashell*, and for this reason the *textual* markers of authorship are of more significance than the particulars of the debate between individuals. It is within this context that I consider both Dulac and Artaud as having similar conceptions of the film and compatible impulses behind its realization. For the present analysis, I thus emphasize the correspondence of authorial voices.[22]

To attempt to describe the "plot" of *Seashell* is to immediately situate oneself within its central problematic, for the film consists of a series of moments connected associatively without any regard for narrative logic or causality. It is precisely the unpredictability and confusion of dreams that Artaud sought in his scenario, a succession of images "in a film constructed according to the dark and hidden rules of the unconscious," images that would follow each other despotically, arbitrarily, relentlessly in a "poetry of the unconscious . . . which is the only poetry possible."[23] This pure poetry of visual elements was intended to approximate subjectivity by recreating the impact of the dream *as it is being dreamed:* "[*The Seashell and the Clergyman* attempts] to find, in the occult birth and wanderings of feeling and thought, the deep reasons, the active and veiled impulses of our so-called lucid acts[.] [This] scenario can resemble, can be related to *the mechanism of a dream* without actually being a dream itself. [It seeks to] restore the pure work of thought."[24] Thus a simple outline of the visual situations that follow each other for no apparent reason is the closest one can come to a narrative description, for the significance of each sequence of images comes from its suggestive relationship (its representation of thought processes) rather than from its content (its motivation through character development).

A clergyman (Alex Allin) fills beakers with a black liquid from an oyster shell, then lets them shatter on the floor; a general (Lucien Bataille) arrives and brandishes his saber; the clergyman follows him through the city streets to a church, where an astonishingly beautiful woman in eighteenth-century attire (Génica Athanasiou) suddenly appears. There is a confrontation in the confessional, as the officer abruptly becomes a priest; after tossing the priest from a cliff, the clergyman takes the latter's place in the confessional, then, confronting the woman, rips off her bodice, which turns into a carapace of shell-shaped armor. There is next a wildly dancing society crowd into which a royal couple (the general and the woman) arrives, followed by the clergyman brandishing first the seashell and then the carapace; as he momentarily sees another apparition of the woman, he drops the carapace, which disappears in flames. His coattails then grow and expand across the parquet floor; suddenly, he is chasing the woman down a country road, as she metamorphoses (through close-ups) into a series of facial distortions; he continues to chase her through several hallways with closing doors until, finally, he enters a room where there is a large globe on a pedestal. He beckons to the unseen woman, captures her head, and places it inside the ball; now jauntily trying his key on a number of doors, the clergyman again sees the royal couple and this time pursues them both through the hallways and on the country road. Pounding fists wake the clergyman, who is asleep on a hammock on a ship; he spies the general and the woman kissing, a sight that prompts an attempt to strangle her fantasized neck in a movement that initiates a series of dreamlike images of glittering stalactites, islands, shimmering water, a tiny sailing ship, mist. Abruptly, a corps of maids emerges into a room, busily dusting as the woman, now a governess, takes charge; there is a couple (an unseen man and the woman) with tennis rackets, then a return to the maids who clean the globe as a group of butlers arrives. A return to the tennis scene precedes the arrival in the room of the clergyman and the woman now as a wedding couple; a close-up of the clergyman's head initiates a series of dream-images which are displayed on four different portions of his face. Suddenly, the headless clergyman descends the stairs, holding the glass ball; he then arrives in the room as the servants line up; a panning shot of their eyes causes the clergyman to drop the globe, which shatters on the floor, his face emerging among the shards. He stands, now with the oyster shell in his hand, then drinks from the shell that has his head in it, and the film ends as he drinks the black liquid—and his own image—which pours from the seashell.

Again it is Artaud's words that clarify this apparent narrative confusion and indicate the profound systematicity at work beneath the film's surface disorientation. "*The Seashell and the Clergyman* does not tell a story, but develops a series of states of mind, just as one thought derives from another, without needing to reproduce a logical sequence of events. From the clash of objects and gestures, *true psychic situations* are derived, and from these, rational thinking, trapped, can only seek a subtle escape."[25]

What is particularly illuminating for the purposes of this chapter is the manner in which an emphasis on psychic processes eliminates the distinction between internal and external necessitated by the conventional fiction film, for it is precisely this latter kind of film that must develop narrative alibis and rational explanations for the appearance of every one of its images. In the traditional film, a veneer of narrative complications acts as an explanatory frame for the arbitrariness of the subjective images, whereas in *Seashell*, the absence of this frame allows the spectator to actually participate in the fantasmatic process.

Far from being a facile depiction of dream associations on the screen, therefore, *Seashell* attempts to reproduce—*for the spectator's active engagement*—the actual production process of desire, its perpetual metamorphoses as it circulates from representation to representation. And it is no coincidence that this is associated specifically with the representation of the female figure, for throughout the text the elusive quality of the female figure is equated with that of desire in its evanescence. The woman's image is repeatedly generated as a fantasm of vision throughout the film—femininity is thematized as desire itself. Therefore, conceptions of the "feminine" do not disappear from *Seashell*, but are reoriented so that they are associated more fundamentally with unconscious processes.

Artaud's understanding of this is quite apparent in his description of the female character (portrayed by the woman with whom he was still passionately and desperately in love, although he was at the time in the process of ending their long and intense affair): "The woman displays her animal desire, she has the shape of her desire, the spectral shimmering of the instinct which drives her to be at the same time one and ceaselessly different in her repeated metamorphoses."[26] In the film, Dulac was able to emphasize the fantasmatic quality of this female figure through expressive lighting, through soft-focus and hazy iris effects, and through sudden appearances and disappearances that enhanced her ephemeral status as an apparition. The figure of the woman thus emerges in *Seashell*, repeatedly in different guises, as a concrete, visual manifestation of unconscious forces of desire. According to Artaud, again, the woman was meant to portray "a role which is entirely instinctive, one in which a very surprising sexuality takes on an air of fatality that goes beyond the character as a human being and attains the universal."[27] It is clear from both Artaud's intent and Dulac's cinematic articulation of it, then, that the mediations of the subjective consciousness of a character, the rationalizations of narrative complications are not only unnecessary, they are strictly forbidden: This image of the woman is continually presented *as* representation. Thus rather than a figure with a referent in the actual world, a personality with depth of characterization, Génica Athanasiou's appearances materialize the actual production process of the image itself—an image of the woman *as desire*. However, it is extremely important to understand that both Artaud and Dulac in no way attempt to ascertain "the truth of woman" in this film, nor do they posit any social generalities of gender. Rather than suggesting an essentialist association of woman and instinct, or the particularities of personality, both scenarist and filmmaker place their emphasis on the dynamic and protean variations that the woman's form assumes. By foregrounding the fantasmatic nature of this image of the woman—as an imaginary production, with the capacity of simulacrum, of memory, of hallucinated vision—the female figure in *Seashell* thus provides a sustained reflection on the construction and production of femininity both in the film and within its cultural and psychic contexts.

Another point to be made in relation to Artaud's positing of sexuality over personality in the construction of the female image concerns his reference to the "surprising" sexuality of the woman (in the passage just cited). Like most of Artaud's language, the term "une sexualité très curieuse" defies literal translation, for the very "curiosity" that seems self-evident in its meaning explodes in a number of allusive directions once it slides from French to English. What is peculiar to the meticulous or inquisitive investigator—attracting and retaining the attention of the pursuit—becomes almost meaningless as an attribute when used to modify "sexuality." What remains, instead, are the strange, the surprising and the singular—qualities of the rare and the extraordinary. How contradictory, then, that Artaud should choose a word designating an astonishing uniqueness in order to describe the characteristic that makes his female "universal." It is precisely within this complication that Dulac chose to situate her elaboration of "femininity" in this film, for the very elusiveness of definition is what characterizes her female form.

A brief exploration of Artaud's descriptions of the feminine figure in the scenario and Dulac's cinematic actualizations of them might be useful in this light. As previously noted, at a very superficial level, none of the "characters" in *Seashell* conforms to traditional notions of character elaboration and development. Yet even at the outset, by virtue of her ephemeral quality and the clergyman's fascinated pursuit, the woman's image is secured as central to the cinematic fiction. This "very beautiful" woman's figure, in various aspects, characterizations, and symbolic forms, constantly and unexpectedly appears throughout the film, as the clergyman, a consciousness in search of itself, pursues her.

However, in order to avoid an immediate and superficial reading of the film as romantic quest, I should point out that *Seashell* neither begins nor concludes with this pursuit of the woman. Rather, if an interpretation must be posited (and it should be noted that Artaud had excised "everything that had a poetic or literary quality" in the *découpage* he sent to Dulac), the film has as much to do with the clergyman's quest for identity as it does with romantic aspirations. The film thus both opens and closes with the clergyman alone, in a circular reiteration of images that assures the association of clergyman, liquid, seashell, and self. This equivocation of interpretations is intentional: Artaud and Dulac were less interested in the character's psychological narrative—be it of identity or of romance—than they were in dramatizing fundamental operations of the psyche. Instead of a single protagonist—male or female—used to focus and organize the identificatory processes of the spectator, then, there is a multiplicity of positions available within the fantasmatic scenario, a scenario which, in fact, comprises the entire film. It is this form of dispersed subjectivity that puts the viewer, rather than the character, in the place of the desiring producer of the fantasm, and in so doing, unfixes notions of the singular self, and of "masculinity" and "femininity" as well. Numerous relations of identification with both characters and functions make the film's "story" a series of dramatized relationships and narrative moments in a psychosexual dynamic—and the spectator perpetually slides between and among them.

A form of spectatorial identification with fantasmatic activity itself thus allows the female figure to function as a *representation* in the dream-space of the film, a generalized social and psychic articulation of "femininity" as it is produced from situation to situation. It is in this sense that the overall "narrative" structure of both scenario and film achieves the dream-logic so important to Artaud, and thereby permits the rendering of sexuality as a process unrestricted by prior definitions. Both Dulac and Artaud agreed that a film's structural coherence should emerge from within the text itself rather than from an organizing principle external to it. In fact, Artaud was not against the notion of the dream per se, but against its use as an alibi to justify the bold technical maneuvers of the film. In his preface to *Seashell*, immediately after his famous disclaimer ("I will not seek to excuse its incoherence by the easy loop-hole of dreams"), Artaud is quick to point out the importance of the film's internal logic: "Dreams have a logic of their own—but more than that, they have a life of their own in which nothing but dark and intelligent truths appear. This scenario seeks out the somber truth of the mind, in images emerging uniquely from themselves, images which . . . draw their meaning . . . from a sort of powerful inner necessity which projects them in the light of a merciless obviousness (*évidence sans recours*)."[28]

But although his evocation of these "somber truths" demonstrates a profound understanding of the mechanisms of the unconscious, Artaud most definitely objects to traditional notions of psychology, personality, and behavior. Thus he emphatically counterposes this self-engendering power of the image to the facile explanatory coherence of narrative or of psychology. Again in the preface he is quite explicit on this point: "In the scenario that follows I have attempted to realize this idea of a visual cinema in which even psychology is devoured by acts. No doubt this scenario does not achieve the absolute image of all that might be done in this direction; but at least it points the way. Not that the cinema must renounce all human psychology. That is not its principle. On the contrary, *it must give this psychology a much more vital and active form*—and this without those discursive connections which attempt to make the motives for our actions appear in an absolutely stupid light instead of exposing them to us in their original and profound barbarity."[29]

And it is here that the distinction critical to a feminist reading of the film emerges, for in eliminating psychology as a means of rational explanation or interpretation, the full psychic force of the unconscious as a signifying system becomes apparent. Screen images and sequences thus become violently evocative stimuli for the viewer's own intuitive and psychic processes, chosen for their powerful immediacy and capacity to move rather than for their discursive ability to delineate fictional constructs, male or female. In this context, then, the viewer is continually engaged in the activity of meaning-production through textual instances that actualize psychic forces: "characters" become generalized cultural constructs—symbolic representations of masculinity and femininity, of patriarchal authority and female sexuality in a circuit of desire. It is along these lines that the appearance of the woman's figure in the film—as spectral apparition rather than as substantial character—must be understood. Through each incarnation, through each elusive moment, the woman in *Seashell* achieves exactly that directness of the "purely visual situations whose dramatic action springs from a shock designed for the eyes, a shock founded . . . on the very substance of the gaze"[30] that Artaud called for and that the dream-work implies. It is in this sense that the images of libidinal violence, of perverse sexuality, and of passion must be understood.

There is an even more important point: Artaud envisioned *The Seashell and the Clergyman* as the film that would tear the cinema away from its status as reflection, reproduction, and representation of the real, and in so doing demonstrate its capacity to signify the unrepresentable—the fantasmatic world of hallucinations, metamorphoses and desires. Yet it is only—and specifically—the figure of the woman that bears the full weight of this project. For while the clergyman remains clothed in his ecclesiastic frock throughout the film, the patriarchal figure likewise alternating between military uniform and priestly robes, it is the female figure alone who undergoes no fewer than ten transformations of attire. From billowing eighteenth-century gown and feathered bonnet to slender black silk dress with train, from a flowing Empire-style garment to the dark high-collared outfit of a governess, from the contemporary tennis outfit of pleated skirt and sweater to the filmy simplicity of a wedding gown, the image of the woman perpetually reappears, as variable as she is elusive. Her changes of costume correspond to changes of function in the representation of the sexual dynamic, as she repeatedly forms a different couple with each of the men at different times. A closer look at her varied appearances throughout the film will demonstrate the way in which a sense of almost "physical intoxication" is achieved through these repeated metamorphoses of the visual embodied in the female figure.

The first indication of the woman in *Seashell* emerges unexpectedly: She is seated in a horse-drawn carriage beside the officer whom we recognize from the film's first sequence. Artaud's scenaric indications are even devoid of a verb—the officer is simply seen "with a very beautiful white-haired woman."[31] This sudden emergence of the female figure is depicted in the film by means of the first in a series of "impossible" points of view. The initial two shots of the carriage show it traversing the frame from different sides, intercut with images of the clergyman crawling in the street. As he crawls around the corner of a building, we see him suddenly lurch upward, as a close-up reveals a horrified expression on his face. The "reverse-shot" is a close-medium-shot of the woman seated in the carriage, making our first encounter with her one signalled by her status as *an object of vision*. As spectators, we see the woman in a way impossible for the clergyman, given both his distance from the carriage and his position behind it. Yet his reaction is vividly portrayed, and the force of the woman as haunting vision, replayed throughout the film, is secured from the start.

As the scenario describes it, the officer and the woman enter a church; once they are in the confessional together, the clergyman leaps on the officer, who turns into a priest. At this point, Artaud indicates that the priest should appear differently to the clergyman and the woman. Dulac conveys this sequence in a way which emphasizes the ephemeral beauty of the woman: As the woman and the officer form a primal couple in the confessional (a shot that opens and closes the sequence, its repetition acting as a frame), shots of the clergyman begin to alternate with shots of the woman, alone in the frame. A close-up of the clergyman's eyes, framed by a soft iris, initiates a strikingly lovely shot of the woman—a frontal close-up of her face, isolated and enhanced by the hazy lighting that surrounds it. The episode in which the clergyman strangles the priest is elaborated in a separate sequence. Artaud designates a number of separate close-ups of the priest to indicate his different demeanors, "aimiable and complaisant when [his face] appears to the woman, savage, bitter, and menacing when it considers the clergyman." In a sequence of roughly twenty-five shots, Dulac utilizes a variety of technical devices, including an original and inventive use of split screen, superimpositions, a wide range of high and low angles, distorting lenses, and larger or smaller close-ups to convey the violence of the episode and the gamut of expressive attitudes evoked by the scene. At this point, the female character's face expresses love or shock, concomitant with the emotions designated by the scenario.

In a subsequent episode, it is now the woman and the clergyman who are in the confessional, and as the clergyman's rage develops, the film follows the scenario's description fairly closely. Allin's anger is accompanied by pounding fists and paroxysms of gesticulation, while the image of the woman maintains its evanescent stature. Once again, a close-up of astonishing beauty, this time of Génica Athanasiou's eyes surrounded by a gauzed iris, renders the woman in all her seductive loveliness while the scenario says simply, "The woman stands before him, looking." Through the metonymy of the close-up of the eyes, Dulac thus materializes the act of looking in a provocative way, making the eyes, which look themselves, the object of the (spectator's) gaze. I will return to this shortly.

The responding shot, a masked close-up of the clergyman's eyes, initiates the next sequence, one which has, because of its violence and the fairly obvious misogyny of its literal denotation, been seized upon by traditional feminist criticism. The clergyman "throws himself upon [the woman] and tears off her bodice as if he had wished to lacerate her breasts. But her breasts are replaced by a carapace of shells." Yet this can only be interpreted as an act of psychologically motivated violence within the context of a conventional narrative film; here, I maintain, both Dulac and Artaud are interested in the libidinal force of the gesture—in its function as a representable instance in the dream-work—and in these terms it is one of many "purely visual situations" that constitute the film.

Therefore, the apparition of the woman, a spectral vision that freezes the clergyman in terror or incites him to violence throughout the film, must not be interpreted as a sign of Artaud's sexist fear of women. Rather, these sudden, disturbing unexpected appearances—at once horrifying and seductive—are instances of the visual shock "founded on the very substance of the gaze," images in which the woman—as a figure of desire—evokes ambivalent sexuality, passionate obsession, and libidinal violence. In a subsequent episode of the film—after another of the woman's protean transformations into a queen in a royal couple, her absorption into the air (done through a dissolve), and her reappearance in a different corner of the room (this time portrayed in hazy iris as a mythical figure in flowing white robe and long hair)—the clergyman reacts: "This apparition seems to terrify the clergyman," indicates the scenario, as he drops the carapace-breast-plate he has been brandishing. This sequence, then, makes use of the cinematic reaction-shot to convey pure dynamic emotive processes, for, as Artaud maintains, "There is no hidden significance of a psychological, metaphysical, or even human[istic] kind."[32]

This initiates another sequence which condenses a number of the "repeated metamorphoses" intended by Artaud to convey that "fantasmatic shimmering" of desire. As the woman and the clergyman run wildly, distractedly in the night,

> Their flight is intercut with successive apparitions of the woman in diverse attitudes [another translation refers to this as "hallucinatory sequences with the woman in various guises. . . . "]: Sometimes her cheek is enormously swollen, sometimes she sticks out her tongue, which stretches out to infinity as the clergyman clutches it as if it were a rope. Sometimes her chest swells out horribly.
>
> At the end of their course, we see the clergyman entering a hallway and the woman behind him swimming in a sort of sky.[33]

These words are in Artaud's description, and Dulac utilized the full extent of her skill and imagination to transform these to the screen. All of the distortions are filmed against a very black background, something that contrasts with the intense sunlight of the chase sequence with which they are interspersed; this also emphasizes the spectral and illusory quality of these varied metamorphoses. Through the use of distorting lenses, wipes, superimpositions, and rotating prisms and lenses, a number of deformations are wrought on the feminine figure. Yet in some strange way, none of these is as horrific as the images of Monsieur Beudet in the earlier film, although many of the same devices are used. This demonstrates fairly graphically, therefore, that while the effects in *Beudet* are aimed at conveying an *interpretation* of character already formulated when the film was shot, the focus here is on *processes*—the conditions of representability at work in both unconscious and filmic figuration which it is *Seashell*'s project to represent.

Shortly after this, a sequence of the film occurs that has lent itself to the strongest attacks by traditional feminist criticism. The clergyman "raises his arms in the air as if he were embracing the body of a woman." Then, once his hold is secured, he throws himself upon it, strangling it "with expressions of unheard-of sadism," introducing the severed head into a glass bowl. Standard interpretations of this sequence find still another instance of violence wrought on women, yet a reading of both the scenario and the film's images reveals other meanings instead. The scenario clearly indicates that what the clergy-man grabs hold of is a "shadow, a sort of invisible double," thereby permitting the "*elle*" on which he flings himself to be interpreted as *either* the woman or the shadow (which is feminine in French). And although it is true that the head that gradually appears in the ball in close-up is a woman's face, throughout the film the textual work has established an association between the woman and the clergyman's identity, between his pursuit of her and his quest for self. Substantiat-ing this is the fact that near the close of the film, it is the *clergyman's* head that appears amid the shards of the broken glass ball. And it is this head that is placed on the oyster shell, the clergyman's own head, which "melts" and becomes the dark liquid that he drinks in the film's final shots. Indeed, it is not a "real" female character which has been captured and subdued in the film, but an *image* of the woman, as phantom, as specter, as shadow of desire.

As noted before, there are other transformations of the female figure in the film: she appears as a governess, as a young girl, and as a bride. Yet one additional sequence stands out in the film, for it materializes the libidinal force of the primal scene in a sequence of eight shots whose very economy seems to illustrate Artaud's belief in the powerful directness of the cinema and its ability to bypass the distortion of verbal language and rational thought. Artaud's descrip-tion in the scenario is as follows:

The clergyman finds himself in a ship's cabin. He gets up from his bunk and goes out to the ship's bridge. The officer is there, in chains. Now the clergyman seems to meditate and pray, but when he raises his head, at the level of his eyes, two mouths which touch each other reveal to him, at the side of the officer, the presence of a woman who was not there a moment ago. The body of the woman rests horizontally in the air.

Then a paroxysm shakes him. It seems as if the fingers of each of his two hands were seeking a neck.[34]

Dulac renders this in a sequence whose shots (one action per shot) are all connected by dissolves, contributing to the nocturnal, dreamlike quality of the episode. Six shots constitute the crux of the sequence, laying out this miniature scenario of vision in terms of positions held by its protagonists. First, the officer is seen in long-shot, standing, asleep, by a pile of boxes on the ship's deck. The clergyman enters the frame from the left foreground, and turning, assuming a position of half-wakeful spectatorship, leaning against a pillar as if in a daze or a dream. A dissolve to the next shot reveals the officer, now in medium-shot, looking up slowly (decelerated motion) toward the top right edge of the frame. A parallel movement in the next shot discloses Allin, in close-medium-shot, looking slowly down and then left. The next shot, a medium-close-up of the officer, is interrupted by the spectral appearance, through a dissolve, of the woman's head; she leans over and kisses the officer. Now, as can be anticipated, a shot discloses all three figures—the "parental" couple in the background, kissing (as the woman's leaning body appears horizontal), and the clergyman in American-shot in the foreground, making his characteristic clutching gesture. Finally, the sequence is terminated by a close-up of Allin's head; he first looks off frame right toward the couple, then turns his head frontally, revealing a horrified expression.

This scene-within-a-scene encapsulates and reiterates the fantasmatic drama of spectatorship, a drama which, in *The Seashell and the Clergyman,* is played out through the circulation of figures of desire, figures of generalized sexual identity whose movements are not justified by narrative peregrinations. And it is here that the cinematic image of the woman assumes its full erotic force. As spectral illusion, as hallucinated vision, she is the reappearing phantom who draws the clergyman—and the viewer—into seeing things which are not there. And precisely because of her ephemeral quality, an undecipherability as powerful as it is evasive, the feminine figure allows something of Artaud's vision of the spectator to be achieved: "The mind is affected outside of all representation. This sort of virtual power of the image finds hitherto unutilized possibilities in the very depths of the mind."[35]

It seems appropriate to return now, momentarily, to the scene of the confessional, for it condenses a number of the film's procedures with a kind of striking immediacy. All of *Seashell*'s sequences, in one way or another, actualize psychic processes, and their method of doing so can be categorized as follows: 1) the representation of the dispersed subjectivity that places the viewer at the center of a generalized psychic experience; 2) the use of male and female "characters" as cultural and symbolic constructs; 3) the use of shots or sequences that foreground vision, such as the staging of the primal scene or the emphatic elaboration of the gaze; 4) the representation of a dreaming consciousness as evidenced by the apparition of metamorphosing objects and fantastic visions; and 5) the depiction of the subjectivity turned in on itself, as exemplified by the film's conclusion, which repeats its beginning in a parable of film spectatorship, the clergyman consuming his own image in an act of narcissistic absorption. One brief moment in the confessional—a simple exchange of two shots—articulates all five of these categories in such a way as to produce a microcosm of the film itself.

This pair of shots is the "eyeline match" par excellence, for it is, quite simply, the alternation of two large close-ups of eyes (gauzily masked to render everything else in the image a hazy blur)—first the woman's, then the clergyman's. This exchange, embedded within sequences that dramatize religious hypocrisy and erotic violence, seems, by its very energy, to erupt from the more narrational instances that surround it. This is how Artaud's scenario describes the action: "The woman and the clergyman are praying in the confessional. The clergyman's head quivers like a leaf, and all of a sudden it seems that something begins to speak inside him. He pushes up his sleeves and gently, ironically, knocks three times on the partition of the confessional. The woman gets up. Then the clergyman bangs with his fist and opens the door like a fanatic. The woman stands before him and looks at him. He throws himself on her and tears off her bodice as if he had wanted to lacerate her breasts."[36]

In keeping with her usual practice, Dulac renders—in detailed images and gestures—each action described. Yet for one small moment she diverges from the written scenario to depict these eyes, and this is highly significant. For it is precisely in their capacity to act as signs that these haunting, elusive images function to evoke exactly those processes of unconscious figuration which are central to the film in its effort to create, *for the spectator*, the experience of the fantasm. In their isolation, their fragmentary status, they aid the dissolution of character and the redirection toward psychic processes by emphasizing vision itself. In so doing, these pairs of eyes create an ambiguous space of interpretation for the viewer, a site in which character psychology is only one option among many others in determining the symbolic value of the shot. It is possible, for example, to regard this exchange of glances as one instance in the circulation throughout the film of cultural signifiers of femininity and masculinity—hers the alert and watchful eyes of a female victim, his the lustful eyes of a violent brute. This is, after all, a confrontation with an extensive representational heritage. From another standpoint, these shots can be seen to take their place in a paradigm of subjective images and dream distortions; it is generally this sort of close-up that is linked to the flow of glistening castles, shimmering water, and the like in the film.

Yet there is something different about these shots as well, a difference that recalls the slide of subjectivity back into itself. Although Artaud's script specifies only the gaze of the woman (as opposed to that of the man), Dulac chose to emphasize the actual fact of looking in a reciprocity of vision that blurs the distinction between characters. This slippage is characteristic of a film that associates the clergyman's pursuit of the woman with his own quest for self. But more important than that, here Dulac is able to give *both* characters the privilege of visuality, and in so doing she reaffirms the psychic reality that is the mainspring of the film. There is a remarkably similar close-up of eyes in *The Smiling Mme Beudet,* where it was used to amplify our understanding of the character, her desperate need for escape, and her imaginative capacity to envision flight. When this type of shot reappears in *Seashell,* however—in what amounts to an echo of the earlier film—it reinforces the latter film's project, not of recounting the dream or the daydream, but of portraying the unconscious figural processes of dreams themselves. And this foregrounded visual exchange which slides, as it does, between the masculine and feminine configurations of the gaze, represents nothing less than the double scenario of sexuality and vision—a dramatization of desire for both "character" and spectator that plays itself out on the psyche's unconscious stage.

Fantasy and/as the Woman

From the foregoing analyses it should be clear that there is an undeniable *feminist* consistency in Dulac's film work, a plurality of intersecting concerns that links her early explorations of "female fantasy" in *Beudet* to the more sustained examination of the very mechanisms of unconscious desire in *Seashell.* Thus her preoccupations—with cinematic language and its constructions of the viewer, with structures of the fantasm, and with the possibilities for representing woman's desire— converge in her filmmaking practice, while the explicit manifestation of these interests varies from film to film. For this reason, from the more overt feminism of the earlier film to the analysis of cultural and psychic representations of femininity (through work on signification) in the later one, Dulac's entire oeuvre can be said to represent the feminist project of conceptualizing differing ways of articulating women's relation to language and the body.

This is precisely the postulation of an alternative feminist cinema formulated in Mary Ann Doane's article, "Woman's Stake: Filming the Female Body," in which she asserts: "The most interesting and productive . . . films dealing with the feminist problematic are precisely those which elaborate a new syntax, thus 'speaking' the female body differently, even haltingly or inarticulately from the perspective of a classical syntax."[37] Doane calls for a kind of filmmaking that will posit a complex interrelation between the female body and psychic and signifying processes, because, for her, a pathway out of the essentialist impasse lies not in the abandonment of the body altogether, but in theories that "attempt to define or construct a feminine specificity (not essence), theories which work to provide the woman with an autonomous symbolic representation."[38] And one of the ways this representation can come about is to be found in the very problematization of the woman's image engendered by both *Beudet* and *Seashell,* for in each of these films Dulac is concerned—albeit in different ways— to determine new forms in which the woman's body is "spoken" by the cinematic text.

Regarded in this light, each film suggests a way of thinking "femininity" in its multiple meanings, and of understanding these meanings in their relation to the signifying processes of the unconscious. As such, they represent attempts to appropriate the construction and representation of the woman's image in its social, psychic, and cinematic contexts—attempts which, for Dulac, inflect her continuing research into the language of the cinema at every point. Whereas *Beudet's* early example of representing female desire can be seen as an effort to give the woman both a vision and a voice, *Seashell* offers an abstract meditation on the processes that produce these at the level of the unconscious. Thus in *Beudet* the female character thinks (or dreams) in images, while in *Seashell* the female character is, in fact, the image itself.

In the earlier film it is possible to understand Dulac's depiction of her heroine's dreams, hallucinations, and fantasies as evidence of an assumed definition of female desire, for both Madame Beudet's

The Seashell and the Clergyman (Summary)

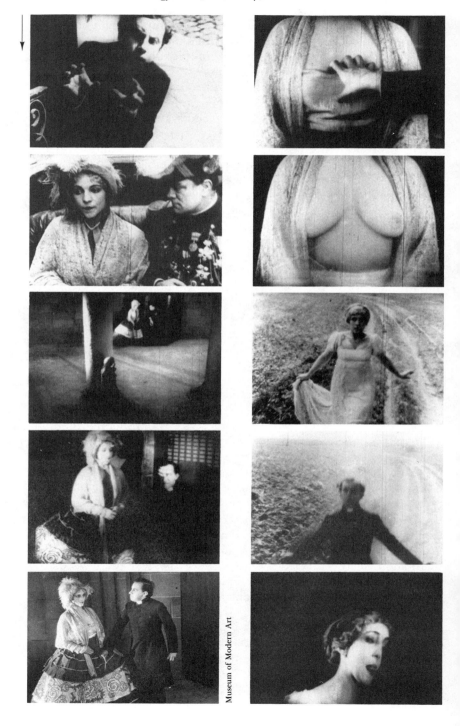

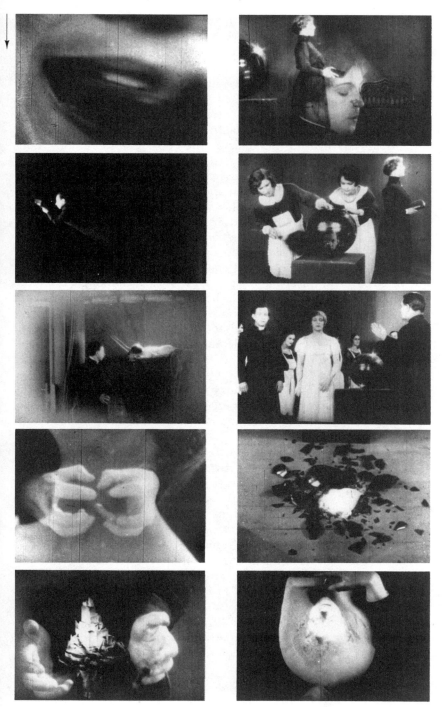

phantom lover and her reveries of escape participate in the certainty of familiar meanings. Yet the very certainty with which Dulac can be said to "know" her heroine's fantasy already becomes problematized within that same film when she confronts the issue of representing her female character *differently*. You will remember that, as a result of her solitary thoughts, Madame Beudet loads her husband's gun and subsequently engages in a frantic attempt to remove the bullets before a tragedy occurs. Sitting in her bedroom the following morning, she contemplatively brushes her hair as she considers, in remorse and desperation, how to slip undetected into her husband's study. It is here that, for one striking moment in the film, Dulac gives us an image of arresting beauty as Madame Beudet's face, lavishly surrounded by her flowing hair, is replicated in her triple mirror. This reiteration of the woman's image, framed and enhanced as it is by the multiple borders of the mirror, suggests a considerable departure from what was already being established at the time—the conventional representation of the woman as object of spectacle and of the desiring gaze. For in contrast to an erotic image of the woman looking—offering herself to the viewer as an image of her own desire (and thus recalling the culmination of this in Marnie's fascinated, self-absorbing gaze)—Dulac here fractures the masculine mode of visual pleasure in an activity which disperses and problematizes that very image. The tripartite framing of the woman's face, then, represents a reflection on the image as a *mode of representation*—a refusal to simply generate an image of female beauty constructed in masculine terms. And it is just such a dislocation of the visual language used to represent the woman's body that begins the challenge to dominant articulations of femininity and their structures of the gaze.

The Seashell and the Clergyman extends this work by activating the female image as representation itself, for it is here that the female body—and the very processes of desire that constitute it as "feminine"—undergo a sustained investigation throughout the film. It is therefore no accident that the film of Dulac's that most assertively takes the "language of the unconscious" as its subject should offer multiple modes of figuring the feminine, not only in terms of the different types of costuming and the positions suggested by these, but also in its use of explicit nudity and its focus on body parts. The facial close-up itself exemplifies these procedures in a highly interesting manner. In *Beudet,* the close-up of the heroine's face—which was for Dulac, as noted before, the psychological shot par excellence—is used to convey access to Madame Beudet's interiority and her desires. For this reason, the connection between the head and the rest of the body

Marnie (Alfred Hitchcock)

The Smiling Mme Beudet

The Seashell and the Clergyman

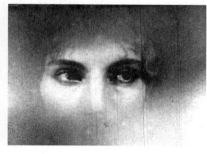

(1)

(2)

(3)

(4)

(the face as a metonymy of the person) is not only maintained, it is reinforced. However, in *Seashell* it is precisely this close-up, this disembodied woman's face, which becomes the site of transformations and hallucinations, in an obsessive reworking of feminine features used to produce the psychic atmosphere of the dream. Beyond this, *Seashell* contains several shots of bare breasts, which would have been shocking at the time, in addition to various other erotically charged bodily fragments such as the neck, the ankle, the shoulder, and so forth. In each instance, the shot brings us closer to a reinforcing physicality, aligning femininity with the body, while at the same time creating a breach between the image and its referent. It thus obliges us to read the image as a sign circulating in the textual space of the film.

In this context, it is important to note that the "characters" in the film are not simply generalized symbolic forms that interact, but, precisely, *sexually differentiated* figures whose very distinction comes about in relation to a concept of the body. From this perspective, *Seashell* is less about the narcissistic identity of its hero than it is about sexual identity in general, for it gives us not the conclusion of a solidified character to emulate, but the production processes of femininity and masculinity themselves—cultural processes which overlay psychic trajectories. In her move from the particularized representation of a female character in *Beudet* to the generalized social and psychic representation of "femininity" in *Seashell*, Dulac thus demonstrates her growing understanding of sexuality as a process rather than a content. Her interest in unconscious processes of desire is the constant between the two films, as is her exploration of the constitutive elements of "femininity." But it is in her shift from the representation of the content of the fantasy to its very operations that the consequences for thinking the woman's relation to language and the body can be found.

In its foregrounding of processes of signification, then, *Seashell* activates that syntactic disequilibrium which challenges both fixed meanings and notions of sexual identity from the very start. The excess of meaning provoked by its random and incongruous images, the circulation of its unexpected signs, suggests the impossibility of stable comprehension, or at least implies a kind of signification exceeding the borders of established reason. In the proliferation of meanings, the film offers diverse positions of viewer subjectivity and in so doing puts into relief the complex relations of language and desire. Therefore, Doane's positing of a feminist filmmaking which "attempts to construct another syntax," one that "threatens the 'idea of language' " based on intelligibility, finds a model here.[39] In *Seashell*, the female body is represented *differently* as the film reworks conventional modes of articulation, organizing its flow of images according to "other" rules. Its disrupted, disordered syntactical relations suggest something of the dynamism of unconscious forces and in so doing evoke possible alternative constructions of the "feminine."

I am arguing that this work at the limits of meaning, taken in the context of feminist concerns, can be understood as a way of circumventing established structures of thinking, a way of reinscribing desire into the process of signification itself. When analyzed in this light, Dulac's formulation—of an abstract cinema endowed with the capacity to passionately move the viewer—takes on new force: "Yes, lines, volumes, surfaces, light, envisioned in their constant metamorphoses, are capable of taking hold of us by their rhythms if we know how to organize them in a construction capable of responding to the needs of our imagination and our feelings. . . ."[40] This solicitation of each spectator's potential for direct, affective access to the cinematic image suggests a reconceptualization of desire not restricted to preformulated categories of meaning, and by extension, it implies the blurring of fixed definitions of masculine and feminine as well. The liberation implicit in this reconceptualization has important consequences for feminist cinema, for in rethinking sexuality by way of a profound exploration of the deepest foundations of all meaning-production, Dulac is able to contribute to the formulation of an alternative cinema based on new articulations of the body, language, and desire. And it is in this sense that, for all their differences in emphasis, both *The Smiling Mme Beudet* and *The Seashell and the Clergyman* provide significant contributions to the development of a forceful new theory of sexual difference in cinematic representation.

NOTES

1. J. Laplanche and J.-B. Pontalis, *The Language of Psychoanalysis* (New York: W. W. Norton, 1973), p. 475.

2. Germaine Dulac, "Les procédés expressifs du cinématographe," *Ciné-magazine*, no. 28 (July 11, 1924): 68. This is a transcript of a talk Dulac gave on June 17, 1924, at the Musée Galliera. All translations from the French are my own unless otherwise noted.

3. Both films are available from the Museum of Modern Art, 11 West 53d St., New York, NY 10019. It is possible that the print of *Seashell*, if ordered from another distributor, is in an incorrect order. See note 23 below.

4. Wendy Dozoretz, "Dulac Versus Artaud," *Wide Angle* 3:1 (1979): 51.

5. Jacques B. Brunius, *En marge du cinéma français* (Paris: Editions Arcanes, Collection Ombres Blanches, 1954), p. 138.

6. Ado Kyrou, *Le Surréalisme au cinéma* (Paris: Editions Arcanes, 1953), p. 186.

7. Germaine Dulac, "L'Essence du cinéma: L'Idée visuelle," *Les Cahiers du mois*, nos. 16/17 (1925): 64. An alternative translation of this article by Robert Lamberton, can be found in *The Avant-Garde Film: A Reader of Theory and Criticism*, ed. P. Adams Sitney (New York: New York University Press, 1978), pp. 36–42.

8. Dulac, "Les Procédés," p. 68.

9. Germaine Dulac, "La Musique du silence," *Cinégraphie*, no. 5 (January 15, 1928): 78.

10. Dulac, "La Musique." The identical statement appears in Dulac's "Films visuels et anti-visuels," *Le Rouge et le noir* (July 1928); anthologized in *L'Art du cinema*, ed. Pierre Lherminier (Paris: Editions Seghers, 1960), p. 71.

11. See Richard Abel's insightful discussion of the film in *French Cinema: The First Wave, 1915–1929* (Princeton: Princeton University Press, 1986), pp. 340–44.

12. This categorization of subjective images is proposed by Jean Mitry in *Esthétique et psychologie du cinéma*, vol. 2 (Paris: Editions Universitaires, 1965), pp. 61–79.

13. Germaine Dulac, "Les Procédés expressifs du cinématographe," *Ciné-magazine*, no. 27 (July 4, 1924): 17.

14. Germaine Dulac, "Le cinéma d'avant-garde," in *Le Cinéma des origines à nos jours*, ed. Henri Fescourt (Paris: Editions du Cygne, 1932), p. 359. An alternate translation can be found in *The Avant-Garde Film* ed. Sitney, pp. 43–48.

15. Dulac, "Les Procédés," *Cinémagazine*, no. 28 (July 11, 1924): 67.

16. Virginia Woolf, "Modern Fiction," in *The Common Reader* (1925; repr. New York: Harcourt, Brace, Jovanovich, 1953), p. 154. There is much suggested by the parallels between Dulac and Woolf, not the least of which are the "multiple and contradictory interior impressions" that form the cornerstone of each woman's artistic practice. The possibilities for a study along these lines are endlessly suggestive.

17. Laplanche and Pontalis, *The Language*, p. 318.

18. Anonymous, "Un rêve à l'écran," *Cinégraphie*, no. 2 (October 15, 1927): 32. This appears to be a press release announcing the opening of the film at the end of October, a screening that in fact never took place. There is reason to believe that this text (or portions of it) were written by Yvonne Allendy, Artaud's close friend (and, ironically, the same person who was instrumental in the subsequent attacks on Dulac for having "distorted" the scenario by, among other things, calling it a "dream").

Once the initial agreement with Germaine Dulac was reached, Yvonne Allendy increased communiques to the press announcing the film; she continued to do this during the film's shooting, and once completed, in the weeks preceding its opening; the accent was always placed on the film's uniqueness in being *made of a single dream*. In the beginning of October

1927, Yvonne Allendy wrote an advance publicity release (we do not know if it was ever published and are working from drafts [provided by Colette Allendy]) which carried the same assertion and whose prospective titles (A Dream-Scenario, A Dream in the Camera, A Dream on the Screen) are sufficiently characteristic. (Editors, *Les Oeuvres complètes d'Antonin Artaud*, vol. 3 [Paris: Editions Gallimard, 1978], p. 327.)

(Further references will be noted as *OC;* this volume contains all of Artaud's film scenarios, letters, and texts concerning the cinema. The edition date is important, as each edition of *OC* contains new material and different pagination.) A number of Artaud's scenarios and texts on the cinema, translated into English, can be found in *TDR* 11:1 (Fall 1966): 166–85, as well as in the Susan Sontag anthology, *Antonin Artaud: Selected Writings* (New York: Farrar, Straus, and Giroux, 1976).

19. Laplanche and Pontalis, *The Language*, p. 318.

20. Alain Virmaux and Odette Virmaux, *Les Surréalistes et le cinéma* (Paris: Editions Seghers, 1976), p. 29.

21. See chapter 2, note 49.

22. Although Dulac's film follows the scenario, image for image, with extreme precision, there is still a very complex relation between the two texts, and this is what I explore in detail in my article "The Image and the Spark: Dulac and Artaud Reviewed," in *Dada and Surrealist Film*, ed. Rudolf E. Kuenzli (New York: Willis Locker and Owens, 1987), pp. 110–27, where I discuss the Dulac-Artaud debate in terms of conflicting aesthetic theories of Symbolist poetic fusion and Surrealist juxtaposition. I trace the actual conflict between Dulac and Artaud over the production of the film in detail in my Ph.D. dissertation, "Women, Representation, and Cinematic Discourse: The Example of the French Cinema," University of California at Berkeley, 1982.

23. Antonin Artaud, letter to Jean Paulhan, January 22, 1932, reprinted in *OC*, pp. 259–60. A translation by Helen R. Weaver can be found in Sontag, *Antonin Artaud*, p. 281. To further confuse matters, a very serious error exists in some American prints of the film, something that continues to be corrected, but that has already led to some critical misinterpretations. For some reason, when the film's three reels were initially spliced in the United States, the last reel found its way into the middle of the film, making American prints end with an image of the woman's severed head inside a glass ball. Both the correct version of the film and the scenario itself end with the clergyman drinking the black liquid from the shell. Within each of the three reels, however, the order of individual shots is correct, making the basic sequence structure uniform in all prints of the film. It is the *order* of the sequencing that is incorrect in the U.S. prints, and although the Museum of Modern Art has rectified this mistake, other distributors have failed to do so. William Van Wert's widely read article, "Germaine Dulac: First Feminist Filmmaker," for example, bases its entire argument on the incorrect sequencing and its mistaken ending.

24. Artaud, "La Coquille et le clergyman," *Cahiers de Belgique*, no. 8 (October 1928) reprinted in *OC*, p. 71.

25. Artaud, "Le cinéma et l'abstraction," *Le Monde illustré*, no. 3645 (October 29, 1927) reprinted in *OC*, pp. 68–69, emphasis added.

26. "Le Cinéma et l'abstraction," *OC*, p. 69

27. Ibid.

28. Artaud, "Cinéma et réalité," *La Nouvelle revue française*, no. 170, November 1, 1927, reprinted in *OC*, p. 19. Artaud had wanted to clarify his position about the scenario in relation to Dulac's film, and proposed an article to Jean Paulhan, stating, "I have something to defend, and an article could help me defend my film without attacking anyone, in order to more clearly determine my position in relation to this film" (letter to Jean Paulhan, August 29, 1927, reprinted in *OC*, p. 127). "Cinéma et réalité" was suggested for the October issue of *La NRF*, but actually appeared in November, functioning as an introduction to the scenario. Alternative translations of this text are widely available. For a more thorough discussion of this particular passage in relation to the film's strategies, see my " 'Poetry of the Unconscious': Circuits of Desire in Two Films by Germaine Dulac," in *French Cinema: Text and Contexts,* ed. Susan Hayward and Ginette Vincendeau (London: Methuen, 1989).

29. "Cinéma et réalité," *OC*, p. 19; emphasis added.

30. Ibid.

31. The scenario for *The Seashell and the Clergyman* is reprinted in *OC*, pp. 18–25. There is a translation by Victor Corti in *TDR* 11:1 (Fall 1966): 173–8.

32. Artaud, letter to Dulac, September 25, 1927, reprinted in *OC*, p. 128.

33. Scenario, *OC*, p. 22.

34. Scenario, *OC*, p. 23.

35. Artaud, "Sorcellerie et cinéma," *OC*, p. 66. Written at the time of the shooting of *Seashell,* this article does not appear to have been published until 1949, when it appeared in the catalogue of the Festival du Film Maudit, Biarritz, July 29–August 5, 1949. Translations are in *TDR*, pp. 178–80, *The Avant-Garde Film*, pp. 49–50, and *The Shadow and Its Shadow: Surrealist Writings on Cinema*, ed. Paul Hammond (London: British Film Institute, 1978), pp. 63–64.

36. Scenario, *OC*, p. 21.

37. Mary Ann Doane, "Woman's Stake: Filming the Female Body," *October*, no. 17 (Summer 1981): 34.

38. Doane, "Woman's Stake," p. 33.

39. Ibid., p. 36.

40. Dulac, "Du Movement, des harmonies, et du rhythme: A la Symphonie visuelle," p. 6, chapter 8 of an unpublished manuscript of texts collected by Marie-Anne Colson-Malleville.

FIVE

Marie Epstein:
A Woman in the Shadows

MARIE EPSTEIN'S CAREER AS A FILMMAKER offers something more of a challenge from the standpoint of an argument that seeks to establish an alternative tradition of feminist cinema, for while Germaine Dulac's filmmaking practice can be seen to demonstrate a consistent project of resistance to traditional cinematic norms—from the dual perspective of both aesthetic issues and feminist theory—Epstein's work is, in fact, fairly exemplary of French filmmaking in the thirties. All of the major directors of the period conceived of their films as efforts to establish a national cinematic identity—each in their own way posing a form of opposition to the dominant commercial cinema of Hollywood by making films "in the French manner." However, Marie Epstein's films can also be seen to resist this French standard, placing her work in the status of double-rupture in relation to the cinematic mainstreams of both Hollywood and France. For one thing, Epstein is virtually unknown to the conventional film histories, and for this reason her very specific marginalization implies a position at the borders of the cinematic activity of the time. But more important for the purposes of this study, Epstein's concerted focus on "feminine" questions—issues of the maternal, of the domestic, of female bonding—and her reworking of basic cinematic structures of point-of-view and identification along these lines, offer a form of textual resistance whose challenge to the mainstream can only be discerned in terms of sustained analysis of her films. To begin the work of elaborating Epstein's significant contribution to a feminist theorization of the cinema, then, a form of "feminist archaeology" is first necessary.

Any discussion of Marie Epstein as a film auteur will encounter numerous problems from the outset, for she is truly a woman "hidden from history," to borrow Sheila Rowbotham's perspicacious phrase. It is hard to avoid a certain sense of irritation at the realization that work as important as Epstein's has been relatively invisible for so long; she has, in fact, been an active participant in several of the most critical periods of the French cinema's development. It is, perhaps, a sign of the times that this type of anger has become increasingly prevalent as the "discovery" of active and creative women in all fields of work (in part inspired by the women's movement and the accompanying interest in women's issues) becomes more widespread. Likewise, meeting Marie Epstein is sure to evoke a frustrating paradox: her shyness and self-effacement—her surprise that film scholars would take an interest in her, and her constant deflection of attention away from herself to other filmmakers—is in direct contradiction to the inspiration of her galvanizing energy and her considerable achievements.[1] Marie Epstein's filmmaking career spans two of the most productive decades in French cinema and covers all major levels of cinematic production. Initially she started acting in films, and jokingly refers to herself as a frustrated actress. Her work as a scenarist also began early in her career, when she started writing treatments and scenarios for the films of her brother, Jean, in the 1920s. Although in the twenties she worked as scenarist on four films and co-directed three silent films, her major directorial work consists of the eight sound films she co-directed with Jean Benoît-Lévy during the 1930s. In addition, Marie Epstein is a consummate editor, having both created brilliant montage sequences in her own films and done restoration and reconstruction work as director of technical services at the Cinémathèque Française. In fact, until her retirement in 1977, at the age of seventy-six, her work at the Cinémathèque went far beyond film preservation; not only did she reconstitute numerous films and coordinate all the technical work in film reproduction, but her devotion, energy, and knowledge also have earned her the affectionate title of "nerve center of the Cinémathèque" from the countless scholars whose work on the French cinema owes a major debt to her.

Marie Epstein comments that her original interest in working in films involved the desire to be an actress: "I never really had it in mind to be a director. I wanted to be an actress. I really had the desire to be an actress." Early in 1920 Epstein had written to Germaine Dulac, the only woman filmmaker in the French industry at the time, for advice on how to become an actress. Epstein recalls that Dulac was approachable and generous during the half-hour interview she had with her at

Sandy Flitterman-Lewis

the Film D'Art studio in July 1920. As far as an acting career was concerned, Epstein was at somewhat of a disadvantage, given that most actors in the cinema of the time had come directly from the theater. With no formal training, Epstein essentially had to rely on the fortuitous fact that her brother Jean was beginning to make films of his own.

In Jean Epstein's first film for Pathé-Consortium, *L'Auberge rouge* (1923), Marie Epstein appears in several shots early in the film, one of which is used as an illustration in the 1974 edition of Jean Epstein's *Ecrits*. This brief appearance was simply an example of a common practice that recurs in the films of avant-garde filmmakers today— that of placing friends in minor roles. In *Coeur fidèle* (1923), Jean Epstein's second film, Marie Epstein has a more substantial role, and this was to prove the major part of her acting career. Epstein plays Mademoiselle Marice, a crippled young woman who lives next door to the heroine of the film (Gina Manès) in a shabby third-floor apartment. Epstein's role is central to the film's resolution: she shoots Manès' drunken husband (Edmond Van Daele), thereby allowing the woman to reunite with her true love (Léon Mathot). Epstein's performance reveals considerable talent, a fact noted by Léon Moussinac and others who reviewed the film. However, *Coeur fidèle* was a financial flop in spite of its strong critical acclaim, and Epstein only acted in one more film—a secondary role in her brother's *Mauprat* (1925), a fantasy with elements of Gothic romance.

Although *L'Auberge rouge* and *Coeur fidèle* antedate Epstein's actual work as a director, they play a significant formative role in terms of her entire oeuvre. With both of these films, her brother Jean was to begin the work in the highly evocative subjective cinema which, as we have seen with Dulac, was the hallmark of French filmmaking in the twenties. Although their subject matter is quite different—*L'Auberge rouge* is based on a Balzac novella and interweaves past and present in a nightmarish tale of crime and vengeance; *Coeur fidèle* is a contemporary romance whose poetry of the waterfront combines a sordid realism with a stunning visual lyricism—both films are early evidence of Jean Epstein's concern with exploring the expressive possibilities of the cinema. In *L'Auberge rouge,* as Richard Abel maintains, "Instead of developing [the hero's] story conventionally through dramatic confrontations . . . Epstein emphasizes simple patterns of rhetorical figuring and several ambiguous sequences of privileged subjectivity."[2] These stylistic features in *L'Auberge rouge*—the reiteration of figures, repetitions of haunting images from the past, and the use of significant objects as recurring motifs that structure the narrative at the level of the psyche—all find their way into Marie's most accomplished work as a director, *La Maternelle* (*The Nursery School,* 1933). Likewise, Jean Epstein's interest in the expressive value of the image through the systematic use of close-ups and the rhythmic relations of shots—a dynamic montage that orchestrates a variety of unusual camera angles—can be found in the most evocative sequences of Marie's sound films, where they seem to emerge with a kind of poetic force. Again *La Maternelle* is the best example, although all of the films show some evidence of this.

In addition, both *L'Auberge rouge* and *Coeur fidèle* make use of an astounding and memorable close-up of their protagonists staring hauntingly through a window. In *L'Auberge rouge,* the hero's nightmare is intercut with a series of hallucinatory close-ups as his face seems streaked and beaten by the driving rain. In *Coeur fidèle,* it is Gina Manès' face (as she looks out of the dirty bistro window)—in a stunning and beautiful image that seems to hover over the narrative itself—that floats over the water of the squalid, dismal harbor. It is precisely this type of shot that forms the climax of *La Maternelle,* as its young protagonist gazes first at a shop window and then into the river where haunting images of her desire seem to float before her eyes.

Both of these early films demonstrate Jean Epstein's concern to articulate the subjective vision of a character's inner life with the objective conditions of an oppressive social milieu—a concern that reappears throughout his sister's films in the thirties. But there is also something else—a detail almost unnoticed in *Coeur fidèle* that will form the thematic core of all of Marie's later work. As previously mentioned, *Coeur fidèle* is a love story in which Marie Epstein plays a minor but significant role as the crippled neighbor of the heroine. As the lovers are reunited (enabled by Marie's shooting of the villainous and drunken husband), the heroine's sick child remains in the dingy apartment as Mademoiselle Marice, dazed by her violently provoked action, cradles the infant on the wooden stairs. These are the last images of Marie, intercut with shots of the happy couple on the carnival ride that had been the scene of their separation. Richard Abel sees Mademoiselle Marice as a kind of double for the heroine, "as if all her suffering were projected onto the crippled woman, who then assumes all the guilt of revenge. . . . "[3] But beyond that—and critical to the priority of the themes of childhood and the bonds of caring that bind women and children in Marie Epstein's films—this image in which Marie participates as an actress will become the highly charged thematic icon that will characterize all of her work as a director.

Marie Epstein's work as a scenarist began, close to the same time she started her acting career, with the lighthearted anecdote she tells about her entry in a contest. In May of 1923, shortly before production started on *Coeur fidèle*, Epstein had entered a scenario competition sponsored by Pathé-Consortium. She won the first cash prize with a script entitled *Les Mains qui meurent*, a Maupassant-type story of a violinist who deliberately injures his highly insured hands to satisfy an obsession with gambling. Although the film itself was never made, Epstein is still pleased with its central concept, an ironic core that seems to inform at least two of the films she scripted for her brother, *L'Affiche* (1925) and *Six et demi-onze* (1927). Epstein refuses to discuss another film that she scripted for her brother Jean, *Le Double amour* (1925), which remains unedited at the Cinémathèque; it appears to have a similar story to *L'Affiche* and uses the same actress for the leading role.

There is a double narrative to *L'Affiche*—the story of the film's production and the story of its narration. The first story begins with Marie Epstein sending a five-page scenario to the newly established Russian emigré company, Films Albatros, in the spring of 1924. When she went to discuss terms for the scenario with Alexandre Kamenka, the director of the company, Epstein brought along her brother Jean for moral support. This story ends happily: Kamenka both bought the scenario from Marie, and engaged Jean, who had just broken his contract with Pathé, to direct it, along with several other film projects. The story of *L'Affiche* is not so happy. Beginning with a woman's seduction and abandonment—a common motif or narrative trope of the time—the film winds its tragic course to the conventional happy ending. "Disturbed to realize her youth is passing, a flower-market worker (Nathalie Lissenko) spends the night with a man who disappears the next morning, leaving her pregnant. Once the baby is born, she enters its photograph in an insurance company's contest for the most beautiful baby in Paris. Soon after she wins the 15,000 francs prize, the child grows ill and dies. Her grief is all the more poignant because the company's advertizing campaign has covered the walls of Paris with hundreds of posters of her child. Once the company discovers her plight, it is revealed that the man who abandoned her is none other than the director's son. He recognizes his sacred debt of love and the film ends happily."[4] Epstein's description of how she wrote the scenario for this film is illuminating for a number of reasons. It gives an indication of her work process in writing and thereby provides some insight into the development of her scenarios for later films such as *Peau de pêche, La Maternelle, Hélène, La Mort du cygne,* and *Le Feu de paille,* all of which are only loosely based on novels. It also exemplifies her continual concern with events and ambience taken "close to life," a quality that characterizes all of her later films with Benoît-Lévy. Although she gives all the credit for the cinematic techniques, editing, and mise-en-scène of *L'Affiche* to her brother Jean, she does say she was responsible for the five-page scenario on which the film is based, which she says she wrote "like a novel." Her inspiration for the story came in fact from an advertizing poster for Cadum Soap on which "un magnifique bébé, le Bébé Cadum" was depicted with a bar of soap. Epstein says she got the idea for the film's story when she was told that the baby on the poster had died. She concludes: "There you have it, that was the idea! The best scenarios can be found in journalistic fillers (*les faits divers*): People are always asking me, 'Why do you read the newspapers, you know, the fillers, accidents, all that?' Well, because 'all that' is a nest of scenarios, that's where you can really find scenarios, in all the little details of life."

In fact, the narrative of *L'Affiche* is quite complicated, and what emerges over and above the conventional love story is a series of dramatic moments involving the relations of adults to children, all conveyed with a kind of powerful intensity that transcends mere romantic love. It is not only the haunting image of the dead child on the poster—sending the grieving mother into a destructive frenzy as she slashes the billboards throughout Paris—around which Epstein organizes her scenario. Numerous other sequences demonstrate the tenderness and intimacy between parents and their children, and all bear the weight of meaning in the film. For example, as the heroine sews flowers late into the night in her tiny room, she is "like so many other women without husbands, suffering for their children without fathers." As she ponders entry into the contest, her thoughts are described: "It is not so much the prospect of the money, but of the pride she would feel if her child were chosen." And in a bit of visual irony that serves to elaborate the most important plot complication of the film, the insurance company director praises his son for his business sense (it is, in fact, the son who is the father of the child) while simultaneously, across Paris, the mother softly croons a lullabye about the happy future of her son (whose father is unknown to her), thereby contrasting the masculine world of commerce with the scene of maternal desire.

It is also this company executive who has a little daughter (the details of age difference seem not to have been a concern for Epstein), and it is this child's illness that leads to her father's compassionate realization, an acknowledgment that resolves the film into its conclusion. Charged with punishing the woman for her destruction of the advertisements, the company head is determined to send her to prison. At this point his daughter, gravely ill, begs her father to take down all of the posters himself, "so the mother of that baby won't cry anymore." The father agrees, and, as if this act of compassion had curative powers, the daughter's health is restored. His son assumes his responsibility and marries the woman he had previously abandoned, as the father's blessing concludes the film. Thus the baby's mother becomes a daughter and its father, a son, as the romantic couple pales in relation to the parental bonds of love. It is as if the romantic love interest itself were merely a slim pretext, an insignificant framework around which Epstein chose to build the first of her elaborations of the drama of the maternal (or parental) and the preeminence of the child which this implies.

It is important to note the central function of the photographic image in *L'Affiche*, for example in sequences where the woman is confronted with the huge posters of her dead child. Epstein speaks enthusiastically about this motif when describing a film such as Feyder's *L'Image* (in which three men are led to their destruction by falling in love with the photograph of a woman), and it is taken up again in *Six et demi-onze* (*6 1/2 x 11*). Epstein remembers composing a one-page treatment of the scenario for this latter film, then working out a "*découpage*" with her brother before shooting began in the spring of 1927.[5] This can be seen to mark the unofficial directorial debut of Marie Epstein, representing as it does the transition from simply writing a scenario to the conceptualization of a film in terms of individual shots (composition, angle, lighting, camera movement) and their organization through montage.

"The sun and a Kodak [camera] are in the credits of the film—as American movie-stars."[6] *6 1/2 x 11* (the title gives the dimensions of the Kodak print) is about two brothers who are deceived separately by the same woman. The photographic image plays a central role in the film because it is through a photograph taken by the younger brother that the elder one realizes the woman's deception. The film is narrated through a system of parallel alternations that provide an elaborate and original doubling structure. The first half of the film deals with the younger brother's love for the woman, his discovery of her infidelity, and his abrupt suicide attempt. The second half repeats the first, with a difference: it is now the older brother who falls in love with the woman and discovers her infidelity. The ironic doubling reaches its peak when, in the very house the younger brother had bought for the woman, the older brother realizes that he has unknowingly loved the same woman. The climax of the film involves a complicated alternate montage sequence in which shots of the older brother walking round a country house and garden (remembering the photograph he had found and developed) are juxtaposed with shots of the woman wandering on the beach; both collapse simultaneously.

Equally illuminating are Epstein's comments about her choice of scenario for this film: "*6 1/2 x 11?* I was always looking for ideas which had a visual point of departure; so, Kodak . . . I thought of a photograph developing in the chemical bath, developing little by little, like that, and you see, gradually, a face appearing. I looked for a dramatic situation around this face which appears little by little, because it was a visual idea, an image. It's like *L'Affiche*, which also began with an image! It's completely visual!" And indeed her brother Jean made a very visual film, for its narration is composed almost entirely of images; very few intertitles punctuate the action. Not only is there a repeated duplication of narrative events, owing to the film's double structure as the older brother reenacts his sibling's liaison, but there is also a complex patterning of visual figures, as sunlight, camera, photograph, and woman's face all circulate to elaborate and define the relationships of the characters. This, too, finds its counterpart in *La Maternelle* (which represents, for me, a culmination of Marie Epstein's film work) in which the visual and metaphoric repetition of traumatic moments provokes a crisis for its little heroine that results in the climax of the film. Thus it is possible to see, even in this early phase of Marie Epstein's career, an interest in an almost whirlpool-like cinematic construction—an organization of visual echoes and reiterated narrative events that counters classical teleology with a mode of signifying "otherwise."

Marie Epstein's cinematographic collaboration with Jean Benoît-Lévy began in these early years of film work with her brother. Although the collaboration was a happy and productive one, it has proven to be rather a mixed blessing: of the eleven films they made together, all of them are credited to Benoît-Lévy alone in the standard histories and reference books. A typical example is *Le Cinéma français,*[7] in which Georges Sadoul attributes four of their collaborative films simply to Benoît-Lévy, first when comparing *La Maternelle* with another contemporary film dealing with childhood, *Poil de carotte* by Julien Duvivier, and then when discussing the remainder of Benoît-Lévy's career.

A slight cut above this total effacement is the very brief mention made of her by Marcel Lapierre in *Les Cents visages du cinéma:* "Marie Epstein, sister of the director of *L'Or des mers* was also his collaborator; it was she who wrote the very original scenarios for *L'Affiche* and *Six et demi-onze.* She also does directing with Jean Benoît-Lévy."[8]

Even Benoît-Lévy himself, in his book *Les Grandes missions du cinéma,* where he frequently discusses the films he made with Marie Epstein, always discusses them in the first-person singular. In fact, he only refers to Epstein in a footnote which, despite its charm and sincerity, can hardly compensate for his appropriation of their collaborative work, particularly in a book that discusses in great detail the collective process in making those films.

> If I may be permitted, I should like at this point, by way of dedication, to pay a grateful and affectionate tribute to one who has been my precious collaborator and who remains a very dear friend, both to myself and to my family. When she reads these lines, I would like Marie Epstein to feel that all the professional joys and sorrows through which we have lived together are reflected in this essay on the art we both love. I am certain that, over there, in the country of tragic heroism, she, like myself, retains the hope that soon we shall be able to revive our old group and, through our "fine art," attempt to express what we feel we have yet to say![9]

It is finally Henri Fescourt, in *La Foi et les montagnes,* who manages to characterize both Marie Epstein's accomplishments and her curious invisibility. Yet even Fescourt, although discussing both Benoît-Lévy and Epstein and their films with admiration, tends to see Marie Epstein in a conventional way. Describing her as bringing "the full force of her feminine sensibility" to their work, he concentrates on ideologically loaded details, such as Epstein's knowing how to get the best expression of despair on a child's face by threatening to break a favorite doll. Nonetheless, the footnote remains as a kind of minor testament to Marie Epstein and her unacknowledged yet indispensable participation in French filmmaking of the twenties and thirties. "Marie Epstein, who stands in the shadows because she is too discrete, is one of the most complete *cinéastes*, as much for her ideas as a scenarist as for her work as a director and editor. She was, for both her brother and for Jean Benoît-Lévy, a collaborator of the most inestimable efficacity."[10]

How did this long-standing and productive collaboration come about? Not without some irony, Marie Epstein relates the transition from her work with her brother to her work with Benoît-Lévy as the shift of so many goods and services from one boss to another. From the early twenties, Jean Benoît-Lévy was a producer and maker of educational films; his filmography includes approximately three hundred educational films, and his book *Les Grandes missions du cinéma* is an extensive elaboration on his theory and practice of making documentary educational (as well as feature) films. During the early twenties he was also an associate of La Sirène, the avant-garde publishing house that had published Jean Epstein's first theoretical writings, *Bonjour cinéma!* in 1921.

In 1922, Benoît-Lévy offered Jean Epstein, who had become secretary of La Sirène in the summer of 1921, the opportunity to direct a feature-length documentary about Louis Pasteur. On the strength of this film Jean Epstein was given a ten-year contract with Pathé-Consortium to make commercial fiction films.

Speaking of her early career as an actress, Marie Epstein says that originally when her brother began making feature films in 1923, she had not even considered directorial work for herself. But when Benoît-Lévy suggested to her that she act as "first assistant" on one of his films, she recalls being "very happy to approach the cinema from the standpoint of *mise en scène*." Epstein recounts the beginning of their collaborative work in the following way: "My brother had made the film *Pasteur* from Jean Benoît-Lévy, who was the producer of the film. And then, my brother all of a sudden had a contract with Pathé-Consortium; so, he had to leave Benoît-Lévy. Jean Benoît-Lévy was, in fact, a bit aggravated that my brother was leaving him, and my brother told him: 'Well, I'll leave you my sister in my place.' That's how it happened, as simple as that!"

Benoît-Lévy had at the time decided to expand his film production to include commercial fiction films and as a result of his "legacy" of Jean Epstein's sister, asked her to help with the scenario of *Ames d'enfants* (1927). Epstein continues: "First he asked me to help him write the scenario. So we began the scenario together, and we got along very well. Then we did the *mise-en-scène* together, and after that we were still getting along very well, so we did the editing together. You know, it's a collaboration, and I can't see it any other way than on the basis of a perfect friendship, because if you can't get along together, then I don't see how you can collaborate."

On this perfectly egalitarian basis (perhaps a little too perfect, in terms of a blend that has historically molded them into one "auteur" with the name of Jean Benoît-Lévy) Epstein and Benoît-Lévy went on to make two more silent films during the twenties (*Peau de pêche*, 1928, and *Maternité*, 1929) and eight sound films during the thirties, plus—after World War II—a short series of television documentaries on the ballet, *Ballets de France*.

When Marie Epstein speaks of collaboration in filmmaking she insists on its necessary and constant base of friendship; she asserts that for her it would not have been possible to collaborate on different films with several different filmmakers. Likewise, she says that an editor whose job it is to edit first one film for one director, then another film for another director, would not be capable of the kind of collaborative work she and Benoît-Lévy have done. This is not meant to deny that there were disagreements and differences of opinion on their various film projects, but rather to emphasize the intimate knowledge of every aspect of the work—and of each other—that was necessary for the collaboration to be successful, to be a "true" one according to Epstein. With respect to several of their films that rely heavily on a naturalistic sense of ambience, such as *La Maternelle* (which takes place in a nursery school in a Parisian slum), *La Mort du cygne* (*The Dying Swan*, 1937, which takes place backstage at the Paris Opéra), and *Hélène* (1936, which takes place at the University at Grenoble), Epstein emphasizes the weeks of location research that they did together before writing the scenarios. In discussing work further on in the production process, she relates how they always viewed the daily rushes together and mutually made corrections and suggestions; she admits that there was necessarily one person who did the actual editing (Epstein is credited with this on most of the films), but that the decisions for this editing were generally made collectively.

In fact, Marie Epstein is so tenacious about the mutuality of collaborative work that she resists an almost automatic separation that can be made as a conclusion from viewing their films—the tendency to attribute a moral dimension to Benoît-Lévy's contribution while locating the concern with feminist issues and formal experiment with Marie, and the assumption of gender hierarchies which this implies. It is clear from Benoît-Lévy's book that he considers the cinema to have a moral imperative: its most important function is to instruct its audience ethically ("The principle aim of all motion pictures is to educate . . . The motion picture represents potentially the greatest advance in human intercommunication since the invention of printing"). Epstein, on the other hand, asserts "I was always, and above all, interested—passionately involved—in making films which were alive and close to life!" But when offered the suggestion that in their films, perhaps, the moral was provided by the narrative action itself, while its transposition into images was more lyrical and more specifically cinematic, Epstein refuses to agree to this type of division of labor. "Yes, that's true, one expresses a certain subject by the cinema . . . it's a means of expression. . . . But listen, it's very difficult to put boundaries on the work of collaboration—I'm not capable of doing that. You work together, you discuss things all the time, you think of certain things . . . but who came up with this idea, who came up with that? That I really can't tell you."

And continuing to emphasize the reciprocity between moral instruction and cinematic technique in their films, as well as the impossibility of attributing a single thread to either of the filmmakers, Epstein goes on: "[The spectator] won't be touched at all if you don't show him life. If you show him things of conventional morality, etc., he won't be moved, you will make no impact, it will have no effect. . . . When you write something, or create something, if you think about the public at the beginning: 'I must touch the public, how am I going to move the audience,' well, it's ruined from the start."

Finally, although it might be said that Marie Epstein simply worked as Benoît-Lévy's assistant, an assertion that has in fact been made by some historians, Epstein is quite emphatic about the nonhierarchical nature of their collaboration: "It is very difficult to delimit a collaboration, when you work together, you know. . . . We both signed the films. Very well, take it for what it's worth. That's all!"

The films that Marie Epstein and Benoît-Lévy signed together span more than a decade, beginning before the very first experiments with the uses of sound and continuing to the eve of World War II. Between 1927 and 1939, their collaboration produced one film a year, with the exception only of 1932 and 1935. A brief enumeration and description of these films will suggest some conclusions about a general thematics that characterizes their oeuvre. Later, a more detailed discussion of *La Maternelle* will focus on its specific textual operations in order to provide an analysis of the ways in which its filmic system subverts the basic structure of the classical Hollywood model, particularly in its articulation of fantasy scenes and its reorganization of point-of-view. For the moment, capsule plot summaries of the individual films reveal a concern with childhood and social conditions, with women who struggle with difficulties in daily life, and with parental relationships. These are not the subjects of grand spectacle, nor can they be specifically classified as the familial conflicts of bourgeois melodrama. What can be said, however, is that for the most part these films are textured with the milieu of ordinary daily life, and that the quotidian proportions of the depicted situations give the films a feeling of intimacy that can best be described (in Epstein's words) as "close to life." Yet within the context of this study, it is not only the intimate and domestic scale of these films—and the naturalness and vitality that come as a consequence—that make Epstein's work so important for feminism. What marks the peculiar sensibility of many of these films is not simply that they are about domesticity and children's lives; they are, rather, about a particular relation to childhood which has to do, powerfully and fundamentally, with feminine desire. On a thematic level there is an overriding concern with female identity, as issues of relevance to women's lives continually intersect with the careful depiction of the social milieu. And this shift of narrative focus to the scene of the feminine (that is, from woman as object to woman as subject of desire) often implies a transformation in cinematic structures as well.

The three silent films all deal in one way or another with childhood, and even at this point an interest in questions of female desire is evident. Likewise, they contain the seeds of what is to become a major element in *La Maternelle*—the depiction of children's lives in the milieu of the Parisian slums. *Ames d'enfants* (1927) and *Maternité* (1929) are what Epstein calls "propaganda films," by which she means instructional or agitational films about different subjects.[11] *Ames d'enfants*, says Epstein, was made in the style of other educational films on the subject of hygiene for example, or human physiology, or culture, or geography; that is, the type of film that Benoît-Lévy made during most of his career, and that he discusses at great length in his book. *Ames d'enfants* argued for sanitary, healthy housing conditions as against the miserable slums where children have neither air nor light. Equally a propaganda film, *Maternité* is remembered less enthusiastically by Epstein, who dismisses it with a laugh as "a very bad film": it agitated for women to have lots of children.

Yet despite her dismissal of these films, they both—*Maternité* in particular—constitute a matrix of concerns that will inform the later films in a particularly interesting way. Taken together they represent an early preoccupation with what can be formulated as the two reciprocal elements contained in the concept of "maternal desire": the child's desire for the mother (the locus of childhood) and the woman's desire for the child (the site of motherhood). *Ames d'enfants* moves two families from a Paris tenement into a model housing project (City Gardens) and then contrasts the virtuous, industrious Valereux family with its chaotic, irresponsible counterpart, the Berliets. Both families confront the daily problems of an impoverished working class, but while the Valereux children blossom in these surroundings—due in no small part to Madame Valereux' immaculate housekeeping—the Berliets' slovenly behavior forces them to be evicted from this public housing. However, while the film's moralizing surface extolls the virtues of hard work, the real interest of the film is conferred on the younger members of both families, and on the familial ties that connect them. Even the film's title ("children's souls") bears this out. Epstein's primary concern with the children themselves is present to such an extent that the love interest, a romance between Simone Valereux and Mimile Berliet, is deflected onto a mutual concern for Mimile's ailing little brother. In fact, the relationship between Simone and Mimile itself is depicted as one of fraternal bonding, for the film's resolution involves Simone's arrangements to have little Charlot Berliet cared for in the sunlight and warmth of the City Gardens. "You've saved me . . . and my family!" exclaims a fervent Mimile at the film's end as a large close-up is followed by clasped hands and the sunlight through trees, "Thank you, Simone!" The narrative has served as a support for the more focussed elaboration on the quality of children's lives, depicted through such lyrical passages as one linking air and sunlight, little hands reaching upward, roofs, birds, and boys playing, or the one involving plants being watered in the garden, a large close-up of a flower, and a child's laughing face.

Maternité makes use of such visual lyricism as well, but toward different ends. If one is to go by Marie Epstein's assessment of it, one can expect a fairly awful propaganda film. However, a screening of *Maternité* reveals an astounding complexity, both in its evocative visual poetry and in the subtle psychological issues it treats. The film involves a childless woman who comes to regret her decision and who, by the end of the film, discovers other forms of nurturing that will enable her to experience an alternative kind of bonding. The film begins with a contrast: While the frivolous and flirtatious Louise Viguier, daughter of an affluent farmer in the Auvergne, mocks her father's desire for grandchildren, Marie, a worker on the farm, gives birth to a child out of wedlock. A proud and loving mother, she is nonetheless ordered off the farm by Louise. This proves to be to Marie's advantage, for in the city she finds Pierre, the baby's father, and he marries her. Although the baby dies (scenes intercut with Louise fussing over her Pekingese puppy), they start a new family—six children of whom Jacquot is the youngest. The years pass, and Louise takes over the farm upon her father's death; Jacquot arrives to help with the harvest. Although Louise has been insensitive and cold, Jacquot comforts her when her dog dies, and a bond is formed between them.

When Jacquot is injured in a fall, Louise cares for him, although she is saddened to find that upon awakening he cries out for his real mother. Marie arrives and, thanking Louise, explains that Louise's nurturing attention to her son is what motherhood is all about. Later Jacquot's sister marries a local herdsman, and the birth of their baby is another occasion for Louise to experience regret. At a country dance, as Jacquot dances with his mother, the herdsman with his, and the new baby is tended to by his, Louise feels useless and isolated, and so decides to leave. Along a country road she sees a tree being destroyed "because it no longer bears fruit," and deliberately stands in the path of its collapse. Nursed back to health by a Dr. Laurent, Louise is able to take a job as director of his daycare center, and so "finds courage in the fact that she is helping mothers," and in her own special position in "the continuity of life."

The plot, in and of itself, seems to be in keeping with Marie's assessment of the film, for it reveals the pressure of patriarchal ideology in its advocacy of traditional conceptions of mothering and female self-fulfillment. Yet, here too, it is a plot that functions merely as a support for what constitutes a fundamental thematic matrix defining all of Epstein's work. In its lyrical passages, its repeated motifs, the psychological realism of its evocative images, and in its focus on specifically feminine questions (of maternal desire, of female reciprocity, of women's emotive capability) it demonstrates a powerful incisiveness and a concern with female identity that informs all of Epstein's subsequent films. It is in this sense that, amid an ideologically charged backdrop of paeans to fertility, a profound reflection on female subjectivity emerges: "Being a woman" involves capacities for empathy, compassion, and caring that have only been *channeled into* a concept of motherhood by a culture that automatically assimilates these qualities to it. The film presents a way of understanding that the intense, affective bonds formed between women and children are not the unique province of mothers alone, and that there are alternative roles for women which can provide the means to sustain nurturing desires. At the same time, the film suggests that there is something specifically feminine at the core of these bonding needs.

There are sequences, for example, which fairly exult in the natural process of giving birth, such as the opening segment with Marie, on a pillow of hay, surrounded by mountains, clouds, and sky, or the springtime benediction ritual with its panoramas of livestock and mountainous countryside, or Marie's daughter's childbirth with its lyrical facial close-ups, its tears, its timed-release flowers. But these are offset by sequences in which mutual ties of compassionate understanding are shared between women and children, and it is this very reciprocity that leads Louise to discover her own possibilities and sources of caring. In an extremely beautiful sequence, a homesick Jacquot buries his face in his mother's shawl while Louise simultaneously attends affectionately to her dog, indicating not the absence of feeling but its displacement. Louise will learn to draw on these emotions in her care for impoverished city children as the film conveys its message that intensity of feeling and the capacity for love are shared by all women, mothers and non-mothers alike. Likewise, Jacquot comforts Louise in an exchange of highly moving close-ups, a reciprocal structure repeated when Marie's daughter tells her of her love for the herdsman, as Louise looks on. While the former scene makes Louise the recipient of filial love, here it is her position as observer to a scene of maternal warmth that will inspire her own desire for a kind of sharing that she will eventually achieve through her work with children.

Repetition through reiterated visual motifs—another stylistic device that recurs throughout Epstein's films—is also put in the service of this complication of meaning, this refusal of ideological definitions of femininity as equivalent to maternity. Just as Louise's regret at the lost possibility of motherhood is conveyed through parallel sequences that place her by a window, so, too, is the suggestion of other modes of nurturing made via parallel, highly poetic sequences at the daycare center, first early in the film and later at its close. The moments with Louise by the window form part of a paradigm of cyclical repetition in which an essentialist conception of femininity links it with biology. The daycare sequences posit a more materialist notion of femininity in that they generalize the possibilities for caring not tied to nature. The dialectical articulation of these two strands provides the structural mainspring of the film. In these ways the conventional association of the woman with fertility and nature—the surface meaning of the film—is challenged and reworked by the figurative structures that form its textual system.

It is easy to see how this surface meaning could lead Marie Epstein to dismiss *Maternité* as "a very bad film," for its advocacy of fertility could have been nothing but painful to her. Yet already, here, there is the sensitivity and imagination with regard to the feminist problematic that will mark the rest of her filmmaking so fundamentally. As such, *Maternité* constitutes an early and important challenge to the patriarchal representation of the woman, for it articulates its confrontation both in terms of the ideology of motherhood and in terms of representing female subjectivity. The formulation of another discourse—of desire in the feminine—is already present in this film; in its attempt to redefine female desire, it suggests a different relation to the female body than patriarchy prescribes. In rupturing the association of female identity with fertility, the film posits another conception of femininity, one not grounded in biology, but nonetheless related to it in a very specific way. The central emotive core of the film concerns a series of problems posed—precisely for women—around the issues of motherhood and female bonding, and it does so in terms that must take feminine specificity into account. In light of contemporary debates surrounding surrogacy, maternal questions, and other forms of nurturing, *Maternité* is an undeniably modern film, and one whose complexity and beauty make it a profoundly significant contribution to the formulation of a feminist cinema.[12]

Peau de pêche (1928) receives its title from the main character, a little boy who presumably blushes (like a peach) when he gets excited. Social criticism is made in the form of depicting the child's unhappy life in the city; this is contrasted with his life in the country where, after his adoption by gentle country folk, he becomes happy. Benoît-Lévy has written about this film, in terms of its narrative content, as a film that depicts a nine year-old boy's sudden awareness of mortality. The boy is obsessed with the current war, both in the games he plays and the pictures of toy soldiers he collects. The death of his close friend, son of the farmers who have adopted him, brings him to a military cemetery. "Faced with a forest of crosses, he discovers the horror of reality, which he expresses tragically by the mere depth of his look."[13]

Shifting the emphasis of recollection significantly, Marie Epstein comments that this film was more about a kind of ambience and emotional atmosphere than about specific narrative events. And, characteristically, its main plot (involving a romance between the grown-up Peau de pêche and a young woman from the village, and the subsequent rivalry over her with his best friend)[14] recedes into the background in light of the sensitive evocation of children's lives that constitutes only part of the film. Continuing in the tradition already established by *Ames d'enfants* and *Maternité*, the urban social environment's effects on impoverished children forms much of the film's texture, as the "*style Poulbot*" finds its cinematic equivalent on the screen. Poulbot was a late-nineteenth-century illustrator whose popular depictions of children of the Paris streets created an enduring and widespread cartoonlike imagery of ragged urchins and their milieu. *Peau de pêche* makes these figures of children literally come to life. And so powerfully did Epstein and Benoît-Lévy's location shooting contribute to the contrast of urban poverty and the restorative powers of the countryside that one critic claimed: "Finally, here is a film that leaves behind the stifling, miserable limits of the studio, with its conventional decors and illusory techniques, a film where one can breathe the vigorous outside air . . . a film where there are no dance clubs, music halls, or worldly salons, but where, by contrast, there are admirable and restful perspectives of fields, of lovely rivers, and farm houses, so marvelously peopled that one would like to remain there the rest of one's days."[15]

Epstein and Benoît-Lévy's first sound film, *Jimmy Bruiteur* (1930), continues the focus on childhood while at the same time representing an original and innovative experiment with the new dimension of the cinematic medium. Starring Le Petit Jimmy (who had played the young Peau de pêche in the previous film), it, too, is about a little boy, but here instead of poignancy there is imagination: the boy takes over his grandfather's job as a sound-effects man in a small provincial theater. In *Peau de pêche*, little Jimmy Gaillard had entertained a collection of laughing village children with his imitation of Maurice Chevalier. In *Jimmy Bruiteur* the sound effects themselves create the humor, for as he seeks to match appropriate sounds with the theatrical performance, the results are calamitous. He confuses everything, creating the effect of a sputtering automobile while the singer is singing, a raging storm while the lovers kiss, and a number of ridiculous sound effects that do not correspond at all to the scene being acted. Epstein recalls the film with laughter, pointing out that the comedy is created entirely by the use of sound.

In 1931, Epstein and Benoît-Lévy made *Le Coeur de Paris*, their first sound film to continue the thematic concerns of their silent films—the intensity of affective relationships and the lives of children in an urban (usually Parisian) setting. A street urchin, again played by Jimmy Gaillard, shows an American around Paris and ends by taking him home to meet his family. The foreigner falls in love with the boy's sister, but she marries the street vendor whom she has loved for a long time. Reflecting on this film, Epstein recalls, "well in fact, it shows you Paris, but it's not really a good film." One can only speculate, but judging from Epstein's quick dismissal of *Maternité*, it is possible that there are evocative, poetic sequences in this film as well, sequences that suggest a formal and thematic consistency with the entire oeuvre.

Released in 1933, *La Maternelle* (which will be discussed in detail in chapter 7) is by far the most successful and widely acclaimed of the Epstein Benoît-Lévy films, in addition to being the only one distributed in the United States.[16] Georges Sadoul praises its "touching vision of childhood," as well as its "authentic depiction of Parisian neighborhoods, in the best French tradition."[17] When it was reviewed in the *New York Times* upon its exhibition in the United States in 1935, the reviewer hyperbolically called it a film "of great subtlety and almost unendurable power; a film of extraordinary insight, tenderness, and tragic beauty."[18] As noted in the introduction to this book, the film concerns a young woman named Rose who takes a job as a cleaning lady in a nursery school (*école maternelle*) where an abandoned little girl develops a love relationship with her. When the school director proposes marriage to Rose, little Marie relives the trauma of the first abandonment by her mother, a prostitute, and attempts suicide. But the film ends happily as she reconciles with Rose and accepts her fiancé, giving another level of significance to the title.

La Maternelle represents a thematic and textual crystallization of Epstein's work, and thereby constitutes a culminating point toward which the early films proceed and to which the later films return. As is the case with *Ames d'enfants*, the focus on the child makes all else recede into the background—even the woman's desire to be a mother, which ostensibly forms one of the main narrative motifs in *La Maternelle*. Thus, although Rose assumes her employment at the nursery school out of a love for children—and a fear that she might never have children of her own—it is truly *Marie*'s story that the film tells. And it is the emotional intensity surrounding the little girl's longing for the mother that allows the film to shift its focus from the traditional masculine Oedipal narrative to the complex relations of female desire.

This is, in fact, what distinguishes *La Maternelle* from other films about children, films that form a characteristic subgenre of French cinema of the thirties. To be sure, the typical atmosphere of these "childhood" films is present in *La Maternelle*, for, as with *Peau de pêche*, the "*style Poulbot*" is everywhere apparent—even more so because the Léon Frapié novel on which *La Maternelle* is loosely based (a collection of stories that won the Prix Goncourt) is itself heavily illustrated with

Poulbot's drawings. Mademoiselle Paulin (the "titular head maid"), some of the children (Marie Coeuret, Fondant, little Jules, and others), and the entire atmosphere of the nursery school with its benches and baskets, the children's smocks, and so forth, appear in the book as Poulbot's images. But when *La Maternelle* is seen in relation to Julien Duvivier's *Poil de carotte* (both 1925 and 1932 versions), Jacques Feyder's *Gribiche* (1926) and *Visages d'enfants* (1925), Christian-Jaque's *Les Disparus de Saint-Agil* (1938), and even Jean Vigo's *Zéro de conduite* (1933)—with which it is sometimes compared—several important features set it apart.

For one thing, in many of these films the atmosphere of childhood is infused with the spirit of boyish anarchy—these films project what is essentially a masculine universe rendered in miniature. The latter two films in particular depict a spirited dynamics of revolt against authority, a theme which, although present in *La Maternelle* in the form of sequences illustrating gleeful childish rebellion in the nursery school, is not its central focus. But even in those films that do share with *La Maternelle* its emotive emphasis on the maternal rapport, these other films about childhood concentrate on the *male* child's relation to the mother (and the father) and the problematic but necessary intensity of that particular bond. Thus *Les Disparus de Saint-Agil* and *Zéro de conduite*, both set in boys' schools, fairly reverberate with the collective masculinity of early adolescence, while *Visages d'enfants* and *Poil de carotte* locate structures of subjectivity within their youthful male protagonists. In all cases, it is the powerful emphasis on the masculine hero (singular or plural) that makes an exploration of masculine consciousness the primary concern.

In contrast, *La Maternelle* depicts a virtual society of women. All of the major characters are female, from Rose and Marie, to Madame Paulin and the school's principal, to Marie's actual mother herself, present throughout the film even in her absence in its second half. The men in the film, on the other hand, are simply masculine functions, positions around which the dramas of female desire circulate—from Dr. Libois (the director who proposes to Rose) and the famous professor who visits the school, to the brutal, drunken Pantin (father of two of the children at the school) and the seedy character who runs off with Marie's mother. Beyond that, the primary focus on the intensity of the affective bond between the female child and the maternal figure distinguishes this film from its superficially similar counterparts. It is in the *reciprocity* of female desire—a mutuality of relationship that affects every level of the film, from its structuring thematic and its concentric organization of narrative moments to its patterned reiteration of visual figures and motifs—that the film derives its singular force. The silent Epstein/Benoît-Lévy films had already posed this reciprocity as a central matrix of the oeuvre by establishing a dual concern with both the locus of childish longing and the site of maternal desire. *Maternité* extended the exploration of the problematics of mothering by proposing a dialectical conception of motherhood that combined what might be seen as a conventional lyricism about mothers and children with a critique of traditional views of maternity (the proposal of alternative nurturing structures and channels of compassion).

It is possible to see *La Maternelle* as a kind of inversion of the work begun in *Maternité*, for what is prominent in the earlier film (the woman's desire to be a mother) gets shifted to secondary status as the focus on the child (and her desire to have a mother) becomes the central concern, while the overriding organizing issue of motherhood remains intact. This can be seen in the comparison of each film's climactic suicide attempt: *Maternité*'s Louise throws herself in the path of a collapsing tree because she cannot be a mother, while little Marie throws herself into the river because she has lost the hope of having one. And it is precisely this focus on the child that necessitates *La Maternelle*'s alternative discursive structure, its modification of terms of address, and its reorganization of point-of-view. In locating the affective intensity within the province of the child, while nonetheless maintaining a profound preoccupation with the parameters of feminine desire, the film must generate new modes of spectator-identification, structures other than those implied by the traditional cinema of masculinity. As desire for the woman is articulated in terms of the female child's longing for the maternal object, the figure of the woman becomes reconstituted as another object—and subject—of vision. In this complex of formal, thematic, and enunciative (textual) concerns *La Maternelle* achieves its important exemplary status in the Epstein oeuvre.

Epstein and Benoît-Lévy turned to more distant location shooting for *Itto* (1934), their most exotic film. Filmed in the Moroccan desert with the participation of nonprofessional actors from the Schleu tribes of the Atlas mountains, this film's dramatic tempo is heightened by rhythmic editing patterns characteristic of Soviet montage of the twenties.[19] In fact, because there is little dialogue, and much of this is in the native language of the tribespeople, the film relies heavily on music and the impact of the visual image for its effect, which gives it the striking quality of a silent film. Despite its moralizing tone and unselfconscious transmission of colonialist values, *Itto* is a powerful and exciting film. A French doctor and his wife care for the nomads engaged in a fratricidal war. An infant born out of a Berber version of *Romeo and Juliet* is left orphaned when its rebel mother is killed. The doctor's wife adopts the baby as the film ends on an image of peace among the races.

There are several things to note in relation to *Itto,* for although its North African location makes it atypical of Epstein's work, it demonstrates a certain consistency of theme and motif that connects it strongly to the other films. Here, again, preoccupations of the maternal retain priority, even though the film fits comfortably into the colonial tradition in other ways.[20] If one can look beyond the time-bound contrasts of European and Arab cultures with their propensity for hegemonic stereotyping, one finds that the nomad lovers in *Itto* are little more than children themselves, torn tragically by the economic and social circumstances of their particular milieu. Likewise, the representation of femininity characteristic of the colonial film— the femme fatale's cliches of exoticism, opulence, and alterity—does not find its equivalent here. Rather, the film seems to displace the conventional notion of romantic passion as it argues for a universal humanity, one based on profound bonds of love associated with (the film makes this quite clear) maternal desire. The film's closing image, a union of clasped hands, repeats what has been a consistent visual motif throughout the Epstein oeuvre and reinforces its project of articulating a different desire.

Hélène (1936) is about a single woman who struggles to raise her child alone amid the myriad difficulties she must confront. In discussing this film Epstein resists any conventional attribution of a feminist intent: She insists that Benoît-Lévy chose the story out of his admiration for the novel *Hélène Wilfur* by Vicky Baum, but adds that she was pleased with the choice. The milieu of the film is university life at the Faculté de Grenoble, where Epstein and Benoît-Lévy spent several weeks among the students, studying their lives and noting details for the scenario, and the displaced love affair makes the film thematically consistent with its predecessors. The initial situation recalls *L'Affiche:* A young student named Hélène[21] is abandoned by the father of her child when he commits suicide out of an inability to deal with paternal responsibilities. At the same time, the wife of one of the professors leaves him to pursue a singing career. Hélène and Professor Amboise come together out of mutual love for their work. Despite her disavowal of feminist intentions, Epstein recalls the film in terms of the woman's struggle ("It was the struggle of a single woman meeting life's obstacles. . . . ") and mentions episodes in the film such as Hélène's consideration of abortion and her subsequent decision to keep the child.

It is easy to see how the complexity of the maternal problematic first articulated in *Maternité* and developed in *La Maternelle* achieves a kind of synthesizing force in *Hélène*. All of the earlier themes are here—the enduring emotional support that work can provide, the intensity of a woman's bond with children, the sustaining power of mutual friendship, and alternative forms of compassion and love. But with *Hélène*, Epstein returns to the adult again and reinstates her concern with female identity, for it is here that the systematic reflections on both the social and the psychic constructions of femininity are dramatized in narrative form. It is as if, having explored the primacy of the maternal bond from the child's point of view, Epstein returns to the woman with renewed interest in mapping the parameters of female desire. The power of a film like *Hélène*, then, lies in its positing of an alternative—a redefinition, in fact—of the terms of love and fulfillment as they are engaged in and by women's lives.

Along with *La Maternelle*, *La Mort du cygne* represents the most accomplished blending of detailed location ambience, children's lives, and narrative action in the Epstein/Benoît-Lévy films.[22] Set in the backstage areas of the Paris Opéra, it also concerns a maternal relationship, this time between a young ballet dancer and her idol, the star of the corps de ballet. In preparing the scenario, Epstein and Benoît-Lévy had spent several weeks at the Opéra, observing the young dancers in the corps de ballet and absorbing a sense of the milieu. Both Epstein and Benoît-Lévy wanted this film to portray the drama behind the scenes of the performed spectacle. As Benoît-Lévy notes in his book: "Like every theater, the Opera has two sides to it: one made of velvet and gold, magic and pleasure; the other of dust and painted canvas, reality and work and self-sacrifice"; they wanted to portray the latter side.[23]

This film, which was awarded the Grand Prix du film Français at the 1937 Exposition, concerns a twelve-year-old ballerina who adores the star of the corps de ballet (Yvette Chauviré). When she fears this star will be dethroned by a rival dancer (Mia Slavenska), little Rose Souris opens a trap door as the rival dances, causing her to have a serious accident. Forced to give up her career because of this, the crippled star becomes an instructor. But the other star ballerina also gives up her career—she gets married and leaves the theater. Finally, little Rose and her "victim" are reconciled through love of their art.

The film is based only loosely on a story by Paul Morand; Epstein explains that everything up to and including the accident was in the book, but a scenario was written, with Morand's approval, for everything after that point. Agreeing that the story of the accident alone is a bit "artificial," Epstein acknowledges that the more interesting complications in the film deal with complex interpersonal relationships among females. A woman's relationship to her work (as in *Hélène*) is explored in the drama of the crippled dancer; the maternal relationship (as in *La Maternelle*) is illustrated by the dancer's pardon of the younger ballerina who had caused the accident; and the mutuality of a productive work relationship is encapsulated by the crippled star's statement to Rose at the film's end: "I will make you the dancer that I couldn't be."

However, because the film proceeds through fairly straightforward narrative exposition, it lacks the power and poetic beauty of *La Maternelle*. Where the latter film achieved its depth and effectivity through a complex visual patterning which reiterated actual, remembered, and fantasized images in the mind of the child, articulating repeated scenarios of vision and desire within its narrative frame, *La Mort du cygne* avoids such suggestive evocations of the psyche altogether, and thereby fails to resonate in quite the same way. The intimacy of relationships is there, as is the feminine focus, but because its methods are essentially discursive it does not achieve the intensity of psychic atmosphere generated by *La Maternelle*'s provocative use of silent film techniques. Although it is tempting to associate the two films on the basis of their similar concerns, it is clearly *La Maternelle* that represents the achievement of the Epstein oeuvre. Still, the excitement and dynamic energy of a spectacle behind the scenes and the focus on emotive relationships among women are enough to mark the film with a peculiar sensibility that distinguishes it from its more commercial counterparts.

Altitude 3200 (1938) appears to be the Epstein/Benoît-Lévy film closest to a thesis-play. It is in fact based on a play by Julien Luchaire, who wrote the scenario and dialogue. The film's two previous titles, *Le Grand rêve* (*The Great Dream*) and *Nous les jeunes* (*We, the Youth*), are perhaps more explicit about the utopian nature of the film's project: Seven young men, disgusted with modern life, found a sort of commune at a chalet in the Alps. When six young women lose their way in the mountains, the chalet becomes the site of a newly founded "republic" based on friendship. However, the inevitable quarrels over romantic rivalry and disputed authority erupt, and the group disbands. Their communal experiment having failed, the young people go their separate ways.

It is important to note that this film's view of a society in microcosm is not too different is some respects from other films made by Epstein and Benoît-Lévy. *La Maternelle, Hélène,* and *La Mort du cygne* all depict miniature social systems with their own specific codes of conduct and systems of rules to regulate behavior. In these three films, the nursery school, the university, and the corps de ballet are the social milieux of the action, but in each, rather than simply providing dramatic background, these social milieux structure the relations and interactions of the characters. It is at this level that these films can be seen to provide a very sophisticated type of social commentary while at the same time maintaining a consistent preoccupation with specifically "feminine" concerns.

The last feature film that Epstein and Benoît-Lévy made together was *Le Feu de paille* (*Straw Fire*) in 1939. Combining the themes of childhood in *Peau de pêche* and *La Maternelle* with the theatrical milieu of *La Mort du cygne,* this film concerns a child actor and his father. This is the only collaborative film in which Marie Epstein is listed as "assistante" in the *Catalogue des films français de long métrage (1929–1939)* by Raymond Chirat. The film concerns Antoine Vautier, an unsuccessful actor. When a director comes to town to audition children for a film he is making, Vautier's son Christian is chosen. The child becomes a popular star, and his father suffers pangs of jealousy. But when Christian's second film is a disaster, the father forgets his jealousy in face of his son's failure.

Benoît-Lévy is particularly fond of this film precisely because it contains a sequence, the children's audition, which is a replica of Epstein's and his own procedures of interviewing children for films. The scene begins as the director tells the little boy that the two of them are "friends. . . . All people you see in the studio aren't here at all; there's only you and I." As the boy regains confidence, Benoît-Lévy continues to describe the sequence: "he and the director really do appear to be the only two people in the studio. Then occurs that phenomenon of suggestion, that transmission of thought, which permits the director to communicate with the child. There is a real visual dialogue expressed in alternating close-ups of each one as seen by the other, which enables the child to be placed in exactly the same situation as the character whose reactions he is externalizing. In this way, the author can almost invariably make his choice, which, in the last analysis, depends on the child's sensitivity to coaching and his receptivity to the film author's mental reactions."[24]

As I indicated at the beginning of this chapter, any discussion of Marie Epstein's authorship is a fairly complicated task. The very fact of her "invisibility" from the standard film histories necessitates a kind of foregrounding of her activity in an effort to redress the balance; it involves a work of reconstruction as well. This is because, paradoxically, that same process of collaboration that enabled her to contribute such a significant body of work to the tradition of French filmmaking was responsible for her effacement. Furthermore, when authorship is considered textually, it becomes necessary to displace this collaboration of individuals into a synthetic conception of textual instance, a complex of thematic and stylistic preoccupations and enunciative strategies that I have chosen to call "Epstein." For this reason, I have referred to "Epstein/Benoît-Lévy" when speaking of the actual production of the films and the "Epstein oeuvre" when discussing their thematic consistency, textual processes, and feminist concerns.

There is no doubt that, judging from the films themselves, Marie Epstein can be considered an auteur in her own right. In their concerted focus on childhood, on intimate female relationships, on maternal issues and their reciprocal relations of desire, and on feminine identity, the films demonstrate a coherence of project more rigorous than, say, the work of an acclaimed woman director such as Dorothy Arzner or Ida Lupino. This strongly supports my assertion (the assertion of this book, in fact) that the theorization of a feminist counter-cinema has more to do with the signifying and textual relations of a particular body of work than with attention to individuals simply because they are women. Beyond the elaboration of a consistent thematics there are other levels of analysis as well, other elements of Epstein's authorship that mark her profound contribution to a feminist cinema. In posing an authorial voice from another site of desire, Epstein's films engage new modes of organizing meaning, new articulations of the gaze, not only in their poetic texture, but in their fictional structures as well. But perhaps most important of all, what continually emerges from the ensemble of these films is a unique and different construction of the woman's image—and a redefinition of the desiring relations in which it is taken up. From this discussion, then, it should be quite clear that Marie Epstein's films are important not simply in terms of the "discovery" of a woman's work, but rather, in terms of the highly significant contribution they make—on a thematic and a textual level—to the formulation of feminist cinematic alternatives.

NOTES

1. A strong example of this contrast can be seen in Epstein's nearly anonymous collecting and editing of her brother Jean's theoretical writings (*Ecrits sur le cinéma*, Paris: Editions Seghers, 1974), for which she refused to have her

name appear on the title page. I was very fortunate to have the opportunity to interview Marie Epstein in May and June of 1977, thus enabling me to begin to bring her film activity to public attention. She spoke engagingly and interestingly on a whole range of topics, from her own film work to that of others. I am extremely grateful to her both for her information and for the example of her incredible energy and dynamism. Her comments in this chapter are taken from these interviews. All translations are my own.

2. Richard Abel, *French Cinema: The First Wave, 1915–1929* (Princeton: Princeton University Press, 1984), pp. 353–54. Portions of his book are based on information he received in interviews with Marie Epstein, and he warmly acknowledges her in his book. Both *L'Auberge rouge* and *Coeur fidèle* were screened at the Museum of Modern Art in New York City in 1986 and 1983 respectively.

3. Abel, *French Cinema*, p. 366.

4. Edmond Epardeaud, "*L'Affiche* de Jean Epstein," *Cinéa-Ciné-pour-tous*, no. 34 (April 1, 1925): 27–28. *L'Affiche* was screened at the Museum of Modern Art in 1983.

5. Jean Dréville, "*Six et demi-onze*," *Cinégraphie*, no. 3 (November 15, 1927); the *découpage* and shot continuity are found in Dréville, "Six et demi-onze," *Cinégraphie*, no. 2 (October 15, 1927).

6. Epstein, *Ecrits sur le cinéma*, vol. 1, p. 61.

7. Georges Sadoul, *Le Cinéma français (1890–1962)* (Paris: Flammarion, 1962), pp. 70, 83.

8. Marcel Lapierre, *Les Cents visages du cinéma* (Paris: Editions Bernard Grasset, 1948), pp. 161–62.

9. Jean Benoît-Lévy, *Les Grandes missions du cinéma;* translated as *The Art of the Motion Picture* (New York: Coward, McCann, 1946), p. 186. It should be obvious from this quote that the book was written in exile; Benoît-Lévy had gone to the United States when he fled the Occupation.

10. Henri Fescourt, *La Foi et les montagnes (ou le septième art au passé)* (Paris: Paul Montel, 1959), pp. 402–8, 311.

11. Both *Ames d'enfants* and *Maternité* were part of the Museum of Modern Art's series, Rediscovering French Film, Part 2 in the winter and spring of 1983.

12. Part of this discussion is indebted to conversations with Sharon Flitterman-King and her comments on the issue in *Ms Magazine*, April 1988.

13. Benoît-Lévy, *Les Grandes missions*, p. 175.

14. This discussion draws, in part, from Abel's treatment of the film in *The French Cinema*, p. 137.

15. Robert Trevise, "*Peau de pêche*," *Cinéa-Ciné-pour-tous*, no. 126 (February 1, 1929): 26, cited by Abel in *The French Cinema*, p. 137.

16. *La Maternelle* is available for rental from the Museum of Modern Art, 11 West 53d St., New York, NY 10019. I base my analysis and discussion, however, on prints seen at the Cinémathèque Française in Paris, the Pacific Film Archive at the University Art Museum in Berkeley, Calif., and the UCLA Film Archive.

17. Sadoul, *Le Cinéma français*, p. 70.

18. *The New York Times,* October 15, 1935.

19. I was able to see *Itto* at the Department d'études et de recherches cinématographiques de l'Université de Paris III.

20. For an extremely interesting discussion of the colonial film as a genre of French film of the twenties, see Abel, *The French Cinema,* pp. 151–60.

21. Hélène is played by Madeleine Renaud; Jean-Louis Barrault has a minor role in the film as the fiance. Marie Epstein takes pleasure in relating the fact that Renaud and Barrault met for the first time on this film and subsequently married and became the famous theatrical team of the Théâtre National Populaire ("It was here that they fell in love for the rest of their lives!"). The film is unavailable in the United States but exists at the Cinémathèque Française; a small portion of a sunny picnic scene between Barrault and Renaud appears in a documentary on Jean-Louis Barrault shown on Public Television, confirming both Epstein's version of their meeting and a sense of the film's visual poetry.

22. The only print of *La Mort du cygne* available in the United States is a noncirculating print at the UCLA Film Archive. The film was screened at the Museum of Modern Art during Part 2 of its Rediscovering French Film series in 1983; my discussion is based on the UCLA print and the one at the Cinémathèque Française.

23. Benoît-Lévy, *Les Grandes missions,* p. 151.

24. Ibid., p. 170.

SIX

Epstein in Context:
French Film Production in the Thirties

HAVING ESTABLISHED WHAT DISTINGUISHES the Epstein oeuvre for feminism, a closer look at the context in which Epstein and Benoît-Lévy
worked will help to discern to what extent their films are exemplary
of the general economic and aesthetic atmosphere of the time. As I
have argued in the introduction of this book, the thirties represent the
second period of resistance to Hollywood cinema, a period whose
creative challenge to American dominance produced some of the most
brilliant examples of a French cinema truly expressive of a national
character. A particular combination of economic factors and aesthetic
solutions produced what critics have called the Golden Age of French
cinema, manifested in the films of such directors as Jean Renoir,
Jacques Feyder, Marcel Carné, René Clair, Julien Duvivier, Jean
Grémillon, and, from a slightly different standpoint, Marcel Pagnol.
The films made by Epstein and Benoît-Lévy share important characteristics with this work, and, as such, reflect that "Frenchness"—the
national cinematic identity for which the period is known. My discussion will cover three areas of French film production in the thirties:
1) collaborative work as a socioeconomic fact of filmmaking at the
time; 2) the aesthetic context of "Poetic Realism"; and 3) the specific
production methods and techniques that resulted as a consequence of
the first two factors.

The work of Marie Epstein and Jean Benoît-Lévy represents one of
the earliest and perhaps longest examples of filmmaking collaboration
in France in the 1930s. At that time, the French film industry, particularly at the level of production, was unstable, fragmented, and faced

with heavy foreign competition. In 1929, the previously considerable output of French film production fell to fifty feature-length films per year. Hollywood dominated the world market, with approximately 85 percent of the films shown throughout the world coming from the United States.[1] In France, the cooperation that grew up more or less spontaneously between certain directors, scriptwriters, cameramen, art directors, and technicians can in some way be seen as a sort of joining of collaborative forces to stimulate French film productivity. At the same time, the dispersed and chaotic situation of the industry enabled a degree of creative freedom that permitted an unusual amount of cooperative reciprocity among members of a film's production team.

Financial anarchy reigned in what Raymond Borde calls "one of the most brilliant and fruitful periods of the French cinema.... [T]he French film industry was fragmented, atomized, and vulnerable. It went from swindles to bankruptcies. As dubious schemes emerged, it had every chance to founder—and yet it produced masterpieces."[2] While the two major French companies that had dominated the silent film market went bankrupt (Gaumont-Franco-Film-Aubert in 1934 and Pathé-Nathan in 1936), hundreds of small, fly-by-night operations emerged, creating a climate of haphazard speculation as companies with limited capital would form around such variables as a famous actor, a commercially popular story, or single idea in order to make only one film—and then disband. Basing his observations on Raymond Chirat's catalogue of French feature films produced between 1929 and 1939,[3] Borde calculates that "it appears that 426 production companies, theoretically independent from one another, produced in 10 years 681 films, approximately one and a half films per company."[4] Georges Sadoul has characterized this period as "The reign of the street vendors and speculators."[5]

Yet this fragility and dispersion of the industry meant less control by large production companies modeled on the Hollywood "majors." As Sadoul points out, this decentralization led to a certain amount of freedom because any director with popular appeal would be given a free hand by an undiscerning backer, while the large companies had rigid selection committees who preferred conventional subjects: "[These financial] risks assured a relative freedom in the choice of subjects. The personal influence of a filmmaker could convince an artisan producer, while non-standard subjects were pitilessly eliminated by the Board of large companies. From the poverty of French cinema was born its richness, thanks to the reestablishment of (relatively) free competition."[6]

The fragmented production situation meant something else—the substitution of a more craftsmanlike process for the strict division of labor (into producer, director, scenarist, dialogist, cameraman, and art director) of the Hollywood studios and their bureaucratic, centralized coordination. The flexibility that resulted from this more personal and "democratic" interaction meant that the director was able to discuss and modify the script, was able to work with actors in a more reciprocal fashion, was able to defend the project against an executive producer whose only interest was financial, and was able to have the right of final cut. As a consequence, in this stimulating climate of cooperative work, some of the most enduring and important cinematic collaborations were born. Thus, in addition to the Golden Age directors, French cinema of the thirties is known for the significant work of scenarist-dialogists like Charles Spaak, Jacques and Pierre Prévert, and Henri Jeanson; cameramen like Georges Périnal, Eugen Schüfftan, and Kurt Courant; and art directors like Lazare Meerson, Eugène Lourié, Jacques Krauss, and Alexander Trauner. The most important mark of collaborative work in the French cinema of the thirties is the 1936 collective film, *La Vie est à nous,* directed by Jean Renoir (plus Jacques Becker, Henri Cartier-Bresson, J. P. Le-Chanois, and Jacques Brunius, among others), the original credits of which read "A film shot collectively by a team of technicians, artists, and workers" with no individual credits.

Given this environment of immensely productive collaborative activity, it is possible to see the Epstein/Benoît-Lévy association as typical of its time. And yet two things distinguish it from its collective context. In the first place, the scenarists, cameramen, and art directors all worked on different projects with different filmmakers at different times. Thus a writer like Charles Spaak is credited with major scenarios for Feyder, Renoir, Duvivier, and Grémillon, while the set designs of Lazare Meerson, for example, are found in films by Clair, Feyder, Duvivier, and Allégret, often with very different stylistic emphases. In contrast, all of Epstein's work as a director is done with Benoît-Lévy; both Epstein and Benoît-Lévy share the title of "co-director," an equality of function that stands apart from the other collaborations. The second difference emerges from the first: Where traditional histories often accord secondary status to writers, cameramen, art directors, and the like—in an ideological assertion of the individual as auteur— this background status has been conferred on Epstein on the basis of her sex. Therefore, while the context of collaboration in the thirties perhaps facilitated collective work for Epstein and Benoît-Lévy, the larger cultural bias based on gender made it more difficult to acknowledge Epstein's particular contribution.

It is within the aesthetic context of Poetic Realism that the films of Epstein and Benoît-Lévy can be understood as representative expressions of their time, but discussions of Poetic Realism itself are fraught with problems from the start. Although there is an acknowledged tendency—a set of characteristics that gives films of this period their "typically French" allure—there are two contrasting definitions of the Poetic Realist cinema. There is general agreement as to the "poetry" embodied in the lyricism of these films, however, the precise nature of the "realism" that they seem to project continues to be argued. Dudley Andrew paraphrases Grémillon, who, according to Andrew, borrows his key phrase from Bazin on Renoir: "French cinema is surpassingly realist and most French when it brings out formerly hidden relations between 'objects and beings,' between the outer world and the inner."[7] Yet two very distinct conceptions of this realist tendency emerge, depending on whether the "outer" or the "inner" world is emphasized. In emphasizing the former, the first strain's populism of subject and setting—its attention to quotidian detail—conveys a vitality and closeness to life that the French film designer Léon Barsacq has called (in relation to Clair's *Sous les toits de Paris*, 1930, actually a precursor of the movement, but Renoir's *Le Crime de Monsieur Lange*, 1936, could do as well) "the image of a good-natured people's Paris."[8] In films of this category there is always an element of social critique, a vision of the complexity of life tempered by astute class analysis and an attentiveness to the intersecting web of economic and social factors. In emphasizing the "inner" world, on the other hand, the second strain projects a pervasive atmosphere of fatality, one that film historian Michel Marie describes as "a tragedy based on an individualistic problematic which gives way to failure and bitterness, this with a background of metaphysical dimensions."[9] Two examples are Carné's *Quai des Brumes* (1938) and *Le Jour se lève* (1939). Here a rigorous inevitability in the narrative is matched by a decor of foggy shadows, mysterious nocturnal streets, objects glistening with rain or mist—in short, an urban environment charged with angst. Andrew summarizes this contradiction between populism and fatality in a formulation which suggests that the very interaction of these two strains is at the core of the aesthetic definition: "The tension between the drive toward realism and an impulse to transcend or essentialize reality is the defining characteristic of poetic realism."[10]

Both strains of Poetic Realism find their definitions bound up with set design—a harmonizing of action and atmosphere that makes every detail of decor highly charged with significance. Whether it is the vibrant social fabric of French working-class life or the damp nights and heavy atmosphere of a hostile, alien universe, the Poetic Realists' emphasis on set design meant that location provided more than simple background ambience: it was the signifying texture of the film itself. Lazare Meerson is said to have transformed French film design through his imagination, virtuosity, and careful attention to closely observed detail. His first work with both Feyder and Clair demonstrated his considerable talent and set the precedent for making a film's atmosphere function as a character itself. For Clair's *Sous les toits de Paris*—a film that set the tone for Poetic Realism although it is not actually considered part of the movement itself—he created a large set depicting a corner of an old Parisian faubourg, extending the realism of sets he had devised for Clair's *The Italian Straw Hat* (1927), and firmly establishing the idea that national character could be conveyed by significant decor. Barsacq, whose definition of Poetic Realism fits well into the first category, claims that Meerson's work was a major factor in these films' characteristic style. The meticulous care in documenting his sets enabled Meerson to provide a new standard of authenticity for French film design, yet he was also capable of a kind of artistic abstraction and stylization that made these sets something more than "realistic." Another film whose use of "significantly Parisian" decor makes it fairly radiate with the "Frenchness" and vitality of the first category of Poetic Realism is Renoir's *Le Crime de Monsieur Lange*. Here, too, there is a mixture of authentic detail with a kind of condensed stylization. The bustling central courtyard (designed by Jean Castanier, who also co-wrote the scenario) created an evocatively picturesque and proletarian atmosphere that Sadoul praises for its skillful depiction of "the Paris of *concierges*, laundresses, and printshop workers, like the ones already seen in Emile Zola or Auguste Renoir,"[11] both masters of their respective realist traditions of literary and pictorial representation.

Set design in the second category of Poetic Realism is best exemplified by the work of Alexander Trauner—whose artistic direction for both *Quai des Brumes* and *Le Jour se lève* represents an apotheosis of the atmospheric style, for it is thanks to these decors that a psychological and symbolic dimension reverberates throughout each film's realist texture. This is due, in some sense, to the fact that Trauner had a distinctive and personal method of freely utilizing documentary material, a mode of interpretation that gave his sets a realistic, authentic appearance while maintaining a forcefully suggestive dimension. Trauner's sets define a certain quality of the French quotidian that is powerfully infused with an air of fatality, a paradoxical blend of minutely detailed realism with symbolic, suggestive effects.

A cinema of atmospheres, Poetic Realism placed its meticulous observation of the random detail in the service of expressive ends, combining works of great lyrical beauty with subtle psychological insight. The concern with decor and the tone it could set had its corollary in the dramatic function of environment. So much so, in fact, that the integration of ambience and theme, of set design and script, would become a defining feature of the movement itself: "[U]nlike the Germans, for whom deranged inner states or impulses served as pretexts for imagistic conjurings, and unlike Americans, for whom melodrama and plot resolution became ends in themselves, the French poetic realists remained firmly within the world of the everyday, even as they let the atmosphere of the everyday become the final dramatic point. In modulating through strong tones . . . French poetic realism arrived at an aesthetic balance, [a balance] which . . . insists on a relation between character and decor that is so strong it radically reduces the function of plot."[12]

This reciprocity of character and milieu forms the thematic matrix of each Poetic Realist film, for as environment impinges powerfully on the lives of its inhabitants, it is this consistent interaction that generates the text. This is equally true for films that fall into the first category as for the second. The collective or popular protagonist of the first strain of films must invariably deal with situations resulting from social circumstances, and the very interconnectedness of the proletarian milieu provides the atmosphere which is the drama itself. The second type of film focuses on the doomed, alienated hero, a pessimistic loner who inevitably succumbs to the fatality imbued in every aspect of the surroundings. It is from this latter strain that Poetic Realism derives its characteristic aura of anxiety and meta-physical ennui, but it is also here that the overwhelming aesthetic cohesion and economy of means associated with the movement finds its purest expression.

In either case, the "atmospheric totality" generated in both types of film signifies an integration of action and milieu that speaks profoundly of French life and culture of the time. It is difficult to precisely define what is peculiarly French about such an atmosphere, to specify—in terms of a national identity and style—what connects such different cinematic currents under the single rubric of Poetic Realism. Not clearly a movement, school, or style, although it has been identified as all three, it is nonetheless quite evidently a national cinema, one undeniably French in texture and tone. And it is precisely this "Frenchness" that is relevant for an argument about resistance, for in constructing a body of work so characteristic of their culture, these filmmakers offer a cinema at the opposite pole of its Hollywood counterpart.

However, efforts to determine a national style are complicated by a kind of critical vagueness: By what parameters can the construction of this "Frenchness" be defined? A look at the economic context of one aspect of French production in the thirties might provide a possible way of categorizing stylistic alternatives—elements that produced the characteristic French feel of these films. For purposes of this discussion, I will consider Marie Epstein and Jean Benoît-Lévy's production methods against the background of an established mode of mass-production, a working system which, although having been abandoned by 1934, had set the tone for the rapid creation of stylistically neutral films for wide consumption.

With the advent of sound came the construction of giant American film factories near Paris, most notably Paramount's "European Hollywood" at Joinville-le-Pont, a Paris suburb. In the early thirties, these studios, with their numerous Hollywood directors and technicians, mass-produced each sound film in as many as fourteen or fifteen different language versions for distribution throughout the world. The Paramount formula and its assembly line techniques consisted of general overall scenarios where details of dialogue were unimportant; interchangeable casts of different nationalities; cheap and easily constructed sets; and cosmopolitan subjects to appeal to a generalized international audience. The accelerated production tempo of this rigidly organized, factory-style system could provide finished films within the space of two or three weeks. Although all but a few of these studios were closed by 1933, and Paramount itself went bankrupt in 1934 (having produced primarily boulevard comedies and frothy social satires until the end), it is against this background of a certain type of culturally unspecified mass-produced film that the carefully crafted, collectively produced works of Poetic Realism and other French films of the thirties, with their unmistakable populist appeal, emerged. Although there is no direct relation of response to the Hollywood system on the part of these latter films,[13] their individually tailored quality and their specifically cinematic creation (as opposed to those films "fabricated like canned goods")[14] gives them the mark of a decisively French alternative to Hollywood.

The first area in which this can be seen concerns the written script. At a time when early sound production meant exciting new possibilities for the use of dialogue, the French were at first alarmed by its prospective ability to reinforce U.S. dominance: "Must we look forward to the day when American sound films will spread over the world, submerge

it, and drown national productions?"[15] This was not simply idle paranoia, for an unnamed American filmmaker had reputedly set the tone
by making the claim that "sound film will not reduce our market in
France, because, in six months, all those people who are interested in
movies will speak American."[16] The specter of Hollywood with its
standardized productions had found its concrete manifestation in the
uniform scenarios of European Paramount. Written to be filmed in
multiple language versions for interchangeable national casts, scripts
had to have a universal dialogue without the national specificity that
regional dialect, informal conversation, and slang could provide. Sequencing, for example, might consist of one general shot to be used
in all of the versions, followed by repeated scenes acted by the different
national casts. Thus, generalized dramatic situations found no use for
the particular words and phrases of spoken dialogue and for the
national character that went along with them.

In contrast, French cinema of the thirties is known as a writers'
cinema. The work of scenarist-dialoguists Jeanson, Spaak, and Prévert
had much to do with this, as they created original scripts for specifically
cinematic texts. Rather than producing adaptations, something that
would have left the cinema basically tied to theatrical roots, these
writers constructed works that emphasized the filmic aspects of their
construction, a foregrounding of *film as film* in a musical construction
of mood, atmosphere, and tone. And part of this ambience is set by
meticulous attention to culturally specific dialogue, as language is
inflected with local expressions, accents, and slang—the popular spoken language of the working-class revealing the social basis of linguistic
practice and contributing to the overall feeling of the film.

The Epstein/Benoît-Lévy films are exemplary of this in the characters' pervasive use of slang. Thus in *La Maternelle,* one important
contribution to the film's atmosphere is the babble of the school children, which makes particular use of street language, familiar expressions, and ungrammatical phrases. Several sequences that appear to
have little direct bearing on the narrative itself function, instead, as
fragments of naturalistic detail, the children's comments serving to
enrich the ambience of the film and to give it its "Parisian" quality. As
a consequence, one level of the film defies translation. For example, a
typical interaction early in the film between Rose and a little boy with
a black eye ("Ça te fait mal, eh?" "Je chanterais beaucoup plus que ça,
hein") translates into subtitles as the simple display of juvenile bravado
rather than the slang it is, a particular form of Parisian slum street-
smartness prematurely visited on a five-year-old.

Epstein maintains that written dialogue served primarily as a point of departure for spoken language in the film, particularly where the children were concerned. During the filming, the children were familiarized with the parts of the story in which they were to act, and then encouraged to respond spontaneously. Sequences were rehearsed as little as possible in order to retain that spontaneity; thus as is typical of French films of this time, dialogue achieves the naturalness of ordinary speech, and the reality of popular language enriches the poetic texture of the film.

The second area that might provide some insight into the development of a specifically French tradition of filmmaking in the thirties concerns actors. By the middle of the decade, French cinema was solidly an actor's cinema. Rather than operating on the model of the Hollywood star system, in which certain actors were linked to particular studios (and thereby to the production apparatus) by contract, French film production was able to rely on the popular appeal of certain well-known stars in order to attract audiences to small, diversified productions. Because of this, and the dispersed production situation discussed earlier, film projects could be created on the basis of viewers' interest in the actors rather than in the film itself. The popular "Saturday night cinema" abounds with the names of famous French actors and instantly recognized character types, even in minor productions.

Raymond Borde distinguishes two generations of film actors in the thirties, all of whom retained a certain degree of power over their films because of their free-agent status from production to production.[17] Experienced Parisian stage actors, both from legitimate and boulevard theater, such as Gaby Morlay, Jules Berry, Elvire Popesco, Harry Bauer, and Pierre Fresnay, were able to fill the void left by silent film stars unable to make the transition to sound. By 1935, a new generation of actors emerged, actors such as Jean Gabin, Danielle Darrieux, Jean-Pierre Aumont, and Arletty. Trained specifically in the cinema and skilled at developing a particular naturalistic, popular acting style, these are the figures most readily identified with French cinema's Golden Age. And of course, instant audience recognition and appeal were possessed by such character actors as Carette, Marcel Levesque, and Saturnin Fabre, among others.

But another aspect concerning actors—one more relevant in terms of the contrast I am suggesting between mass-produced culturally neutral films and the specificity of the French tradition—involves the authenticity and "freshness" to be gained from using nonprofessional actors. The formula for mass-production involved either interchangeable casts from different countries or established stars with solid international reputations. Against this background, French directors seeking a characteristic national tone could use nonprofessionals—ordinary people involved in their daily activities—in order to achieve the variety of French life itself. Using nonprofessionals necessitated a kind of reciprocal work between the director and the actor, as each worked equally to produce a "character" over a "performance." This is another important aspect of the teamwork that typified French cinema of the thirties (films were often referred to as being made by a team—"une équipe"), in which the final film was the result of a collective effort rather than the distinguished work of a significant individual—filmmaker or actor. This reciprocity between actor and director was thus another facet in the creation of the "atmospheric totality" that marks these films.

The example of Epstein and Benoît-Lévy can be seen in *La Maternelle* and *La Mort du cygne,* both films in which the directors use the spontaneity and naturalness of children to the best advantage. Each film literally bursts with life as the children set a tone of uncontained excitement for the dramatic action. This serves a dual purpose. First, the atmosphere of vitality created by the Parisian slum children contributes to a defining feature of what I have called the first strain of Poetic Realism—the creation of a populist texture of life over and above the particulars of the narrative. Second, this atmosphere helps the films achieve what Epstein sees as the primary vocation of cinema—a means par excellence for capturing life: "The truly fundamental quality of the cinema is its ability to capture life."[18]

This is apparent in Epstein's discussion of the pre-production procedures in making their films. Their kind of detailed analysis of a location and its inhabitants (the school for *La Maternelle,* the Opéra for *La Mort du cygne*) was more than an effort at verisimilitude, it was a fundamental structuring element of the films themselves: "It's a sort of principle of approaching the truth of things: By starting from the truth you are able to draw inspiration from life itself. What really touches us is to show things which are real, which are close to life. Or better, a kind of poetry which escapes life, but yet which takes life as its starting point. A poetry which has its roots in life, which isn't conventional, or artificial—that is what really touches us."

A primary factor in Epstein's and Benoît-Lévy's ability to attain this feeling for "the truth of things" was their successful orchestration of the work of untrained actors—especially children—into the overall aesthetic structure of their films. For *La Mort du cygne,* they lived backstage at the Opéra for one month in order to get a sense of the daily milieu of the young ballerinas. For *La Maternelle,* children were transported from a real nursery school in a crowded, impoverished section of Paris to the studio, where a set had been constructed. Epstein says that it was the children themselves who transposed the atmosphere of the nursery school to the studio.

The naturalness provided by the children was augmented by Epstein's and Benoît-Lévy's insistence on a form of acting that was as untainted by professional and artificial mannerisms as possible. Madeleine Renaud, whose experience in La Comédie Française produced too declamatory a style, was encouraged to "forget about her profession" in order to attain a more lifelike characterization. When describing this in his book, Benoît-Lévy emphasizes the importance of a nontheatrical acting style, noting that "the story she would be living was more important than the words."[19] Benoît-Lévy details his and Epstein's efforts to extract naturalistic, "lived" performances from actors by having them absorb the locales of the films rather than emphasizing the dramatic possibilities of their roles.

The filmmakers found that the contact with nonprofessionals, chosen from the environments in which their films were set (the ballet, the nursery school, the university, the Moroccan desert, and so forth), had an important effect on the professional actors, enabling them to perform in a more convincing (because less artificial) way.[20] Elaborating on the importance of improvisation, Epstein uses an example from one of her brother's films about Breton fishermen, *Finis terrae* (1929), noting that Epstein tore up his original scenario and recomposed the film with the collaboration of the fishermen themselves. "It's the same for all truly sincere filmmakers," she concludes. Thus, the use of nonprofessionals was much more than a drive toward authenticity—it was a source of aesthetic and thematic coherence. The meticulously detailed milieu, an important source of the film's atmosphere, had thematic significance as well, for each of these films, in their texture of the quotidian, speaks of the continual impact of environment on the social beings who constitute a culture.

A third area of consideration in determining the precise national quality of French cinema of the thirties is set design, an area in which it made a profound contribution: "If any narrative cinema . . . can be said to make a difference to film art, then poetic realism did indeed alter our conception of decor. . . . Every element of the sets of these films challenges us with its verisimilitude. Nothing by itself seems forced or out of place. And yet all inessential props and lines have been systematically removed until the decor assumes the role of a 'figure' representing a key emotional complex. . . . "[21] With French cinema of the thirties, the physical setting of the action attained symbolic proportions, not only in terms of defining a national character, but of conveying an ambient constellation of attitudes as well. For this reason, art direction became not simply a matter of conceiving a background decor, but of designing sets that would have a significant narrative function, sets that would "speak" the dreams and desires of the characters who inhabited them. Clearly, these sets differed from the culturally anonymous decors of the mass-produced cinematic spectacle.

Using Joinville as a model for Hollywood-style assembly-line production, it is possible to determine a certain formula for set design in the dominant cinema. Working on the same principle that necessitated interchangeable casts of actors, the Joinville studios required films to be made with cheap and easily constructed sets, usually consisting of geographically unlocalizable atmospheres of cosmopolitan luxury, such as nightclubs and hotel ballrooms. In addition to the generalized appeal they had for large international audiences, these sets had the virtue of being able to be easily set up and dismantled, thereby enhancing the speed of production.

By contrast, French cinema of the thirties is known for the authenticity of its detail and the evocative power of its decors. Every locale—from Paris bistros to seedy hotels, from the canals of the 10th arrondissement to the pensions on the streets of Nice—radiates cultural specificity. Thanks to the consummate skill of its art direction, this cinema would be recognized throughout the world as indigenously and characteristically French. The lyrical combination of precisely recorded detail and poetic evocation produced a cinema that was fundamentally a "drama of locale." It found its fullest expression in the work of Meerson, Trauner, and Krauss, but it was not without historical precedents.

Already in the 1890s, Georges Méliès was using photographic documents and sketches of actual sites in order to paint the backdrops of his reconstructions of historic events. His constant care for realism led him, for example, to visit Westminster Abbey, enlisting the aid of clergymen and an authentic chamberlain in the filming a re-enactment of the coronation of Edward VII. Then, as plywood and staff constructions replaced painted backdrops and new specialists such as carpenters, sculptors, and housepainters were brought into set design, the impetus for authenticity in films increased. A typical example is the publicity for a 1911 film that promised a "realistic drama on the life of miners": "The Eclair company brought from Charleroi a crew of miners who built a whole series of galleries on the Epinay estate, in exact conformity with the layout of a real mine. Efforts were made to keep as close as possible to reality."[22]

Later, the desire for authenticity in set design and the concomitant interest in depicting the everyday milieu of the proletariat produced three major works initiating this realist trend in narrative feature films: Louis Delluc's *Fièvre* (1921), Jacques Feyder's *Crainquebille* (1922), and Jean Epstein's *Coeur fidèle* (1923). All three of these films successfully integrated location shooting with studio sets, producing works whose popular nature of subject and setting endowed them with a particular kind of populist poetry. Although Feyder and Epstein were responsible for the production design in their two films, *Fièvre* benefitted from the work of a professional art director, and as Léon Barsacq points out, has the distinction of being the first French film to emphasize the creation of ambience in its construction: "For the first time in France, a film strove for atmosphere, in its choice of characters from the lowest strata of Marseilles society, in the lighting, and in the realistic sets designed by Robert Jules Garnier."[23] Robert Mallet-Stevens, one of the first designers to use contemporary architecture in film sets (particularly in L'Herbier's 1923 film *L'Inhumaine*), summed up this characteristic attitude toward set design as articulate detail in the following way: "A film set, in order to be a good set, must act. Whether realistic or expressionist, modern or ancient, it must play its part. The set must present the character before he has even appeared. It must indicate his social position, his tastes, his habits, his life-style, his personality. The set must be intimately linked with the action."[24]

Epstein and Benoît-Lévy were clearly interested in carrying on this tradition. Three of their sound films used production design by major French art directors. *Le Coeur de Paris* was designed by Hugues Laurent, who worked with French film decor very near its inception in the teens, first at Pathé and then at Eclair. During the thirties Laurent worked on several important Renoir films, notably *Boudu sauvé des eaux* and *Les Bas-Fonds* (with Eugène Lourié). The Alpine chalet sets for *Altitude 3200* were designed by Jacques Krauss, known for his powerfully evocative sets in several Duvivier films considered to be classics of Poetic Realism (*La Bandéra, La Belle équipe,* and *Pépé le Moko*). Epstein and Benoît-Lévy's last feature film, *Le Feu de paille,* was designed by the same man who had designed the sets for *Fièvre*, Robert Jules Garnier, an art director very highly regarded by Barsacq for, among other things, his work with Louis Feuillade. Barsacq maintains that Feuillade had a decisive role "in setting a section of French cinema on the path to poetic realism" with *Fantômas* (1913-14), *Les Vampyrs* (1915), and *Judex* (1917), for he combined detailed interiors with evocative shots of Parisian streets to generate an atmosphere of mystery and the fantastic, creating an emotional and psychological aura that transcended the fullness of the naturalistic detail.

Yet while these three films had sets designed by well-known art directors, the four films comprising the central section of Epstein and Benoît-Lévy's work appear to have been designed by relatively minor artists. *Itto,* their only film shot on location, does not even list an art director. Both Epstein and Benoît-Lévy extensively describe their research and documentation for the remaining three films: *La Maternelle, La Mort du cygne,* and *Hélène.* Because these three are considered to be their most important films—and are, in fact, the ones in which the creation of ambience plays a major signifying role—it seems likely that Epstein and Benoît-Lévy had a substantial part in the production design themselves.

Both co-directors wanted the atmosphere in these films to have a significant function, and therefore chose a project of faithful observation of documentary material in order to achieve the maximum effect from random details. They carefully researched the sets for these films, visiting (and in some cases living in) the milieux and studying the people as they performed their daily routines. Epstein describes this procedure for *La Mort du cygne* in the following way: "It wasn't the Opéra which came to the studio, it's we who went to the Opéra, and who lived for an entire month at the Opéra, from morning to night, in the wings, in the loges, in the large rooms where the ballerinas worked. We really lived the Opéra. . . . In order to prepare the scenario we spent weeks noting things down, observing details, on the spot, noting things which later helped us in the editing, and in the *découpage.*"

Likewise, for *La Maternelle,* Epstein and Benoît-Lévy spent several months at different schools in the most crowded, impoverished parts of Paris, observing the children and gaining their confidence. In this way they were able to construct a set that both functioned dramatically (as an intricate part of the film's emotive texture) and provided a kind of authenticity through an abundance of detail. And because the studio sets were exact replicas of the schools visited, they offered a faithful reconstruction of the framework and atmosphere of the children's everyday lives. The decors, therefore, in all of these films were able not only to render a "sense of place" with a sensitivity, attentiveness, and intimacy unknown to the more uniform backgrounds of the mass-produced spectacle, but they were also able to attain a powerful degree of cultural specificity.

And it is this intimacy that figures in the fourth category of comparison, for French cinema of the thirties can be distinguished by its subject matter. To the enormity of the large Hollywood-style productions with their cosmopolitan subjects and generalized international appeal was posed the more ordinary and domestic scale of the French quotidian, the socially or economically marginal, and the working class. In a sense, it is as if the intimate and popular quality of these craftsmanlike films was reflected in the very material that these films chose to represent. Both types of Poetic Realism shared this interest in the everyday, and in the subjective and emotional atmosphere that the concentration on the random and fleeting moments of life could evoke. Thus Sadoul can praise Renoir's 1935 film *Toni* for its sensitive portrayal of ordinary daily life, its quasi-documentary depiction of the immigrant worker's situation, and its naturalistic use of both French countryside and spoken dialect as "opening . . . the way for an authentic realism,"[25] while Andrew can consider Grémillon's *La Petite Lise* (1931) as an initiator of Poetic Realism because it "sought a tone in which a simple melodrama would suggest a clarifying rhythm capable of universalizing the situation and our response to it."[26]

With the exception of *Itto,* all of the Epstein/Benoît-Lévy films concentrate on everyday gestures and intimate themes, a fact that led one reviewer to say that the directors were "more adept at miniatures than large-scale murals."[27] But more important than the familiar proportions of the subjects they treat, their attentiveness to daily realities points to a defining characteristic of French film of the thirties, for these intimate details of daily life are made to function narratively in a poetic texture that combines the reality of precisely defined ambience with the subjective techniques of the most lyrical cinema of the twenties. Details taken from life do more than enhance the realist texture of the film; they can have a structuring function in the overall organization of the text, as two examples from *La Maternelle* illustrate.

The film opens with an incident in which little Marie Coeuret is devastated because Madame Paulin has caught a mouse in the school's assembly room and has dumped it into the stove. Marie's anger and her tears identify her as a spirited and sensitive child, but beyond that, the mouse initiates an image-paradigm of animals that will circulate throughout the film, occuring in narrative episodes (a rabbit), in conversation (baby wolves), and in the surrounding decor (a canary), in a reiteration of metaphoric figures that gives poetic density to the text. Even more important, however, is the fact that it is by way of a certain repetition of this motif—Madame Paulin's restaging of the scenario of a trapped and forsaken mouse—that the film's resolution comes about.

Other aspects of the film's realist material take on important symbolic functions as well, making the film proceed in terms of the articulation of visual figures instead of the traditional linear narrative progression. Points of locale become structuring matrixes as the film interweaves associative chains from the particulars of everyday detail. Thus a second-hand dealer's shop window in which a model ocean-liner is displayed becomes the site of the child's longing just as it signals her reiterated fear of abandonment. And charged with symbolic significance, the minutia of everyday life attains an emotive intensity infinitely more affecting than those dramas of grander scale.

Finally, although my discussion here has attempted to demonstrate how Epstein's and Benoît-Lévy's films are strongly rooted in their time and typical of the national cinematic identity that French filmmakers of the thirties sought, it is important to note a major difference—a difference which is located, significantly, around a certain representation of the woman and the conception of female sexuality that it implies. As I noted in the previous chapter, what distinguishes the Epstein oeuvre from the work of her contemporaries is the concentration on a kind of subject matter more relevant to women's lives, and with that a distinctive sensibility which builds dramatic intensity on relations of the feminine rather than on those of conventional romantic tropes. Taken in the light of the foregoing definitions of Poetic Realism, some interesting conclusions can be drawn. For while I have established that the Epstein/Benoît-Lévy films partake of the populist strain, *both* categories of Poetic Realist films involve a highly codified sexualized representation of the female figure—one that is nowhere apparent in the Epstein/Benoît-Lévy work.

A good example of a film that combines both populist and fatalist trends is Renoir's *La Chienne* (1931), a film which he himself has said "came near to the style that I call poetic realism."[28] In it, the "bitch" of the title causes the downfall of a pathetic soul: "The story in a nutshell was about the downward drift of a clerk who robs his employer to satisfy the demands of a little tart."[29] The film is a texture of culturally precise detail, from the warring class accents of the dialogue to the gurgle of Parisian sewers and the variety of neighborhood people in the streets. But more important for my argument, the fate of the doomed hero—although in this case he possesses a little less than the moody force of the typical Poetic Realist protagonist of the second trend—is bound inextricably with the destructive sexual energy of the femme fatale. And it is precisely this disruptive sexuality which the female represents that forms the textual center of the Poetic Realist films. No matter what the individual film is ostensibly about, it needs the troubling presence of the woman to generate the conflict. The figure of the feminine, defined in dominant terms, is the mainspring of any and all narratives, which may differ from text to text.

This production of femininity across the representational terrain of the Poetic Realist text tells us much about the conventional function of the woman's image within the operations of the cinematic apparatus itself. For, in spite of the decidedly "French" tone, the pervasive cultural atmosphere of these thirties' films—and they do represent a significant and highly visible French alternative to Hollywood production—the female figure functions in much the same way in films produced both in Hollywood and in France. Always the sexual center, a figure of erotic force, the woman and her function are continually and irrevocably defined in masculine terms. Whether it be as the femme fatale (in the literal sense of the association) whose disruptive alterity is tied to the hero's destruction (either through innocent but ill-fated love as in *Quai des Brumes,* or through mysterious attraction as in *Gueule d'Amour*), or as the desired woman who implicitly engenders the social collapse (as in *La Belle équipe*), or as the elusive erotic object around which masculine heroes stabilize their desire (as in *Pépé le Moko* or *Hotel du Nord*), this sexualized conception remains constant, a particular representation of femininity at the heart of the Poetic Realist text.

However, the films of the Epstein oeuvre redefine femininity from the start. Although the woman exists as desired object, the subjective source of that desire is radically different. Particularly in the three sound films that constitute the core of the work—*La Maternelle, La Mort du cygne,* and *Hélène*—the relations of the maternal form the primary emotive crux. The female figure is thus still constituted as central to the representation, while the terms of that centrality are reformulated along different lines. Therefore, examination of Epstein's paradoxical status in relation to the aesthetic and economic context of her time yields the following conclusion.

Although a substantial and convincing argument can be made about the cultural difference of French filmmaking in the thirties—as a

cinema that poses a challenge to the dominant institution of Hollywood—we must look to another level to find an alternative that profoundly reworks the signifying structures of the cinema as an apparatus of desire. And it is precisely in the Epstein oeuvre and its
articulation of female desire that the distinctive cinematic imprint of
"another voice" can be found. As the editors of *Re-Vision: Essays in
Feminist Film Criticism* maintain, the project of feminist film theory
involves a displacement of critical emphasis "from 'images of' to the
axis of vision itself—to the modes of organizing vision and hearing
which result in the production of that 'image.' "[30] The analysis in the
following chapter—an analysis of *La Maternelle*'s reorganization of
the gaze, its redefinition of the site of spectatorial desire, and its
rearticulation of the structure of the fantasm—will demonstrate just
how profound an alternative that critical displacement yields.

NOTES

1. Léon Moussinac, *Panoramique du cinéma* (Paris: Au Sans Pareil, 1929),
p. 17. See also Moussinac, *L'Age ingrât du cinéma* (Paris: Les Editeurs Français
Réunis, 1967), p. 238.
2. Raymond Borde, " 'The Golden Age': French Cinema of the 30s," in
Rediscovering French Film, ed. Mary Lea Bandy (New York: Museum of Modern
Art, 1983), pp. 66–81; here, p. 67.
3. Raymond Chirat, *Catalogue des films français de long métrage: Films sonores
de fiction 1929–1939* (Brussels: Cinémathèque Royale de Belgique, 1975).
4. Borde, "The Golden Age," p. 67.
5. Georges Sadoul, *Le Cinéma français 1890–1962* (Paris: Flammarion,
1962), p. 67.
6. Sadoul, *Le Cinéma français*, p. 71
7. Dudley Andrew, "Poetic Realism," in *Rediscovering French Film*, ed.
Bandy, pp. 115–19; here, p. 115.
8. Léon Barsacq, *Le Décor du film* (Paris: Editions Seghers, 1970); translated
as *Caligari's Cabinet and Other Grand Illusions*, edited and revised by Elliott Stein
(Boston: New York Graphic Society, 1976), p. 76.
9. Michel Marie, "Les Années trente," in *Défense du cinéma français* (Paris:
La Maison de la Culture de la Seine-St-Denis, January–March 1975), p. 41.
10. Dudley Andrew, "Sound in France: The Origins of a Native School,"
Yale French Studies, no. 60 (1980): 94–114; here, p. 109
11. Sadoul, *Le Cinéma français*, p. 72.
12. Andrew, "Poetic Realism," pp. 118–19.
13. In fact, in "Sound in France," Dudley Andrew convincingly argues that
"far from being a belated strategy coming in the wake of the collapse of
Paramount and the retreat of Tobis, French realism, sponsored by French
producers, was one immediate response to the potentials of sound." These

potentials, represented by the work of Renoir in *La Chienne* and Grémillon in *La Petite Lise* (both 1931), although "submerged for a while by the loftier claims of Clair and Pagnol and by the stronger advertizing of Paramount and Tobis who backed them, . . . would ultimately have the more lasting effect."

14. Sadoul, *Le Cinéma français*, p. 54.

15. Jean Allary, "Le Film sonore et ses problèmes," *L'Europe nouvelle*, February 9, 1929, p. 167.

16. Quoted by René Jeanne in "L'Invasion cinématographique américaine," *Revue des deux mondes*, February 15, 1930, p. 868.

17. Borde, "The Golden Age," pp. 70–72.

18. Epstein's comments are taken from interviews conducted in 1977. See chapter 5.

19. Jean Benoît-Lévy, *Les Grandes missions du cinéma;* translated as *The Art of the Motion Picture* (New York: Coward McCann, 1946), p. 158.

20. This mixture of nonprofessionals and actors occurred to such an extent on *La Maternelle* that the children, not realizing that they were working with real actors, treated Madeleine Renaud and Mady Berry as if they were actual nursery school maids. Another incident from the production of *La Maternelle* illustrates the extent to which naturalness was emphasized. Very little makeup was used; thus when Alice Tissot (who played the principal of the school) noticed an excessively made-up woman on the set, she told her to wash her face. Unfortunately, the woman was actually a nursery school director visiting the set.

21. Andrew, "Poetic Realism," p. 119.

22. As quoted in Barsacq, *Caligari's Cabinet*, p. 14.

23. Barsacq, *Caligari's Cabinet*, p. 40.

24. Robert Mallet-Stevens, *L'Art cinématographique* (Paris: Félix Alcan, 1927); as quoted in Barsacq, *Caligari's Cabinet*, p. 126.

25. Sadoul, *Le Cinéma français*, p. 70.

26. Andrew, "Sound in France," p. 110.

27. *New York Times*, January 29, 1936.

28. Jean Renoir, *My Life and My Films* (New York, Atheneum, 1974), p. 105.

29. Renoir, *My Life*, p. 109.

30. Mary Ann Doane, Patricia Mellencamp, and Linda Williams, eds., *Re-Vision: Essays in Feminist Film Criticism* (Frederick, Md.: University Publications of America and the American Film Institute, 1984), p. 6.

SEVEN

Nursery/Rhymes:
Primal Scenes in *La Maternelle*

To indicate what fantasmatic
weft supports the textual weave. . . . [1]

LA MATERNELLE CONTEXTUALIZES ITS FOCUS on the affective relationship
between a maternal figure and the female child within a detailed,
highly realistic description of life in the Parisian slums. It thus combines crucial elements in a dramatic psychic scenario of familial relations with the populist French films' concern for contemporary social
problems and the accuracy of quotidian detail. The double entendre
of the film's title reinforces the thematic duality of the film: Literally
the "nursery school" where most of the film's action takes place, *la
maternelle* symbolically refers to the emotive relationship that constitutes the film's core. As previously described, a little girl, having been
abandoned by her prostitute mother, relives the trauma of this separation when her new maternal figure (a maid at the school) becomes
engaged. The child's witnessing of the proposal triggers an unsuccessful suicide attempt, which is rendered in a series of images representing actual, remembered, and fantasy scenes of couples. *Nursery rhymes:*
In *La Maternelle*, the trauma of the child's vision of the "parental"
couple is repeated and rhymed in a structure of concentric fantasmatic
scenes, and it is this psychic reiteration which forms the basis of the
film's textual system.

The Three Dramas

The film's plot is fairly straightforward in its causal linkage of narrative
events.[2] Circumstances force a young woman named Rose (Madeleine

Renaud in her first film role) to take a job as a cleaning lady at a nursery school. As the film begins, Rose is at a ball with her fiance; the next sequence opens as she is being interviewed by the principal of the school. The interview, which makes reference to Rose's abandonment by this fiance, is interrupted by a telephone call from Dr. Libois (Henri Debain), the school director who is also acting as its doctor.

Once hired, Rose enters the main schoolroom just after little Marie (Paulette Elambert) has tried to stop the other maid, the rotund and good-natured Madame Paulin (Mady Berry), from killing a trapped mouse by placing it on the stove burner. Little Marie develops a passionate crush on Rose, which becomes even more fierce when her own mother (Sylvette Fillacier) abandons her to run off with a man whom she's met in a cabaret. When the principal learns that Rose actually has a college degree, and thus ought to be a teacher rather than a maid, she says she must dismiss her. Dr. Libois then proposes marriage ("I've found a job for you. . . . "). Marie, despondent at what she interprets as a second abandonment, attempts suicide by throwing herself into the river.

She is rescued by a witness and subsequently revived by Madame Paulin in the school cantine. Dr. Libois makes his peace with her in a bit of heroism staged and instigated by Madame Paulin: He gains Marie's friendship and trust by freeing another mouse that has been caught. Rose joins them as they shake hands, and the drama is resolved in the last moments of the film, the triumphant ending of which is signalled by sprightly music over the image of happy children leaving school.

The second drama is that of the psychical conflict which structures the film; it traces the process whereby the female child is made to renounce exclusive possession of the maternal object and thus to accept the necessary union of the heterosexual couple. But where traditional Hollywood cinema casts this "happy sliding from the familial to the conjugal"[3] in Oedipal terms, here the focus is decidedly on maternal aspects of the psyche, and on the reciprocity of female desire which these aspects of the psyche entail—the little girl's longing for the mother, and, conversely, the woman's desiring relation to the child. Thus, although the Hollywood film's repeated project is the constitution of the culturally sanctioned marital couple, here such a unity can only function as resolution when the *child* acknowledges and thereby accepts it. The scenarization of psychic conflicts in *La Maternelle*, then, is articulated in terms of the female child's recognition of the heterosexual duality rather than the masculine hero's achievement of it, and this locates the film's central identificatory mechanism within the consciousness of the little girl.

The drama of the psyche that *La Maternelle* represents thus involves a process of transition from the dynamic reciprocity of mother and daughter to the mediations of the patriarchal third term, the child's renunciation of the maternal in the name of the cultural order of male-female relationships. Yet so powerful is the force of this primary relation of the maternal that the constitution of the couple which the narrative ostensibly achieves is continually displaced to secondary status by the textual processes of the film. This displacement occurs by means of three rhyming structures whose shifting symmetrical relations crystallize the narrative meaning. Each of the three core sequences—the mother's departure with the man in the cabaret, the proposal, and the suicide attempt—condenses the major thematic elements of the film in a kind of textual meshwork: the child's desire for maternal love, the heterosexual couple perceived by the child as an obstacle, rivalry for the maternal object, the child's perception of exclusion and abandonment, and the traumatic consequences of this perception. Each of the sequences is articulated through and structured around the point of view of the child, and, not arbitrarily, the child's vision always entails the scene of "sexual" activity by a "parental" couple. The repetition of symbolic configurations is mirrored by a repeated cinematic figure: Each of the three sequences is marked by a consistent and systematic use of the reverse-shot structure. Therefore, in each instance meaning is generated by a relay of looks, and the position of looking is emphatically and comprehensively defined as that of the child.

The third drama, the "drama of spectatorship" that the child's look entails, has several important consequences when considered in the light of feminist cinematic alternatives, for the repetition of the primal scene in these three scenarios of vision involves a transformation of the central enunciative structure of the cinema. This transformation yields "another" vision within the dominant apparatus by 1) defining the controlling point-of-view as that of the child, and thereby reorganizing the structure of the gaze; 2) locating the site of spectatorial desire not within the province of masculine imperatives, but in terms of feminine desire for the maternal object; and 3) rearticulating the structure of the fantasm such that the concentric reiteration of the primal scene fantasy replaces the teleology of the classical narrative and its Oedipal trajectory. Thus *La Maternelle* sustains a different logic, a different production of cinematic desire, and in so doing represents, perhaps, a greater challenge to the dominance of Hollywood than other more highly visible strategies of subversion would seem to imply.

As elaborated in the introduction to this book, classical cinema achieves its power on the basis of the production of a viewing subjectivity, a subjectivity defined in masculine terms. By restructuring the desiring look through repeated versions of the primal scene, *La Maternelle* is able to achieve a profound modification in the mechanisms of cinematic identification which produce this subjectivity. As I have maintained, viewer subjectivity in the cinema is continually inscribed by means of that most elusive of processes, the gaze. The theory of enunciation explains how, in some sense, the spectator is a "construction" of the apparatus, and how the desiring power of "the look" is built into the cinematic apparatus itself. It is in this sense that the cinema-spectator is an "artificial" construction, a specific effect of belief created by the cinematic apparatus as it articulates the signifying operations of the filmic text with the psychic organization of the viewing subject. Most often, the specific "regime of belief"—in which the spectator is positioned as the producer of the cinematic fiction—is activated by means of the point-of-view structure. Through this mobile visual exchange, the viewer is made to experience situations simultaneously with the characters by seeing the action from their different viewpoints. Conventionally, the point-of-view structure is dispersed, repeated, and varied across the film and its characters; in every case, it is a means of locking the spectator into the fantasmatic world projected on the screen. And, as film theory has pointed out, in the classical Hollywood cinema this distribution of looks, the organization of desiring vision, is located firmly within the terms of masculine subjectivity and patriarchal power.[4]

It is precisely an inversion of this power that the text of *La Maternelle* enacts. Because it is fantasy—and more specifically, the child's fantasy of the primal scene—that structures the film, rather than the masculine standard of the Oedipal regime, the film puts into play a counter-model of textual desire, one not organized according to a cultural and psychic logic that privileges the male. In *La Maternelle*, the mechanisms of spectator-involvement negotiated by point-of-view operate on two levels, each of which profoundly modifies its classical counterpart, for both primary and secondary identification powerfully coalesce in each primal scene, and in so doing, reorient the cinematic gaze. In terms of the narrative trajectory—the film's secondarized sequence of events— three instances depict the child's vision of the couple as she moves toward renunciation of the maternal in the name of the parental duality. For the spectator, this involves a form of "secondary identification," identification, that is, with the characters and the situations in the fiction. But this identification with *what is represented* is only possible once the spectator's "primary identification" is secured. In describing the encoding of the look in the cinematic apparatus, Jean-Louis Baudry outlines the formative coincidence of looks of camera, spectator, and character. "The spectator identifies less with what is represented, the spectacle itself, than with what stages the spectacle, makes it seen, obliging him to see what it sees; this is exactly the function taken over by the camera as a sort of relay."[5] This spectatorial identification with *that which renders visible* is achieved through a complex relay of point-of-view structures, a relay that constantly centers the look of the viewer in a comprehensive assumption of the projected scene.

This primary identification is evidenced in *La Maternelle* by the "drama of spectatorship" played out through the mechanism of the look. But it is also here that both primary and secondary identification are blended together with evolving complexity as the viewer's increased participation in the child's vision of the couple is engaged. It is thus through a series of primal scenes—within the diegesis, and in the viewer's situation—that the child's vision of the parental couple and the spectator's production of the cinematic fantasm come together. In this manner, the enunciative function of the look—which regulates the viewer's identification with both the image and the fiction—is made to operate so that an alternative vision, a feminine reorganization of the gaze, is achieved.

A look at these important "episodes of vision" in *La Maternelle* will aid in the analysis of the complex enunciative mechanisms which support this feminist restructuring of vision.[6] As I maintained, a tremendous condensation of effects is centered on the look of the female child. As the film builds in narrative intensity, the spectator is brought completely over to the side of this child, sharing her point of view and thus participating in her traumatic vision. This focus represents a significant departure from Léon Frapié's novel of the same name, on which the film is based. (Although the film's credits state that it is adapted from the novel that won the Prix Goncourt, it is really composed from incidents and episodes in several of Frapié's works.) Between 1900 and 1930, Frapié, a social reformer, wrote many texts concerning education and the very young, among them *Les Contes de la maternelle, L'Institutrice de province, L'Ecolière, La Boîte aux gosses, Gamins de Paris,* and of course, *La Maternelle.*

But although Frapié's novel centers on Rose, tracing her development from a well-educated but morally naive and unconcerned bourgeois student to a socially conscious and responsible woman, the film clearly emphasizes the child's point of view. In fact, the intensely charged relationship between Rose and Marie Coeuret is something created by Epstein and Benoît-Lévy in their scenario, existing only in the most skeletal form in the book. Although he was quite pleased with the film, Frapié was far less concerned with this sort of psychic dynamic than with the detailed description of social conditions. Furthermore, while the possibilities for female identification with the character of Rose and with her desire to have children are present in the film, they are relegated to a secondary position. The film is recentered and structured in such a way that the spectator is made to identify increasingly with the child, to see with the eyes of this child, and to participate in her fantasmatic vision. As such, the spectator is made to experience the intensity of the desire for the maternal object that such a constellation entails.

The Cabaret (Seduction)

The first of the primal scenes occurs in the cabaret sequence, the locus of Marie's first abandonment. It establishes a matrix of shot set-ups, angles, montage patterns, images, and figures that will be reiterated, in modified form, in the two later core sequences, the proposal and the suicide attempt. The unity and coherence of this segment are strongly marked in several ways. Punctuating devices, in the form of a close-up of an accordian and a fade to black, frame it. Music on the soundtrack—first the diegetic music of the cabaret, then melodic background music composed of themes in the cabaret—accompanies the sequence in its entirety. With the exception of one harshly whispered admonition ("Attention, la p'tite" [Watch out for the child]) and its gruff reply ("Bah, ces mômes me pigent pas. . . . " [These kids don't bother me. . . .]), there is no spoken dialogue throughout the sequence. And finally, the entire segment takes place outside of the school: the three places where it occurs—the smoky Paris bistro, a second-hand shop window, and little Marie's room—are all locations critical to the psychic scenario. They therefore resonate with symbolic intensity and contribute to the highly charged emotional atmosphere of this portion of the film. These factors all combine to create the sequence's profound systematicity and homogeneity, and when this unity is coupled with the striking and poetic use of close-ups, the sequence achieves the evocative power of a silent film, all the more so because it is embedded within the larger cinematic context of a uniquely experimental sound film.

The triadic eyeline exchange between mother, man, and child that takes place in this sequence truly constitutes the core of the film: It is in this important emotive relay of eyeline matches between "parental" couple and child that the textual threads of vision, knowledge, sexuality, and desire are most condensed. The exchange of glances is accompanied throughout by a chanteuse's song of passion and flight. As the mother and the man attempt to kiss, they are forcefully disrupted by the angry and forbidding look of the child.

At first the couple (in close-up) merely listens to the song as Marie begins to peel an orange. Then a close-up of legs seen from under the table discloses the woman's high-heeled foot caressing the man's pants leg. (Obviously, this shot is missing from the American prints of the film.) This acts as prelude to the attempted kiss that will ensue, in much the same way that its framing shot—a close-up of the same legs unhooking some eleven shots later—will indicate the prevention of this kiss. It is important to note that at this point in the film, these shots of legs seen from under the table depict that which the spectator alone can see, and that which the child must only surmise. When these shots are reiterated in the suicide sequence, they take on a different function, coalescing the fantasmatic vision of the child with that of the spectator, a point to which I will return.

Subsequently, a series of eyeline exchanges involving close-ups of the couple and medium-close-ups of an increasingly angry Marie dominates the remainder of this portion of the sequence.[7] The pattern consists of a number of variations of angle on the shots of the couple alternated with a repeated and consistent angle and type of shot of Marie. The couple (always portrayed within a single shot, sometimes including more of the woman, sometimes more of the man) exchanges significant glances, turning slightly to begin to kiss; Marie scowls. Then, just as the mother begins to offer her face to the man for the kiss, she looks down toward the right edge of the frame. An angry Marie looks back. The man turns to look off in Marie's direction. The responding shot is a medium-close-up of Marie, whose frowning disapproval is reinforced by her gesture of angrily brushing a pip from her mouth. A return to the look of the man, a shot of the feet unhooking under the table, and then the reverse-shot completes the exchange between mother and daughter as the woman moves her head away from the man's.

As the singer begins a new theme, a close-medium-shot of the couple, Marie seated in the foreground with her back toward the spectator, mirrors the shot that had preceded the entire exchange of close-ups before the singer began her song. The man puts on his hat and angrily gets up to leave, an action that contrasts his gesture of tossing his hat and gaily sitting down in the parallel shot at the beginning of the sequence. Marie and her mother follow him with their eyes. Then a four-shot exchange between Marie in medium-close-up and her mother in close-up depicts the mother's silent appeal for understanding as she apologetically, pathetically, attempts a smile—and Marie's accusing, unstinting glare. The section is completed by a long-shot of the cabaret, as the singer finishes her song and is lifted down from the stage by the bartender.

In this silently eloquent dynamic, the power of the child's gaze to disrupt the "parental" couple is displayed. But beyond this conclusion, derived from the manifest narration of the action, lie a number of significant questions that structure and organize the psychic drama of the film: How does knowledge act as a function of vision? What kinds of knowledge are obtained by seeing, and what are the consequences? How does this visual relay redefine the "regime of voyeurism" at the heart of any cinematic eyeline exchange? To answer these questions we must turn to the dynamic reciprocity of the looks in question. As each character responds to the gaze of another, meaning is communicated through the look. The mother knows what the child thinks because of the glances exchanged. The man suggests both his threatening power and his lust for the woman by the expression of his eyes. And the child communicates both the intensity of her love and her fierce protection of it by concentrating all of her force in the significance of a stare. Thus "parental" recognition of and reaction to the fact of observation is depicted in terms of each adult's specific looks. But here the observer is a child—a female child who has a particular stake in the spectacle of sexuality before her eyes. Therefore, although the woman is still constituted as the desired object via the gaze, she is such an object not only for the male. She is all the more powerfully and decidedly an erotic figure, here, because she is the maternal object of the child's desire. In this sequence, then, there is a battle for the woman, but the rivals are not equal and they are not both men. And yet, the more powerful adversary, the man, is not victorious, or not at this point, because in the cabaret, at least, the power of the gaze belongs to the child.

Already at this initial stage, the spectator's position is more heavily aligned with the child's highly charged admonishment than with its object. The spectator is literally transected by this trajectory of looks, functioning as a relay point which, necessarily, coincides with the child's point-of-view. This is the enunciative crux from which the looks repeatedly emanate, to which they constantly return. As this constellation of looks is reiterated in the later segments of the proposal and the suicide attempt, the identificatory pull of the child's look becomes increasingly powerful, until the object of her vision is purely fantasmatic, a memory-trace of couples both perceived and imagined.

By the time this scene embracing child and parental couple is reacti-vated in the suicide sequence, there is no longer an *exchange* of looks, but a *projection* of vision, and the consequences for a reformulation of the cinema's erotic investment in looking are dramatically staged.

The Cabaret (Abandonment)

After the man has left the table, the mother's hurried departure from the bistro (little Marie in tow) inaugurates the final section of what I have termed the "cabaret sequence." This involves an alternation between two spaces—a second-hand shop window and the impover-ished lodgings of Marie and her mother—an alternation whose short accelerated montage at the end of the sequence crystallizes the themat-ics of the couple, abandonment, childish despair, and vision. The first of the rare instances of extra-diegetic music in the film accompanies the remainder of the sequence, and significantly, this theme is echoed in the suicide sequence much later in the film. The diegetic accordion and vocal music of the cabaret is replaced by a new instrumental version of the dance hall and singer's "voyage" themes.

Marie and her mother stop in front of a second-hand dealer's win-dow in which a huge model of an ocean-liner is barely discernable behind its glass pane. The paternal figure's disruption of the maternal dyad is rendered when the reflection of the man from the cabaret—an imaged intervention—surges up from behind the figures of Marie and her mother, causing Marie's expression (in the subsequent medi-um-close-up) to shift from delight to despair. Marie pulls her mother away from the window in an effort to lead her toward home. The mother kisses Marie and sends her off, while she herself runs back toward the window and the man, the soundtrack building an instru-mental crescendo. The final shot of this unit is a medium-shot of the man and woman as they embrace, seen from inside the window, the ocean-liner in soft focus in the foreground. In a condensation of figures of the window, the boat, the reflection, and the kiss—figures dispersed throughout the film in varied constellations—the child's unhappy perception of the "parental" couple is thus evoked even as she is absent from the scene.

This nine-shot section of the second-hand dealer's space is now matched by a section of nine more shots depicting Marie's room. The extra-diegetic music is continuous, although the instrumentation varies. Three shots depict Marie in bed while clarinet and flute versions of the voyage theme are softly played. As a new musical theme begins, played on a high register saxophone with jazzy connotations of sensual-

La Maternelle (The Cabaret)

ity, the mother enters the room and starts to pack. The remaining six shots of this section cover her departure, which is punctuated by a close-up of Marie—whose face reveals a lipstick "scar" left by the mother's kiss—and a plaintive violin theme.

The alternation of these two nine-shot units is then condensed into a more rapid alternation, denoting simultaneity and interweaving one shot of each space for four shots. Prefaced by the trembling hesitation of the final pizzicatto notes over the first of these four shots, the soundtrack breaks into a full orchestration of the voyage theme for the next shot. The final two shots of this section, and thus of the entire cabaret sequence, are accompanied by an attenuated violin repetition of this theme in a minor key.

The first shot, a medium-close-up of Marie looking mournfully through the bars of her bed, is followed by a close-medium shot of the couple seen from the second-hand shop window, in a passionate embrace, a portion of the ocean-liner out of focus in the foreground. The third shot is identical with the first, a despairing Marie looking sadly through the bars of her bed. And the final shot, taking up from where its predecessors left off, depicts the couple, seen from the shop window, as they advance down the dimly lit street toward a sign marked "Hotel," almost invisible at the back of the frame. Then there is a fade to black.

At the outset of this chapter I noted that Epstein's modification of the enunciative function of the cinematic look could be understood in terms of primal scenes in *La Maternelle*, scenarios of vision set up both in the diegesis and by the apparatus. Consequently, the film's reorganization of the gaze to permit the spectator's experience of the primal scene along with Marie, the articulation of this scene from the female child's perspective, and the concentric structuring of the film in terms of these repeated visual scenarios, suggest just how fundamentally *La Maternelle* departs from dominant cinematic structures. In psychoanalytic theory, the primal scene is defined as the child's observation of sexual scenes between adults, usually parents, often creating a traumatic state, or producing anxiety of some sort. It is therefore possible to understand this exchange of shots involving a child's bedstead look and the scene of a couple's embrace as a cinematic rendering of the primal scene across the cut, the most literal representation of this psychic structure in the film, and one of the most profound examples of it in all of cinema.

For a child, the vision of parental sexual activity is likely to connect the ideas of sexual excitement and danger. Individual factors will determine what the child perceives, how he or she interprets these perceptions, and what mental connections are established. For example, identification with the parent of the same sex can affect the child's interpretation of the perceived scene. In any case, "sexual satisfaction" is linked by the child with "danger" in this psychic constellation.[8] Freud defines the situation even more concretely when he discusses the dream of the "Wolf Man" in one of his case histories: *"It was night, I was lying in my bed.* The latter is the beginning of the reproduction of the primal scene."[9]

The cabaret sequence of *La Maternelle* can be described as a number of variations on the child's traumatic vision of the scene of the couple. In fact, the entire dramatic action of this sequence is a series of looks exchanged, a triangulation of vision with important psychosexual consequences for the child. In this context, the last four shots of the sequence—which alternate the vision of the child from the bedstead (through the railings of the cot) with the observed scene of the couple's embrace—can be seen as a materialization of this psychoanalytic matrix.

"The *observed* scene of the couple's embrace." The critical question here, in terms of cinematic enunciation, is, *Who* is watching this scene? The child in the film cannot logically see the couple by the second-hand shop window, yet the logic of implication produced by the conventional eyeline-match structure (the alternation of seeing/seen) establishes this conclusion. It is, in fact, the spectator who sees. By virtue of the montage that matches Marie "seeing" with the couple "seen," the spectator is given the power of vision, made to see from the (impossible) viewpoint of the child and thereby made to experience the primal trauma.

Through this structure of embedded positions of viewing, the primal scene is reiterated: The parental couple, actors who are seen but are unaware of it; a child who watches, separated from the scene by the head of the bed; and an ultimate spectator, beyond the immediate fiction in a position to view both scenes, the watched and the watcher.[10] Thematically, this whole sequence associates sexuality with danger for the child by depicting the trauma of abandonment as a consequence of the couple's union. For the spectator, this miniature episode of a primal scene across the cut prepares the way for fantasmatic participation in Marie's suicide attempt and puts into play the drama of cinema viewing.

The Proposal

La Maternelle's second core sequence in terms of primal scenes involves Dr. Libois' proposal to Rose. In the proposal sequence, the doctor's

The Primal Scene

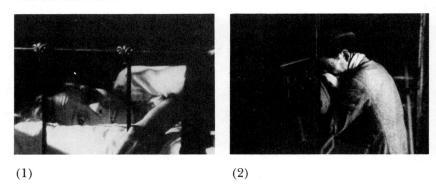

(1)   (2)

The Primacy of the Visual

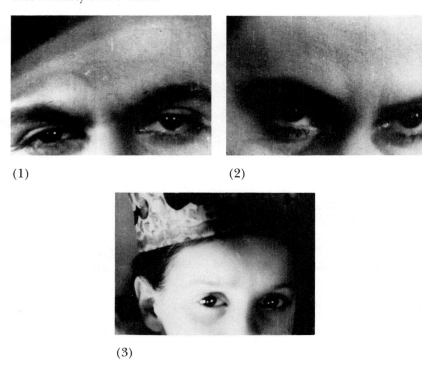

(1)   (2)

(3)

offer of marriage is made in the school cantine and witnessed (by virtue of the windows connecting the cantine to the surrounding main room) by Marie, the principal, and Madame Paulin. At first, only the couple is depicted: American-shots of Rose and Libois alternate with close-ups of Rose for four shots. Then, the appearance of the child— a frontal close-medium-shot of Marie watching through the window— initiates a new alternation, thereby inaugurating the film's second primal scene configuration. It is thus the child's gaze that confers symbolic "parental" status on the couple composed by Rose and Libois, and the "drama of vision" begins.

American-shots of Rose and Libois (with the back of Marie's head in the right foreground corner of the frame) then alternate with medium-shots of the main room as the principal and Madame Paulin come in to watch. This is accompanied on the soundtrack by an alternation of silence and a bird's chirp. Immediately following this, an extremely striking relay of looks—punctuated by silence on the soundtrack and alternating between the space of the cantine and the main room—depicts in quick succession: Rose's sudden shock at noticing that Marie has observed the scene, Marie's head and raised shoulder framed by the window, Rose's astonished face, Madame Paulin, Rose, the principal, Rose and Libois, the principal.

Finally, Rose comes into the main room and notices Marie seated on the bench, initiating a charged visual relay of three shots between maternal figure and child. An eyeline exchange, intensified by silence on the soundtrack, alternates extreme close-ups of Marie's eyes with a close-up of Rose. When the second close-up of Rose occurs, the voices of Dr. Libois and the principal are heard offscreen, indicating their presence and predicting the following shots, an American-shot of the principal and Libois, Marie and Rose. In the last close-up of this exchange, Rose shuts her eyes and turns out of the frame.

The sequence ends with an alternating series of shots which secures the spectator's position firmly on the side of the child. This effect, in fact, has been installed in this sequence by the first appearance of Marie, then highly reinforced by the extreme close-up of Marie's eyes, a type of shot that literally draws the spectator into the representation of vision. Now this last part of the segment begins with a medium-close-up of little Marie sadly looking out at the spectator over the clasped hands of Libois and Rose in the foreground. The triangular structure of this shot has a dual function: in its symbolic configuration of child's vision and parental union, it restages the primal scene; in its powerful invocation of the spectator's vision by the direct appeal of the child's gaze, it virtually engages the primal scene of the cinematic viewing situation. This is alternated with American-shots of Libois, Rose, and the principal talking excitedly. The segment ends with Rose adjusting her hat, powdering her nose, and leaving, as Madame Paulin stands chuckling delightedly in the main room.

The echoes of the cabaret scene are striking, but important transformations have occurred. While the interplay of desiring looks in the cabaret sequence was charged with sexuality (seduction) and interrupted by the child's disturbing gaze, here the illicit aspect is defused (a marriage proposal is more legitimized and culturally sanctioned than seduction) and the focus is placed on the act of observation itself, as it is dispersed across the activity of several witnesses. And, while Marie's expression in the cabaret is one of anger at the constituted unity of her mother and the man, now the child's expression is tempered with the resigned knowledge she has gained from observation: an exclusive relationship with Rose is not possible. But the intensity of the child's vision is here condensed in two ways: First, by the extreme-close-up of her eyes, a privileged textual moment, and then by the structure of the single shot which places child, gaze, and couple in direct solicitation of the spectator's view. Thus desire, so prevalent in the sequence in the cabaret, is now within the limits of the law (the matrimonial couple), while its sexual component is displaced, in a kind of textual immediacy, to the vision of the child. And this vision, by decisive implication, is also that of the spectator, an equivalence that the film has worked increasingly to define.

Another factor that supports the evolving concentration of identificatory effects with the psyche of the child concerns the two "maternal" reactions—first by the mother in the scene in the cabaret, and here by Rose in the proposal sequence. In the earlier moment of childish prohibition, you will remember, the mother had answered with a pathetic, plaintive smile. This appeal was met with Marie's unyielding scowl. Here Rose's reactions involve first a sudden gasp, and then a closing of her eyes as she turns out of the frame; in each case, there is no visual dialogue to engage. Thus although it might have been possible, for a moment, to psychically "take the mother's part" in the cabaret, here the viewer can only identify with Rose as a function of the child's desire. As viewer-identification becomes more firmly rooted in the place of the child, then, the possibilities for identifying with the maternal figure are reduced. It is in this sense that there is a refinement of effects that can be traced from one instance to the next, a paring down of identificatory mechanisms that prioritize the child.

In addition, the extreme close-ups of Marie's eyes echo those of an initial exchange between her mother and the man when they had first entered the cabaret. These extreme close-ups of pairs of eyes—the mother's and the man's in the cabaret, Marie's in the proposal sequence—are the only shots of this kind in the film. They thus focalize a kind of textual intensity on vision itself. Their substitutive relation, that is, the shot of the eyes of the child replacing the shots of the eyes of the man and of the woman, traces the psychic movement of the film. Where the child's look onto the scene of the couple in the seduction sequence is rendered through a series of medium-close-ups of Marie, as the film moves toward its climax, it increasingly condenses its focus on the child. Here the isolated concentration on Marie's eyes both reinforces the signifying aspect of her accusing stare (a silent communication between herself and the maternal object), and brings the spectator into a more active, participatory role in the fiction. Thus through the differential echo of figures which accentuate the look, the psychic intensity of the film's climactic moment is prepared.

The Suicide Attempt

The climax of *La Maternelle* is, of course, Marie's suicide attempt. This is not simply because it is the result of a dramatic buildup, but, more important, because it represents the central point of focus for a number of identification mechanisms; in this episode of the film, the centrality of the little girl's point of view achieves its strongest elaboration. It is thus in the suicide sequence, a fantasmatic condensation of perceived, remembered, and imagined images, that the child in the fiction and the spectator in the theater coincide to produce the fantasmatic vision on the screen, and it is here that *La Maternelle*'s most substantial challenge to the classical structures of spectatorship can be found.

Little Marie's witnessing of the proposal reactivates the memory of the cabaret, and her anticipation of a second abandonment by the maternal figure summons up a sense of loss and despair. She runs to the river, where a nearby couple reflected in the water triggers an associative relay in which all of the traumatic couples of her memory are evoked. She tries frantically to erase these images of couples by throwing gravel and stones into the water, and then she throws herself in.

In this sequence, all of the elements of the psychic scenario which structures the text are replayed in a new symbolic configuration, making it an intensified and condensed version of the entire film. In addition, extra-diegetic music, which repeats the melodic themes of the cabaret sequence, isolates and unifies this sequence and recalls the evocative power of the silent film suggested by the earlier sequence.

La Maternelle (The Proposal)

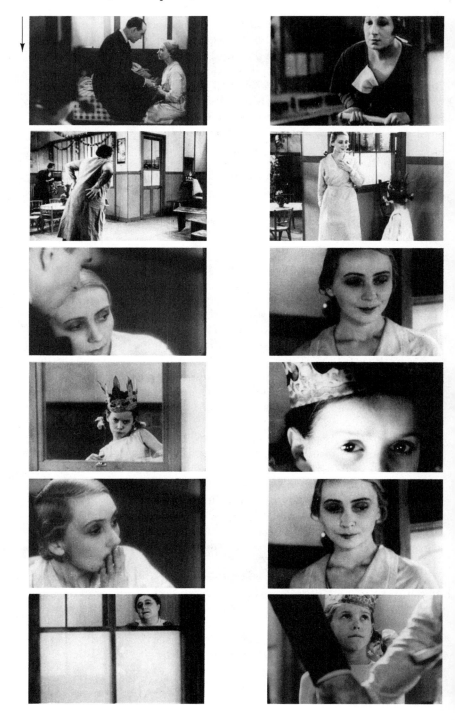

The first few shots depict Marie by the second-hand dealer's window, providing both a visual and a musical echo of the two previous scenes at this location. But there is repetition with a difference: The former scenes had shown a maternal dyad (Marie with her mother, and later with Rose) ruptured by a paternal third term (first the man, then Dr. Libois). Now Marie is alone, and as she simply looks at the ocean-liner, the constellation of meanings from the past—voyage, separation, abandonment, loss of the mother—bears the burden of signification.

Marie next runs over to the quais by the river as a very high angle shot discloses a couple seated on a barge, locked in an embrace. Then, as the cabaret singer's theme is picked up in strings, a close-up portrays Marie looking sadly out, presumably at the water. This shot initiates a series of five shots (with one exception) depicting Marie at various focal lengths and angles, alternately looking sad and throwing stones into the water.

The second shot in the series is of the nearby couple, now in medium-shot, seen from a low angle as they kiss, silhouetted against the sky. The camera angle and position are meant to indicate that this couple is seen from Marie's point of view, and this shot will be repeated later in the sequence, when it forms a frame encasing the series of quick images of remembered and imagined couples. In this way, a bit of everyday detail—signifying the "Frenchness" of barge life on the Seine—achieves a symbolic function in the psychic scenario of the film.

A new series of shots then alternates Marie with the reflection in the water of the couple on the barge. The alternating structure of seeing/ seen/ seeing, still anchored firmly in the reality of the diegesis, traces Marie's increasing anxiety and frustration as she tries frantically to erase the image of the couple. The reflection of the embracing couple is shown in medium-shot, a realistic rendering of how this would be seen from Marie's point of view. This is alternated with American-shots of Marie, first spitting into the water, then throwing handfuls of gravel, and finally heaving a huge boulder. This last effort is punctu-ated aurally by a chord, then silence. Each time, the corresponding shot of the couple's reflection shows concentric ripples in the water, leaving the image undisturbed. The realm of the fantasmatic has yet to be engaged.

Suddenly, it is a reflected image of Marie's mother, in a large, upside-down close-up, which is shaken by ripples of water circling out around her mouth.[11] The recession into fantasy is thus marked by a transition from the reality of the perceived couple to the memory of the maternal figure. The mother, then, is the first indication of Marie's fantasmatic projection; Marie has now moved from the perception of an actual couple reflected in the water to the remembered image of the mother she lost. This is virtually the first wholly subjective image in the film, initiating as it does an image sequence combining memory, loss, and sexuality in the mind of the child.

After a return to a shot of Marie, this time in medium-close-up, shoulder up in her characteristic pose of despair, another image from the cabaret appears. This time it is a shot that emphasizes the man's face instead of the mother's (remember that the sequence had been composed of a whole variety of unusual angles on the couple). It is important to note how this reiteration of the exchange of looks between the seducer and the forbidding child is modified. In the cabaret sequence, this exchange had signalled the adult's recognition of the child's vision and its consequences; the child had been able to prevent the kiss momentarily through the force of her gaze. When this image is replayed as a part of Marie's memory, however, it takes on the elusive aspect of fantasy. Just as in a dream, the dreamer's cry fails to halt the progress of the action, now the child's attempts to disturb the fantasmatic image of the couple have no effect at all.

The medium-close-up of Marie returns, followed by another remembered image. This time it is a memory of the proposal: Rose's face in large close-up reflected, upside-down, in the water. Libois' head leans out of the image as the concentric ripples continue over the image of Rose. There is a marked similarity between the two images of maternal figures; the mother and Rose are both shown in large, upside-down reflections. The parallel indicates a transition from remembered absence to anticipated loss. In both cases it is the maternal, a fiction of reciprocity denoting the impossibility of desire, which heralds the crossing over into an imaginary "elsewhere."

The return to the medium-close-up of the despairing Marie, shoulder up, is matched by Rose's whispered admonition, "Marie, tiens-toi droite" [Marie, stand up straight], repeated three times. The soundtrack thereby reinscribes the fantasm by carrying an imagined maternal imperative, emanating not from the reflected image of Rose, but from the child's memory. Because this is the only verbal material in the sequence, it evokes its counterpart in the cabaret sequence, another admonition ("Attention, la p'tite!" "Bah, ces mômes me pigent pas. . . . "), but pronounced by woman and man. And, importantly, this exclamation is addressed to Marie, while that in the cabaret reinforces her exclusion.

These whispered phrases are the only instances of verbal language in sequences that otherwise consist entirely of images and music. They therefore form a sort of echo structure whose transformation is significant. Whereas in the cabaret, the whispered exchange had signified the heterosexual couple, its illicit union, and the exclusion of the child, here, the language in the suicide sequence verbally signifies the maternal relationship, and thus, necessarily, the centrality of that child. Because the mother's image triggers the fantasm and signals the subjective memory, the verbal command that issues from the maternal figure provides aural reinforcement. But more than that, it addresses the child in a relationship whose very reciprocity is the image of that child's desire. Led to attempt suicide by the perceived impossibility of that rapport, Marie is able, by fantasmatic means, to evoke what she feels she cannot possess in reality. And thus her fantasy is born in a moment of loss.

Rose's whispered admonition triggers a highly significant sequence of shots which is intensified by the silence on the soundtrack. In rapid montage, a series of images of couples—both perceived and imagined, remembered and fantasized—flashes on the screen *as if before Marie's eyes*. A staging of the fantasm is thus produced for both child and viewer alike. And it is in this sequence of images that a psychic truth is demonstrated: Both fantasy and the look share a relation to loss. The psychoanalytic notion of fantasy has its roots in the infant's "primal hallucination" of the breast. In the absence of milk, the infant seeks to reproduce not the real object (which would satisfy need), but a representation, an image of the satisfaction associated with feeding (a production of desire). The fantasmatic structure thus originates in a moment of separation, "leaning" on a loss which is the definition of the drive. In this primal moment in the film, then, the fantasmatic maternal image surges forth at the child's most intense desire, and in so doing provides the viewer with a powerful example of the cinematic fantasy, one rarely equalled in the history of film.

And it is here that the viewer finally becomes locked irremediably within the child's vision, for it is indeed the spectator before whose eyes these fantasmatic images pass. The structural pattern of seeing/seen/seeing that had alternated shots of Marie with shots of the couple reflected in the water, and then with one shot of the mother and one shot of Rose, now becomes the unmediated vision of the child, whose position the spectator takes as the *seen* images flash quickly on the screen—unnegotiated by any shot of Marie *seeing*. Thus in quick succession, a medium-shot of the couple on the barge, kissing; a close-up from the cabaret sequence in which the man looks at the mother; a medium-close-up of the brutal Pantin, buried in Rose's neck in a forced embrace in the schoolroom; the reverse-shot of this, a close-up of Rose's pained expression; a medium-close-up of Pantin's hand grabbing Rose's waist, the children tugging at her skirt; a medium-close-up of the mother's leg rubbing against the man's seen under the table at the cabaret; a close-up of the mother, looking up at the man; a medium-shot of the couple on the barge, an exact repetition of the first shot in the series.

A return to the medium-close-up of Marie that preceded this quick succession of shots reiterating the film's couples marks her despair as she falls over into the water, out of the bottom of the frame. The man on the barge (seen from a high angle) dives in to save her as the final shot depicts Marie's little paper crown floating away on the swirling water.

Marie's suicide attempt can be understood as the traumatic fantasy of separation and loss occasioned by the child's sense of danger, a feeling of anxiety associated with the vision of the "parental" couple. Its cinematic rendering is through visual reactivations of the film's primal configurations. The fantasmatic repetition of the child's distressing sight—portrayed here in a quick montage of couples—is nothing other than the reiteration of a scene played out several times before in the film.

In addition, this rapid succession of images of couples reinforces the effect of textual condensation by combining, in one signifying constellation, the repeated associations of water, voyage, abandonment, reflection, couples, and the kiss. Furthermore, the two shots in the cabaret sequence that the child could not have possibly seen—the legs seen from under the table—take on a new meaning in terms of unconscious production in the suicide sequence. Whereas in the cabaret sequence they represented the spectator's—and only the spectator's—vision, here they become incorporated into the structure of the fantasm itself. They are thereby given the same fantasmatic status as every other couple image in this quick succession: all are metonymies of sexuality, and all are the child's hallucinations. In the suicide sequence, then, the brutality of separation is associated with the vision of sexuality to combine memory and fantasy, desire and loss in a moment of textual density in the psyche of the child.

It is as if this sequence of memory-traces, built from the child's gaze onto various scenes of couples (from which she is excluded), is a momentary replay of the entire film itself. And it is no accident that at precisely this moment the spectator ceases to have a mediated vision of the scene—becoming the vision of the child, remembering the images of the past. When this is considered in the light of Thierry Kuntzel's work on textual systems and their relations of vision and desire, the implications for cinema spectatorship are quite powerful:

"The Most Dangerous Game is uncanny because it stages, puts into play, my 'love' of the cinema; that is what I go to see (again) with each new film; my own desire—endlessly repeated—for re-presentation."[12]

The Child and the Fourth Look

The three "scenarios of vision" in *La Maternelle* thus trace the maturation process of the female child, for it is as a result of this final suicidal fantasm that she is able to renounce the maternal object and accept the paternal hand. But in terms of the radical restructuring of vision and identification that *La Maternelle* represents, the development of the "drama of spectatorship" is even more important. As each subsequent scene of the couple is rendered, the viewer is increasingly brought over to the child's side, making spectatorial subjectivity ever more powerfully an effect of identification with the female child's point-of-view: There is a constant recentering of the viewer's position so that the young girl's fantasm becomes the spectator's vision.

In a film whose central emotive constellation is built on the look of the child and her desire for the mother, the cinematic alternation of seeing/seen becomes the fundamental motor of the text. But how does this fact modify the enunciative structures of the film? The modalities of point-of-view allow us to differentiate between the characters' positions and that of the camera, assigning to the spectator a number of possible placements in relation to the film. Four types of looks interact in cinematic representation: The look of the camera onto the pro-filmic event, the look of the spectator at the screen, the diegetic looks between characters within the fiction, and the look of the character directly toward the camera. It is this fourth look, conventionally disavowed in classical cinema, which gives access to the elusive enunciative mechanism by implicating the spectator directly, condensing all three other aspects of vision within a single gaze. When the look of the character coincides with that of the spectator in this fourth look, the viewer's fantasmatic participation in the cinematic fiction is reinforced.

Therefore, when Marie looks straight toward the camera lens—and by implication directly at the spectator—in each of those primal moments of the text, the primary cinematic identification with *that which stages the spectacle* is heightened, permitting, by both its nontraditional focus and its intensity, an alternative formulation of enunciation and the gaze. By means of this operation an important relationship is engaged, one that links the structure of the fantasm to the child's viewpoint—and places the spectator firmly at the center of this. Thus by rendering a conventionally suppressed scenarization of childhood

La Maternelle (The Suicide Attempt)

fantasms, placing the female child at the core of the textual drama, and positioning the spectator there by means of the fourth look, the film posits another economy of vision, another site of textual desire.

Teresa DeLauretis has suggested that the project of a feminist counter-cinema is "to articulate the relations of the female subject to representation, meaning and vision: to set out the terms of another measure of desire, the conditions of presence of another social subject."[13] She reminds us that while feminist film theory maintains that the "place of the look" defines the cinema and governs its representations of the woman, it is the task of resisting filmmakers to explore the possibilities of varying, shifting, and exposing that look.[14] From this perspective, the kind of density of spectatorship achieved in *La Maternelle*, through its repeated stagings of the primal scene and its complex organization of visual structures, redefines the "desiring look" and recasts it in feminine terms. And it does so not only from the source of enunciation, but at the site of spectatorship as well. The subject of enunciation is no longer aligned with the masculine Oedipal standard, just as reciprocal maternal longing speaks of feminine desire. While so central a mechanism of the apparatus as the primal scene is dramatized for the spectator, it is structured according to a different logic, dispersing the possibilities for identification along feminine lines. In this, DeLauretis' "other positionalities of desire" which "address the spectator from an elsewhere of vision"[15] find their actualization in Marie Epstein's film.

Over and above a new content that reworks patriarchal definitions of motherhood, the film resituates the viewer as producer of the fantasm not in terms of Oedipal desire but of female longing—both child for mother and mother for child—instead. And it is precisely the use of the primal scene fantasy as a structuring matrix that suggests a multiplicity of spectator-text relationships, even though, by the film's end, all of these identification mechanisms are concentrated in the child. Up until the traumatic final moments of Marie's suicide attempt, each vision of the couple entails a complicated production of feminine desire. In this, the exchange and doubling characteristic of fantasy finds an alternative elaboration in feminine terms. When the first primal scene enables Marie to prohibit the "parental" kiss in the cabaret, it is not only the child's attachment to the mother which is dramatized. There is also the contradictory emotional complex of the mother's feelings: She is torn between her passion for the man and her bond with the daughter, and the spectator is made to participate psychically in these emotions as well. The second part of the sequence (the child's bedstead gaze) extends the film's process of marshalling enunciation for the child by constituting the mother as the (hopelessly unattainable) object, while the child becomes the sole focus of the play of vision, subjectivity, and desire. The second sequence of the primal scene, the witnessed proposal, likewise involves the possibility of "maternal" identifications, this time with Rose. She is transected by the same contradictory play of feelings as the mother, torn by the same conflict of desire. But where the mother's acquiescence to the paternal term had signified abandonment of her maternal role, here Rose's acceptance of the proposal facilitates—and even requires—her potential fulfillment of that same function. By this point in the film, however, the possibilities of viewer-position have been even further concentrated in the locus of the child. It is in the final sequence of the child's suicidal vision, a fantasmatic sight of couples that is both produced by trauma and productive of trauma itself, that *La Maternelle*'s transformation of the cinema's central enunciative structure finds its most dramatic elaboration. The logic of masculine desire so central to classical narrative film is destablized, displaced, and rearticulated from another source, while the feminine figure is constituted as the object of a "different" vision, and it is for these reasons that the film represents so powerful, yet subtle, a challenge to the dominant cinematic form.

However, I do not wish to make it seem that the simple existence of the primal scene in a film—nor even its occupation of such an important structuring position—is enough to constitute that film's alternative status. In fact, excellent examples of the primal scene exist in Hitchcock's films, films which repeatedly demonstrate the centrality of classical Oedipal logic. In *Notorious,* for example, the witnessing of a primal scene by one of the main protagonists is the turning point in the film: Once Alex Sebastian comes upon his new wife, Alicia, embracing Devlin, the American agent, he immediately understands his wife's treachery and begins to punish her, thereby transforming his characteristic passivity into action and maturing from "boy" to man in the process. The primal scene is significant in *Marnie* as well, for it is from the heroine's childhood vision of adult sexual activity that all of her neuroses flow, and it is this vision as well that provides her husband, Mark Rutland, with the key to the enigma of his wife; Marnie's primal scene is thus the condition of their union. Therefore, what the primal scenes in both of these films do, in fact, is simply corroborate, by dramatizing another register of, each film's classical project: the stabilization of the hero's desire in the legitimized constitution of the couple. In this they fulfill quite successfully the function of any structure based on the logic of masculine subjectivity; they reinforce the social and psychic articulation of patriarchy. However, to cite again an important formulation by Teresa DeLauretis: "an interruption, a dis-alignment of the triple track by which meaning and pleasure and narrative are constructed from [Oedipus'] point of view, is necessary for women's work and pleasure in cinema and in the world."[16] The feminist significance of *La Maternelle* is that it achieves precisely this kind of radical reworking, not only by systematically organizing its visions in terms of this childhood fantasy, but also by making the articulation of (reciprocal) maternal desire its very structuring core.

NOTES

1. Thierry Kuntzel, "Savior, Pouvoir, Voir," *Ça/Cinéma*, nos. 7–8 (May 1975): 96 (my translation). This chapter reworks material presented in my article in *enclitic*, "Nursery/Rhymes: Primal Scenes in *La Maternelle*" 5:2/6:1 (Fall 1981–Spring 1982): 98–110.

2. *La Maternelle* is available for rental from the Museum of Modern Art; although the museum's prints are far from adequate in a few portions of the film (see below), they are the only ones in circulation in the United States. As stated in chapter 5, note 16, I base my analysis on prints seen at the Cinémathèque Française in Paris, and at archives at Berkeley and UCLA. I am grateful to Marie Epstein and to Dugald Williamson for assistance on the Cinémathèque print.

3. Raymond Bellour, "Segmenting/Analyzing," in *Genre: The Musical*, ed. Rick Altman (London: Routledge and Kegan Paul, 1981), p. 118. I have modified the translation.

4. See my discussion in the Introduction, particularly the section entitled "The Enunciative Apparatus," pp. 11–19.

5. Jean-Louis Baudry, "Ideological Effects of the Basic Cinematographic Apparatus," *Film Quarterly* 28:2 (Winter 1974–75): 45. This article is anthologized in *Apparatus*, ed. Theresa Hak Kyung Cha (New York: Tanam Press, 1980), pp. 25–37 and in *Narrative, Apparatus, Ideology*, ed. Philip Rosen (New York: Columbia University Press, 1986), pp. 286–98.

6. The establishment of a reliable version of the text of *La Maternelle* for scholarly analysis presents a number of problems. The most complete version of *La Maternelle* exists at the Cinémathèque Française in Paris; all prints in the United States have various sequences or numbers of shots missing, most probably due to censor's cuts when the film was released in 1935. (Many of the suppressed shots are images of haunting beauty, scenes that recall the nocturnal Parisian photographs of Brassaï, whose *Paris de nuit* was published in 1933. His *The Secret Paris of the Thirties* (1976) and *Paris by Night* (1987) indicate the current renewal of interest in his vision of Paris.) The noncirculating print at the Pacific Film Archive in Berkeley is the most complete in this country to date. Unfortunately, two of the sequences treated in my analysis (the cabaret and the suicide attempt) are among those submitted to the cuts.

I have tried to indicate, where possible, the differences between prints. These generally consist of missing shots, while the overall structure of the sequences and their main articulations remain intact.

7. Seven shots of the exchange are missing from the Pacific Film Archive print of the film, including the main exchange between the man and Marie. The Museum of Modern Art prints are missing several more, including some of the those at the very end of the sequence. In fact, after having seen the film in its entirety, the MoMA print looks disturbingly inadequate. Still, the museum does make the film available for rental, and for this they are to be gratefully acknowledged.

8. c.f., Otto Fenichel, *The Psychoanalytic Theory of Neurosis* (New York: W. W. Norton, 1945), pp. 214–15.

9. Sigmund Freud, *Three Case Histories* (New York: Collier Books, 1963), p. 228; emphasis in the original.

10. This is adapted from Thierry Kuntzel's description of the primal scene in *The Most Dangerous Game*, "Sight, Insight, and Power: Allegory of a Cave," trans. Nancy Huston, *Camera Obscura*, no. 6 (Fall 1980): 109.

11. This shot, along with the following three, are missing from the American prints of the film.

12. Thierry Kuntzel, "The Film-Work 2," *Camera Obscura*, no. 5 (Spring 1980): 63. I have slightly altered Nancy Huston's translation.

13. Teresa DeLauretis, "Oedipus Interruptus," *Wide Angle* 7:1&2 (1985) pp. 34–40, here, p. 38.

14. Teresa DeLauretis, *Alice Doesn't: Feminism, Semiotics, Cinema* (Bloomington: Indiana University Press, 1984), p. 138.

15. DeLauretis, *Alice Doesn't*, p. 83.

16. DeLauretis, "Oedipus Interruptus," p. 40.

EIGHT

Agnès Varda and the Woman Seen

UNLIKE GERMAINE DULAC, Agnès Varda did not come to the cinema with a set of publicly formulated feminist principles, although these did evolve in the course of her work. And unlike Marie Epstein, she has not been totally ignored in accounts of French film production. On the contrary, Agnès Varda has enjoyed a considerable amount of success as both a feminist and a filmmaker, although much of this is recent and long overdue. From the point of view of this study, Varda's films suggest important questions that are absolutely central to any formulation of a feminist counter-cinema, for they raise the issue of precisely how to define the "feminism" of a body of work. For example, although Varda's more avowedly feminist films, such as *L'Une chante, l'autre pas* (*One Sings, the Other Doesn't,* 1977), are quite explicit in their concern with women's issues, they fail to offer a serious challenge to dominant structures of representation, a challenge which forms the core of any alternative cinema. On the other hand, *Cleo From 5 to 7* (1961) and *Le Bonheur* (1965) do posit a feminist critique of patriarchal structures through their critical explorations of both the production of femininity and its representations, yet they are often not understood as such. It is only with the complex and disturbing beauty of *Sans toit ni loi* (*Vagabond,* 1985) that Varda's status as a feminist filmmaker has been undeniably established, yet this film, too, finds a contradictory reception among feminists themselves. It is precisely this problem that makes Varda's work so important to a feminist analysis of the cinema, for it is through these films and their ambiguous critical stance that we can understand the importance of conceiving resistance to the dominant model in textual terms.

The crux of the problem lies with the complicated issues surrounding feminist essentialism and the response to it formulated by feminist theory. Where the essentialist position assumes that a fundamental feminine nature preexists both language and culture, feminist theory asserts that only a sustained analysis of gender constructions—an interrogation of their production and representation in discourse—can lead to an understanding of feminine specificity (not essence). Logically, a film subscribing to the essentialist position will pose its images as, in some way, conveying the "truth" of real women, whereas feminist film theory necessarily posits that this "truth" is (always already) produced in and by complex discursive and cultural practices. When Varda's films are seen in terms of these arguments, a basic contradiction emerges: While *L'Une chante* expresses an assertively feminist content through fairly traditional cinematic means, the latter films (two of which are, in fact, earlier chronologically) make the critique and analysis of cinematic language a fundamental part of their discursive structures, and thereby challenge essentialist notions of a preexisting feminine nature.

L'Une chante (and to some extent, *L'Opéra-Mouffe*, 1958) operates on the assumption that the image of the woman is unproblematic. Thus the expression of a female consciousness (as in *L'Opéra-Mouffe*) or the delineation of social issues (such as women's solidarity, contraception, and child-care in *L'Une chante*) are presented by images that are taken as self-evident. There is a simple equation between the women depicted in the films and real, active women in the actual world, while the multiple and contradictory systems of representation that produce these images of women are not reflected upon, or to the extent that they are, this reflection is not embedded in the structure of the films.

L'Opéra-Mouffe presents a much more complicated problem, however. Antedating most of the nouvelle vague films by a year or two, the poetic-essay form of this short-subject film produces some extremely interesting experiments with cinematic language and narrative organization. Although Varda herself rejects the essentialist interpretation, choosing to see the film as both a personal and a social diary, it is around the question of "femininity" that the film's main shortcomings crystallize. Because (in spite of its interest in social perceptions) the film's project is the treatment of pregnancy from a woman's point of view, it appears to support a biological definition of woman, one that, through the glorification of female

Sandy Flitterman-Lewis

bodily functions, suggests an essentialist ideology. It is possible to interpret the film as an idealization of the woman's body, thereby associating femaleness with pregnancy and confirming the equivalence of femininity and biology; this implies that being a woman is fundamentally grounded in nature. Although the film offers a powerful contrast to traditionally codified images of maternity, it can also be seen to represent a politics of simple inversion by implying that the feminist view of pregnancy merely recasts the dominant notion in feminine terms while retaining the ideological project of "naturalizing" a discursively produced femininity. Therefore, although the film is highly interesting from a cinematic standpoint, its possible essentialist content prevents it from offering a truly viable alternative for feminist filmmaking practice; precisely what constitutes this "woman's point of view" remains in question.

On the other hand, both *Cleo* and *Le Bonheur*, and later, *Vagabond*, analyze the definitions of "woman" and the constructions of sexuality as complex social processes, doing this in ways that foreground the signifying work of cinematic structures. The problematics of vision and of feminine desire have always assumed a central role in Varda's filmmaking. When these are combined, as they are in all three of these films, with a reflection on the very production process of the images used to articulate these issues, the result is a profound understanding and demonstration of "femininity" as a complex intersection of social and cinematic representations.

As a consequence, Varda has continually posed the question of cinematic language in her work, maintaining that the issue goes much deeper than simple formal innovation: "I learned to seek my language, and not simply my style."[1] The statement has important implications in terms of a feminist cinema, for Varda's formulation suggests the necessity of discovering a new cinematic language to articulate an utterly different content, a language born of visual conceptualization with its own specific properties and identity: "I always attempt to utilize the plastic vocabulary of the cinema before my ideas about the film are firmly fixed in words."[2] For Varda, this ongoing research into new discursive strategies is profoundly connected to a consistent preoccupation with vision. "In my films I always wanted to make people see deeply. I don't want to show things, but to give people the desire to see."[3] But it is not simply the fact of seeing, or of seeing cinematically; Varda is committed to exploring the feminist dialectic of the woman seeing/the woman seen. In other words, the woman's status as both subject and object of vision is continually posed throughout her work, whether this is the film's explicit subject matter (as in *Cleo*) or its underlying structuring thematic (as in *Vagabond*). In this sense, the vision of the woman (both meanings of the phrase) and cinematic discourse come together in a reformulation of feminist cinema as articulation—an articulation of constructions of "the feminine" with the problematics of the gaze.

Between 1954, when she was twenty-six, and 1989, Varda has made a total of twenty-seven films, twelve of which are shorts (*court-métrages*). It is a prolific filmmaking career in which a constant interweaving of documentary material and fictional structures has yielded complex cinematic constructions that perpetually call into question the traditional distinction between these two modes. Varda has discussed this concern in terms of what she sees as a dialectical process informing all of her work: "All of my films are based on the principles of contradiction-juxtaposition. *Cleo:* Objective time/subjective time. *Le Bonheur:* Sugar and poison (suave cliches of happiness/cruel gesturing of happiness). *Lions Love:* Historical truth and lies (television)/ collective self-deception and truth (Hollywood). *Nausicaa:* History (the Greeks after the coup)/mythology (the Greek gods). *L'Une chante:* Daydreams and documentary."[4]

Although this conceptualization is basically thematic, all of Varda's films, in one way or another, work on a textual level as well, contesting or subverting the main codes of the dominant narrative cinema while they invent new forms of cinematic expression along the way. Whether experimenting with modernist techniques of cinematic storytelling (as in *La Pointe-Courte, Vagabond,* or *Jane B. par Agnès V.*), with genre conventions (as in the subversion of melodrama in *Le Bonheur* or *Kung-Fu Master,* of the musical in *L'Une chante,* and of cinema-verité in *Lions Love*), with conventional stereotypes of female beauty and the fetishization of the star (as in *Cleo*), with the poetic-essay format (as in *L'Opéra-Mouffe, Daguerréotypes,* or *Les Dites-Cariatides*), with the fantasy film (as in *Les Créatures* or *7 Pièces, cuisine, salle de bains. . . . A saisir*), with sound conventions (as in *Mur Murs*), with the *ciné-tract* and documentary forms (as in *Salut les Cubains, Réponse de femmes,* or *Une minute pour une image*), her work continually explores the parameters of film language and the varied strategies of cinematic representation these suggest.

This interest in specificity led Varda to coin the term *cinécriture* (a neologism composed of *cinematic* and *writing*) to describe the total visual and aural conception and construction of a film: "I use the word because I find it is the only one which takes into account all the facets of a film's conception and realization. *Cinécriture* is the total concept, the filmmaker's imprint from the writing of the scenario to what occurs during the choice of decor, location scouting, the actual shooting and the editing process. I believe that the visual imagination involves much more than the writing of the scenario and the direction of the film. In *cinécriture*, there is no dichotomy between the scenarist and the director."[5]

In another context, Varda speaks of *cinécriture* in terms of the "untranslatable" quality of film, its capacity to signify according to its own specific systems of meaning, and its fundamentally visual mode of organization. She cautions against taking the meaning of writing in this new concept too literally because for her, *cinécriture* "means cinematic writing. Specifically that. Not illustrating a screenplay, not adapting a novel, not getting the gags of a good play, not any of this. I have fought so much since I started, since *La Point-Courte,* for something that comes from emotion, from visual emotion, sound emotion, feeling, and finding a shape for that, and a shape which has to do with cinema and nothing else."[6] And it is in this sense that the phrase, "Cinécrit par Agnès Varda," appearing on the title credits of *Vagabond,* must be understood—a signature of authorship which signifies at the same time the cinematic specificity that this authorship entails.

After studies in art history at the Sorbonne and the Ecole du Louvre (she had wanted to become a museum curator) and a career as official photographer for Jean Vilar's Théâtre Nationale Populaire, Varda made her first film, a feature-length narrative called *La Pointe-Courte*

(1954, released in 1956). The fact that she had seen very few films before this (notably *Quai des Brumes* and *Les Enfants du paradis*) both distinguishes her from other filmmakers of the nouvelle vague—whose steady cinephilic diet figured greatly in their backgrounds—and makes the achievement of this first effort all the more astounding. Georges Sadoul has called *La Pointe-Courte* "genuinely the first film of the French *Nouvelle Vague*,"[7] and its complicated narrative structure, stylistic innovations, experiments with point of view, and melding of Neo-Realist practices with modernist techniques of subjectivity have marked it as an important turning point in French film production of the late fifties.

The film takes place in La Pointe-Courte, a fishing village located near the city of Sète, where Varda spent most her childhood. It concerns a couple who, on the verge of separating after four years of marriage, return to the husband's native village, and, in a sense, rediscover each other. In the course of the film, two worlds collide—the woman's Parisian background and the husband's fisherman's milieu. Likewise, in an intertwining of distinct fictive modes, the personal problems of the married couple are juxtaposed with the economic and social struggles of the people of the village. Varda's "spirit of contradiction" is evident still further in the constant cinematic shifts between the apparently objective world of things and the ambiguous subjective world of thoughts.

The film is structured on a strict alternation of ten-minute segments, the first concerning the married couple and their personal problems, the second chronicling the economic and political struggles of the local fishermen. This has a double function—the constant shifting back and forth works against spectator identification with the characters, and it inserts these characters in a pervasive social milieu. The problems of the couple are thus only important in relation to the life of the village. But, significantly, this is presented in such a way that it is the spectator who must come to this conclusion. Varda calls this form of presentation "aggressive"; her discussion of it posits a viewer who is reflective, analytic, and critically engaged, a highly politicized position of spectatorship that runs throughout all of her work: "[This method] was even aggressive, in order to allow the spectator to remain distanced, lucid, and even so that we could show the spectator both the situation of the village and the situation of the couple. That's what is interesting—it was not a question of identifying with the couple or with the villagers, but of identifying with a spectator who is presented with situations which are more, or less, moving."[8]

This emphasis on nonidentification with the characters, so important in this first film of Varda's, was to become a constant in all of her subsequent films. In a move that combines techniques of critical distanciation with a conception of cinema-viewing as the assumption of a point of view, Varda has constructed all of her characters in terms of broad social outlines, thereby replacing psychological depth with social complexity. The resulting activity of judgment on the part of the spectator involves a renunciation of emotional identification in the name of critical reflection and evaluation. The consistency in Varda's thinking about this is quite striking; from its earliest formulation with *La Pointe-Courte* to a relatively recent discussion of *Vagabond,* made some thirty years later, Varda's respect for the viewer's critical activity is central to her filmmaking project: "I want spectators to define themselves vis-à-vis Mona. For example, would you give Mona a ride? Would you let her sleep in your car? Would you give her money? It's not the question, but the questioning that matters."[9]

Paradoxically, at the same time that this kind of abstraction outlines the gestures and relationships of the characters, it effectively reinscribes the position of viewing so central in the cinema: "One senses the *photography,* since when one feels distance, he [or she] becomes a voyeur and looks at the image itself."[10] Immediately apparent in this notion of spectatorship is that famous "desire to see," which powerfully suggests both the redirection of voyeurism that feminist cinema calls for and the production of new viewing relations with the cinematic text. Varda's reformulation of spectatorship here entails a decisive shift in the quality of the cinematic look—it is not invested with traditional mechanisms of identification—and thereby posits, from her earliest film onward, an erotics of vision not bound by gender hierarchies of the gaze. For in Varda's work, looking itself is pleasurable, regardless of the sex of either viewer or object.

In keeping with the tendency to depict characters in broad general outlines, Varda objectified the characters of *La Pointe-Courte* still further by associating them with inanimate objects. At the time she was making the film, she was greatly influenced by the philosophy of Gaston Bachelard, whom she'd had as a professor at the Sorbonne. She was particularly interested in his theory of *"l'imagination des matières,"* in which certain personality traits were found to correspond to concrete elements in a kind of psychoanalysis of the material world. Bachelard taught Varda to study writers not by the stories they told, but by the material things they mentioned. Thus in *La Pointe-Courte,* the clash of temperaments is rendered through the association of objects—the opposition of wood and steel. The man, son of a shipbuilder, is associated with wood; he has his roots in the village, feels at ease with trees, and knocks on wood for luck. The woman, "this furious, aggressive character, who questioned not only her marriage, but her position and identity as a woman in relation to him,"[11] is evoked by references to trains, rails, and iron fences. But beyond this particular discursive strategy, what is important to note is that here, in Varda's very first film, she is concerned with conveying a very specific feminine problematic through carefully conceived formal devices, thereby indicating, at the outset of her career, a profound comprehension of the radical possibilities of a feminist politics of form.

Another method of character abstraction that began with *La Pointe-Courte*—and is to recur importantly in Varda's subsequent work all the way to *Vagabond*—is the combination of professional actors with nonprofessionals. This articulation of skilled performance and spontaneous naturalism contributes another dimension of contradiction to the basic dialectics of Varda's work. The couple in *La Pointe-Courte* was played by Sylvia Montfort and Philippe Noiret, both professional actors with established theatrical backgrounds. Although *La Pointe-Courte* was Noiret's first film role, both he and Montfort went on to have significant careers in film. Alongside these two professional actors, the actual inhabitants of La Pointe-Courte provided a "documentary" texture to the sequences of village activity that alternated with the couple; the emphasis on parallel worlds produced a critical commentary on the fictive situation.

With *Le Bonheur* things are somewhat different; there is no clear delineation of fictive and actual worlds. Both the Drouot family (who play themselves) and Marie-France Boyer (who plays Drouot's mistress) participate in a single fictional universe; they are all "characters" whose lives intersect. Varda chose Jean-Claude Drouot, known to French audiences as a television personality, after she had read an article on him and his wife, small son, and daughter in the women's magazine, *Marie-Claire*. In *Le Bonheur* the combination of the Drouot family's unself-conscious acting and Boyer's professional sensitivity creates a filmic texture that is both naturalistic and stylized, again reinforcing Varda's dialectical method. She extends this particular type of dialectic still further in *Lions Love*, which has for one of its topics, appropriately, the notion of the Hollywood star. She combines the self-ironic acting of Viva, the celebrated Warhol superstar, with the ad-lib improvisations of James Rado and Jerome Ragni, author-stars of the popular rock-musical *Hair*, and with the emphatically directed acting of Shirley Clarke, the noted documentary filmmaker. This interaction allows Varda to achieve a montage of acting styles by performers who reflexively comment on the production of the film star.

This method achieves a kind of heightened condensation in *Vagabond*, where a relatively young newcomer to acting (Sandrine Bonnaire) is matched with a highly skilled and important actress (Macha Méril), but more significantly, these play opposite a whole range of "ordinary people"—shopkeepers, shepherds, construction workers, vagrants, migrant workers, mechanics, maids—who compose the diverse spectrum of French society. In this case, the combination of professional and non-professional acting styles creates a kind of infinitely reflecting prism, as we view the main character, Mona, through these divergent perspectives while also seeing these varied aspects of French life as well. Varda explains how this use of actors enabled her to achieve the effect of social observation that she sought in the film: "In a way, *Sans toit ni loi* is a portrait of the South of France in that specific winter and how the people in that region reacted to a girl on the road . . . who is a rebel. And you find that you learn more about them than about her. . . . I used a lot of documentary technique to approach the people in the film, the nonprofessionals, to involve them. And then I turned it into fiction by giving them lines. I put them in a fictive situation using both systems and having them interact with professional actors. You come away knowing it's fiction yet feeling it's true."[12]

In all of Varda's work, her direction of actors is what she calls "concrete." Rather than focusing on the psychologies of the characters, Varda prefers to describe an attitude, a gesture, a manner. It is this materialist conception of acting, linked perhaps to the influence of Bachelard, which permits her to attain an acting style concomitant with her overall social conception. In the words of Corinne Marchand, the heroine of *Cleo From 5 to 7*, "Like all great filmmakers, she '*sees*' the ensemble of her subject, she possesses a global vision of her film before shooting. Often, I didn't exactly understand what she was asking of me or why. . . . In a way, she constructed my personality."[13]

It is this directorial "construction" of a character that forms the basis of *Vagabond* as well. In this film, the effects of Varda's technique of composing the film the night before the shooting, explaining little if anything to Bonnaire, and refusing to let rational interpretation or narrative logic inform her characterization, resulted in one of the most complex and demanding portraits of a character to appear in the cinema. Varda speaks of her "gestural" direction in the following way: "I work on behavior . . . gestures, details. I told Sandrine just how she should touch the strap of her backpack, how she should put it down, how she should fix her boot on a tree-stump, or hold the ruined painting. . . . I would often make her repeat the same gesture over and over again. I demanded a very precise kind of action. . . . But finally the character of Mona emerged."[14]

To return to *La Pointe-Courte*, it is interesting to note just how important a structuring matrix this first film has proven to be, for it sets into place a number of textual mechanisms and preoccupations that recur throughout all of Varda's work—recur, in fact, to such an extent that even her most recent work is entirely informed by these concerns. Take, for example, "a sense of place": It might be easily said that, for many of her films, Varda starts with a locale—a deeply felt sense of the effects of environment, both geographic and social—and works from there. In this way, a vision, an image of a place evokes more than the narrative itself, such that the interaction of the character and the milieu produces the theme or "meaning" of the film. For *La Pointe-Courte*, it was the fishing village of that name; for *Cleo*, it was certain streets of Paris and the Parc Montsouris; for *Les Créatures*, it was the rugged coast of Brittany; for *Lions Love*, it was Hollywood; for *Daguerréotypes*, it was the Parisian neighborhood where Varda lived; for *Mur Murs* and *Documenteur*, it was certain sections of Los Angeles; for *Vagabond*, it was the vineyards in the frozen winter landscape of Southern France. Varda has described her work procedure in the following way: "[W]hen I know I'm going to make the film, I often go to the site which will be the setting of the film. I try to really understand the arrangement of things, so that I can integrate [the character] as accurately as possible into an environment which explains him, justifies him, attacks or contradicts him, so that one understands the dialectic between the character and the environment."[15]

For *La Pointe-Courte*, this process involved extensive documentation, through photographs and interviews, of the location and its inhabitants. Varda spent weeks in pre-production, writing the scenario and deliberately mapping every shot. The result is a peculiar combination of highly polished artistry (due to the film's complicated literary texture, which was inspired by Faulkner's *The Wild Palms*) and a documentary naturalism reminiscent of Italian Neo-Realism. For *Vagabond*, the process of observation and notation was even more important, for in this film, character and environment are inseparable from the start; there is a sense in which geography, as it impinges on the social, forms the basic thematic network of the film. Varda began the film with a few ideas, a few feelings, and allowed herself a kind of openness—through casual travels, chance encounters, observations—that would permit her to seize the occasion to "capture" things. On the basis of a two-page sketch of some preliminary ideas, and in the manner of a sociologist, Varda began to travel through the countryside that was her inspiration:

> I found people, but without seeking them out, without a pre-established program in mind. I informed myself, I oriented myself. Through friends I met some shepherds, and then others. I became interested in these post-68 philosophers who had turned to goat-herding. I travelled around, casually, alone. That's how I had all different kinds of encounters: powerful ones,

touching ones, even strange ones. People hitch-hiking, or in bistros, who spoke with me. At this point it wasn't a question of a film-crew, not even an assistant or a manager. I am a person before I'm a filmmaker, or better yet, a filmmaker who's still a person. In these encounters I didn't even talk about film. I was simply someone speaking to someone else: people told me all sorts of things, and, for the most part, these were interesting to me.[16]

The result is what Varda calls "a fiction film which was nourished by reality and real people."[17]

Although *La Pointe-Courte* was received with great enthusiasm by the critics (among them André Bazin and Jacques Doniol-Valcroze), at the time Varda considered filmmaking "a one-time thing"—a film that was made collectively by a group of friends, with very little money, on the margins of the traditional commercial industry. She returned to the more lucrative still photography—Varda is an excellent photographer—until a few years later, when the French Government Tourist Office, via Pierre Braunberger, commissioned her to make two short travel films, *Ô Saisons, ô châteaux* (1957) and *Du Côté de la Côte* (1958). Varda regarded neither film as a serious cinematic statement; she did, however, view the situation pragmatically, concluding that this might be a way to obtain recognition and financial backing from producers wary of the experimental nature of *La Pointe-Courte*.

The first, a twenty-two-minute color film that juxtaposes castles on the Loire with elegant fashion models in Jacques Heim originals, is filled with incisive wit and humor. Varda calls *Châteaux* something of a didactic film, in which fifteen minutes are devoted to "amuseries" (a ballet by the castle gardeners, a comparison of the models to exotic birds, hats and pumpkins, and so forth), while seven minutes teach a short lesson on architecture (the historic evolution of the chateau from a donjon at Loches to the splendors of Chambord). *Du Côté de la Côte*, also a color film, is a humorous fable in thirty-two minutes about the Riviera and the search for earthly paradise: The crowded, somewhat banal beaches and amusements are contrasted with the serene beauty of the locked, inaccessible private gardens (Varda had wanted to call the film *L'Eden-toc* [*Fake Eden*]). The ideal of rest and relaxation comes up flat against the economic reality of property relations on the Cote d'Azur.

Between these two films Varda made the short film *L'Opéra-Mouffe*. It marked a turning-point for her, as she began to see the cinema as an ideal means to express what she was coming to perceive as her own personal—and feminist—vision. *La Pointe-Courte* had contained many innovations which, ironically, had already been done by filmmakers whose work she didn't know (Luchino Visconti, for example). When the similarities were pointed out to her by her editor, Alain Resnais— who has acknowledged the influence of *La Pointe-Courte* on his own work, particularly with respect to the simultaneous narratives, the shifting discursive registers, and the subjective structures of memory and thought—she acknowledged her cinematic "illiteracy" and determined to educate herself in the traditions of cinema. *L'Opéra-Mouffe*, a seventeen-minute "subjective documentary" made in 1958, is the first achievement of this motivation to find a cinematic language expressive of her own particular voice: "I thought all my films as a woman, because I didn't want to be a 'false man' making films. I was trying to make films about what I knew. When I was pregnant, I made a film about pregnancy, as I wanted people to share it with me."[18]

Shot while she was pregnant with her first child, Rosalie (she gave birth to her second, Mathieu, some sixteen years later), this black and white film traces the varied activities on the rue Mouffetard as seen through the eyes of a pregnant woman. In her characteristic dialectical spirit, Varda interweaves the personal and the social, the subjective and the objective, into a detailed exploration of one specific milieu and of one very particular point of view, and in so doing, delineates the constitutive elements of each.

Beyond the personal motive, Varda says she chose pregnancy as her subject because of the contradiction it embodies. For her, pregnancy does not pose simply the idea of the dialectic, but a "lived contradiction": The expectant mother, alive with hope, must continually confront that hopeless spectacle of daily life that surrounds her. *"L'Opéra-Mouffe . . .* recounts how one can be both pregnant, joyful, happy, and at the same time know that life is nothing but poverty and age, which are particularly omnipresent on rue Mouffetard. There the contradiction interested me even more because it was very striking."[19] But Varda goes further than that—she works the contradiction from every angle until it becomes a deromanticization of pregnancy, a vital feminist illustration that cannot be recuperated by patriarchal definitions. The film's images are sometimes metaphors, sometimes violent absurdist symbols, and most often documentary footage shot in this impoverished section of Paris. Varda describes her filming process as one governed by an almost Surrealist principle of the arbitrary: She went to the rue Mouffetard every day and filmed whatever she had the desire to shoot. In the course of this she became an ordinary fixture of the Mouffetard quarter, as common as the vegetable and shellfish hawkers, the Baudelairean flaneur absorbing and observing Parisian street life.

But this raw material is very carefully selected and structured in ways that indicate a highly subjective point of view: a pumpkin being smashed and scooped out, children in masks, a wire doll with a smaller one inside it, close-ups of weary faces, a chicken embryo, shattered glass, lovers on a brass bed, a tree with branches, and so on. The film is divided by chapter headings ("Lovers," "Drunkenness," "Holidays," "Old Age," "Cravings") that structure the visual material—people shopping, gossiping, drinking, making love, and so forth—into units. The images generate a variety of reflections both on the life process itself (love, death, birth, old age) and on the gentle absurdity of ordinary daily activities.

It is a nonnarrative articulation of images that depends for its coherence on the strong, consistent organizing principle of the central point of view. The subjective consciousness, this gaze of the enunciating subject, is thus the unifying factor that weaves the subtle texture of images of daily life through the subjective structures of memory and anticipation. Varda has spoken of L'Opéra-Mouffe as a film that works at the limit of modesty and immodesty; it is in this sense that this profoundly personal vision becomes inseparable from the social context that produces it. And it is here that the film's most productive feminist meaning can be ascertained. Varda's comments combine an interest in filmic composition with the problematics of the gaze, and in so doing suggest that cinema is, above all, an articulation of vision which is at once both personal and deeply social: "It's the type of thinking which pushes looking (le regard) to the limits of cruelty and of tenderness. I felt that, starting with the minutest sensations, I understood lyricism."[20] L'Opéra-Mouffe's importance for feminists lies not so much in the fact that it is a film both from and about the body of the woman (an essentialist trap, to be sure); rather, it is the emphasis on subjectivity as point of view—on the structuring function of "the look"—that makes this film a significant landmark in feminist cinema.

Varda has continued to make short-subject films throughout her career, and she is unequivocally a master of the form. This is partly because she views each short as a sort of "experimental laboratory" or "exploration," and from these earliest films to the later examples she demonstrates an astonishing originality and versatility in matters of both subject and of treatment. Each film, regardless of its style, constitutes a minor meditation on the topic at hand, whether it be an architectural documentary about buildings in Paris (Les Dites-Cariatides, 1984), a poetic reflection on memory, imagination, and representation (Ulysse, 1982), a fantasy combining fictional modes (7 Pièces, cuisine, salle de bains . . . A saisir, 1984), an inquiry into how we perceive and understand images (Une minute pour une image, 1983), or a mini-homage to a film archive (T'as de beaux escaliers, tu sais, 1986). In some cases, Varda's short films can be seen as sketches in miniature of ideas to be expanded in feature-length form (Ô Saisons, ô châteaux contains the landscape and the palette of Le Bonheur; 7 Pièces . . . A saisir interweaves the documentary and fictive discourses of *Vagabond*, whose working title was *A saisir*).

Speaking of the status of these films as investigations into issues of representation, Varda says, "I love short films. They keep me busy and alive with cinematic ideas." "I have made several films around this kind of research into what we feel, what we see, what emotions we experience in relation to other views, other feelings, other choices— this chain reaction—and this has finally resulted in *Vagabond*."[21] *Ulysse*, for example, is a reflection on a photograph Varda took in 1954; the filmmaker examines her own feelings and memories about the photo, as well as those of others—some involved, like Ulysse, the boy in the photo, some twenty-eight years later; others not, like children who respond to what they see by making their own paintings of the photo. Varda ends with an observation about Ulysse's mother: she is gifted for remembering everything. Varda thus explores a moment in time, combining the discourses of history, subjective memory, and imagination in a reflective texture about human consciousness. She turns to work on narration with *7 Pièces* (the title translates like an ad in the apartment listings of the newspaper: "7 rooms, kitchen, bath . . . Get it now!"), a twenty-seven-minute fiction film in which a large, empty apartment becomes populated with an imaginary family, assorted characters, bizarre decors, disappearing oddities, and the like. Threads of narrative are taken up, dropped, recombined, in a fiction that is at once realist and fantastic. *7 Pièces* has much of the humor, irony, and capriciousness of *L'Opéra-Mouffe;* it, too, interweaves subjective registers in a working of fantasy and imagination as they intersect with the reality of place. Each of these short film "experiments" can be seen as demonstrations of a kind of cinematic manifesto: "This is what cinema is all about. Images, sound, whatever, are what we use to construct a way which is cinema, which is supposed to produce effects, not only in our eyes and ears, but in our 'mental' movie theater in which image and sound are already there. . . . What I am dealing with is the effects, the perception, and the subsidiary effects of my work as proposals, as an open field, so that you can get there things you always wanted to feel and maybe didn't know how to express, imagine, watch, observe, whatever."[22]

Varda's next feature film after *La Pointe-Courte*, *Cléo de 5 à 7* (*Cleo From 5 to 7*, 1961), continues the kind of theoretical research into feminist questions that was begun in *L'Opéra-Mouffe*. This film, which will be discussed in greater detail in chapter 10, is a surprisingly prescient cinematic exploration of many of the issues concerning woman's image and "the gaze." Superficially it is about a pop singer who, awaiting the results of a test determining whether or not she has a

mixed modes into a film-collage that interrogates its own methods. *Vagabond*'s personal testimonials in direct address (modified or not) evoke the frontal pronouncements of *The Married Woman* (and numerous other Godard films), while Madame Landier's "discourse on the plane trees" is wonderfully reminiscent of a similar research (into prostitution) in *Vivre sa vie*. And, no stranger to cinematic rule violation (having excelled with brilliant editing tricks in *Le Bonheur*), Varda has provided in *Vagabond* a virtual handbook of such instances (violations of the 180 degree rule, the axis match, movement and direction matches, and of course, the jump-cut) worthy of *Breathless* itself. Likewise, *Vagabond* shares with Resnais as complicated a temporal construction as can be achieved in film, weaving threads of narration into sequences that disappear and return with a compelling fluidity, while structures of memory (such as the flashback, for example) are rendered with the reality of present perception. Time is expanded in *Vagabond* through the delayed testimonies of characters who have perhaps been forgotten; it is condensed through unexpected ellipses that compress events into nothingness. Along with this goes the circularity of the film itself, ending where it had begun, bringing us back to the image which has haunted us (*Marienbad* comes to mind) from the start. And all the while, the continuity of narration—Mona's story, as she travels throughout the region with no visible purpose in mind—provides the connection for a whole range of "moments." Resnais's interest in subjective perception is here, too, for each account of Mona is an account of the self as well. Other elements are reminiscent of Resnais: The interest in Surrealism (the wine-dregs inserts, curious "clues" at the film's beginning, evoking Varda's *Les Créatures* as well as Resnais's *Muriel*, both paradigmatic Left Bank films); the intricate metaphoric structure which creates a signifying network of recurring motifs (all the references to trees, for example, from plane trees to tree people), and the structure of implausibilities which finally, logically, cohere (Tante Lydie's relation to Yolande, Jean-Pierre, and to Mona herself). To say that *Vagabond* shares its strategies of distancing with Godard and its narrative complexity with Resnais is to attest to the exemplary status of all three directors who, each in their particular way, have pushed the limits of cinematic expression in their simultaneous concern with discursive and visual forms.

There is another way that *Vagabond* is exemplary as well. As we have seen, Varda uses interruption as a structural device, creating moments of narrative suspension that generate our own reflection on the events. But this isolation of episodes into discrete units is matched by a rigor-

through the text; she even says "We have so little time left" in one moment, followed by "We've got all the time in the world" in the next.[25] Likewise, the encounter of beauty and death, the juxtaposition of grotesque aberrations (for example, a man eating live frogs) and brilliant loveliness (Cleo's public image), the visual contrasts of light and dark, artificial and natural, the interweaving of lighthearted musical comedy and tragic drama, coquettishness and anguish, all contribute to the subtle texture of oppositions which structures the film.

As with all of her films, Varda wrote the scenario for *Cleo.* She brings a photographer's sense of seeing to her writing, often using still photographs to stimulate her ideas. However, as noted in her discussion of *cinécriture,* writing for films is necessarily grounded, in all cases, in a visual conceptualization. "And yet [*Cleo*] was not written as a scenario, simply to be translated into cinema. I try to work in a 'disordered' way, because I like for a camera angle to precede a figure in my thinking, at times. I like to go from the site to a 'situation,' from the tracking shot to an emotion, from the tempo of montage to a thought."[26]

What emerges in *Cleo* is a ninety-minute portrait of a woman and a city in which important feminist themes intersect with an almost sociological regard for Parisian life. In a 1962 interview Varda said, "Paris for me is linked with feelings of fear and anguish, and I looked for a subject which dealt with fear in Paris."[27] But this theme and this place are only starting points for Varda—her exploration of both produces a profoundly cinematic articulation of the problematics of vision and the woman's image, generated in the film-text but only formulated verbally some thirteen years later. Abounding in visual ideas, cinematic styles, and film-theoretical questions, *Cleo From 5 to 7* marks another important turning point in the development of feminist cinema.

In 1963, Varda made *Salut les Cubains,* a thirty-minute documentary that she wanted to be both didactic and entertaining. Composed entirely of still photographs that she had shot in Cuba with her Leica (of the 4,000 she took, 1,500 were used), the film attempted to capture the Cuban ethos through the folklore of their revolution, the rhythm of their life, the heat of their climate. Varda, who had been invited to Cuba by the Cuban cinema institute (ICAIC), found the country surprising and joyful, and wanted her film to reflect its combination of "socialism and cha cha cha."[28]

Salut les Cubains marks the first of a long list of political documentary films, both short and feature-length, that Varda has made throughout her career. Her consistent commitment to the Left, and to the struggles against oppression in any form—political, economic, or social—has led her to treat a broad range of topics in these films, from the Black

Power movement in California (*Black Panthers*, a 1968 film dealing with the Oakland trial of Huey Newton) and the Viet Nam war (*Loin du Vietnam*, a collective film in episodes made in 1967), to the situation of Greeks in France (*Nausicaa*, a 1970 television documentary using actual Greek exiles in a fictional chronicle), the Hispanic community in Los Angeles (*Mur Murs*, a 1980 "look" at the murals in Los Angeles and their sociopolitical context), photography (*Une minute pour une image*, 1983, a television documentary of 170 ninety-second films, each about a different photograph), and women's liberation (*Réponse de femmes*, 1975).

This last film, an eight-minute *ciné-tract*, was a response to the question, What does it mean to be a woman?, which was posed by a television station for a program entitled *F comme femme*. Varda's film, an affirmation of women's bodies, which had to be edited for television and was later remade as a *ciné-tract* for regular theatrical distribution, emerged from the following impulse: "I said everyone is always talking about the feminine condition and the role of women; I'd like to speak of the woman's body, our body."[29] Although there are overtones of essentialism in this—associating the feminine with the biological, the natural, and the physical—Varda is quick to point out the political implications of this position: "For me, 'being a woman' is first of all having the body of a woman. A body not cut up into more or less exciting parts, a body not limited to so-called erogenous zones (and classified by men). . . ."[30] Thus, possible essentialism is tempered by theoretical reflection, for it ties in very clearly with the important feminist recognition that definitions of femininity and of sexuality are cultural constructs rather than predetermined essences.

In other words, female pleasure, the power over one's own body, the right of choice over pregnancy—all of these are seen as fundamentally political questions that must be claimed by feminists. A concern with the socio-political, as it is lived, marks all of Varda's documentary films, a fact that places the filmmaker's perspective immediately within the subject itself, rather than outside of it, authoritative and distanced. This characterizes the bearing of Varda's political commitment, which was best expressed by her in 1977, in terms of the films she would like to make: "I still have many films I'd like to make, not on problems, but films based on the subject of the people who live these problems. And then, ideas, propositions, departures, active utopias. . . ."[31] As a filmmaker, then, she sees her work of documentation as a political project and engages with a variety of issues and people "not in order to do journalism, but to nourish my imagination with feelings, with things seen, observed, detailed."[32]

Le Bonheur (1965) is one of Varda's most complex, playful, and misunderstood films. Overwhelmingly lush in its visual and aural impact, profoundly feminist in its concerns, it has often been dismissed as a reactionary film by those who fail to understand the multilayered, ironic twists that form its textual core. Ostensibly a philosophical study of happiness that explores the interfaces of cruelty and personal well-being, Le Bonheur offers an extensive critique of traditional feminine roles and social constraints. The film concerns a young carpenter's family; during the course of the family's ritual activities, the husband falls in love with a postal worker in a neighboring town, attempts to manage two simultaneous love affairs, and waxes poetic about the bounties of life; his wife is found drowned, and his mistress comes to replace her in the snug family unit.

One of the most remarkable things about the film is its systematic, antinaturalistic use of color. From the very outset, this color, accompanied by amplified strains of Mozart on the soundtrack, signals the reflective, contemplative distance that the film requires of its spectator. More than an investigation into the nature of happiness, and perhaps more than an analysis and critique of social relations, Le Bonheur represents an exploration into the processes of cinematic representation. In other words, it examines how both the emotional and the societal, the psychological and the political, are mediated by signifying modes that construct our sense of "reality."

Therefore, in Le Bonheur the color is used not so much to enhance the realism of the film as to call attention to itself as material or as dramatic element. For example, the character of Emilie, the postal clerk, is associated with lavender, a color that virtually explodes on the screen after the wife's death. Likewise, the clothing of the Drouot family is coordinated with the springtime and autumnal tones of the family picnics, the fronts of the houses are painted in vivid, dominant hues, while the sexual passages are highlighted in warm, pastel shades, and the fades between sequences are not to the usual black, but to gradations of blue, white, or red. In this Varda was not attempting a kind of color symbolism that would equate happiness, for example, with yellow. Rather she was outlining the parameters of a color system that would interact with other structures of meaning in the film-text to provide sociocritical commentary on the emotional material of the plot.

Varda had already manifested a strong sense of color dynamics in her black and white films like La Pointe-Courte and Cleo; indeed, she has said that black and white are colors too.[33] There the sharp contrasts displayed an almost Manichean compositional duality which recalls the films of Antonioni. "Le Bonheur was my first color [feature] film,"

Varda said in a 1971 interview. "It was essentially a research of the palette, in the sense that I sought combinations: yellow, green, violet, or red, pink, orange or blue. I tried, with a very simple subject, to do Impressionist painting. . . . "[34] Her debt to the Renoirs, both father and son, is even made explicit in the film: an insert from Jean Renoir's *Le Dejeuner sur l'herbe* appears at one point on a television screen, while Varda implicitly evokes Impressionist painting theory in her use of analytic color shading (violet as the shadow of orange, for example). This interest in color remains throughout Varda's career, and in 1967 she made a small hommage film to someone whom she felt was partially responsible for this. In discussing this twenty-minute color film about her painter-hippie Greek relative who lived on a houseboat (*Oncle Yanco*) she says, "I made a short film about my Uncle Yanco, this father of dreams who I only found later in life. He was fabulous and tender. He spoke wonderfully of colors, and of his own painting; he said, 'between desire and the canvas . . . there's a little bit of bitterness, a shadow passes.' That moved me quite a bit. There is no light without shadow, and shadow is beautiful. I look for that—bright shadows."[35]

The audience reaction to *Le Bonheur* was extremely varied. Some found the film alienating because of its stylization of gesture and decor, its structure of repetitions, and its refusal to develop characters with psychological depth. Some criticized the depiction of Drouot's work relations while others were troubled by the lack of a strict moral message. For Varda's purposes, this was all to the better, as she was primarily interested in stimulating critical reflection on the part of the spectators. When people left the film they were asking themselves— and each other—questions concerning the nature of happiness, of sexual relations, of social constructs, and so forth. "Finally, it's a spectacle which demands a certain kind of activity from its spectator. . . . [I]t became a matter of confrontation, of consciousness, of *prise de conscience*. . . . The film exposes a situation. Obviously, each spectator draws his [or her] own conclusions, judging the characters by personal criteria. I think that's really good."[36]

One of the ways Varda achieves this is through the analytic use— and subversion—of cliches. "*Le Bonheur* is not the psychological story of an egotistical man torn between two blonds. Rather, it is a minute exposition, almost obsessional, of the images and cliches of a certain happiness; it's the gesture, and the function of this gesture up to the point where its signification explodes."[37] Through this kind of extended exploration, which involves, as does caricature, the exaggeration of certain details and the distortion of others, Varda produces an analytic view of the functions of the bourgeois housewife, of patriarchal dominance, of the ideological consequences of a certain concept of well-being, of the necessary interrelations entailed by personal actions—and casts these all in the light of feminist critical evaluation. It is a form of Brechtian outlining of a social situation that highlights certain elements while leaving the spectator in the productive position of forming his or her own conclusions. Varda discusses this procedure in terms of an interesting distinction between *problems* (a reified notion implying a specific solution) and *questions* (a concept involving productive dynamism and one's participation in the search for a solution). "I'm not really interested in problems, but in certain questions. [Even the spectator who goes to the cinema primarily for entertainment needs certain films which pose questions.] In the end, I think that people have a taste for reflection. . . . I like a film which acts as a sort of discoverer [*révélateur*] . . . . I try to pose these questions in a way which is both clear and ambiguous, so that the spectator may pose them to himself [or herself] in turn."[38]

In posing both psychology and morality as social constructions, in organizing her film as a series of didactic "situations," Varda also engages in an implicit critique of one of the conventional forms of cinematic storytelling. The circular structure of *Le Bonheur*—which opens on a Drouot family picnic in the springtime and ends with an autumnal family outing (with the important difference that the mistress now takes the place of the wife and thus fulfills the maternal function)—substitutes a symmetrical organizing pattern for the traditional linear plot. The film proceeds by a series of repetitions, refrains that highlight the ritual, episodic nature of the familial (and sexual) interactions.

But these effects of symmetry also result in underscoring what film theory has designated as the textual logic of the classical Hollywood model. The work of Raymond Bellour, for example, has demonstrated the ways in which rhyming effects and relations of differential repetition structure the development of the narrative in dominant cinema. In analyses of textual production, these substitutive relations and effects work at every level of the film, creating a kind of productive textual volume beneath the linear flow of the plot. It appears that in *Le Bonheur,* by laying bare these effects of symmetry and regulated difference and forcing them to a position of prominence in the film, Varda has effectively outlined this traditional narrative impulse. Thus, in exaggerating the conventions of both the melodrama and the musical, and in objectifying the codic operations of symmetrical repetition-resolution, Varda produces in *Le Bonheur* a level of formal critique of commercial narrative cinema, just as certainly as she challenges patriarchal social relations.

Varda continued this exploration of narrativity with her next feature, *Les Créatures* (1966). A "science-fiction" fantasy (Varda's term, emphasizing the combination of speculative science and fictional manipulation) that blends black and white photography with occasional flashes of red tinting of different intensities, the film carries distancing techniques still further as symbolic characters embodying both social and instinctual forces interact in a highly stylized drama that examines the nature of fiction, language, power relations, and sexual roles. The narrative concerns a writer (Michel Piccoli) and his wife (Catherine Deneuve), who live in a fortress-like tower on the rugged Brittany coast, in Noirmoutier-en-l'Isle. The wife, who has lost the power of speech in an auto accident, becomes pregnant, and the film interweaves two parallel themes—the creation of a novel and the birth of a child—within a texture that explores the problematics of social isolation and despotic dominance implied in any fictive creation.

While the wife communicates solely through written words and mute gestures of both affection and apprehension, the husband roams the island in search of material for his novel. And as the wife's pregnancy grows closer to term, the neighboring townspeople are incorporated more vividly into the husband's inventions. The dialectic of stasis and mobility, gender-defined and associated with two types of creation (equally gender-defined), thus becomes the framework for an eventually inextricable intermingling of fantasy and reality. Finally, the two parallel plots, one actual and the other developing in the mind of the novelist, intersect at the film's climax: the birth of the baby is counterposed against a bizarre chess game in which the novelist competes with a maniacal scientist in manipulating the relationships between the "characters" on the island.

What does it mean for Varda to use a woman deprived of the power of speech as a figure in her parable of fictive domination? Perhaps an essentialist reading would find "true" creative force in the woman's life-giving capability. However, more important, the film's primary concern is with discursive processes, with the relationship of people in and through language. Varda has said that her interest in the notion of the couple in *Les Créatures* was different from that in either *La Pointe-Courte* or *Le Bonheur*. *Les Créatures* does not simply deal with two people in love whose mutual comprehension, or lack of it, makes them capable, or incapable, of overcoming loneliness; rather, it deals with two people who have very specific problems of their own to work out, and the focus is on the particularities of each character's situation.[39]

Both of these situations are fundamentally concerned with language. The husband, a writer, is continually engaged in an attempt to give fictive life to the products of his imagination. The wife, incapable of speech, is involved in consistent efforts to communicate her thoughts and feelings in the most material of circumstances. Language is posited as a social space of intersecting relations, the discursive texture through which all human interaction must flow. Thus the problematic of the couple is seen in terms of a linguistic relation, and this relation in turn is posed as the basis of all sociality.

Therefore, rather than a simple love story, *Les Créatures* is a story of desire in language. Part philosophical essay, part thriller, the film was received by its audience largely as a science-fiction adventure film. (Henri Langlois had wanted to program the film at the Cinémathèque with a series of Méliès shorts.) Varda acknowledges this by noting that the film's subject matter evokes critical reflection and contemplation while its treatment is that of an adventure film. By this very procedure, *Les Créatures* is the kind of film that Varda posits as successfully instructive: "We shouldn't forget that the movie is a popular art; people go to movies to have a good time. They don't want to be taught all the time. That's why we have to change the image of women, but we have to be careful not to become such bores that no one wants to listen to anything."[40]

In 1969, Varda made *Lions Love;* an ambivalent, critical-affectionate view of movie-making in its attested "mecca," this reflexive semidocumentary uses Hollywood as a metonymy for American culture in order to explore the mass-media constructions of the American ethos. Varda prefers to think of *Lions Love* as a "film-collage" in which a variety of intersecting elements, from movie myths and the American underground to psychodrama and political assassination, combine to produce an analysis of the peculiar intertwining of sex and politics that forms American cultural ideology.

In a 1971 interview, Varda outlined the subjects treated in this "collage" in a fairly systematic fashion. What follows is a general paraphrase of her categories and explanations, with one or two additional comments of my own.

1. Stars: New stars of the Pop scene, Viva as a "space-age Mary Pickford"; nostalgia for past stars, "Jean Harlow" in Michael McClure's *The Beard;* politicians as stars, the Bobby Kennedy assassination; the attempted assassination of Andy Warhol.

2. Making a film in Hollywood: Some self-referential strategies; a conversation about the financing of a movie in America; the episode of Shirley Clarke's "attempted suicide," directed by Varda; Clarke as the epitome of the filmmaker who struggles for an Independent American Cinema in the face of commercial traditionalists.

3. Liberation and quest: The three actors live freely, but not simply in sexual freedom; a sort of mystical quest involving love and the search for happiness; alternative "familial" relations and roles.

4. Hollywood: The magic of the city, its boulevards, its studios.

5. End of youth: The Viva-Ragni-Rado group are too old to be hippies, too young to be adults; flower children and other kids; "I showed the whole movie to an audience of children, aged about twelve or so, and they loved it."[41]

6. Contradictions: Between political events and private life; the tragic event of an assassination reduced to the contours of a television set; the intimacy of three people having breakfast in bed, projected on a gigantic screen.

7. The assassination of Bobby Kennedy: The death of a hero; the continuation of the Shakespearean tragedy of the Kennedys; Viva: "What can we do if not try to amuse ourselves when the national pastime is televised death?".

8. "In resume: The film has as its subject, stars, films, freedom in love, freedom in editing, California trees, tv, the end of youth, plastic flowers, political heroes, swimming pools, red glasses, rented houses of Hollywood, coffee, and who must get out of bed first in order to make it."[42]

One of the striking things about *Lions Love* is Varda's uncanny sense of what might be called "politics of milieu." As noted previously, in her almost sociological cinematic explorations of cultural situations, Varda has consistently emphasized the effects of place on the social relations she analyzes; this has been a recurrent thread in her work from *La Pointe-Courte* onward. While her utilization of Brechtian critical distance implies a type of characterization which deemphasizes personal psychology, her sensitivity to the importance of locale has formed the basis for her social delineation of character. This interest informs *Daguerréotypes* (1975), a feature-length documentary, filmed in color, about the people and the street where Varda lives when in Paris. In keeping with her sense of social environment, Varda has described the film as "an attentive look at the silent majority, the portrait of a local neighborhood family, their relations with illusionism, a magician, immobility."[43]

As with *L'Opéra-Mouffe* some sixteen years before, Varda made the film while she was pregnant, and used it as a means of exploring both her specific point of view and her surrounding environment. Both films have punning titles, and a comparison of these wordplays can indicate a minor shift in emphasis in Varda's work from an attested personal vision to a more broadly social concern. However, this is simply a slight transformation rather than a complete change of subject, for as my discussion shows, both films depend on an integration of the personal and the public for their particular treatments of their material. The musical title of *L'Opéra-Mouffe* stresses the lyrical concern with the spectacle of life observed on the rue Mouffetard; "l'opéra-bouffe" is French for comic operetta. The different sensations, cravings, and curious particularities that pregnancy confers on this vision are orchestrated into a kind of poetic light opera. *Daguerréotypes* plays on three words: the rue Daguerre in the XIVth Arrondissement of Paris, the ordinary people who inhabit this street (*les types*), and the daguerreotype, that early photographic portrait on a silver-coated metallic plate. The film's title thus produces a condensation of people, milieu, and processes of representation—an exploration of ideology as it is lived.

Varda speaks of her procedure for *Daguerréotypes* as a "*double démarche*," in which the approaches of a documentarist and a feminist combine to examine the specific nature of the political world view that constitutes the "silent majority." The film explores her own ambiguous relation to the quarter and uses the situation of her pregnancy in order to produce a feminist reflection on the issues. These are people with whom she has daily, quasi-personal encounters; there is a similarity of quotidian experience and activity, a shared sense of the domestic. And yet, an overwhelming difference of political perspective (for example, regarding such issues as abortion, the death penalty, the CIA involvement in Salvador Allende's death) creates a distance that firmly delineates two separate worlds.

In an attempt to convey a sense of the limitation that pregnancy imposes on a filmmaker's freedom, Varda firmly circumscribed the area she filmed to conform to the exact amount of space of her apartment. Concomitant with the implied domesticity of her situation, Varda employed a technique of documenting the ordinary, an attention to detail that she feels is an important part of her feminism: "[*Daguerréotypes* uses] a completely quotidian approach—I sought to capture the people's way of life, their smallest gestures. . . . In this simplicity I touch on another aspect of feminism: filming in a simple way the simplicity of daily life. . . . I preferred to make a testimony [*un témoignage*] of the world open to women, rather than making a film about a woman who simply goes shopping."[44] In other words, Varda approaches the important political questions by means of an immersion in the everyday, allowing this vision of the world available to women a more critical effectivity than the fictional description of a character's experience.

In doing this Varda also attempts to avoid the aggressivity toward the subject involved in most conventional documentaries. Her solution is a procedure that mediates the look of the camera in order to film people without violation, while the emphasis on the camera's position as a position of looking is maintained. Varda achieved the first effect by inserting herself as filmmaker into the milieu: she spoke to the people of rue Daguerre about her interest in understanding their gestures, the rhythm of their lives, and at the same time gave her own answers to the questions she asked of them, for example, their name and age, occupation, and dreams. But the film itself, consistent with Varda's continual preoccupation with vision, asserts the look of the camera as an unavoidable presence: "The general idea was that of a camera which was always present, supple, discrete, a bit mute, a bit immobile."[45] In the final analysis, however, it was the filmed image's power of fascination that endured. Speaking of a projection of *Daguerréotypes* held for the people of rue Daguerre in an effort to stimulate discussion of the political issues raised by the film, Varda noted that the people were mainly captivated by the images of themselves: "The image had a magical power, not a political one."[46] An inadvertant object lesson in the cinema's fascinating hold was thus achieved.

Between 1966 and 1975, Varda was generally unable to obtain financial backing and thus made only a few films (notably *Lions Love, Nausicaa,* and *Daguerréotypes*). During that time she wrote four scenarios, *Christmas Carole, Hélène au miroir, Viveca le Sage,* and *Mon corps est a moi,* the latter inspired by collective discussions with feminists. Finally, in 1976 she received an *avance sur recettes* (an interest-free advance on box office receipts) for *L'une chante, l'autre pas,* a color feature film that was released in 1977. Varda calls the film, which spans fifteen years in the lives of two women and traces the development of the women's rights movement between 1962 and 1972, a "feminist musical." In this fable of feminine identity, the two protagonists "live the classic events of women's lives"[47] as a variety of women's issues are presented and analyzed: the result is a form of "double textual work" which weaves fictive and documentary, imaginary and actual in a sort of female bildungsroman with a feminist content.

For the part of the film concerning feminist issues, Varda provides a ready catalogue: "Maternity, on all fronts at once. Free and guiltless abortion. Non-possession of children. Horror of parental authority. Love for children, other people's as well. Contraception. New laws. Sex education. Love for men. Desire to have children. Fatherly tenderness. Disrupted family. Vitalizing pregnancy. Freedom of identity, with or without children. It's no longer a film, it's an encyclopedia."[48]

Many of these issues focus on traditional concepts of the family and the subordination of women implied by these definitions. In her explorations of what it means to be a woman, then, Varda focusses on conventional constructions of femininity and women's experience of oppression within these constraints. Characteristically, her research for the film involved the close observation of the people around her, a sensitivity to the small changes going on in her friends' lives, and an awareness of the articulated problems of women she knew or came in contact with.

In *L'Une chante* she combines this quasi-sociological documentation with the depiction of a fictive universe in which her two protagonists experience the need for political strength and women's solidarity. However, as usual, Varda tries consistently to denaturalize her fiction by providing elements of subversion that work against the production of too realistic a texture. One of her strategies is a narrator's voice-over commentary (spoken by Varda herself); this voice never hovers over the action in a position of omniscience, but rather inserts itself into the fiction as another character, a critical yet sympathetic female voice. Another distancing device is the use of musical comedy conventions such as songs, storybook images, dreamscapes, and saturated color, all of which provide a reflexive commentary on the genre film. Finally, the film offers a subversion of the romantic novel by parodying traditional nineteenth-century narrative structures through the insertion of female characters into conventionally masculine roles such as the chance encounter, the attraction, the establishment of a relationship, and so forth.

However, a problem arises when one considers these devices and strategies in terms of the essentialist debate, for from this perspective they merely produce a cinematic politics of simple inversion, substituting "female" meanings into "male" structures. As such, they can only provide one level of feminist resistance. By having women's relationships and political struggles as its subject matter, *L'Une chante* can make only a limited critique of patriarchal structures; it cannot work profoundly on the level of representation and symbolic relations. It is one thing to discuss the "dreams and desires" of actual women in society, but quite another to work at the level of the production process of those desires. More important, an effective feminist analysis should attempt to understand how the figure of the woman functions in broader desiring productions of the cultural formation. This places *L'Une chante, l'autre pas* in the somewhat paradoxical position of being an avowedly feminist film while having only limited application in a theoretical context. Shortly, I will discuss how Varda resolves this critical problem with extraordinary clarity and vision when she takes up these issues eight years later, in *Vagabond.*

In fact, the work was already begun with *Documenteur* (1981), for in this film Varda attempts a reformulation of the very notion of textual space by allowing a fictive and documentary interplay to work across two different film-texts, thereby creating the reflection on representation that was lacking in *L'Une chante. Documenteur* (whose parenthetical title, *An Emotion Picture,* plays on its fictional nature) is a sixty-five-minute narrative about a divorced woman with a child who works as a secretary and struggles to make ends meet. It is a companion piece to *Mur Murs* (a pun on "walls" and "whispers") which is a documentary about the murals in Los Angeles that is, briefly, but only tangentially, referred to in *Documenteur.* When both films are screened together, as is the intention, constant intersecting references are made to the nature of representation, to the inevitable mediation of lived experience in and through language, and, by extension, to the symbolic structures that underlie all human interaction. This double screening is also, as Varda herself asserts about her film practice in general, a way of moving the audience emotionally in order to have it reflect on critical questions.

In a sliding of pronominal functions that matches the intermixing of documentary and fiction, subjective and objective visions, *Mur Murs* is a documentary in the first person—a personal look at the Los Angeles mural scene—while *Documenteur* is, paradoxically, an autobiography in the third. Its "fictional" narrative is quasi-autobiographical; made around the time Varda and her husband Jacques Demy separated (although they have since gone back together), the film explores the situation of a newly unmarried French woman living alone in Los Angeles with her young son. But the characters and events are acted, staged; if Varda's own son Mathieu plays the boy, Varda's editor, Sabine Mamou (and not Varda herself) acts the part of the woman, and a number of other fictive characters are played by friends and acquaintances. The problems and preoccupations of filming *Mur Murs* form part of the fictional texture of *Documenteur,* so that its highly emotional narrative framework of a woman's personal problems intersects with critical reflection about the nature of film.

The title pun, a combination of "documentary" (*documentaire*) and "liar" (*menteur*), evokes the complex problematic of documentary "fiction" and filmed "truth." This kind of questioning has run throughout Varda's work, from the intermingling of materials in the two parallel plots of *La Pointe-Courte* to the critical examination of Hollywood's fictive construction of "reality" in *Lions Love*. In fact, Varda's discussion of the original title for this latter film provides some useful insight into the intersecting threads of meaning in *Documenteur*.[49] At first entitled *Lions, Loves, and Lies*, the film got its final name from the more expedient *Lions Love* on the clapper during shooting. "Lions" referred to the fact that actors are something like lions; a constellation of meanings combined the imperious quality in the notion of the star, the MGM logo, and politicians as actors. "Love" referred to the relationship of the three main characters, whose interaction was provoked by the question, How does the post-Hippie generation conceive of conjugal life? And "lies," the theme everywhere apparent in the film but excised from its title, resurfaces with the notion of "menteur" in the later film. For Varda, a series of questions implicit in any filmmaking project, or in any consideration of the ideological bearing of the cinema, came together in the term "lies." Are actors liars? Are politicians? What is the Hollywood lie? Is a Hollywood film on the new stars a documentary or fiction? Is it cinema-lies (*cinéma-mensonge*), as opposed to the traditional notion of documentary as cinema-truth (*cinéma-vérité*)?

In fact, Varda's conceptualization of her own cinematic practice is much more fluid and integrated than this seemingly rigid dichotomy of truth and fiction would suggest. For her, films consist of a studied articulation of certain subjects, such as milieux, people, and issues, with the formal and discursive concerns of cinematic structure. To emphasize the content side of this dialectic by focusing on the referential aspects of Varda's films is to neglect the importance of the signifying operations that make the rendering of this material possible. It is the inextricability, the inseparability of elements in this dialectical process that Varda stresses: "I really try for a Lumière/Méliès cinema. Using this superb cinematographic matter which is the faces of people really enmeshed in their situation (daily lives), though not surprised nor spied on. . . . And using, as well, this imagery from the dream-cinema, all the baggage and iconography—depending on the case—of our mental world. And forms. And colors which attach themselves to words of dialogue rewritten on the very day of shooting, but structured one or two months before. The internal music when one films—that's the tempo."[50]

This complex intersection of cinema/reality, truth/fiction finds its most cogent formulation in theories of cinematic meaning-production. What this means for feminists is a shift away from the content of films in terms of feminist issues or women's lives toward a more theoretically based consideration of representation itself. Consequently, agitational cinema around specific questions, traditionally the province of feminist filmmaking, must give way to the kind of work aimed at more fundamentally social concerns, such as the constructions of meaning in a particular cultural formation. In fact, when Varda discusses the position of the woman filmmaker, she implies that an awareness of this critical problem of cinematic meaning is at the core of feminist cinema: "Finding one's identity as a woman is a difficult thing: in society, in private life, in one's body. This search for identity has a certain meaning for a woman filmmaker: it is also a search for a way of filming *as a woman* [*filmer en femme*]."[51]

This manner of "filming as a woman" is precisely what Varda powerfully achieves with her remarkable 1985 feature film, *Sans toit ni loi* (*Vagabond*), for it is here that she brings to bear a distinctly feminine authorial voice in exploring the social articulation of vision and (feminine) identity. As a film, it resumes all of the issues and discursive strategies associated with Varda's work: The basic sense of dialectics that informs her films; the interest in narrational processes that blend documentary and fictional modes; the narrative fragmentation and temporal dislocation of episodically structured texts; the production of a critically engaged spectator; the redirection of the gaze into a dispersed erotics of looking; the sociological investigation of a cultural milieu; the concern with women's issues and the representation of the female body. And precisely because of this, it is here in *Vagabond* that we see most clearly what has arguably been Varda's central concern all along: constructions of "the feminine" as they are visually and culturally inscribed.

The film depicts, in a sort of heterogeneously composed flashback, the last days in the life of a teenage vagrant named Mona, and it is this "construction" that forms the textual and thematic core of the film. Found frozen to death in a ditch at the film's beginning, this fierce and solitary vagabond is described by the variety of people who had encountered her as she strode defiantly across the icy winter landscape of the Languedoc. Each of them—workers, peasants, hippies, professionals—has a different recollection, a different interaction, a different observation. As these "characters" (both actors and nonprofessionals) remember their impressions, the plurality of discourses—documentary, direct testimonial, fictional construct—creates what Varda calls an "impossible portrait" of Mona. At the same time, the complex interweaving of their testimonies constructs a social vision of French culture as well. Varda refuses to offer us the security of a fixed identity for her character; rather, through her careful orchestration of these diverse visions, she invites us to participate in the construction of meaning—of this woman, of her situation, of the necessary social context for all of human activity.

This set of strategies poses significant challenges to both the established conception of authorship and to traditional modes of representation, and it is from this perspective that, although it offers no positive female role model, the film represents a highly productive feminist cinematic alternative. In this light, Varda's comments are very suggestive:

> For this film, I invented a character who rejects me. It's someone who is very different from me, that attracts and repels me at the same time; someone I cannot completely understand. I placed myself in a very peculiar "auteur" situation since I don't know much more than the witnesses who saw her pass through. Sometimes I am very close to her, sometimes very far.

> More than just Mona herself who always eludes us, who is too reserved, too closed, the film addresses "the Mona effect" on those she came in contact with and inevitably affected. She is a catalyst, someone who forces others to react and adjust themselves in relation to her. This is true for the actors in the film and also for the audience. I hope for personal reactions to my films and allow for varying opinions. We are not with Mona because she is dirty, selfish, unappealing. [On the other hand] we are with her because she walks freely; she carries something of ourselves with her, some of our dreams, our struggles.[52]

In reformulating her authorial stance in this way, Varda interrogates the notion of the filmmaker as punctual source of truth and raises philosophical questions about the discursive production of that truth. She initiates the interrogative mode very near the beginning of the film, as her own melodious voice-over glides on the surface of endless dunes, track-lines of erosion patterning the sand: "I wonder, do those who knew her as a child still think about her? People she had met recently remembered her . . . she left a mark on them. She impressed those she met last; they spoke of her as if she wasn't dead, or they didn't know that she had died. I know little about her myself, but it almost seems to me that she came from the sea."

Varda thus immediately foregrounds her presence as enunciative source while simultaneously relinquishing all authoritative certainty. She marks herself as distributor of the visions we are about to see, but yet retains no power over those visions—she simply offers them to us for our own active judgment. This is a process that renders enunciation dialectical, calls into question the text's controlling force. Intrigued by Mona herself, Varda sets into play a number of contradictory impressions, visions of characters that she creates but does not control, and thereby reflexively comments on all fiction-making processes—both within the film and beyond it. Varda dedicates *Vagabond* to Nathalie Sarraute, a French "New Novelist" whose concern with perception and consciousness parallels her own: "It is a tribute to her, because I try in my films to do what she does in her writing, to give people the chance to feel the connection between the work and what they have felt at some time. The artist is one who shows you the feeling without telling you what you have to feel. I love films that allow the filmmakers not to decide what is good and bad, not to make statements."[53]

Because the film takes the form of an inquiry, the characters are all figured as witnesses who contribute their testimonies to the construction of Mona. As we have seen, this sociological eye of Varda's goes all the way back to her very first film, *La Pointe-Courte,* and finds its most accomplished elaboration in *Daguerréotypes,* where the filmmaker, in fact, refers to the activity of "witnessing" daily life. Here, again, Varda refers to these diverse representatives of French society as "witnesses," this time in relation to a fictional construct that she—and they—have created: "These witnesses get close to her, stand back, warm up to her, reject her, criticize her, but empathize as well, etc., always contradictory positions. . . . "[54] The idea of witnessing, itself, combines both verbal and visual registers in its meaning and thus implies that essentially visual discursive construction embodied in Varda's concept of *cinécriture.* For what are witnesses if not those who relate to experience from a position of viewing, and what are their testimonies if not the verbalization, the putting into language, of these visions? *Vagabond* itself is a perpetual testimony to the verbal and the visual—discursive— construction of reality.

And finally, Mona herself, this "impossible portrait"—this wanderer, this homeless person, this . . . woman. In this film, Varda as filmmaker asks the questions—the social and psychic questions of femininity. And in posing a central character who remains an enigma, she offers us, and her characters, the possibility of engaging in the process of meaning construction. The woman is posed as enigmatic precisely to allow us to explore the production of that enigma. We see her from a variety of perspectives, each discourse constructing another vision of her. Speaking of the detailed reconstitution of a portion of the shooting that was published in *Les Cahiers du cinéma,* Varda refers to each technician's version of one day of work as *"Rashomona."*[55] This work of continually engaging with meanings, then, is something shared by author, production workers, characters, and viewers alike, for Mona becomes the cinema itself. It is not so much that the film posits Mona as "unknowable," then, but that it offers all of us the profoundly social activity to *trying* to know, engaging with her (and ourselves) in the production of cultural meanings. As a consequence, we are led to this conclusion: The "Mona effect" is nothing other than the riddle of femininity politicized.

NOTES

1. Agnès Varda, "Propos sur le cinéma récueillis par Mireille Amiel," *Cinéma 75*, no. 204 (December 1975): 50. All translations from the French are my own unless otherwise noted.

2. Agnès Varda, "Avant-propos," *Cléo de 5 à 7* (scénario) (Paris: Editions Gallimard, 1962), p. 7.

3. Cited by Roy Armes in *French Cinema since 1946*, vol. 2: *The Personal Style* (Cranbury, N.J.: A.S. Barnes, 1970), p. 108.

4. Agnès Varda, "Entretien avec Jean Narboni, Serge Toubiana, et Dominique Villain," *Les Cahiers du cinéma*, no. 276 (May 1977): 25.

5. Agnès Varda, "Interview: A Personal Vision," *Passion*, June–July 1986, p. 20.

6. Agnès Varda, "Agnes Varda: A Conversation with Barbara Quart," *Film Quarterly* 40:2 (Winter 1986–87): 4.

7. Georges Sadoul, *Dictionnaire des films* (Paris: Editions du Seuil, 1965), p. 196.

8. Agnès Varda, "Entretien avec Hubert Arnault," *Image et son: La Révue du cinéma*, no. 201 (January 1967): 44.

9. Agnès Varda, in Annette Insdorf, "Filmmaker Agnes Varda: Stimulating Discomfort," *International Herald Tribune*, June 11, 1986.

10. Agnès Varda, in Jacqueline Levitin, "Mother of the New Wave: An Interview with Agnès Varda," *Women and Film*, nos. 5–6 (1974): 66.

11. Varda, "Mother of the New Wave," p. 66.

12. Varda, "A Personal Vision," *Passion*, p. 20.

13. "Entretien avec Corinne Marchand," publicity release from the distributor of *Cléo de 5 à 7*, Rome-Paris Films, 1961.

14. Agnès Varda, "Agnès Varda de 5 à 7," *Cinématographe*, no. 114 (December 1985): 21.

15. Varda, "Mother of the New Wave," *Women and Film*, p. 66.

16. Agnès Varda, "Mona, nomade," *Cinéma 85*, no. 322 (December 4–10, 1985): 2.

17. Agnès Varda, "Entretien avec Agnès Varda," *Cinébulles* 5:3 (1985): 6.

18. Varda, "Mother of the New Wave," *Women and Film*, p. 63.

19. Varda, "Propos sur le cinéma," *Cinéma 75*, p. 45.

20. Agnès Varda, "La grace laïque: Entretien avec Agnès Varda par Jean-André Fieschi et Claude Ollier," *Les Cahiers du cinéma*, no. 165 (April 1965): 48.

21. Varda, "A Personal Vision," *Passion*, p. 20, and Varda, "Entretien," *Cinébulles*, p. 7.

22. Varda, "A Conversation," *Film Quarterly*, p. 7.

23. Varda, "Propos sur le cinéma," *Cinéma 75*, pp. 47–48.

24. Varda, "Avant-propos," p. 9.

25. Noted by Varda in Ibid.

26. Varda, "Avant-propos," p. 7.

27. Agnès Varda, "Interview with Mark Shivas," *Movie*, no. 3 (October 1962): 33.

28. Varda, "Propos sur le cinéma," *Cinéma 75*, p. 53.

29. Ibid., p. 48.

30. Ibid.

31. Varda, "Entretien avec Jean Narboni et al.," *Les Cahiers du cinéma*, p. 26.

32. Varda, "Mona nomade," *Cinéma 85*, p. 2

33. Agnès Varda, screening of *Kung-Fu Master*, Museum of Modern Art, April 19, 1988.

34. Agnès Varda, "Entretien," *Jeune Cinéma*, no. 52 (February 1971); cited by Charles Ford, *Femmes cinéastes* (Paris: Denoël, 1972), p. 113.

35. Varda, "Entretien avec Jean Narboni et al.," *Les Cahiers du cinéma*, p. 25.

36. Varda, "Entretien avec Hubert Arnault," *Image et son*, pp. 41–42.

37. Varda, "Propos sur le cinéma," *Cinéma 75*, p. 49.

38. Varda, "Entretien avec Hubert Arnault," *Image et son*, p. 41.

39. Ibid., p. 44.

40. Varda, "Mother of the New Wave," *Women and Film*, p. 65.

41. Agnès Varda, "The Underground River: Interview with Gordon Gow," *Films and Filming* (March 1970): 10.

42. Agnès Varda, "*Lions Love*: Entretien avec André Cornand," *Image et son: La Révue du cinéma*, no. 247 (February 1971): 98.

43. Filmography provided by the American distributor of *Mur Murs* and *Documenteur*, Tom Taplin, TET Films, 1981.

44. Varda, "Propos sur le cinéma," *Cinéma 75*, pp. 40–41.

45. Ibid., p. 40

46. Ibid., p. 45.

47. Varda, "Entretien avec Jean Narboni et al.," *Les Cahiers du cinéma*, p. 22.

48. Ibid., p. 24.

49. Varda, "*Lions Love*," *Image et son*, p. 98.

50. Varda, "Entretien avec Jean Narboni et al.," *Les Cahiers du cinéma*, p. 25.

51. Varda, "Propos sur le cinéma," *Cinéma 75*, p. 46.

52. Agnès Varda, "Press Book" for *Vagabond*, p. 8, prepared by the American distributor, International Film Exchange Ltd.; special thanks to Stephanie Holm.

53. Agnès Varda, in John Harkness, "Agnès Varda: Improvised Inspiration," *Now*, June 19–25, 1986.

54. Varda, "Entretien," *Cinébulles*, p. 6.

55. Agnès Varda, "Un Jour sous le ciel," *Les Cahiers du cinéma*, no. 378 (December 1985): 15.

NINE

Varda in Context: French Film Production in the Early Sixties—The New Wave

AGNÈS VARDA'S RELATIONSHIP to the filmmaking context of her time—that explosion of cinematic energy and experimentation in the late fifties and early sixties that has been loosely but unmistakably defined as the New Wave—is a complex and paradoxical one. Credited by many with making the first authentic film of the New Wave (five years before the "initiating" and paradigmatic *Breathless* by Jean-Luc Godard)[1] and continuing, throughout her career, with a consistent commitment to what have been interpreted as the aims, ideals, and critical formulations of the group—although Varda herself asserts that there was never a formalized group nor a specific program—she is given only scant attention (if any at all) in most of the accounts of that film movement. As I maintained in the introduction to this book, the New Wave represents the third "period of cinematic resistance" to the traditional commercial norms of Hollywood (and established French) production, and as such defines itself in terms of a newly conceived national and cinematic specificity. The powerfully innovative, energetic, and imaginative work of such directors as Jean-Luc Godard, François Truffaut, Claude Chabrol, Eric Rohmer, Jacques Rivette, and secondarily, Alain Resnais, Chris Marker, and Varda herself, is associated with the "Nouvelle Vague" rubric, and although it does not imply a school or a specifically constituted group, the term *New Wave* automatically suggests that spirit of formal innovation, personal expression, sociopolitical commitment, and technical renovation associated with these filmmakers. This chapter will assess the status of Varda's work in relation to the New Wave in an effort to define both her affinities with that group and what I perceive to be the "feminine difference" of her filmmaking.

Each of the women directors in this book has experienced a situation of "double rupture," first in the context of a national French cinema, which saw itself in opposition to Hollywood dominance, and second in relation to her male colleagues who formed that national cinema in each of these periods. Germaine Dulac participated fully in the atmosphere of her time, a climate of experimentation in the 1920s fostered by intensive filmmaking, journalistic production, and ciné-club activity. The feminist significance of her films grows out of her cinematic experiments with abstraction and musical evocation. As a consequence, the plurality of meanings suggested by her later, more abstract and "poetic" works significantly challenges patriarchal structures of thought while the work of Delluc, Epstein, Gance, and L'Herbier has always remained firmly within a narrative tradition. With Marie Epstein, the discussion of French filmmaking in the 1930s has demonstrated both what she shares with her contemporaries—the decidedly "French" texture and tone of a realist aesthetic and lyrical style—and what distinguishes her—the thematic focus on feminine problematics and its concomitant reworking of fundamental enunciative structures. The film work of Agnès Varda shares characteristics with both of her female predecessors; while (like Dulac) she participates in the atmosphere of radical challenge and work on cinematic language that forms the foundation of filmmaking in her time, she retains (like Epstein) the feminine focus on issues of concern to women and explores new possibilities for a cinematic discourse capable of expressing feminine realities.

Definitions of the New Wave vary because of its lack of solidification as a programmatic school of directors, but there is widespread agreement that the term undeniably characterizes the spirit of a whole new generation of filmmakers who literally erupted onto the cultural scene. Between 1958 and 1961, more than one hundred filmmakers made their debut; many of those whose first films were released during this period would come to embody the definition of modern French cinema itself. And the creative impact of their films and their theorizing about the cinema would be felt on various new national cinemas all over the world, in places as diverse as Japan and Brazil. The exciting and vibrant context that the New Wave provided for both theoretical work and original cinematic production has been said to "crystallize a generation gap" by creating films that were "offhand, free and easy, irritating, Parisian, and aesthetic."[2] Moreover, the New Wave combines the research into the language and syntax of film so prevalent in the 1920s with that focus on the "poetry of milieu" that marked French films of the thirties. In this way, this "new wave" of cinematic experimentation collects and resolves what has preceded it in the history of the French cinema, and it does so in order to create films that are expressive of a profound new understanding of the signifying potentials of the medium.

Initially, the term *New Wave* did not apply specifically to filmmakers. It was first coined in 1958 by Françoise Giroud, a journalist for the left-liberal weekly *L'Express*, to denote a certain new spirit evident in a whole youthful generation of the French population. However, because this emergence of fresh aspirations and ambitions into French political life coincided with the appearance of numerous new filmmakers whose work—independently financed, relatively cheaply made, and artisanal in conception and inspiration—emphasized concomitant values of personal expression and freedom, the term *New Wave* came very quickly to refer to the cinema. In its very specific (and limited) usage, it stands for those directors who entered into filmmaking with a theoretical grounding in film history and aesthetics, for they began as critics for the influential film journal, *Les Cahiers du cinéma*—Godard, Truffaut, Chabrol, Rohmer, and Rivette (and, to a lesser extent, Jacques Doniol-Valcroze and Pierre Kast). Importantly, this was the first truly film-educated generation of directors, filmmakers prepared to understand a specific cinematic tradition that they would be working both within and against. It is their continual preoccupation with the language of film, with forms of narrative organization, and with strategies of cinematic discourse, which expands the definition of New Wave to include Resnais, Varda, and Marker, as well as Jacques Rozier, Marcel Hanoun, Jean-Daniel Pollet, Jean Rouch, Jacques Demy, and Louis Malle, among others.

The *Cahiers* critics are credited with shaping the New Wave cinematic practice, and they did so, essentially, around three theoretical concepts that all pointed to an understanding of the cinema as a discursive system of signs. The first originates in Alexandre Astruc's extraordinary and seminal article of 1948, "The Birth of a New Avant-Garde: *La Caméra-Stylo*," in which he elaborated an exciting new theory of film "authorship": "Direction is no longer a means of illustrating or presenting a scene, but a true act of writing. The filmmaker/author writes with his camera as a writer writes with his pen."[3] This is not merely an advocation of personal expression in the cinema, however; Astruc's concept of authorship is firmly rooted in a notion of film as a specific mode of organizing meanings, a cinematic language that is at once both individually and culturally inscribed. In conceiving of film language in this manner, he astutely paves the way for experimentation and contravention of the cinematic codes, a reinvention of the cinema that is both personal and social at its source: "The cinema of today is capable of expressing any kind of reality. What interests us is the creation of this new language. We have no desire to rehash those poetic documentaries and surrealist films of 25 years ago every time we manage to escape the demands of a commercial industry. Let's face it: between the pure cinema of the 1920s and filmed theatre, there is plenty of room for a different and individual kind of filmmaking."[4]

With this claim, Astruc suggests that alternatives to the dominant filmmaking tradition will emerge in the work of directors seeking to express themselves through purely cinematic means, for the demands of a new kind of cinema (cultural) and of a unique and distinct vision (personal) will converge in the elaboration of new cinematic forms. Although Varda never read Astruc, nor any of the critical texts of the time, it is, in fact, in terms of Astruc's writings that Varda's theoretical and conceptual affinities with the New Wave are most evident.

Astruc's revolutionary claim that filmmaking could be "a means of writing as flexible and subtle as written language"[5] had a very specific appeal to the *Cahiers* critics, for as they delved more fully into the traditions of both French and American cinema, they became interested in defining the particular authorial stamp of directors who had produced what they considered to be true works of cinematic art within the Hollywood studio system. The "auteur theory" associated with the *Cahiers* critics, and thus with the New Wave, has its roots in a polemic that was elaborated in Truffaut's 1954 article, "A Certain Tendancy of the French Cinema,"[6] refined in André Bazin's 1957 critique, "La Politique des auteurs,"[7] and solidified in the creation by those critics themselves of a pantheon of "men [*sic*] of the cinema." In the simplest terms, it consisted of finding a formal and thematic consistency in the body of work of an individual director, and thereby defining a cinematic oeuvre as a specific articulation of the language of film. Bazin, who founded *Cahiers du cinéma* with Lo Duca and Jacques Doniol-Valcroze in 1951, makes this concentration on cinematic specificity central to the definition of authorship when he argues against what appears to him as a capricious distinction between the true "auteur" and one who is simply a "great director." For him, this distinction disappears as soon as one considers the concept of authorship as a complex *interaction* of individual and material:

> To a certain extent at least, the *auteur* is a subject to himself; whatever the scenario, he always tells the same story, or, in case the word "story" is

confusing, let's say he has the same attitude and passes the same moral judgements on the action and on the characters. Jacques Rivette has said that an *auteur* is someone who speaks in the first person. It's a good definition; let's adopt it.

The *politique des auteurs* consists, in short, of choosing the personal factor in artistic creation as a standard of reference, and then of assuming that it continues and even progresses from one film to the next.[8]

Authorship, then, is defined as a stance, a position within cinematic language that can be determined through close analysis of specific texts. But Bazin is eminently careful to emphasize the social inscription of this personal stance and the theoretical foundation on which it rests. In this context, directors like John Ford, Howard Hawks, Fritz Lang, Alfred Hitchcock, and Orson Welles are appreciated not only for their ability to "speak" cinematically, but also for their capacity to integrate a social vision into a particular style of cinematic narration. Bazin concludes his essay with a concise formulation of the basic premise of his article, which is to restore to criticism a look at the films themselves, over the "cult of personality" that auteurism is in danger of becoming: "*Auteur*, yes, but of *what?*"[9]

It is thus from the perspective of auteurism that the New Wave critics (and soon-to-be directors) regarded American cinema with ambivalence: Once again, as in the twenties, both appreciative fascination and cautious distance characterized the French view. In their renewed attention to the Hollywood product, the incipient filmmakers of *Cahiers* would seek to emulate the formal sophistication and profound understanding of the medium demonstrated by American directors, while at the same time conceiving of alternative cinematic styles that would resist the dominance of the commercial American model. The *Cahiers* critics thus wrote incisively about the films of certain Hollywood directors whose consummate artistry, they felt, enabled them to produce works that transcended the limitations of mass production. In addition to Hitchcock, Lang, Ford, Hawks, and Welles, Otto Preminger, Samuel Fuller, Vincente Minnelli, Nicholas Ray, and Douglas Sirk, to name a few, all received lengthy paens in the pages of *Cahiers*. And it is in this context that Godard could write of Sirk's "attempt to assimilate the definition of cinema itself to that of his heroes,"[10] or state categorically that "the cinema is Nicholas Ray."[11] The *Cahiers* critics' fascination with Hollywood culminated, in a sense, with a special issue in 1955 devoted to the "Situation of the American Cinema" and dedicated to Orson Welles, which had, among other things, Astruc stating, "The American cinema is the greatest in the world . . . because its directors are not contemptuous of *mise en scène*"; Rohmer equating Hollywood to the

Florence of the Renaissance and Rivette welcoming its "breath of fresh air"; and the established master Jean Renoir owing the essentials of his formation to Hollywood, stating that "the American cinema can have a very favorable effect, for example, in accustoming foreign directors to appreciate technique."[12]

The third theoretical armature of New Wave criticism (after "writing" and "auteurism") is "genre," and it, too, owes an important debt to Bazin's formulations. For, in keeping with the need he felt to dialecticize the personal inflection of auteurism, Bazin sought to emphasize the highly conventional and structured aspects of the cinematic language that these pantheon directors "spoke." The concept of genre— a shared set of cinematic conventions and audience expectations that describes the narrative and stylistic parameters of the film—provided him with that context, for it encompassed both cultural spectators and individual texts in its definition. Thus all genre films (westerns, musicals, gangster films, screwball comedies, for example) depend to some extent on audience recognition for their success, just as they afford each director an opportunity to manipulate the cinematic codes. For Bazin, the concepts of author and genre are intertwined; the ability to work within a genre is one manifestation of what makes a filmmaker an auteur, but it is also what binds that director to his or her culture.

> Thus, a certain kind of popular American culture lies at the basis of Minnelli's *Lust for Life*, but another more spontaneous kind of culture is also the principle of American comedy, the Western, and the gangster film. And its influence is here beneficial, for it is this that gives these cinematic genres their vigour and richness, resulting as they do from an artistic evolution that has always been in wonderfully close harmony with its public. . . . [A]bove all a Western [is] a whole collection of conventions in the script, the acting, and the direction. . . . What is *Stagecoach* if not an ultra-classical Western in which the art of Ford consists simply of raising characters and situations to an absolute degree of perfection[?][13]

And it is with the concept of genre that the New Wave's self-conscious emphasis on cinematic language is most readily engaged. From the standpoint of these filmmakers who began as critics, fundamental questions about the nature of the cinema as both an institution and as a language became transformed; what were originally the preoccupations of journalistic activity evolved into cinematic "problems" to be posed, evoked, or worked out in the course of the filmic text. Considering films in terms of genres meant thinking a film's codicity—its structured organization of lighting, camera work, editing patterns, sound, and narrative processes—and it meant considering the viewer's position as well. In New Wave films, the component elements of the genre are often broken down and foregrounded so that viewers can engage in a process of critical reflection about the images that flow before them. For this reason, these films are often marked by a dialectical interaction between genre conventions and reflexive commentary, placing the viewer in a position of new awareness about the processes of cinematic meaning-production. And, as a consequence, "looking" in the cinema is redefined.

The French film historian and critic Bernard Eisenschitz has provided a useful framework for discussing the cinematic and cultural achievements of the New Wave. He has correctly noted that, as a concept, the New Wave broadly covers three related areas: economics, ideology, and aesthetics.[14] Briefly stated, as an economic concept the New Wave provided an atmosphere of encouragement for the promotion of low-budget films, and less costly projects in turn permitted new methods and techniques of shooting, and the consequent evolution of new cinematic forms. As an ideological concept, the youthful exuberance of the New Wave characterized the spirit of the beginning of the Fifth Republic: young films representing a young country. And as an artistic concept, the New Wave elaborated a new set of aesthetic principles that reformulated the cinema as a specific discursive system conceived in opposition to the stale academicism and slick technical proficiency of the preceding generation.

A number of specific economic factors were responsible for permitting the New Wave to generate a different kind of filmmaking practice. Because of government legislation—guidelines to curb Hollywood competition, aid and development laws for the French film industry, the development of a system of avance sur recettes, allocations for a series of prizes for outstanding films, the establishment of a network of cultural and recreational centers with a full range of film programs (Maisons de la Culture), and laws that provided financial and artistic incentives to young filmmakers—there was a greater opportunity to make films without the old-fashioned professional training and normal apprenticeship of routine commercial production. As a consequence, New Wave films were generally shot quickly and cheaply, using small crews (often consisting of friends), available locations (rather than costly sets), and nonprofessional actors. Enlightened producers such as Georges de Beauregard and Pierre Braunberger, and the reduced financial risk in establishing small companies, also facilitated low-budget film production. In addition, Roger Vadim's 1956 *Et Dieu créa la femme* (*And God Created Woman*), whose enduring historical importance has quite a bit to do with the captivating presence of Brigitte Bardot in her first major film, is credited by many with opening the commercial industry's doors to low-budget, innovative production, due to its international box office success in spite of its modest production costs. And due, as well, to the then unknown Vadim's ability to produce a work of imagination within the context of the industry, a work that proved the commercial viability of original and fresh ideas.

Technical developments in high-speed film stock, light-weight portable cameras, and 16-mm equipment led to another important element associated with the New Wave—the live recording of "direct" cinema. Many of the effects of this are owed to Jean Rouch, a pioneer in the ethnographic and documentary film, whose highly interesting narrative and technical explorations brought out the fundamental contradictions between the innocence of "life caught unawares" and the manipulations of film—the dialectic between the "real" and the fictive that founds the cinema. Live recording on the scene meant new procedures of filming: reduced shooting schedules, small crews, natural lighting and locations, and day and night shooting in the streets. Concomitant with this type of shooting are the techniques of reportage—hand-held camera, an "interview" acting style, a directness of approach. Live recording implied a new narrative mode as well. In the words of French semiologist Michel Marie, "Events no longer 'pre-exist' shooting; they are created by it."[15] The procedures of direct shooting perfected by Rouch—and characteristic of much of the New Wave at the start, particularly Godard, Varda, Resnais, Marker, and Rozier—then permitted a new discursive mode in which each film, in a sense, created itself. The intersection of live recording, location shooting, and improvised dialogue with fictional narration and constructed situations disturbed the traditional (ideological) distinction between documentary and fiction, and provoked the questioning of the nature of cinematic reality itself. Varda's inheritance of all this is quite evident; from her earliest films to those made most recently, such issues are her major concerns.

When considered as an ideological concept, the New Wave combines filmmaking practice with a general cultural politics to produce an ethos of rebellion on a variety of levels. In more broadly political terms, the New Wave embodied the youthful spirit that characterized the beginning of the Fifth Republic. Much of the freshness, exuberance, and vitality associated with New Wave films, both in terms of style and of theme, was seen in direct relation to the political climate of the time. In addition, it was the Fifth Republic that created a Ministry of Cultural Affairs, maintained by André Malraux, and although this is seen by some critics as establishing a hierarchy of social practices that opposed culture to education, it did respond to a general need for government support of filmmaking activity.

When the ideological aspect of the New Wave is expressed in terms of film, it involves the spirited rejection of "papa's cinema" that characterized some of the early *Cahiers* writing. Essentially an attack on the "Tradition of Quality" that had preceded it, the rebellion consisted in criticizing the films of Yves Allégret, Henri Décoin, René Clément, Jean Delannoy, Claude Autant-Lara, and André Cayatte, among others, as overly literary, conventional, and uninspired studio productions. This polemic against the established French art cinema of the forties and early fifties, with its classical structures, its elegant decors, and its academic scripts, was formulated in terms of an emerging understanding of cinematic language. The failure to conceptualize a film cinematically thus formed the basis of the critique. In "Une certaine tendance," Truffaut deplored the conventional literary techniques and uninspired psychological realism of the "Tradition of Quality." Blaming commercially established scriptwriters such as the team of Jean Aurenche and Pierre Bost, who specialized in literary adaptations, he wrote, "I consider an adaptation of value only when written by *a man of the cinema.* Aurenche and Bost are essentially literary men and I reproach them here for being contemptuous of the cinema by underestimating it."[16] Following Astruc's powerful new formulation, then, the New Wave replaced the function of scriptwriter with the director who, often writing his (or her) own scenario, conceived the material from an essentially cinematic standpoint.

Five years later, Godard sharpened the assault on the "false technique" of the cinematic old guard by addressing twenty-one major directors: "[Y]our camera movements are ugly because your subjects are bad, your casts act badly because your dialogue is worthless; in a word, you don't know how to create cinema because you no longer even know what it is."[17] Although Varda did not participate in this particular "assault on the fathers," she has had other patriarchs to challenge, and her work on constructions of femininity and the expression of a female point of view partake in the spirit of rebellious contestation that characterizes the New Wave.

Eisenschitz's third defining category of the New Wave is aesthetic, and this is articulated by these directors, in one way, through the development of a film form in direct contrast to the Tradition of Quality. A random, improvisational style, a fragmentation of narrative cohesion, a concern to renovate fictional forms, a disruptive, jolting kind of editing practice, a reliance on the chance occurrence made possible by location shooting (as well as its pervasive sense of cultural milieu), a research into the language and syntax of film, and a new construction of the viewer—all were engaged in order to discover new ways of telling stories cinematically. In the words of Jacques Siclier: "*Breathless* is both an *auteur* film and the manifesto of the *Cahiers du cinéma* generation. . . . A categorical rupture with all the customary technical rules, an obvious sense of provocation, have led Jean-Luc Godard to reinvent the cinema. His film has all the marks of a spontaneous creation, a continuous explosion, because it is written directly [*une écriture directe*]. . . . *Breathless* is the newest of all the 'new wave' films."[18]

The work of formal innovation, experimentation, and reevaluation allowed the New Wave to make significant contributions to an oppositional filmmaking practice. Resistance to established traditions and the reassessment of certain American directors, for example, led to the construction of an alternative cinematic tradition, one marked by an appreciation of a director's work in terms of his understanding of the language of film. For some New Wave directors this led to a commitment to the kind of self-reflexive cinema that did not falsify or mystify its procedures, a notion that embeds filmmaking in a profoundly historical, materialist conception of its function. By reasserting the active, productive work of the director in the filmmaking process, by redefining the function of the spectator, and by attempting to think those processes constantly in social terms, the New Wave can be credited with producing significant new forms in the evolution of a counter-cinema. And it is in terms of what I have loosely defined as the aesthetic conception of the New Wave that Varda's connection to the group is the clearest.

It is an almost craftsmanlike definition of the New Wave, one that understands the filmmaker as an "artisan of language," that establishes Varda's link with a film movement for which she is both a precursor and, some thirty years later (with the possible exception of Godard), its strongest contemporary practitioner. Although the New Wave officially "ended" shortly after the publication in 1962 of a special issue of *Cahiers* devoted entirely to it, and although some of its prime directors went on to have commercial preoccupations and careers, some New Wave filmmakers—Godard, Resnais, and Marker, in addition to Varda herself—have retained the original commitment to the cinematic elaboration of a politics of form in all of their work. And Varda's connection to the New Wave, with both its first and its most recent manifestations, is clearly borne out in both theory (writing) and practice (filmmaking) as well.

As noted, it was Astruc's 1948 essay on the "*Caméra-Stylo*" that presented a kind of manifesto for the New Wave; in calling for a "written" cinema, he established the necessity of both the formulation of a personal voice and the conception of a cinematic language in any discussion of film as an art. Varda's concept of *cinécriture* demonstrates an interest in those same principles, for with this composite notion of both authorship and film—appearing as a signature in her films of the eighties—Varda newly emphasizes the act of writing inherent in the filmmaker's task. It was Astruc's important and lucid observation that the cinema functions like a language which made his idea of authorship so central to the thinking of the New Wave and infused it with such contemporary critical implications. In a statement that brilliantly condenses the cinema's evolution from a public novelty to a signifying system, he asserts its capacity for structured organization as the basis for its expressive force:

> To come to the point: the cinema is quite simply becoming a means of expression, just as all the other arts have been before it, and in particular painting and the novel. After having been successively a fairground attraction, an amusement analogous to boulevard theater, or a means of preserving the images of an era, it is gradually becoming a language. By language, I mean a form in which and by which an artist can express his thoughts, however abstract they may be, or translate his obsessions exactly as he does in the contemporary essay or novel. That is why I would like to call this new age of cinema the age of the *caméra stylo* (camera-pen). This metaphor has a very precise sense. By it I mean that the cinema will gradually break free from the tyranny of what is visual, from the image for its own sake, from the immediate and concrete demands of the narrative, to become a means of writing just as flexible and subtle as written language.[19]

Varda echoes this inspiration when she speaks about her concept of *cinécriture*, whether it is in terms of the personal conception of the author ("*Cinécriture* is a word that refers to the recognizable universe of a filmmaker"),[20] or in terms of the total process encompassing all aspects of a film's creation ("To write a film is not a screenplay, but the creation of the film itself. What I do in the editing room is writing. Deciding [on the] music . . . is part of the writing").[21] She speaks about filmmaking as the creation of a state of availability, a kind of readiness that allows the director to improvise, to capture things as they come up, and allows the film to be an essentially visual texture developed in the process of shooting. This, too, contributes to her notion of direction as cinematic writing. "This is why I am committed to the expression, even a bit pretentious, '*cinécrit par Agnès Varda*.' A film isn't 'written.' For a painting, there is certainly the word 'painted.' Written and directed by . . . doesn't work either: [In *Vagabond*] there was no written script! This sort of directly cinematographic writing which is practiced from location-scouting through the editing, with a scenario written during the actual shooting itself—that's *cinécriture*. You could say 'composed by' as you do in music . . . But I prefer cinematic references. Thus, to be the author of a film is to *'filmécrire.'* It's *cinécrire.*"[22]

Vagabond, the first feature of Varda's to bear this signature on the screen, is in many ways a film about the interrelationships of people and things, an essayistic meditation on the social nature of all human activity and the complexity of that interconnection. In this it is almost a cinematic demonstration of ideas first expressed by Astruc:

> Every film, because its primary function is to move, i.e., to take place in time, is a theorem. It is a series of images which, from one end to the other, have an inexorable logic (or better even, a dialectic) of their own. We have come to realize that the meaning [in cinema] exists within the image itself, in the development of the narrative, in every gesture of the characters, in every line of dialogue, in those camera movements which relate objects to objects and characters to objects. All thought, like all feeling, is a relationship between one human being and another human being or certain objects which form part of his universe. It is by clarifying these relationships, by making a tangible allusion, that the cinema can really make itself the vehicle of thought.[23]

Thus, twenty years before critical parlance created a vocabulary to describe this "materiality of the cinematic signifier," Astruc was calling for the kind of filmmaking and criticism that would take this into account. And Varda, almost forty years after Astruc's essay, would make a film whose very conception and organization would be a cinematic enactment and elaboration of his ideas.

There is a second way that Varda participated in the earliest formulations of the New Wave, and that is through her filmmaking. In his excellent 1961 assessment of the emerging cinematic movement, *Nouvelle vague?*, Jacques Siclier establishes Varda's important function, with *La Pointe-Courte*, as a significant "precursor" of the New Wave. In a book that subscribes to the strict definition of the New Wave as those five critics who wrote for *Cahiers* (plus Kast and Doniol-Valcroze), Siclier discusses what he sees as the formative influence of five directors—Varda, Astruc (as a filmmaker), Jean-Pierre Melville, Vadim, and Louis Malle, this latter, a "brilliant stylist," a precursor in chronology only. Citing Astruc as a director who "said 'I' with every shot" due to his rigorous stylistic concern for angle, framing, and lighting; Melville as a filmmaker's filmmaker whose capacity to make "the typical example of a total *auteur* film" earned him the title of "inventor of the new wave"; and Vadim as an actor's director who, by "creating the mythology of the 'new wave' . . . indicated what direction the young cinema should follow"; Siclier claims for Varda the responsibility of having made the film that "was the prologue to the economic revolution of the young French cinema" and earned for her the accolade: "The young cinema owes everything to her."[24] Seeing Varda (along with Melville) as a pioneer in independent production, he cites *La Pointe-Courte*'s creation outside of commercial circuits, its estimated cost of a scant seven million francs, its cooperative production crew, its restricted shooting schedule, and its natural locations as factors in its innovative status. But beyond the economic specifics of its production, Siclier praises the film for its studied literacy which is, importantly, combined with a concern for its viewers. This essentially intellectual film (he quotes Varda's claim that it was "a film to be read") was made with its public in mind. For Siclier, Varda's early concern with audience engagement in the production of meaning is what makes the film a true precursor of the New Wave, beyond any achievements of independent production.

But it is also the concern with temporality, the interfacing of subjective realities, the articulation of discursive modes, the combination of fictive and essayistic structures, the pervasive "sense of place," the aspect of research, both sociological and linguistic, the interest in permutations of the narrative form, the techniques of distancing and of cultural critique, the redefinition of spectatorship, the self-reflexivity about cinematic meaning, and the challenge to establish forms of cinematic storytelling that make *La Pointe-Courte* a New Wave film. These concerns, in fact, obtain in all of Varda's films, right down to *Kung-Fu Master* and *Jane B. par Agnès V.* (both 1987). As I stated before, the New Wave was a cinema of formal innovation, experimentation, and reevaluation. Many, although not all, New Wave directors saw their films as part of an ongoing research into the language and syntax of the medium, posing the questions, What constitutes the cinema?, How does one narrate in film?, and How does the spectator come to understand the filmic image? at the start of their cinematic explorations. Varda's film work can be associated with this kind of profound interrogation of the fundamentals of the cinema. Beneath this questioning are basic premises of cinematic meaning-production involving the fictive manipulation of "reality" at the core of any filmic construction. The dialectic posed at the beginning of the cinema's history and questioned by Varda herself (chapter 8)—Lumière's "documents" of everyday life and Méliès's magical creation of the fantastic—was reformulated by the New Wave in order to explore its false dichotomy between "truth" and "fiction" into an understanding of all cinematic practice as discursive. This is exactly the suggestive process that *La Pointe-Courte* enacts. But these are also the kinds of issues that both *Kung-Fu Master* (a fictional "melodrama" of the contemporary woman and her desire) and *Jane B. par Agnès V.* (a sustained reflection on the politics of representation and on women both in front of and behind the camera, initiated by the intersecting work of both "artist" and "model" as they imaginatively explore how they see themselves and their work) take as their central concerns almost thirty-five years later.

Another way to cast Varda's affinities with the New Wave is through a shared interest in self-reflexive cinema. For the most part, New Wave films are marked by a self-consciousness about cinematic procedures, for example, the emphatic use of jump-cuts and elliptical editing practices; the reflexive use of sound and narration; the pervasive emphasis on camera techniques, with special attention to the moving camera; the widespread utilization of "quotations" and intertextual references to other films; and the amalgamation of disparate elements and materials. All of these stylistic traits can be understood as the rejection of the classical grammar of filmmaking, a form of resistance to established commercial practices that constitutes an ongoing challenge to structures in dominance. Since early in her career, Varda has made cinematic self-reflexivity a primary interest, from *Les Créatures* (an imaginary game of the fantastic about making fictions, both literary and human) and *Lions Love* (a collage-construction whose real subject is filmmaking itself) to *Mur Murs* (another film about another kind of filmmaking), *Vagabond* (a film that explores the fictional component in anyone's perception of reality) and *Jane B. par Agnès V.* (a film portrait in which fantasies, fantasms, and fictions are used to dialectically explore the production of the woman's image by a filmmaker who uses the means of a painter and a writer). This interest is another way that Varda has continued the concerns of the New Wave in her filmmaking practice long after the group officially ended as a viable cinematic alternative, although Varda herself remains ambivalent about being associated with any formal conception of the group.

One final way of thinking of Varda's relation to the New Wave is through the concept of the "Left Bank Group." Considered a subgroup of the New Wave (they share a cinematic chronology), it basically consisted of four filmmakers—although there are others—who were also friends and who happened to share certain formal, thematic, and sociopolitical preoccupations: Resnais, Marker, Varda, and William Klein. Although Varda maintains that there was never anything more shared by the group than friendly conversation and a love of cats, Claire Clouzot, who developed the concept of the group and named it in her 1972 book, *Le Cinéma français depuis la nouvelle vague,* describes it in this way: "The filmmakers of the Left Bank are inspired by an artistic eclecticism. As creators they are interested in the flow of mental processes, rather than in a cinephilic fanaticism. It is not theoretical criticism which draws them to the cinema, but an interest in filmic writing, and the relations this might have with literary production."[25] Clouzot, in fact, in her highly detailed and comprehensive study of the group, considers these filmmakers not as a faction of the New Wave, but, rather, as a distinct group in opposition to it. Clouzot's a literary emphasis; she takes "authorship" literally in her discussions to mean the essentially novelistic preoccupations with time, memory, narration, and form that characterize the group. And although her extensive treatment of every aspect of the group is quite perceptive— from formative concepts, literary relations, shared interests, and technical training to constants of thematics, character, decor, and style (elements of cinematic writing such as camera movements, editing, direction of actors, compositional style, and sound)—it brings up the problems that any kind of labelling involves. Some of her Left Bank directors fit comfortably into her category, whereas others, such as the undeniably New Wave Godard, fit equally as well, particularly when she states categorically, for example, "The shadow of Brecht and the New Novel hovers over their themes. The anonymity of certain characters, the 'flux' of situations . . . the distancing of the spectator in relation to those depicted on the screen, the simultaneous time of action and time of thought, all this is taken up. The 'Left Bank current' affirms itself as a cinema of non-identification. . . ."[26]

Still, there is a way in which the preoccupation with modes of cinematic discourse united both groups in a common pursuit—the particular inflection in this research is what distinguishes them. Take, for example, the short-subject film (*court-métrage*). Many of these filmmakers, both New Wave and Left Bank, excelled in the form, and it is here that, as Siclier claims, the freedom of expression and creation extolled by the New Wave's "*politique des auteurs*" finds its clearest elaboration. It was the atmosphere of economic encouragement for independently financed small productions that enabled the flourishing of the short-film format in the late fifties and early sixties, and allowed Varda, Resnais, Marker, and Godard among others to create some extraordinary cinematic examples of their talent. Because of the short's low production costs and relatively limited institutional control, it could act as a sort of training ground for future filmmakers, who were then able to produce works of great vitality, imagination, and originality based on these early conceptions. In fact, much of the freedom and expressiveness of personal vision attributed to the New Wave comes directly out of cinematic explorations such as these, in which the director of a short could assume something very close to total control over the work. At least one critic sees in these short films the origins of all the new trends and tendencies associated with the New Wave.[27]

It is the achievement in the short-film format that allows others to group Varda, Resnais, and Marker under the Left Bank rubric. Varda, who has continued to make shorts throughout her career, sees this kind of film as a sort of experimental laboratory: "That's what you can do in shorts: investigate the *feel* of cinematic impressions, cinematic emotion, powerful visions that make people grow into their own imagination. . . . This is what a short film means to me, how it grows into a longer film. It's like a painter who makes a little painting, but he likes the theme so much that he makes a bigger painting."[28] Because of the experimental nature of the form, its suggestion of an essayistic format, and its foregrounding elements of cinematic language, Varda has been able to make short films that associate her with either group. *Ulysse* (1982), for example, shares the preoccupations with perception, memory, and time of the Left Bank Group, while *Les Dites-Cariatides* (1984) has as much a sense of the Parisian landscape as any early short by Godard, Rouch, or Rohmer. And because she has consistently found the short film a rich field of cinematic investigation, Varda has been able to continue one of the most important contributions of the New Wave—its spirit of innovation.

It is significant that, in terms of the foregoing discussion, Varda solidly partakes of the three historically defining features of the New Wave, strictly conceived. Her affinities with Astruc's founding concept of "cinematic writing" are eminently clear. In addition, the entirety of her oeuvre is a demonstration of the "politique des auteurs," for, as she continues to maintain, "I really fight for the same struggle that I have always been fighting, which is cinematic independence, cinematic vision."[29] Further, the focus on cinematic language and syntax that the theory of genre implies has been a consistent interest of Varda's, from her re-working of genre structures (as discussed in chapter 8) to her continual preoccupation with discursive forms. In addition, Varda's film work can be discussed in terms of all three of Eisenschitz's categories of the New Wave—economic, ideological, and aesthetic—as well. What, then, distinguishes her from the group so radically that she is so overlooked in most accounts—to such an extent that James Monaco's retrospective study, *The New Wave*,[30] the only book of its kind in English, only mentions her name twice in 372 pages, and then only in relation to work by other filmmakers?

Varda herself has provided one answer in suggesting a very precise historical reason: "When the new wave bloomed in '59, I was already there, making films by hand, expressing the way I felt, being free. But I didn't come from the intellectual, *Cahiers du cinéma* tradition. I didn't review films."[31] But I would suggest something else, a reason that has to do, significantly, with Varda's feminist perspective ("Always a feminist, I was born a feminist").[32] Her effort not only to constantly articulate challenges to dominant representations of femininity, but also to express what it means to see—to film—as a woman, means that a profound feminist inquiry is at the center of all her work. In fact, Varda is alone among New Wave directors—with the exception of Godard, a very different case—in her exploration of the politics of representation as they are inflected by questions of sexual difference.[33]

From *La Pointe-Courte* on, through *Cleo From 5 to 7* and *Le Bonheur* to *Vagabond* and even in *Jane B. par Agnès V.*, Varda's concern has been with constructions of femininity as they are socially inscribed. And it is in this sense that even such a fundamental New Wave quality as its spirit of "Frenchness" is infused with perspectives and debates relating to the feminist problematic. *L'Opéra-Mouffe* and *Cleo* show us Paris, to be sure, in the best tradition of the early New Wave films, but they show us a very precise view of that city, one constructed by a female point of view and fully determined by feminine subjectivity. The sociological explorations of a Godard or a Rouch are likewise put in the service of an incisive critique of patriarchal social relations, in *Le Bonheur*, for example, where masculine attitudes are subjected to the scrutiny of irony. And *Vagabond* continues the interrogation of French culture, but it does so, as well, in terms of a character about whom, Varda has repeatedly stated, it makes all the difference that she is a woman. Finally, *Jane B. par Agnès V.* continues Varda's work of perpetually doing something new in each film, presenting a quasi-fictional, quasi-essayistic structure that expands the limits of cinematic meaning as it explores ways of thinking about representation and the constructions of gender. There is an undeniable consistency in Varda's work in terms of what could be described as "New Wave practice," but over and above that is a feminist consistency, which has, ironically, distinguished (if not excluded) her from that very practice. Agnès Varda is an exemplary filmmaker: historically exemplary because she so fully embodies the project of the New Wave, but more important than that, exemplary from a feminist standpoint because she so consistently enacts her desire to *film as a woman.*

NOTES

1. See, for example, Georges Sadoul, in *Dictionnaire des films* (Paris: Editions du Seuil, 1965), p. 196, as cited in the discussion of *La Pointe-Courte* in the previous chapter. The film is recognized as a precursor of the New Wave by numerous critics, including Ephraim Katz, *The Film Encyclopedia* (New York: Crowell, 1979), p. 866; Richard Roud, *Cinema: A Critical Dictionary* (New York, Viking Press, 1980), p. 1019; and Jacques Siclier, *Nouvelle vague?* (Paris: Editions du Cerf, 1961), pp. 58–60.

2. Raymond Borde, in " 'The Golden Age': French Cinema of the 30s," in *Rediscovering French Film*, ed. Mary Lea Bandy (New York: Museum of Modern Art, 1983), p. 81. Because my focus in this chapter is on Varda in context, this is an abbreviated discussion of the New Wave itself. Economic and ideological issues are given fuller treatment in my dissertation, "Women, Representation, and Cinematic Discourse," University of California, Berkeley, 1982.

3. Alexandre Astruc, "The Birth of a New Avant-Garde: *La Caméra-Stylo,*" in *The New Wave,* ed. Peter Graham (Garden City, N.Y.: Doubleday, 1968), p. 22. The article originally appeared in *L'Ecran Français,* no. 144 (March 30, 1948). Graham's excellent collection of translated articles by Astruc and Bazin ("The Evolution of Film Language" and "La Politique des Auteurs"), as well as articles by Godard, Truffaut, and Chabrol, among others, is unfortunately out of print. This seems to be the only place where one can find the complete English text of Astruc's brilliant article.

4. Astruc, *"La Caméra-Stylo,"* p. 21.

5. Astruc, *"La Caméra-Stylo,"* p. 18.

6. François Truffaut, "Une certaine tendance du cinéma français," *Cahiers du cinéma,* no. 31 (January 1954): 15–28; translated and anthologized in *Movies and Methods,* vol. 1, ed. Bill Nichols (Berkeley: University of California Press, 1976), pp. 224–37.

7. André Bazin, "La Politique des Auteurs," in *The New Wave,* ed. Graham, pp. 137–55. This is translated from "De la politique des auteurs," *Cahiers du cinéma,* no. 70 (April 1957) and is also collected in *Cahiers du Cinéma: The 1950s,* ed. Jim Hillier (Cambridge: Harvard University Press, 1985), pp. 248–59.

8. Bazin, "La Politique des Auteurs," pp. 150–51. It has been one of the projects of this book, in fact, in discussing the work of three women auteurs, to recast this "first person" in the terms of contemporary enunciative theory and the textual operations that this specific perspective implies. The theories first advanced during the period of the New Wave provide an important critical foundation for my discussion of Varda, Epstein, and Dulac as film authors.

266 / To Desire Differently

9. Bazin, "La Politique des Auteurs," p. 155. I have slightly modified Graham's translation for purposes of clarification.

10. Jean-Luc Godard, review of *A Time to Love and a Time to Die*, in *Cahiers du cinéma* 94 (April 1959); translated and anthologized in *Godard on Godard*, ed. Jean Narboni and Tom Milne (New York: Viking Press, 1972), p. 138. *Godard on Godard* is a collection of Godard's writings on the cinema between 1950 and 1967; it contains practically all of the *Cahiers* articles.

11. Review of *Bitter Victory* in *Cahiers du cinéma*, no. 79 (January 1958); in *Godard on Godard*, ed. Narboni and Milne, p. 64.

12. *Cahiers du cinéma*, no. 54 (Christmas 1955), pp. 73, 16, 21, and 79, respectively. Some of these articles are in *Cahiers du cinéma: The 1950s* ed. Hillier.

13. Bazin, "La Politique des Auteurs," p. 153–54.

14. Bernard Eisenschitz, "Histoires de l'histoire: Deux périodes du cinéma français, le muet et la génération de 58," *Défense du cinéma français* (Paris: Maison de la Culture de la Seine-Saint-Dénis, March 1975), p. 30.

15. Michel Marie, "The Art of the Film in France Since the New Wave," trans. Robert Ariew in *Wide Angle* 4:4 (1981): 20.

16. Truffaut, "Une certaine tendance," in *Movies and Methods*, ed. Nichols, p. 229.

17. Jean-Luc Godard, "Debarred Last Year from the Festival Truffaut Will Represent France at Cannes with *Les 400 coups*," *Arts*, no. 719 (April 22, 1959); reprinted in *Godard on Godard*, ed. Narboni and Milne, p. 147.

18. Siclier, *Nouvelle vague?*, p. 71.

19. Astruc, "*La Caméra-Stylo*," pp. 17–18.

20. Agnès Varda, "Interview: A Personal Vision," *Passion* (June–July 1986): 20.

21. Agnès Varda in John Harkness, "Agnès Varda: Improvised Inspiration," *Now*, June 19–25, 1986.

22. Agnès Varda, "Mona, nomade," *Cinéma 85*, no. 322 (December 4–10, 1985): 11.

23. Astruc, "*La Caméra-Stylo*," p. 20.

24. Siclier, *Nouvelle vague?*, pp. 54, 56–7, 62, 60, and 59, respectively. This last is a citation from the journal *Arts*, which Siclier quotes.

25. Claire Clouzot, *Le Cinéma français depuis la nouvelle vague* (Paris: Fernand Nathan-Alliance Française, 1972), p. 48.

26. Clouzot, *Le Cinéma français*, p. 56.

27. Roy Armes, *French Cinema Since 1946*, vol. 2, *The Personal Style* (Cranbury, N.J.: A. S. Barnes, 1970), p. 10.

28. Agnès Varda, in Mary Beth Crain, "Agnès Varda: The Mother of the New Wave," *L.A. Weekly*, August 1–7, 1986, p. 33.

29. Agnès Varda, in "Agnes Varda: A Conversation with Barbara Quart," *Film Quarterly* 40:2 (Winter 1986–87): 9.

30. James Monaco, *The New Wave* (New York: Oxford University Press, 1976).

31. Agnès Varda in Judy Steed, "Director Feels 'Close to Rebellious People,' " *The Globe and Mail,* June 20, 1986, p. D9.

32. Varda in "Director Feels 'Close to Rebellious People.' "

33. See, for example, Laura Mulvey and Colin MacCabe's chapter in Colin MacCabe, *Godard: Images, Sounds, Politics* (Bloomington: Indiana University Press, 1980) for a discussion of Godard in terms of "Images of Woman, Images of Sexuality," and Robert Stam's excellent book, *Reflexivity in Film and Literature from Don Quixote to Jean-Luc Godard* (Ann Arbor: UMI Press, 1985).

TEN

From *Déesse* to *Idée*: *Cleo From 5 to 7*

Strictly speaking, such women love only themselves with an intensity
comparable to that of the man's love for them. . . . The importance
of this type of woman for the erotic life of mankind must be
recognized as very great. Such women have the greatest fascination
for men, not only for aesthetic reasons, since as a rule they are the
most beautiful, but also because of certain interesting psychological
constellations. It seems very evident that one person's narcissism has
a great attraction for those others who have renounced part of their
own narcissism and are seeking after object-love; the charm of a
child lies to a great extent in his narcissism, his self-sufficiency and
inaccessibility, just as does the charm of certain animals which seem
not to concern themselves about us, such as cats and the large beasts
of prey.[1]

THROUGH ITS CENTRAL PROBLEMATIC of woman-as-image, *Cléo de 5 à 7*
(1961), one of Varda's most interesting, accomplished, and beautiful
films, offers a critical examination of reified categories and definitions
of woman while proposing the necessary inscription of sociality in
constructions of femininity. The film traces the process by which Cleo,
the woman-as-spectacle, becomes transformed into an active social
participant, rupturing the oppressive unity of identity and vision and
appropriating the gaze for herself in a new appreciation of others in
the world around her. In the course of the film's ninety-minute running time, and its two hour diegetic time, Cleo undergoes "a profound
transformation of [her] entire being."[2] This transformation is intimately bound up with processes of self-reflection. But, whereas self-

reflection means narcissistic self-absorption in the first part of the film, it means self-recognition—mediated by an awareness of others—in the latter half.

The film concerns a pretty blond pop singer, Cleo Victoire, who passes two anxiety-ridden hours of a long summer day awaiting the results of a medical examination determining whether she has a possibly fatal illness. In Varda's words, *Cleo From 5 to 7* is "about a woman facing a great fear, and that fear makes her think about herself. She discovers that she is a little doll, manipulated by men, a little girl who makes no decisions, *who sees herself only through other people's eyes*. And in that hour and a half she starts to relate differently."[3] Cleo's internal evolution from egoism to communication is thus formulated in terms of a visual problematic: she ceases to be an object, constructed by the looks of men, and assumes the power of vision, a subjective vision of her own.

Cleo's transformation hinges on the turn of a phrase: "How do I look?" This question, traditionally connoted as feminine, is displaced from its passive, objectified meaning ("How am I seen, how do I appear in the eyes of the world?") to its active complement ("How do I see, how is the world viewed by me?"). This shift is hinted at in a subtle yet engaging way fairly early in the film by means of a simple pun. As Cleo and her secretary-companion Angèle get into a taxi, a little repartee ensues:

Cleo: C'est une déesse, j'aime ça. [It's a "goddess," I like that.]
Driver: C'est pas une DS, c'est une ID. [It's not a DS, it's an ID.]
Angèle: Une idée comme une drôle d'idée? [An idea, like a funny idea?]
Driver: Oui, c'est ça. [Yep.]

The letters *DS* and *ID* refer to two different models of Citroën; Cleo and Angèle participate in a short play on words, a game which was, in fact, encouraged by the auto manufacturer at the time. But beyond the double entendre of sounds and initials, the significance of the words (*déesse*/goddess; *idée*/idea) predicts Cleo's emotional trajectory on that summer day. From an alluring female goddess, objectified in the eyes of men (her pianist prefaces a song with a musical paean: "Cléopâtre, je vous idolâtre" [I worship you]), to a reflective individual with a healthy curiosity (Cleo muses near the film's end, "I always have a question for everything. . . . Today, everything amazes me"), Cleo has made the journey from object to subject of vision. And, along the way, Varda has explored traditional conceptions of the woman's (self-) image in an analysis that underlines their social origins.

The textual process of the film traces Cleo's development in terms

of a movement from narcissistic containment to a burgeoning awareness of and empathy for others. Typically, Varda analyzes this movement along feminist lines, situating Cleo's crisis within the feminist
problematic of the woman's image. In so doing, she interrogates the
conventional notion of female beauty not by a radical contestation or
an aggression on visual pleasure, but by dissecting this image into its
constitutive parts, and by equating love with an acceptance of others—
a turning away from the self (the antinarcissistic move) which dialecticizes the image of homoerotic unity. By examining the "narcissistic
woman" as a construction, Varda begins the critical exploration into
sexuality and femininity as transformable processes, thereby initiating
a fundamental questioning of patriarchal definitions of woman.

The turning point of Cleo's transformation occurs during a song
rehearsal session in which lyrics evoking absence, lack, and death
force Cleo into a sudden recognition of her identity, a recognition
concomitant with both a new social awareness and a rejection of established definitions of her. In fact, this sequence occurs at the exact
temporal middle of the film, making it possible to trace Cleo's radical
change through an analysis of the corresponding differences in each
half of the film. The narrative is divided into chapters that delineate
both the chronological time elapsed and the different characters'
points of view; "they color the story, or rather the angle in which the
portrait of Cleo is painted."[4] Thus in its very narrative structure, the
film's format foregrounds the intersubjectivity of identity, revealing
both the image and the self-image of Cleo as functions of vision. It is
precisely Cleo's awareness of this that triggers her new understanding:
"Caprice, caprice, that's all you say . . . but it's you who make me
capricious. Soon I'll be an idiot, incapable, a talking doll. . . . You
exploit me."

The chapter headings themselves, which appear as titles in the film,
provide an outline of Cleo's actions in the period between five and
seven, at the same time that they sketch a revealing profile of her
psychic and emotional growth:

    I.   Cleo from 5:05 to 5:08
   II.   Angèle from 5:08 to 5:13
  III.   Cleo from 5:13 to 5:18
   IV.   Angèle from 5:18 to 5:25
    V.   Cleo from 5:25 to 5:31
   VI.   Bob from 5:31 to 5:38
  VII.   Cleo from 5:38 to 5:45
 VIII.   Some others from 5:45 to 5:52
   IX.   Dorothée from 5:52 to 6:00

X. Raoul from 6:00 to 6:04
XI. Cleo from 6:04 to 6:12
XII. Antoine from 6:12 to 6:15
XIII. Cleo and Antoine from 6:15 to 6:30

After a visit to a fortune-teller who confirms Cleo's fears by predicting that "profound transformation" (Varda labels this the film's "Prologue"),[5] Cleo meets her secretary-companion, Angèle, in the Cafe Ça Va Ça Vient. Cleo and Angèle then stop in a hat shop on the rue de Rivoli, take a taxi across the Pont Neuf to Cleo's apartment on the rue Huyghens, and prepare for a rehearsal session. In her apartment Cleo receives, first, her lover José, then her composer (Bob) and lyricist (Plumitif); one song provokes Cleo's shock of recognition, and her outburst propels her into the Parisian streets, alone, newly contemplative, aware. She wanders through the Cafe Le Dôme, then visits her friend Dorothée at the Académie de Sculpture where Dorothée has just finished posing. They deliver a film to Raoul, Dorothée's lover (a projectionist), and after watching a short silent comedy, Cleo takes a cab to the Parc Montsouris. There she meets Antoine, a friendly, inquisitive soldier on leave who is about to return to the Algerian front. They establish a warm rapport, and he accompanies her to her doctor at the Salpêtrière hospital in exchange for her promise to see him off at the Gare de Lyon.

The disturbing song that Cleo sings in chapter VII is the pivot of the film's bifurcated textual structure. As such, it marks the turning point that permits the contrast between the chapters that precede and follow it. In the chapter titles leading up to this point, there is a strict alternation between Cleo and another character habitually present in Cleo's ordinary routine (either Angèle or Bob); the first chapter title that comes immediately after the song is called "Some Others"—the only title in the film not anchored to an individual character. In addition, Dorothée and Raoul are not a customary part of Cleo's daily existence, and Antoine is an entirely new character in her life. The strict alternation between Cleo and another person that characterizes the chapter headings of the first half of the film, a structure that makes Cleo a recurring reference point, is thus now replaced by a linear sequence—"Some Others," "Dorothée," "Raoul," "Cleo," and "Antoine." Ultimately, the final chapter is entitled "Cleo and Antoine," and is, significantly, the only chapter in the film designated by the names of two characters. Thus the chapter headings themselves trace Cleo's movement from self-absorbed isolation to intersubjective relations, and chart the redefinition of desire that it is the film's project to accomplish.

In the textual work of the film, the viewer is made to experience the

force of Cleo's transformation—from object to subject of desire—
through the intersecting processes of narrativity, continuity, and identification. Thus, the cinematic depiction of Cleo changes as she assumes
the power of a subjective vision; we see Cleo differently as she comes
to see (things and others) differently herself. The first half of the
film installs and reinforces a conventional, fetishized image of female
beauty in ways that objectify Cleo as a spectacle for erotic contemplation. But as Cleo's new vision of herself and the world takes hold, her
image is progressively inserted into a social context; at the same time
that she is given the power of a subjective point of view, the latter half
of the film portrays her as only one face in a multiple texture of human
relations.

One of the most striking ways in which this transformation can be
traced is through the contrasting functions of mirrors in the first and
second halves of the film. Chapter I, appropriately identified as Cleo's
(Varda calls it the "chapter of the tragic-doll"),[6] initiates the fiction
with the reassuring coherence of multiple reflections, asserting the
importance of Cleo-as-image. As she leaves Irma the fortune-teller,
Cleo pauses before a hallway mirror which, through a corresponding
interplay of reflections, offers a seemingly infinite reiteration of her
image (actually, the image is visibly repeated seven times). Then the
spectator is made to participate even more strongly in the contemplation of Cleo's face when the camera zooms in on an unmediated close-
up, the edges of the hallway mirror having disappeared. Confirming
her identity as image, the spectacle of self, Cleo muses in voice-over:
"Being ugly, that's what death is. As long as I'm beautiful, I'm alive,
and ten times more than the others."

When Cleo enters the Cafe Ça Va Ça Vient, once again mirrors
provide her with a unified image; faced with a distorting join in the
mirror, she adjusts her position until the image in its totality satisfies
her. Then, as she worries to Angèle about whether her fear is visible
on her face, a further narcissistic reduplication occurs. Seated with
her back to the cafe's mirrored wall, Cleo's image is repeated three
times (the cafe itself is a hall of mirrors). In fact, the whole first portion
of the film abounds with mirrors and other signifiers of narcissism.
Cleo's self-absorbed display as she contemplates the purchase of a
hat provides a further illustration of her association of beauty and
existence. And her apartment, "a universe over which she presides
like a queen,"[7] is a fulminating world of the archetypal feminine.
Mirrors, necklaces, feathers, flowers, and—most important—cats pro-
liferate in this veritable panoply of masquerade, vanity, narcissism,
and femininity. In chapter V, as Cleo prepares herself to receive José,

Varda's directions make this quite explicit: "She moves about on her bed, more feline than her cats, checks her beauty in the mirror, then smiles when she recognizes her lover's voice."[8]

Thus, at this point, mirrors offer Cleo a reassuring image of coherence, continually providing her with a sense of her own being. Identity and mirror image are firmly united, establishing Cleo's sense of her existence as synonymous with her beauty. And it is from this conception of female character *as image* that Varda begins to explore the parameters of constructions of the feminine. In the second half of the film—after Cleo's critical moment of recognition—the mirrors no longer provide her with this confirmed identity as beautiful object. The first mirror she encounters in her flight from the apartment is one whose surface is disturbed—it is traced with the painted Chinese letters of the Restaurant La Pagode. In a striking contrast to its counterpart, the multiple reflections in the fortune-teller's hallway, this mirror surrounds Cleo's image with the reflected images of other people on the street, offering rupture, dispersion, and fragmentation where unified repetitions had previously prevailed.

Cleo's thoughts on looking at this new reflection extend the contrast: "This doll's face, always the same. And this ridiculous hat. I can't even read my own fear on my face. I've always thought everyone was looking at me, and I only look at myself. It's tiring." Here at La Pagode the first images that greet her eyes are informed by this fresh vision, this heightened consciousness. As the camera moves in to Cleo's mirrored reflection, her face is caught among others in a literalization of the new social view of herself. This prefigures Cleo's final words of recognition and resolution, spoken to Antoine near the end of the film: "Today everything amazes me. The faces of people, and mine alongside them."

Perhaps even more emblematic in terms of Cleo's evolution from woman-as-spectacle to woman-as-social-being is the image that designates chapter XI—the fragmentary shards of a broken mirror. In the scenario, this chapter, the last belonging entirely to Cleo, is prefaced by Varda's description: "She is no longer the heroine of a melodrama, but a woman who is aware of her fear and who feels alone."[9] As Cleo bends down toward the scattered pieces of a pocket mirror that Dorothée has accidentally broken, the only portion of her reflected face visible in these jagged fragments is her eye. This is the last image of a mirror to appear in the entire film; significantly, it announces that this image has ceased to function for Cleo as a reassurance of identity as it confirms the priority of her own vision of the world.

The two cafe scenes, one before and one after the pivotal rehearsal sequence, are also highly indicative of Cleo's transformation. Immediately upon leaving the fortune-teller's, Cleo is shown, in a high-angle shot of long duration, walking on the rue de Rivoli to meet Angèle. The extra-diegetic strains of the theme of Cleo's pop song (later identified by the lyrics with her capriciousness and coquettishness), as well as her boldly patterned dress, achieve Varda's desired effect: "In the street, in the cafe, she is the focal point for all eyes."[10] She enters Ça Va Ça Vient with an evident awareness of the eyes of others. Chapter II, which begins with Angèle's internal monologue ("She needs to be taken care of, she's like a child"), offers the busy social milieu of the cafe as mere background to Cleo's self-absorption. Primarily filmed in crowded long-shot, the sequence is highlighted by two parallel conversations emphasized on the soundtrack above the bistro's noisy din: One is about sex, the other about death.

In contrast, when Cleo enters Le Dôme after her *crise de conscience*, the chapter of "Some Others" begins. Camera position and Cleo's viewpoint coalesce as the subjective vision of social reality imposes itself. Varda's directions could not be more to the point: "Cleo walks forthrightly. She looks. And her curiosity gives others importance. This chapter is like a short documentary on the people who frequent the cafe Dôme and the quarter. We see them with her, faces in the street, serious, closed in on themselves, mysterious or preoccupied. . . . Often the camera is substituted for Cleo's gaze."[11]

A Baudelairean flaneur, Cleo glides through the cafe, hearing snatches of conversations (references to the Algerian war, to artists Miro and Picasso, to children, to memories of the past, and so forth) as she tries to see the impact of her own song, her selection on the jukebox. (Earlier it was this song, "La Belle P.," which had evoked Cleo's narcissistic comment on the quality of the recording when the female cab-driver had played it on the radio. Here in Le Dôme her interest is not in the song itself, nor in her performance, but rather in the *effect* of this song on other people.) The anonymity she craves—the better to observe others around her—is facilitated when she puts on dark glasses. Here dark glasses become the instrument of vision, of insight: By becoming anonymous, Cleo thus sees, and in seeing others, she begins to understand herself. Because in this sequence the camera coincides so often with Cleo's point of view, the spectator now takes Cleo's position as subject rather than object of vision. By making the look of the camera conform to Cleo's gaze, Varda transforms the viewer's position from its characteristic passivity, its contemplation of the object. And, the activity of vision no longer objectifies Cleo as a fixed image. Instead, a productive vision is conferred on both spectator and character alike.

Structurally paralleling and thereby contrasting Cleo's first objectified walk from the fortune-teller's to Ça Va Ça Vient is her walk from Le Dôme to the Académie de Sculpture. The amplified sounds of Cleo's footsteps against a heavy silence replace the extra-diegetic musical theme accompanying the first walk. Likewise, rather than an image of Cleo *seen,* highly marked as the object of the gaze, this second walk conveys the process of Cleo *seeing.* Her subjective vision is rendered by an alternation of past, present, and imagined images, an alternation that intercuts people on the street, seen from her point of view, with remembered images of Bob, Angèle, and José; others from the street and the cafe; and fantasy images of her wig, dressing table, and clock. The chapter ends with the pure subjectivity of unmediated vision, rendered as anonymous as possible to emphasize the fact of seeing: six shots of exceptionally fluid camera movement are highlighted by intense silence broken only by the scraping of sculptor's tools. Varda thus uses a cinematic equivalent—a purely visual and aural construction—to render the theoretical and philosophical transformation of subjectivity. A meditation on vision, femininity, and culture, the film finds its emblematic representation in this pivotal moment at the center of the text.

Significantly, Cleo's new self-awareness is also manifested in her attitudes toward other women. Here, too, we find a contrast between the two opposing halves of the film. The reciprocity of mutual female friendship seems absent from Cleo's life with Angèle. The overtones of a vaguely maternal rapport between them are actually more characteristic of the relationship of servant and mistress. Shared confidences are presented in the stylized form of classical theater. In Cleo's apartment, duenna and charge discuss the vagaries of romance in a camera style that is intentionally flat, distanced, and theatrical. In two frontal tableaux, the two women discuss José's visit in cliches that stereotype both attitude and self-image (Angèle: "All men are egotists"; Cleo: "I'm too good for men"). In addition, Cleo's comments about the woman cab-driver reveal her lack of female solidarity:

Angèle: What a character, that woman.
Cleo: You said it. It's revolting.
Angèle: I found her courageous and charming.

However, once Cleo's self-recognition and social awareness are triggered, her connections with other women—as demonstrated by the sequences with Dorothée—are strengthened. Dorothée is a woman without pretenses whose simplicity is grounded in a healthy acceptance of life. Of her modeling she says, "I'm happy in my body, not haughty. When [the artists] look at me, I know they're looking at something besides me—a form, an idea, I don't know." In other words, for her, identity as a woman is not produced by the looks of others. In the film she introduces the idea of nudity (as opposed to sexual exploitation), a theme later discussed by Antoine. Dorothée's salutary attitude is further rendered in her affectionate exchange with Raoul (Raoul: "Voilà ma poupée" [There's my doll]; Dorothée: "d'amour" [Of love]), which illustrates the way in which reciprocal terms of affection can replace objectifying epithets.

Cleo's car ride with Dorothée is filmed in the aleatory, free-flowing manner typical of the New Wave. The two women talk intimately, like school friends whose shared past provides an enduring bond. Thus when Dorothée playfully utters a familiar reprimand ("You really are a spoiled child") it is said with genuine affection, and balanced by a real appreciation of Cleo's beauty and her talent. Likewise, when at one point "Dorothée looks at Cleo, searching her face for some sign of calm," an implicit contrast is drawn between the woman who looks in the mirror for a reassurance of identity—Cleo in the first part of the film—and the woman who looks into a friend's face out of concern for another's well-being. And Cleo now begins to return this communication in the small gesture of giving Dorothée her hat, significantly a symbol of her vanity in the first part of the film.

As previously mentioned, Cleo's "profound transformation" occurs during a rehearsal session in which lyrics awake in her a sudden perception of mortality and solitude, triggering a new self-awareness which is fundamentally social. As Cleo sings the haunting lines of "Cri d'amour," the camera slowly swings around and tracks in on her until, in an apotheosis of the fetishized woman's image, it isolates her out of all diegetic context of the apartment; a frontal medium-close-up of her face is framed by a black curtain, which now fills the entire background. She begins:

With its doors open,   [Toutes portes ouvertes
Drafty air running through,   En plein courant d'air
I am an empty house   Je suis une maison vide
Without you, without you. . . .   Sans toi, sans toi. . . .]

and as these last words are sung, the camera begins its circular movement while on the soundtrack Bob's piano music suddenly becomes transformed into a full extra-diegetic orchestral chorus. She continues, now without the aid of printed words or sheet music:

Beautiful to no avail	[Belle en pure perte
Naked in the heart of winter	Nue au coeur de l'hiver
I am a starving body	Je suis un corps avide
Without you, without you. . . .	Sans toi, sans toi . . .
And if you come too late	Et si tu viens trop tard
They will have buried me	On m'aura mise en terre
Alone, ugly, pale,	Seule, laide et livide
Without you. . . .	Sans toi. . . .]

The accompanying music, as well as her voice, are dramatically amplified, while the lighting changes from naturalistic to theatrical, as if Cleo were singing on a stage or in a cabaret.

The hypnotic effect that the song has on Cleo is mirrored and reinforced for the spectator by means of procedures that isolate and enhance Cleo's performance. Varda calls this sequence "the hinge of the story," explaining that "the circular movement which isolates Cleo is like a huge wave carrying her off. Her voyage begins after the black curtain of the intermission. She strips herself and changes her appearance."[12] In effect, Cleo explodes in rage at her songwriters, rebelling against the image that they have constructed for her: "You didn't teach me the *solfeggio* just so that you could make me dependent on you. Everybody spoils me, nobody loves me." She then tears off the traditional attributes of stereotypical feminine beauty—blonde wig and feathered satin peignoir—and thereby activates her transformation from object to subject through a change in image. In order to leave the world of those who have defined her as a cliche (lover, composers, secretary-companion), she now puts on ordinary-looking clothing (a black dress, simple jewelry) and with a violent sweep of a black curtain (the time compressed by a jump-cut) she emerges, changed.

"Cri d'amour" is a constellation of signifiers of loss; its lyrics are heavy with the burden of absence, death, mortality. As such it is a crucial textual hinge in another important way. Cleo's development in the film can be understood in terms of a movement from reciprocal narcissistic enclosure, through the painful perception of lack and absence ("without you"), to an acceptance of the necessary intersubjectivity that structures all relations of culture. From the reassuring coherence of identity, in which Cleo is capable of loving only her (reflected) self, Cleo is propelled by an awareness of separation and death into an understanding of the social constitution of her (self-)image. Thus the fundamental sociality at the basis of identity is graphically demonstrated by Cleo's process of coming to consciousness.

Once again this can be traced by contrasting two episodes in the different halves of the film. The first occurs in chapter III, Cleo's confirmation of her beauty as she tries on hats. In a visual tour de force, Varda captures Cleo's image in a maze of reflecting mirrors, sinuous circular camera movements, and plate-glass shop windows that pick up reflections and details from the street outside. In fact, this whole single-shot-sequence can be read as a literalization of the woman-as-image caught up as the pivot within the cinematic apparatus. Varda's directions indicate precisely the effect that binds the spectator to this image: "Passersby perceive, across the large showcase windows, a dream-like creature who glides as if in an aquarium."[13] And, as if she gathers force from this reassuring play of looks and coquettish poses, Cleo says in voice-over internal monologue immediately preceding this shot: "Everything suits me; ah, I could become intoxicated trying on hats and dresses."

The corresponding sequence, or emblematic image, occurs in chapter XI. Someone has just been shot through one of the plate-glass windows of Le Dôme, and as Cleo and Dorothée pass by, they are seen through the cobweblike configuration caused by the bullet-hole. As they stand and stare, snatches of conversation from the surrounding crowd disclose that a man has been killed. In contrast to the hat-shop image, this new depiction of Cleo's face, associated with others and transected by the jagged lines of shattered glass, corresponds to her new social perception of herself. Whereas in the first half of the film, windows had offered up Cleo's own image in a reflection redolent with narcissism, here she is included with a crowd of others, the unity of the reflected image shattered by the trace of death. In the kind of visual economy that we have come to see as typical of Varda, this image points to the necessary social mediation between self and others which is the basis of all culture, and the inscription of femininity in its social definition finds a stunning cinematic image in this sequence of events.

Ultimately, the social foundation of Cleo's self-recognition finds its best expression in the relationship she develops with Antoine. This rapport is established as a reciprocal, human, and nonobjectifying type of sharing unknown to Cleo at the outset of the film. As the fetishized, stereotyped, conventional image of feminine beauty, Cleo has previously been able to engage with men only in terms concomitant with this image. But Antoine presents a different modality of relationship: "With him she can be herself. It is not the grand passion. It is simply a dialogue between a man and a woman which might facilitate mutual understanding and perhaps love."[14]

Antoine, in many ways the masculine counterpart of Dorothée, is secure in his identity. (In fact, Cleo's car ride with Dorothée, depicted for the most part in shots that frame them in a dual relationship, surrounded by the car window, prefigures this rapport.) Inquisitive, curious, gloriously open to the life around him, he represents the opposite of narcissistic containment with its need for a reassuring vision of the coherence of identity (he says, "I believe without seeing"). He begins a conversation with Cleo out of simple gregariousness, refusing to see her as the glamorous doll of her accustomed image.

This is established textually in a striking way. Immediately preceding Antoine's appearance on the wooden bridge in the Parc Montsouris, Cleo engages in an unseen "performance" of her rock song, "La Belle P." She assumes characteristic femme fatale poses as she mouths the words, unaccompanied and unamplified, in what results in a parody of the conventions of female beauty:

My precious	[Mon corps precieux
And capricious body,	et capricieux
The blue of my	l'azur de mes yeux
Audacious eyes.	audacieux.]

Only snatches of the lyrics are audible on the soundtrack ("my eyes . . . charms . . . favors . . . my heart-shaped mouth . . . "), highlighting the fragmentation necessary to fetishization. The significance of the song itself has become modified in the course of the film: whereas Cleo's first reaction to it in the taxi was a self-referential critique of the recording, and in Le Dôme it served to illustrate the ephemeral nature of a mere song, now she mimes it in a manner that foregrounds exactly what it is—a representation of femininity. The gestures and postures of coquettishness are no longer operative for her. The first part of the film had naturalized these gestures by contextualizing them in a notion of character development; now Cleo—and the spectator—understands these attributes of femininity as elements of a constructed image.

In chapter XII, "Antoine imposes his presence with kindness, gently . . . their meeting is natural. The sequence is as well. The chapter is filmed in a single shot, like a deep breath."[15] However, this "natural" is transected by a profound sociality; for Cleo it is not the return to a natural feminine essence of woman, but a retreat from the stifling, objectifying conventions of femininity to a more social form of human relation. Their conversation in this chapter is one of sharing—experi-

Cleo from 5 to 7 (Summary)

Museum of Modern Art

Ciné-Tamaris

Ciné-Tamaris

Ciné-Tamaris

Museum of Modern Art

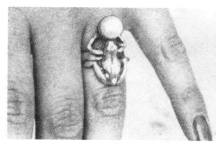

Museum of Modern Art

ences and observations about life, love, and death. In a sense, they complement each other: Antoine says he would like to die for love; Cleo admits that she is afraid to love.

This shared communication has been triggered by Cleo's pronunciation of the dreaded word: Cancer. As soon as she verbalizes her fears, the freedom and openness of this relationship with Antoine is made possible. The transformation hinges on a linguistic formulation of absence, death, and loss, which is, paradoxically, the moment that the profoundly social recognition occurs. Thus, the movement is traced from the first recognition of absence installed by the song ("sans toi . . ."), through the verbal utterance of the world signifying death, to this final liberation which entails a social acceptance of others. Visually this is connoted as a positive thing by Varda's use of an emphatically bleached, sunlit image, and by the amplified noise of birds and other "summer sounds" on the soundtrack.[16]

Ultimately, the film's final chapter, "belonging" to Cleo and Antoine, is one of conciliation. In accepting the possibility of death, Cleo accepts life, and in accepting herself, Cleo begins to accept others. Varda's description of how this last chapter was to be filmed is quite revealing of the intent to depict Cleo's new self-awareness as a social awareness: "The shots are long (in duration) but are very clearly drawn; the interest is equally dispersed on the two characters and on exterior elements."[17] As they walk through the park, then board a bus ("It's more fun than a cab"—sociality over isolation) for the Salpêtrière hospital, Cleo and Antoine discuss a range of topics from nudity to botany; Antoine's enthusiasm for life ("My know-it-all side. Window shopping.") has a salutary effect on Cleo. In addition, the musical theme that had been clearly identified with separate characters and points of view up to this point in the film are now integrated into a harmonic orchestral accompaniment on the soundtrack, assimilating and consolidating musical material in a way that highlights the movement "from conflict to integration."[18] And once they find the doctor, who confirms the illness and refers to a cure, Cleo is able to say, reflectively, "It seems to me that I really feel happy." That this self-reflection is matched by a reciprocal caring for others is rendered visually by the film's last shot. As Cleo and Antoine stand gazing into each other's eyes, the camera zooms back; when it stops, the music starts as the film's final image portrays Cleo and Antoine looking at each other. Thus Cleo has evolved from the compulsion of seeing her own reflection in a mirror to having her gaze now returned by Antoine, this friend, this other.

Finally, the ring Cleo wears (a small golden toad clutching a large pearl) provides an excellent emblematic formulation of the association of vision and motivation underlying the feminist problematic in Varda's film. Early on, Cleo's lover José had referred to her (among other conventional epithets) as "my pearl": Cleo objectified in traditional definitions of feminine beauty. Then once her sudden awareness of life is triggered by the song, Cleo observes a street performer swallowing frogs: Cleo now "sees" reality. But it is ultimately Antoine who condenses these two meanings in his interpretation of the ring's significance: "Pearl and Frog—You and me." He thus makes of this ring a symbol of their rapport, giving the ring a new meaning that combines Cleo's former identity as beautiful object with her new vision of the social world. In this film which exposes traditional meanings conventionally attached to femininity, relations of power are associated with vision. In assuming a vision of her own, Cleo assumes the power to direct her own life—and the power to construct her own image as well. For a woman in patriarchal culture, the two are inextricably related.

This film demonstrates a concern with questions of identity, sexuality, and vision that substantially predates their contemporary status as the currency of critical debate. It is Varda's particular talent to have found a discursive visual language to express these concerns in a way that is at once original, articulate, and profoundly cinematic. Refusing to renounce narrative altogether, and equally committed to the erotics of the gaze, Varda tells a cinematic story that is extremely pleasurable to watch, a story of femininity and its social representations that reveals as much about the character as about ourselves and the culture in which we live. The following analysis of *Vagabond*, a film made twenty-five years later, will demonstrate just how consistently committed to these issues Varda has been, and how brilliantly she has articulated them in a contemporary form.

NOTES

1. Sigmund Freud, "A Note on the Unconscious in Psychoanalysis" (1912), in *General Psychological Theory* (New York: Collier Books, 1963), p. 70.

2. This line of dialogue is pronounced by a fortune-teller at the film's start. All translations from the French are my own. Unfortunately, *Cleo* is not in distribution, but it is currently available on video-cassette. Occasionally the film gets shown at the Museum of Modern Art, the Alliance Française, or universities. The film has been re-released in Paris, where enthusiastic crowds recognized how profoundly ahead of its time the film was in 1961.

3. Agnès Varda in Jacqueline Levitin, "Mother of the New Wave: An Interview with Agnès Varda," *Women and Film*, nos. 5–6 (1974): 63; emphasis added.

4. Agnès Varda, "Avant-propos," *Cléo de 5 à 7* (scenario) (Paris: Editions Gallimard, 1962), p. 8.

5. Varda, "Avant-propos," p. 15.

6. *Cléo de 5 à 7* (scenario), p. 21.

7. Ibid., p. 39.

8. Ibid., pp. 41–42.

9. Ibid., p. 81.

10. Ibid., p. 21.

11. Ibid., p. 63.

12. Ibid., p. 56.

13. Ibid., p. 29.

14. Agnès Varda, publicity release from the distributor of *Cléo de 5 à 7*, Rome-Paris Films, 1961.

15. Varda's directions, Scenario, p. 89. Actually, the chapter is composed of two long (duration) shots, joined together by a cut that violates the 180-degree rule by crossing the imaginary line and filming from the opposite direction.

16. This sequence was actually filmed at 6 in the morning in order to achieve the desired lighting effect.

17. Varda, Scenario, p. 94.

18. Claudia Gorbman has provided an excellent, highly detailed analysis of the music in her article "*Cleo from 5 to 7:* Music as Mirror," in *Wide Angle* 4:4 (1981): 38–49.

ELEVEN

The "Impossible Portrait" of Femininity: *Vagabond*

> *Vagabond* is really constructed about different people looking at Mona—like building together an impossible portrait of Mona.[1]
>
> The first blow against . . . traditional film conventions is to free the look of the camera into its materiality in time and space and the look of the audience into dialectics, passionate detachment.[2]

VAGABOND (1985) IS A FILM about looking, but a kind of looking which is quite precise: in its massive project of reformulating both the cinematic gaze and its object—the body of the woman—it restructures relations of desire, both *in* the text (desire of its characters) and *for* the text (desire of its viewers). As previously noted, the film begins with the puzzling discovery of a woman's corpse, found frozen in a ditch, and then proceeds to recount the last weeks in the life of this young vagrant named Mona, by means of recollections and testimonies of those she had encountered during that time. But this simple description belies the film's deep complexity, on a multitude of levels, as it engages with issues of sexuality and representation, narration and address, in a textual meshwork that is at once a systematic reflection on cinematic meaning and on socially constructed conceptions of femininity as well.

This film, which garnered three major prizes in the year of its release,[3] is described by Varda as follows:

> Adventures and solitude of a young vagabond (neither withdrawn nor talkative), told by those who had crossed her path, that winter in the South of France. But can one render silence, or capture freedom?

The film wanders between Mona and the others. We glimpse their lives, and then move on. I really liked all the characters in this story, here and there, like small "figures" in a winter landscape, where, coming toward us, walking, is a rebellious girl.[4]

In a film that is part social investigation and part feminist inquiry, Varda redefines cinematic visual pleasure just as certainly as she interrogates "femininity" and its cultural representations. And one of the ways she does this is by evolving a new discursive form that blends fictional construct with documentary research in a unique articulation which defies traditional categorization. In so doing, she mounts a triple challenge to the conventions of dominant filmmaking: She devises new textual strategies that rework the function of narration; she disrupts the patriarchal logic of vision by reconceiving the voyeuristic gaze; and she provides a discursive space for questions of sexuality, reflecting on what it means to be a woman and to represent one's own desire.

To trace the narrative movement of the film is to become immediately immersed in these preoccupations, for what emerges from the seemingly random encounters is both a carefully orchestrated story and an integrated vision. Yet it is this very randomness that makes the systematic breakdown into units so complicated, as some chance meetings with Mona connect at the end of the film while others do not, calling for a retrospective determination of meaning for each of the events. Likewise, those people who figure importantly in Mona's last weeks have roles that are distributed between actors and nonprofessionals alike, so a clear distinction between primary and secondary characters becomes disturbed. Even in her production notes, Varda lists seven main actors and thirty nonprofessionals who surround them, yet some of these latter have significant encounters with Mona as well. What follows is a provisional description of Mona's circular trajectory—from the time that her body is discovered in a ditch until the final moments of the film, when she falls, dazed, crying, and isolated, onto the rigid (and ridged) frozen ground—in order to provide some of the conditions of analysis for this highly complex and moving text.

Vagabond is a kind of inverted *Citizen Kane* in two respects. Varda herself refers to Welles's film when she insists on the importance of discursive elaboration over the actual story itself: "[M]ost of my films . . . are very very thin stories. My work is how I use it [how the film *narrates* that story]. If you tell the story of *Citizen Kane* it is not much of a story. An old rich mogul man is dead. He said a word we don't understand. We don't discover so much, just some pieces of his life and finally it is just a sled. Is that a story? It is not much. So what makes *Citizen Kane* so interesting is the way [Welles] told us about the man—intriguing us about what people think about him."[5]

In a playfully perverse move, Varda gives us the total inversion of *Citizen Kane* in *Vagabond:* A young, poor vagrant woman is dead. She died in a way we don't understand. We don't discover so much, just some pieces of her life and finally it is just a pagan ritual of the vine. But Varda has done more than simply substitute the content of the film with its antithesis. *Citizen Kane* is the classic example of a film that proceeds in terms of dislocations between *story* (the chronological reconstruction of events) and *discourse* (their cinematic elaboration as they are presented in the film, the order that is actually seen on the screen). Varda extends this kind of work so that the importance of the story's chronology fades completely. In its move from narrative fragmentation to cohesion, its final revelation of the answer to Mona's death, *Vagabond* brings us no closer to her "truth" than to a satisfying resolution: The interweaving of interpretations, the critical engagement with meaning, the experience of a diverse social tapestry are all of much more consequence to our participation in the text. For Varda, the cinema is above all "a way of narrating,"[6] a discursive process that takes priority over the logic of events themselves. This emphasis on discourse—over the naturalizing function of the story—is only one of the ways that *Vagabond* presents a challenge to dominant forms, but something absolutely central to a theoretical stance. "I'm interested in now and here,"[7] asserts Varda, and in so doing she inadvertently formulates one of the most important deconstructive strategies of the alternative text—the restoration of the discursive marks of enunciation so carefully elided by the story's concealing operations of "then and there."

Thus my outline of the "plot" of *Vagabond* necessarily conforms to its discursive surface; I will enumerate events as they occur to the viewer when the film unfolds on the screen. Mona's story is a complex intersection of narration, vision, and sexuality: Each "witness" who encounters her narrates the account, as the camera renders (either simultaneously, before, or after) a vision of the events, sometimes offering a view unanchored in the narration as well. And all of these texts, both narrated and described, hinge on this curious woman whose existence—framed and identified by her sexuality, her "femaleness"—touches them (and us) deeply in some complicated way.

The film opens on a harshly beautiful landscape of the Languedoc, a vineyard almost golden in the chilly autumn light, as credits are accompanied by a dissonant, contemporary string quartet, the bleak yet compelling tones providing an aural version of the scene before our eyes. This music, written especially for *Vagabond* by the young composer Joanna Bruzdowicz,[8] appears across the film in sharply defined punctuating moments (twelve single-shot sequences, excluding this first one) that trace Mona's progress from a triumphant wanderer with leather jacket and pack to a frozen, crying vagrant in tattered boots and wine-soaked blanket. Suddenly, a vineyard worker gathering black branches in the field discovers the frozen body of a young woman in a ditch; police investigate, take measurements, discuss and determine that this was a natural death. Questions remain, however, as her body and face are covered with wine dregs: Three shots of indeterminate walls being washed clean of purple stains are intercut, a cryptic intrusion that poses the "why?" to the "how" of her death, and instates the interrogative that hovers over the film: "Who?"

It is Varda's own voice, in fact, which frames the question in discursive terms, for the very next shot—an almost abstract tracing of ridges in sand (undecipherable at first) is matched by her words, meditative and reflective, on the soundtrack: "No one claimed the body, so it went from a ditch to potter's field [a pun in French: *fossé à la fosse commune*]. She had died a natural death without leaving a trace. I wonder, do those who knew her as a child still think about her? But people she had met recently remembered her. Those witnesses helped me tell the last weeks of her last winter. She left her mark on them. They spoke of her, not knowing she had died. I didn't tell them. Nor that her name was Mona Bergeron. I know little about her myself, but it seems to me she came from the sea."

The camera, that same scrutinizing eye that had opened *Vagabond* and which marks its status as investigation, a kind of surveillance (the camera/author's, the character's, the viewer's) that never ceases to imply the *social* inscription of vision, slowly moves in the following way: At the words, "I wonder," it begins to track upward and to the left, and moves directly upward on the words "last weeks"; tracking right, it discloses the blue water and lacy waves of an ocean seen in long-shot; and then, at the words "her name was Mona Bergeron," the tiny figure of a woman in the center of this long-shot emerges from the water; finally, after the voice has stopped, the camera remains stationary, at a distance, framing this Botticelli Venus as she walks out of the sea. In this single shot which acts as a sort of delayed preface— and indicates from the outset the kind of temporal dislocations that will structure the film—Varda inserts herself emphatically as enunciative source and establishes a presence of authorship that will be felt throughout the film: "I wonder . . . helped me tell . . . I know little . . .

it seems to me." This is Varda's only "appearance," and yet she is always there, by implication, as orchestrator of the visions (both hers and others'), as manipulator of the fictions (both "real" and not). Yet, importantly, she installs herself as a *questioning* source, assuming a position of investigation that she shares with both her viewers and her characters. Mona eludes Varda just as she eludes everyone, yet the desire to know, and to tell, is deeply felt by all. Thus by making her own position one of uncertainty and doubt, Varda simultaneously foregrounds and disturbs the invisible enunciation of the patriarchal narrative, and offers us a fiction that is problematized from the start.

The next sequence opens as two "motorcycle-types" look at post-cards of women and make jokes about the real woman that they saw on the beach. Then we see them at this beach ("A girl all alone is easy . . . she's got to be crazy to be in the water now"), stopping, looking at Mona, then riding off. In a very condensed way, this short sequence initiates the complicated procedures of narrative and address that structure the film, for a complex interweaving of verbal narration and visual description distinguishes each sequence as well as their interrelation. Sometimes a person will describe an encounter with Mona, which will then be depicted in a viable flashback structure; at other times the verbal account will follow its visual elaboration; or, even further, the opinion or assessment will come much later in the film. In addition, characters who appear as random or unimportant, such as Paulo (Joël Fosse) in this sequence, become primary figures in what emerges as the main narrative by the film's end; others remain secondary and transitory throughout. The viewer thereby becomes enmeshed in the intricate weaving of discourses that traverse the film, shifting temporal registers as well as modes of depiction as each account takes on its cinematic form.

The first of the punctuating musical-interlude shots comes next, as Mona strides emphatically across the shadow-streaked sand, tones of deep blue and gold shining vividly in the cold late-afternoon sun. Abruptly, Mona has a hostile conversation with a truck driver who has picked her up. And then, when he, in turn, tells a friend about the encounter, the friend responds with his own story of finding Mona in an abandoned shack that was about to be demolished. The second "contemplative shot" with music places Mona in a village, whose grey November walls contrast the bright red coat and knit cap of a young girl carrying a baguette. When Mona arrives at a house and asks for water, she learns that she must prime the pump first. Later, she rolls a cigarette, asks a man in a shack for matches, pitches her tent. The girl at the water pump sullenly tells her parents, "I'd like to be free, like that girl with the water." It rains; Mona learns that she's pitched her tent in a cemetery; she asks for work cleaning tombstones. Mona strides across a radiant golden field (the third musical punctuation), smoking; she even smiles. Seated by a rock, she finds her bread as hard as one; she gets a man in a cafe to buy her a sandwich; she fixes her boot with a rock. The fourth punctuating shot discloses a tractor, a stone wall, and Mona jumping behind this wall to avoid a passing police car.

Then the first consistently elaborated "narrative" sequence begins, yet this is still in the register of what will remain ancillary to the major fiction, as it evolves. A garage mechanic tells about the woman he gave work washing cars ("Female drifters are all alike—they loaf and chase men"), as the subsequent series of shots (subdivided into groupings) depicts exchanges of money, looks, and sex, only to return to the mechanic's assessment ("She said 'you've got dirty hands' . . . no, she said, 'you've got a dirty mind.' What nerve!"). Mona, back on the road, resumes hitch-hiking, as a car takes off without her. She comes to a large water pump and fills her bottle while the motorcycle-types (in the foreground) discuss a prospective heist. Paulo commands them to "Leave Yolande out of this." This last sequence represents a transition of what is the most sustained and complicated narrative structure of the film, for its full significance and function can only be appreciated at the end. The connection between Paulo (a petty crook), Yolande (his girlfriend), her uncle (a chateau caretaker), and Tante Lydie (Yolande's employer) is only gradually made clear; at this point in the narration, each event appears in perplexing isolation. But this is how Varda chooses to convey the first in a series of significant relationships between Mona and some others, for it is through the eyes of the hopelessly romantic Yolande that we first see Mona and David (Patrick Lepczynski).

A quick, disruptive close-up of the eighty-four-year-old Tante Lydie (Marthe Jarnias) appears; she rings her bell and calls Yolande (Yolande Moreau). Yolande, in blue housecoat and feather-duster in hand, addresses the viewer directly. The frontality, isolation, and absence of interlocutor in this shot mark it as one of the authentic instances of direct address in the film (there are nine of them, Yolande authorizing four), and make it the important initiator of Yolande's recurring "discourse on love." She tells of her discovery of a couple, asleep in each other's arms, in the chateau where her uncle works; immediately we are with Paulo and Yolande visiting this uncle, and then with Yolande, discovering "the lovers" herself. What follows is a systematic alternation between the "counter-paradise" of Mona and David (he's a hippie squatter in the poorly guarded chateau)—composed of smoking dope, making love, eating meals, and wandering on the grounds—and the sentimental Yolande as she tries to instill some romance into Paulo, an alternation that finally ends with the burglary of the chateau by Paulo and his pals. The entire episode, fragmented structure and all, is concluded by David's direct address as he hunches in a departing boxcar with a bandage on his head: "When I had grass she was nice. But less so when I ran out. When I got slugged, she split. I thought she was a homebody, the staying kind."

Now Mona stands on a windy hill as a train goes by; she sits by her tent and throws a damaged painting (stolen from the chateau) into the fire. Yolande's uncle is interrogated by the police. Mona eats food left outside a local church. She walks past tires, a chain-link fence, frosted corrugated steel in a landscape that is colder, darker, drearier (the fifth musical interlude); she blows her nose in her hand. She wakes up one morning and it has snowed. She continues hitching.

Up until this point, there has been a slow progression of episodes, narrative units that have become gradually more complicated as the film proceeds. The film, in fact, works toward more narrative complexity as Mona herself becomes more isolated, rejecting the opportunity to connect that each encounter brings. What follows is the most extended narrative yet, as Mona arrives at the farm of a goatherd, his wife, and small child. The shepherd, an articulate thinker with a master's degree in philosophy who has chosen the alternative lifestyle of raising goats and making cheese, provides one of the most perceptive indictments of Mona—to her face—and incites in her a hostile rejection. As she engages in what are perhaps her most extensive conversations in the entire film (with one exception), Mona is revealed to be lazy, uncommitted, and entirely without purpose. Rebellious to the core, she appears to have no sense of what she might be revolting against. Asserting the essential importance of human connection, the goatherd says to Mona early on, "I chose a middle road between freedom and loneliness. . . . If you want to live, you stop." He gives her land to plant potatoes and a trailer as a home, but Mona languishes, reading novels and smoking while everybody works. Finally, the goatherd angrily tells her, "You're not serious about anything. . . . You say you want things, but you won't work. . . . You're not a drop-out, you're just out. You don't exist." But he, too, can be criticized for his intolerance; he imposes his own conception of "alternative" on everybody else.

Mona finds a new place to put her backpack; she encounters a prostitute and sells her some cheese. A provincial woman comments to her husband about the young hitch-hiker ("She's got character. She knows what she wants"). And Mona, in the cold, dark night, looks inside at a family watching television (the sixth punctuating shot).

Almost as a complement of the shepherd's sequence (it includes Mona's other extended conversation), this next episode affords the vagabond another significant encounter. It opens as Madame Landier (Macha Méril), a professor and tree expert, talks on the telephone while taking a bath: "I have to tell you about the hitch-hiker I picked up, a sort of vagrant. My lord, how she stank. When she got in, I nearly choked." This shot—which introduces a series of eight short episodes depicting the curiously affectionate rapport between these utterly opposite types ("one is clean, the other isn't; one has a house, the other doesn't")[9]—is strongly marked by the complexity of address. Because the interlocutor is invisible, the address appears direct; because the interlocutor is implied within the diegesis, the address is also indirect; and because the frontal format and *suggested* interlocutor locate it firmly within a system of shots of this kind, it is also a modified direct address. Again, as with other "flashbacks," Madame Landier's preface initiates a series of sequences, moments in which she and Mona, driving through the country and sharing food, drink, and conversation, discuss their ideas about life. Madame Landier tells Mona about her work, a crusade to prevent a disease that has been killing plane trees throughout the region; this is accompanied by a series of three intrusive shots detailing the disease and its treatment and recalling the early wine-dregs shots at the opening of the film. And Mona reveals that she has a degree in stenography.

Their arrival at a plane tree work-site initiates a new sequence and introduces another character who, by the story's end, will also come to figure in the main fiction. Madame Landier's assistant, the agronomist Jean-Pierre (Stéphane Freiss), meets the strange young woman who challenges him with a question: "Do I scare you or what?" Abruptly after this encounter, we are in the bathroom with Jean-Pierre and his wife Eliane (Laurence Cortadellas) who, on stepping out of the shower, refuses to listen to her husband's tale of the girl with "witch's hair," instead insisting that they ought to own his Tante Lydie's huge house. When she nastily says that the young vagrant might be a drug addict, we are quickly shown a needle puncturing an arm. But this turns out to be Mona, donating blood at a blood bank. The seventh musical punctuation shot reveals Mona in a village, walking past the stone surfaces of buildings after shutters have been closed when she asks to buy cigarettes. She tries to fix her boot (the zipper's gone) and then crosses over to a work-site where houses are being built. She looks vacantly as she sits by the fire; village women talk. A construction worker offers his testimony: "To be all alone like that. I should have spoken to her." Mona eats sardines and wipes her hands on her jeans. She loads crates and tells the owner, flippantly, about the plane-tree disease.

A return to Madame Landier shows her narrowly escaping electrocution, as Jean-Pierre turns off the light which she's touched with wet hands. Trembling with fear, and claiming to have seen her life in "bits of images," she tells him that the young woman hitch-hiker kept coming back to her "like a reproach." Again in the form of a narrated flashback, Madame Landier is shown depositing Mona by some woods; she gives her some money to assuage her guilt, but Mona senses the rejection and is hurt. She defiantly answers with a pun, using the play on language that they had shared now as a signifier of separation and defense. The return to Madame Landier's apartment gives us her testimony, told to Jean-Pierre: "Help me. Go find her. I'm worried for her, she's so alone. I should've done something. I don't even know her name."

In the eighth sequence of music, Mona is raped, as a man jumps out of the tangle of bushes and attacks her. Immediately following is the goatherd's testimony: "By proving she's useless, she helps the system she rejects. That's not wandering, that's withering [*C'est l'erreur, pas l'errance*]." The ninth musical punctuation has the camera track past a wall to disclose Mona, cross-legged, looking at some cards. The next shot reveals a close-up of these cards, postcards of paintings and trees.

What follows is the second "relationship" sequence for Mona, an extended interlude in which she stays with a Tunisian vineyard worker named Assoun (Yahiaoui Assouna). In a series of short episodes that alternate inside and outdoors Mona and Assoun work in the vineyards, have meals together, share life. It is only when the other workers return from Morocco, and tell Assoun that Mona must leave, that they are separated. But the sense of rejection begun with the goatherd and continued with Madame Landier is here most forcefully displayed by Mona when "she expresses her anger, her frustration, her sadness,"[10] calling Assoun a coward for giving in so easily to the others. Then the vineyard owner, in formal direct address, gives his observation about Mona's plight (his wife having given hers a few sequences earlier, noting the oddity of a young girl camping alone): "I knew it. Poor girl. Where is she now? So young." It is now nighttime, and Mona, cold and alone, faces the darkness with tears in her eyes. Another testimony, this time by the hippie in the blood bank, adds to the composite portrait ("I wonder why she came—she didn't seem to need the food"). The tenth punctuating sequence uncharacteristically combines narrative with Mona's steps, as she leaves a cafe with a fellow hitch-hiker and then crudely abandons him for a ride.

Yolande suddenly appears on the screen (blue housecoat and all) and continues her meditation on the young lovers, whom, she says, she will never forget. Thus begins the final interconnecting of narrative implausibilities, which now have their own logical coherence. Mona hitch-hikes on a train overpass at night; Yolande and Paulo leave a night club and pick her up. Yolande tells Mona she can stay in Tante Lydie's extra bedroom, then the next morning shares her feelings with the unyielding girl ("You know, I've often thought of you two asleep. I thought it was eternal love"). Mona wears Yolande's housecoat and makes friends with Tante Lydie; the two share a hilarious few moments of cognac and laughter. A furious Yolande expels Mona from the house as Jean-Pierre and Eliane (further complications) come to visit their great-aunt. The threads are woven tighter as Eliane accuses Yolande of aiding the burglary of the chateau (a burglary perpetrated by Paulo) and says she must be fired. At this point, the chain of coincidences binds all of these disparate characters, and we see that all of the "partial views" of Mona and all of the "scenes of provincial life" are interconnected—both narratively and socially.

Mona wakes up in a train station and tries to sell spoons that she has stolen from Tante Lydie. In a rigorously choreographed shot she is shown taking up with other vagrants, hippies, and social refuse in the station. They smoke dope in the abandoned house where they all crash, and Mona kisses a drifter-pimp (Christian Chessa) who wants her to make pornography. They return to the train station, stoned and drunk. Yolande and Jean-Pierre come up the escalator, as Yolande is leaving for another job. In a final address to the spectator she says she had a shock on seeing someone who looked like Mona: "I wonder what's happened to her. I don't even know where she's from." David enters the station, unseen by Mona, who is now creating a disturbance in the coffee shop. Jean-Pierre makes a call in the telephone booth and, to a friend, recounts his assessment (as Mona vomits behind him), answering her question of a much earlier time: "Yes, she frightens me because she disgusts me." Music accompanies Mona in the eleventh sequence as she and the others kick cans, doors, pavement in the street. David enters the hippie house looking for his money, and a fire breaks out in the scuffle that ensues. Mona runs for her life and grabs a ride in a van. The pimp observes, "I miss Mona. She was some piece of ass. I could have made money with her."

Mona huddles in a plastic shed in the freezing night; a dog barks. Assoun stares at us, kisses Mona's scarf, and doesn't say a thing. When morning comes, Mona looks for bread. The village is deserted, when suddenly, she is attacked by "monsters" clothed in burlap and branches, the "tree people" acting out a wild and joyful Dionysian rite. Unable to grasp the codes of a social ritual from which she is excluded, she reacts in a way that dramatizes at once her total isolation and the absolute necessity of human connection. Splattered with wine dregs and screaming in terror, Mona escapes, only to wander, dazed, coughing, and wrapped in a blanket (the twelfth music sequence) around the icy countryside, somber shades of blue, brown, and purple predominating. She continues on, dragging her shivering body along until she trips, falls into a ditch, and, sighing and sobbing as she closes her eyes, assumes the position in which she's found at the beginning of the film. The credits roll over a black background to the tones of a pocket trumpet improvisation.

What follows is a list of "sequences" in abbreviated notation, a graphic demonstration of *Vagabond*'s fragmented, episodic structure and its extremely complicated form.

    1. Credits: Music, landscape.
    2. Discovery of body (a = man; b = police).
    3. Varda, voice-over: "She came from the sea."
    4. Motorcycles (a = postcards; b = watch her on the beach). *indirect address*
I.   5. MUSIC: Blue shadow-streaked sand; Mona strides across the beach.
    6. Truck driver (a = hostile conversation; b = two men talk; c = demolition). *indirect address*
II.   7. MUSIC: Mona smoking; girl with red hat.
    8. Water pump (a = prime pump; b = cigarette/tent; c = girl). *modified direct address*
    9. Mona's tent in rain.
III. 10. MUSIC: Golden field; Mona strides.
    11. Bread (a = hard as rock; b = sandwich in cafe; c = Mona fixing boot).
IV. 12. MUSIC: Tractor, stone wall; Mona hides, then goes on.
    13. Gas station (a = mechanic; b = looks/money/sex; c = mechanic. *modified direct/direct*
    14. Mona hitch-hiking (ends on question-mark). (Men planning heist; "Leave Yolande alone.")
    15. Yolande (a = Tante Lydie; b = Yolande—"lovers"; c = visit uncle). *direct address*

16. Mona and David (a = kiss; b = smoke dope and wander).
17. Yolande and Paulo (breakfast in bed). *indirect address*
18. Mona and David (in garden).
19. Yolande. *direct address*
20. Mona and David (chateau heist).
21. David. *direct address*
22. Mona on hill; burns painting.
23. Uncle (to police). *modified direct address*
24. Mona with food from church.
V. 25. MUSIC: Mona walks by tires, frosted corrugation; blows nose. Colder.
26. Mona's tent in snow; she looks out.
27. Mona hitch-hiking (silent shot, driver's perspective).
28. Goatherd (a = no trespassing; b = conversation; c = outside with goats; d = education discussion, by fire; e = outside, trailer; f = Mona from window; g = Mona eats while others work; h = cheese making; i = Mona and goatherd confrontation).
29. Mona in new place.
30. Mona and a prostitute.
31. Woman (to husband). *modified direct address*
VI. 32. MUSIC: Mona watches couple watching TV; nighttime.
33. Madame Landier (a = telephone; b = Mona and Madame Landier in car; c = car through countryside; d = chi chi's (pastry); e = hands and beer, conversation; f = large house; g = plane tree discourse; h = car again; i = nighttime, champagne). *modified direct address*
34. Plane tree work site (Jean-Pierre meets Mona).
35. Eliane and Jean-Pierre (Jean-Pierre to Eliane). *indirect address*
36. Blood bank.
VII. 37. MUSIC: Mona asks to buy cigarettes; shutters, white walls, crates.
38. Mona sits by fire at house-construction site.
39. Construction worker. *direct address*
40. Mona eats sardines.
41. Mona loads crates.
42. Madame Landier (a = Madame Landier's apartment; b = Mona & Madame Landier part; c = Madame Landier to Jean-Pierre). *modified direct address*
VIII. 43. MUSIC: Mona in woods; rape.
44. Goatherd. *direct address*

IX. 45. MUSIC: Frozen gate; Mona on platform, looking at cards.
    46. Postcards.
    47. Assoun (a = Mona arrives; b = patron; c = Assoun's quarters; d = vineyard; e = inside; f = vineyard; g = dinner; h = patron and wife at TV; i = laundry; j = inside, stay together; k = vineyards; l = Moroccans return; Mona and Assoun leave, white sacks).
    48. Patron. *direct address* (wife had *modified direct address* in segment, 47h.)
    49. Mona, nighttime; tears in eyes.
    50. Blood bank hippie (to attendant). *modified direct address*
X. 51. MUSIC: Mona fills water bottle, leaves man. Old woman.
    52. Yolande. *direct address* (a = "I'll never forget"; b = Mona at night; c = Yolande and Paulo leaving club; d = Mona and Yolande in kitchen).
    53. Mona and Tante Lydie (a = they share cognac; b = Yolande furious; c = Jean-Pierre and Eliane arrive).
    54. Train station; Mona wakes, tries to sell spoons.
    55. Mona, hippies in abandoned house.
    56. Yolande and Jean-Pierre at station; Yolande. *direct address*
    57. Train station; Mona creates a disturbance. Jean-Pierre (on telephone). *indirect address*
XI. 58. MUSIC: Mona and others kick doors.
    59. David enters hippie house; fire, Mona flees.
    60. Pimp (to man in photo booth). *modified direct address*
    61. Mona in plastic hut (a = huddles in blanket; b = night, dog barks).
    62. Assoun. *direct address* (silence)
    63. Tree people (a = Mona wants bread; b = tree people, terror, picks up blanket).
XII. 64. MUSIC: Mona drags herself on, with blanket.
    65. Mona trips, falls, turns over, and crying, assumes pose with hand.
    66. Credits appear over black; pocket trumpet on sound.

The preceding description of *Vagabond's* "episodes" and the complexity of their interaction suggests two primary features which, at the level of narration, characterize the Varda text: the self-conscious manipulation of narrative strategies and the deconstructive use of modes of address. Since her earliest film, Varda has been interested in the particular ways that the cinema could encourage its viewers to investigate their own position in the meaning process through, among other things, its constant permutations of time and space relations. In discussing the way that Faulkner's *Wild Palms* influenced her structural conception of *La Pointe-Courte,* she notes that it was the juxtaposition of parallel stories that held her interest. As she read the novel, she says, "I was trying to notice the effect of that narration on me, [and I learned that] to read it the way it is [two series back and forth] includes disturbance, it includes being frustrated from the narration."[11] *Vagabond* takes up this principle of disruption and interconnection by having certain of its sequences end abruptly, only to be taken up later (Yolande, Madame Landier, the goatherd, Assoun), having other sequences intrude into the texture, almost out of nowhere (the prostitute, the blood bank, the house-construction site, the job with crates, the rape), while still others maintain a kind of narrative integrity that affords a kind of unity within the fragmentary text (David, the train station). Nevertheless, there is a distinct organization into "chapters" (as in *Cleo From 5 to 7*), as we trace the stages of Mona's odyssey, unravel the "truth" of those last weeks of her life. The chapter organization which structures the film in terms of "units of episodic *demonstration*" is typical of Varda; in addition to *Cleo, Le Bonheur, Lions Love,* and *One Sings, the Other Doesn't* all have structures that incorporate strategic distancing into their narrative forms. Yet Mona's progress is the inverse of Cleo's, whose trajectory through Paris leads to self-knowledge and acceptance of others. Mona, in fact, moves farther and farther away from self-discovery as she travels throughout the Midi, and farther away from those social connections that sustain life. However, it is precisely the narrative process of the film—its division into significant episodes—that produces knowledge for *us:* as Mona understands less about her life, we as viewers learn more about ourselves and others.

It is also from the standpoint of narration that, with this film, Varda proves herself to be a true contemporary exemplar of both the New Wave and Left Bank filmmaking of her formative years. In a structure that might be called "Jean-Luc Godard meets Alain Resnais," *Vagabond* connects the political and discursive strategies of a film like *Vivre sa vie* or *The Married Woman* (in which, significantly, Macha Méril starred) with the temporal dislocations and concerns of *Last Year at Marienbad.* With Godard it shares the episodic narration that fragments linear causality into a series of "situations"—each with a demonstrable social lesson, and each with an invitation to the spectator's critical judgment. It also shares his interest in the blending of different discourses and mixed modes into a film-collage that interrogates its own methods. *Vagabond*'s personal testimonials in direct address (modified or not) evoke the frontal pronouncements of *The Married Woman* (and numerous other Godard films), while Madame Landier's "discourse on the plane trees" is wonderfully reminiscent of a similar research (into prostitution) in *Vivre sa vie*. And, no stranger to cinematic rule violation (having excelled with brilliant editing tricks in *Le Bonheur*), Varda has provided in *Vagabond* a virtual handbook of such instances (violations of the 180 degree rule, the axis match, movement and direction matches, and of course, the jump-cut) worthy of *Breathless* itself. Likewise, *Vagabond* shares with Resnais as complicated a temporal construction as can be achieved in film, weaving threads of narration into sequences that disappear and return with a compelling fluidity, while structures of memory (such as the flashback, for example) are rendered with the reality of present perception. Time is expanded in *Vagabond* through the delayed testimonies of characters who have perhaps been forgotten; it is condensed through unexpected ellipses that compress events into nothingness. Along with this goes the circularity of the film itself, ending where it had begun, bringing us back to the image which has haunted us (*Marienbad* comes to mind) from the start. And all the while, the continuity of narration—Mona's story, as she travels throughout the region with no visible purpose in mind—provides the connection for a whole range of "moments." Resnais's interest in subjective perception is here, too, for each account of Mona is an account of the self as well. Other elements are reminiscent of Resnais: The interest in Surrealism (the wine-dregs inserts, curious "clues" at the film's beginning, evoking Varda's *Les Créatures* as well as Resnais's *Muriel*, both paradigmatic Left Bank films); the intricate metaphoric structure which creates a signifying network of recurring motifs (all the references to trees, for example, from plane trees to tree people), and the structure of implausibilities which finally, logically, cohere (Tante Lydie's relation to Yolande, Jean-Pierre, and to Mona herself). To say that *Vagabond* shares its strategies of distancing with Godard and its narrative complexity with Resnais is to attest to the exemplary status of all three directors who, each in their particular way, have pushed the limits of cinematic expression in their simultaneous concern with discursive and visual forms.

There is another way that *Vagabond* is exemplary as well. As we have seen, Varda uses interruption as a structural device, creating moments of narrative suspension that generate our own reflection on the events. But this isolation of episodes into discrete units is matched by a rigorous complexity within these units; the film virtually reads like a lexicon of narrative forms. Because of this, just beneath the aleatory surface that tracks Mona's random encounters, a variety of composition reveals a systematic reflection on modes of cinematic narrativity. The narrative texture of the film can be divided between primary and secondary episodes and these reflect varying degrees of complexity in their structure. Christian Metz's Large Syntagmatic Category[12] can provide a way of distinguishing one type of sequence from another, for in it he delineates eight types of sequencing, eight modes of organization of spatial and temporal relationships between shots. He first divides the sequences between types of autonomous segment: those made up of only one shot and those that combine a number of shots. As already noted, the twelve moments of musical interlude which punctuate *Vagabond* are all "autonomous segments," single-shot-sequences that create periods of reflection and analysis for the viewers as we travel with Mona throughout the land, a terrain which is at once geographic, social, and psychic as well. But there are other "autonomous segments" in the film, and these have a variety of functions. For example, Yolande serves Paulo breakfast in bed in a single shot, thereby allowing Varda to render a Brechtian "demonstration" of the impossible union of crassness and sentiment in their relationship. Another single-shot-sequence depicts Mona, hitch-hiking in the freezing wind, seen from the invisible driver's perspective, with an eerie, windswept silence on the soundtrack—another "demonstration," this time of Mona's isolated life. And, likewise, the numerous testimonies by witnesses appear in this form of framed, outlined, and foregrounded single-shot autonomy.

Metz next divides the sequences made up of more than one shot into chronological (that is, narrative, and related through causality) and nonchronological (that is, descriptive, and related conceptually) modes of organization. *Vagabond* contains its share of nonnarrative syntagmas as well, a fact that contributes to its fragmentary, heterogeneous construction and its pervasive aura of chance. Three types of syntagma, all of which are represented in the film, fall under this rubric: the descriptive (shots suggest spatial coexistence without temporality, for example, to situate the action); the bracket (in the absence of both spatial continuity and chronology, shots are linked by a thematic relation); and the parallel (two motifs alternate without clear spatial or temporal relationship, such as the depiction of rich and poor, city and country). Moments of description occur, for example, when Mona wakes up in the snow, when she pitches her tent in a new place, or when she walks at night, tears in her eyes and the forbidding darkness mirrored on her face. The bracket syntagma occurs as well, and Varda makes use of all its suggestive possibilities in this meditative film: Mona's "life on the road" is presented numerous times in this way, either when she asks for matches, hitch-hikes, munches food left by a church or eats sardines, or huddles, starved and freezing, in a little plastic shack. It is with the parallel syntagma that *Vagabond*'s sequence structure moves over to what I consider Mona's primary encounters—and thus complicates any easy distinction between narrative and nonnarrative forms (as in, for example, the assignation of greater importance to the segments constituted by chronology). For Mona's relationship with Assoun, certainly primary in terms of its significance, is rendered structurally in a parallel mode: The alternation of inside and outdoors presents the theme of "love and work." It is this alternation, in fact, which reveals the basic conflict of their relationship—Assoun works, Mona loafs; Assoun cooks, Mona eats. But even this interpretation is complicated by the fact that, when she must leave, it is Mona who experiences rejection and a sense of loss. Could she have been David's "homebody" with Assoun?

It is, however, true that Mona's primary encounters, for the most part, are rendered in sequences that conform to the chronological, narrative, mode. But even here, under the rubric of chronology, are some random (that is, less central to the "main fiction") sequences as well. For example, the "scene" (Metz's sixth syntagmatic form), in which chronology and narrative consecution are rendered without ellipses in space or time, is present when Mona is in the blood bank, or at the house-building site, or even in some instances when she is camping out. Other encounters that might be deemed ancillary to the main fiction (as it is retroactively conceived by the film's end) also fall into various modes of narrative sequencing shared by the primary characters. Thus the garage mechanic and the train station hippies are both presented in a form that Metz designates as the "ordinary sequence" (there are elements of discontinuity in the consecutive ordering of the shots; Metz calls this the "most cinematic"), while what is certainly a central section of the film—Madame Landier's—conforms to this structure too. As Madame Landier and Mona ride through the countryside, several sequences (all represented in this way) occur that define their growing relationship and the curious attraction-repulsion that characterizes it. Each of these ordinary sequences demonstrates the difference of their two lives, yet the affective similarity of these two women, implicit in their exchanges, will, by the film's end, reinforce an emerging theme: the impossibility of evasive freedom and the necessity of human connection.

Mona's stay with the goatherds is rendered in another syntagmatic form, the "episodic sequence." This type of organization presents a kind of symbolic summary, individual stages in an implied chronological development that suggests a compression of time. In no fewer than nine "mini-episodes," the progress and deterioration of this relation between two kinds of drop-out is depicted, as Mona and the goatherd first exchange philosophies, attempt to put these into action, grow irritated with each other's views and lives, and defiantly conflict. And finally, Mona's relationship with the hippie David (he calls himself a "wandering Jew") is represented by an eighth syntagmatic type, the "alternate syntagma." Along with the ordinary sequence, it can be considered the most fundamentally cinematic as well (Metz categorizes these two together as "sequential narrative syntagmas"), for in its narrative cross-cutting and implied simultaneity it refers back to the cinema's discursive origins. As noted, in the midst of David and Mona's "alternate paradise" a robbery takes place; this is rendered in the classic chase-scene exchange of shots, with the squatter couple in the chateau growing suspicious as noises of the heist are heard. And this itself is embedded in another alternating structure, as Yolande narrates her tale of the idyllic lovers, to Paulo and to us, while we catch glimpses of their "romance"—an interlude in which Mona exchanges names, dope, language, love, music and food with a young man.

It is thus by means of a closer look at the narrative organization of the sequences that we can determine a kind of affective priority in this random, aimless life. What emerges from the foregoing analysis is a parallelism in two of Mona's encounters, giving them a centrality that distinguishes them from other significant interactions. Thus in the two "cinematic" syntagmas, the episode with David and with Madame Landier, Mona is given the possibility of a rapport. To the extent that any of her encounters are sympathetic, these two are; whatever capacity for relating (that exists) in Mona is demonstrated here. Although she rejects the first relationship, and the second rejects her, each of these instances provides her with a possibility of sharing. (The two segments are not only similar in their syntagmatic structure, but also in the content of their exchanges as well, for those things that Mona shares with David are also present, primarily, in her stay with Madame Landier.) One of the conclusions to be drawn from these structurally similar encounters, then, is the possibility they represent. Although neither the isolated, drop-out Eden, nor the suggestion of a social contribution (via work) functions for the aimless drifter, it is *our* consideration, as viewers, on the consequences of these events that yields the social meaning: There is an undeniable social network of human culture in which we must exist.

But even the "narrative" sequences are complicated by the delayed testimonies (the goatherd's, Assoun's), the deferred continuation of events (Madame Landier's episode), and the interweaving of seemingly arbitrary episodes whose connection is only determined later (Yolande's, David's, and Jean-Pierre's). Furthermore, the testimonies of all of these primary figures, occurring as they do in a variety of modes of address (which thereby connect them with the other, secondary, testimonies) complicates the discursive structure even more. And it is with modes of address that *Vagabond* enacts its second challenge to traditional narrative forms.

Varda uses the full range of modes of address for her "witnesses," but refuses to pattern them in any simplistic way. In fact, the attempt to discern a consistent pattern that structures and organizes these disparate views of Mona is frustrated from the start: There is no simple equivalence between a character's importance and the manner in which he or she addresses the viewer. This is another important way that Varda incorporates randomness into the discursive structure, maintaining the atmosphere of chance experience that framed her intention from the start. "[My organization of Mona's encounters] came little by little, here and there as I travelled. I roamed around the region, not knowing where to go next. . . . I decided that the people she'd met would be the ones who spoke of her. She'd be practically silent herself. And that what we learned about her would come from those who'd seen her go by, from what little they might have shared with her, each one. The result would be this 'play of mirrors,' human mirrors which reflected her own image back to her as much as they constituted a little world."[13]

Thus *Vagabond*'s distinction of character—through designations of modes of address—is as complicated as its segmentation into plot—through designations of narrative form—for the division between those who figure in the primary fiction (Yolande, Jean-Pierre, Tante Lydie, Madame Landier, for example), those who interact with Mona in other contexts (the goatherd, Assoun), and still others who simply encounter her along the way (the mechanic, a woman, the construction worker), does not correspond in any way to their significance for Mona nor to the importance of their remarks. Some characters are more extensively enmeshed with Mona, others simply observe. And it is through a complex orchestration of these voices and different types of address—a play of intersections between "characters," "witnesses," and some combination of the two—that we come to have our own impression of this wanderer. As each observer wonders about this woman that all have seen, we wonder along with them; their questioning process is our own as well.

As I noted, the eighteen testimonies in the film (counting those that recur, such as Yolande's, Madame Landier's, and Jean-Pierre's as each constituting one apiece) can be subdivided into modes: indirect address, direct address, and modified direct address. Indirect address is the clearest to discern, and the mode most incorporated into the diegetic world, for it involves two characters within the fictional framework of the film, speaking to each other as the viewer "overhears." Thus the spectator is not overtly solicited, participating instead as the true (auditory) voyeur of classical cinema. The activity of listening is not foregrounded in any way, while, absorbed as they are in the fiction, these observations convey a feeling of naturalness, instead. The motorcycle-types, the truck driver and his pal, Jean-Pierre to Eliane (and later on the telephone)—all are clearly designated as indirect address. Madame Landier, whose first discussion of her encounter with the vagabond takes place during a telephone conversation in the bath, represents a special case, for both of her testimonies can be defined as representing all three modes. They thus signify a condensation of forms of address and attain a kind of priority of enunciation matched only by Yolande. Yet where Yolande's address is always direct, and only emphatic because it occurs four times, Madame Landier's is significant because of the complexity it represents.

It is above all frontality that defines direct address, and this is true whether it is modified or not. When a character speaks in the mode of direct address, the viewer is emphatically evoked; the image appears flat, distanced, and defined—a type of shot that constitutes a true Brechtian device. As there is no interlocutor present, the interview technique of documentary comes to mind; this is another way of reinforcing the sense of "reality" that these testimonies suggest. Yet, paradoxically, at the same time, the very directness that Varda implies by her mode of filming—isolating these shots out of a homogenizing narrative context—emphasizes their use as a distancing strategy, a self-conscious technique to provoke viewer contemplation. Some of the characters who use this type of direct address for their accounts of Mona are significant to the fiction, others are random and uninvolved. Yolande, David, Assoun, and Madame Landier address the viewer directly; so do the mechanic, the construction worker, and the vineyard boss.

But it is those testimonies given in modified direct address that are the most prevalent in the film; they are also the most unique in their complex combination of documentary and fictional modes, and thereby constitute a characteristic element of Varda's *cinécriture*. On first viewing, these accounts seem firmly anchored in the mode of direct address; they are frontal, in close-up (some form of facial shot), and entities unto themselves. Yet each of these witnesses is speaking to someone on the screen; the interlocutor is present, but in a masked and hidden way. He or she is barely seen in the foreground (usually the right-hand corner), thus giving the impression that the discourse is directed at the viewer rather than at them. The effect is that, although these testimonies appear to be direct, they are absorbed in the fiction like any other indirect address. The resulting blurring of distinctions (between direct and indirect address, between documentary testimonial and fictional construct) gives the film a remembered surface impression of a play of countless random observations that continually engage viewer solicitation. It is only on closer examination that their complexity is revealed. The girl with the water pump (to her parents), the garage mechanic (to his wife), the vineyard boss's wife (to him), the blood bank hippie (to an attendant), the drifter (to a companion), and Madame Landier (to Jean-Pierre)—all are represented in instances of modified direct address.

As noted, there is no correspondence between a character's importance and the type of address used, nor consistency of character with a certain address mode. Thus, Madame Landier's first mention of Mona (her curiosity, her surprise) can be seen as modified direct address, although it is also both direct and indirect as well, whereas her later remarks to Jean-Pierre (her sense of guilt and her regret) can be read as indirect, although filmed in direct address's frontal way. Yolande's four testimonies are all direct, while the goatherd has no introduction at all, and his conclusions (to his wife, barely visible in the frame) are rendered in modified direct address. David and Assoun have no introductory speeches as well, yet their summarizing conclusions (Assoun's is silence) are both conveyed in direct address. But even then we cannot assert with any certainty that direct address is reserved for primary characters, for the construction worker and the vineyard boss are also included here. And Tante Lydie, who might have the most significant function in the film, providing Mona with the only pure moment of gaiety and abandon—and connection—she ever feels, has no testimony at all.

The viewer experiences the blending of documentary (the sociological research) and fiction (the characters' interactions) by means of these complicated structures of narrative and address, but it is something conceived by Varda before the shooting even starts: "For me, to make a film I allow myself to be taken on an adventure by the process of documentary research, then I turn it into fiction by choosing. I don't use a casting director. It's a way of being involved with the film with no intermediaries."[14]

The effect of this—in both the conception and the finished film—is such that a redefinition of the parameters of cinematic meaning is continually engaged. The blending of modes and the style of their depiction make every testimony appear to have an equal status. Thus each time a character addresses us, we assume the randomness of the vision: A maid is like a garage mechanic, or a girl at a well. And yet, as the film proceeds, we come to understand this maid, this motorcycle-type, this agronomist, as having functions in a fiction that is only gradually traced out. Finally, all of the characters, even the random ones, become absorbed in the fiction of this rebellious girl. The resulting reflection on the status of reality produces this observation: Reality itself is a fictive construction. But this does not deny the social inscription of that fiction. Rather, the making of meaning and the activity of social exchange are both posed as discursive processes; in their interaction they produce "the signifying text of culture." In speaking of this compelling technique, Varda says "The audience is just continuing the list of witnesses who have seen Mona pass by,"[15] and in so stating she encapsulates the procedure of the film, the movement, in fact, that makes it such a stunning accomplishment of modernism. Finally, we become absorbed in the observational process ourselves, constructing our own fictions of Mona, as well as of the people she meets. In this way, the discursive threads of the text reach out and weave us in, embracing us as viewers while simultaneously keeping us away. The film gives us, its spectators, the same status as its fictive characters; it thereby produces a profound object lesson in the interconnection—the interdependence—of both cinematic and social reality, and an intriguing illustration of the continuity of psychic life.

This interrogation of the processes of cinematic meaning-production is, importantly, intimately linked to the strategies of a feminist counter-cinema; implicit in this activity is an investigation into modes of looking and of constructions of femininity as well. The second aspect of Varda's challenge to dominant cinema, as represented by this film, involves the reorientation of vision, a dispersion of the patriarchal gaze. Laura Mulvey's landmark article suggests some of the possible ways that the dominant look of masculinity in the cinema might be deconstructed: "It is [the] cinematic codes and their relationship to formative external structures that must be broken down before mainstream film and the pleasure it provides can be challenged. . . . [T]he voyeuristic-scopophilic look that is a crucial part of traditional filmic pleasure can itself be broken down."[16]

Vagabond accomplishes this in a variety of ways: Through its visually lush cinematography and its systematic use of color, it redefines visual pleasure; through its singular tracking-shots and surface aesthetic, it provides moments of textual distancing that foreground the viewing process; and through its dramatization of partial visions, it disperses the gendered gaze. Mulvey's dual project—the creation of a self-reflexive, materialist cinema ("to free the look of the camera") and of a self-conscious, critical spectator ("and the look of the audience")—is powerfully achieved in *Vagabond* not through the destruction of cinematic pleasure, but through a gorgeously exultant, alternative view.

In speaking of her own film work, Chantal Akerman acknowledges the sexual pleasure in viewing itself by suggesting the phrase "the ecstasy of seeing" (*la jouissance du voir*).[17] This is a kind of looking undefined by gender hierarchies and dissociated from the objectifying power of the masculine gaze. In *Vagabond,* the image itself is visually opulent, regardless of its content, due to the brilliance of Patrick Blossier's cinematography. The camera never ceases to render images of a fascinating and unexpected beauty, whether these are of a desolate landscape, a provincial building, a woman on a bus bench, or Mona herself. There is a sweep and a scope to these visions, something that defines them apart from sex, yet they never abandon the erotic component of vision. There is another aspect of the camera work as well: it foregrounds the scrutinizing eye. The penetrating gaze of the camera situates the film, from the start, in a register of vision, and at the same time, it suggests that this process is both psychic and social. The film is about a kind of surveillance—of the landscape, of the people, of Mona—but it does not convey the omnipotence of the patriarchal view. Rather, it offers a kind of visual caress that surrounds each of its objects and creates an experience of sensual vision for all of those who share its view. In this it reinforces process over content, and foregrounds cinematic viewing as libidinal play.

Related to this is the film's use of color, an evolving palette that defines Mona's path. The strident hues of brilliant blue and gold match her earliest journeys and her optimistic stride. The more subdued tones, washed with a harsh winter light, characterize the next stage of her wandering, but these are offset by the warmth of interior colors that contrast the outdoors (Mona and David's idyll, the home of Tante Lydie, the bright red surrounding Eliane). Madame Landier is associated with warm browns and shades of rust, colors that link her to the plane trees that absorb her life. Darkness and forbidding tones of blue and black characterize the last parts of the film, the train station and the hippie "house" murky in their confused shades. And finally, as Mona stumbles to her end, there is a curious kind of radiance in the purples and blues that surround her. This, too, is a way that the cinematography renders unconventional beauty in unexpected ways, and restores to the look of the camera that materiality which classical cinema denies it.

Another way that *Vagabond* forestalls traditional structures of voyeurism is by means of its "punctuating shots"—those long, fluid single-shot-sequences that provide periods of contemplation and reflection for the viewer. But these are not the "moments of erotic contemplation"[18] to which Mulvey refers in speaking of the classical cinema: Here the gaze on the woman as erotic object is redefined. There are, instead, moments of critical distancing, textual spaces that provoke the viewer's analytic reflection. As noted before, the twelve musical interludes are rendered by a moving camera that follows Mona and comes to rest on a random object in the landscape—a tractor, a tree, a frozen grate. Varda has called the film "a long tracking shot which is cut into portions where the 'adventures' are inserted,"[19] noting that each of these shots takes up where the last one left off. She is emphatic about the distancing effect of these shots, their disruption of the conventional fiction in the name of a critical view: "As a filmmaker, I wanted to say, let's go with her for a while, without pretending to be totally with her. So whenever Mona is wandering, I use a tracking shot which begins without her—she comes in and then disappears, and the shot goes on, independent of Mona. By staying parallel to her with the camera, you never really reach her. The audience may not be actually aware of it, but it affects them anyway. The important thing was not to confuse the audience with phony emotions—to leave them space and time to feel something on their own."[20]

Thus calling attention to the "aesthetic of surfaces" that the film defines, Varda posits a camera that subverts subjectivity and undermines the psychologizing of the traditional film. There is a refusal to explore the interiority of the character in favor of a look that documents behaviors and evaluates the externals of life. The gaze at Mona is primarily social; the question she represents is the one posed by Varda and suggested by us all: What are the cultural conditions of existence and how do they define the feminine?

The third aspect of *Vagabond*'s deconstruction of traditional cinematic viewing involves its dispersion of vision into a series of partial views. In giving each of the witnesses the power to authorize a look, the film fractures enunciation into numerous component parts. In this the spectator's position is linked to neither male nor female specifically; the composite portrait of Mona traverses gender lines. Certainly some of the witnesses objectify her sexually, but Varda makes this view dialectical by giving us a prismatic definition of Mona, a structure that changes with each encounter that she has. Renouncing the absolutism of an authoritative view, Varda proposes an identification with looking itself, a viewing process that allows a perpetual variability of spectatorial positions and favors indeterminacy over the rigidity of fixed meanings. Taken up in this interplay of moments—demonstrations of social and sexual facts—the spectator participates in the structure of discourse instead of in the seduction of vicarious views.

Throughout this chapter I have tried to maintain that *Vagabond* cannot be understood apart from the concept of sexual difference, for the portrait of Mona is the portrait of femininity itself. The film's complex processes of narration and address, its reorganization of the cinematic gaze, are only significant insofar as they engage with the project of representing the feminine. Every account in this dramatization of vision(s) underscores Mona's sex in some important way: There are those who see her as easy prey; there are those who envy her freedom; there are those who are repelled by her uncommonness (commonness?); and those who are curiously attracted. As Varda says, "The film is really about a woman who has given up all the rules, including the one that says that everyone—especially women—should be pleasant, should try to please. . . . In that minimal situation where you have no home, no bread, where you have to fight just to survive— What is the energy like of simply being alive? That's what I wanted to express. And I thought that that type of character would be much more interesting than a victim. Even though she dies in a ditch, she's a survivor."[21]

Varda has spoken, as well, of her interest in "feminine energy," acknowledging that her attempt to show this over feminist issues themselves in *One Sings, the Other Doesn't* was perhaps a bit cinematically unadventurous. With *Vagabond*, she retains this interest in a feminine force—a resisting force—but does so by refusing to locate it within a single character. Instead, the questioning energy, the spirit of contradiction—associated with femininity from the start and imbued with a long cultural history—becomes Varda's force (and ours) as it pervades the film. It is a vital force of feminism, one not confined to characters.

Mona's situation is expressed in terms of how diverse people see her; there is no assertion of an essential truth. Varda wished to invoke

Vagabond (Summary)

Photofest

Photofest

Ciné-Tamaris

Ciné-Tamaris

Ciné-Tamaris

Photofest

Ciné-Tamaris

Ciné-Tamaris

Photofest

Ciné-Tamaris

Photofest

Vagabond (Agnès Varda, 1985)   *Coeur fidèle* (Jean Epstein, 1923)

Ciné-Tamaris

Museum of Modern Art

Meshes of the Afternoon
(Maya Deren, 1943)

Alphaville (Jean-Luc Godard, 1965)

Museum of Modern Art

Photofest

this process by creating an open-ended work: "I wanted to make a moving [affecting] film which would also be a meditation on several ideas, one of which is freedom, and also a film which would be a puzzle with some of the pieces missing."[22] For Mulvey, classical cinema is structured on masculine desire; its looks coincide with the male protagonist's gaze. In *Vagabond*, it is the "desire to know" (rather than "to possess the woman") that structures the vision, allowing the viewer to identify with the process itself. The spectator's power of vision is not over the female character, a woman constructed as the object of desire, but over all of the images and their interrelation; it is a power of questioning rather than one of possession. In this we see the Oedipal narrative destabilized in favor of a multitude of views, partial impressions offered by each of the narrative "episodes" and by each of the testimonies as well. It is a redefinition of Oedipus' riddle, for in giving her viewers a puzzle to grapple with—instead of the vicarious experience of Oedipus himself—Varda gives us the signifying process, a process which embraces transformation and change.

In *Vagabond*, the body of the woman continues to be a source of viewing pleasure, but it is the engagement with meaning—her meaning—that makes it so. Here Mulvey's look of "passionate detachment" finds its example, for we are both intrigued by Mona yet distanced, analytic. The contemplative gaze of meaning (what it means to be a woman, how being female defines Mona's situation) redefines our fascination—redefines it as a process which does not objectify the woman in the traditional way; in fact, it militates against this by offering a decidedly unglamorous heroine. This is a kind of viewing born of compassion and interest. An example from the film will bear this out. In an extraordinarily beautiful single-shot-sequence—reminiscent of an incredible shot in Jean Epstein's *Coeur fidèle* (Gina Manès, by lace curtains on the bistro window, looking out dreamily over the water's surface), or Maya Deren's famous image in *Meshes of the Afternoon* (Maya looking out of a window, as well, branches reflected behind her hair), or Godard's paradigmatic shot in *Alphaville* (Anna Karina, in lace collar, looking out of a window, again, Eluard's *Capitale de la douleur* clutched against her body)—Mona looks out of a window of the goatherd's trailer. The image is captivating: a shot of the trailer window taken from the outside, lace curtains and branches tracing a reflection across Mona's face as she looks out. But since Varda's project is to avoid sentimentality—to redefine the beautiful as something which does not deny, but rather incorporates, elements suppressed in traditional conceptions of the aesthetic object—Mona opens this window and spits outside. This does not destroy the beauty of this image, but, rather, foregrounds exactly what goes into composing it. As a single-shot-sequence, this image invites our reflection. It is odd to see signs of domesticity (the curtains) on this trailer (signifier of "wandering"), to see something delicate amid the hardy filth of the goat farm as well. It can also be an indication of Mona's inability to understand what it takes to settle—she has been so uncomprehending when the goatherd speaks of a "middle road between freedom and loneliness." At any rate, this image is there precisely to provoke—in the viewer—some form of critical reflection about the character, about the images that give us this character, and about how these, in combination, define the feminine itself. It is certainly a beautiful image of a woman, but one that in no way objectifies her as a spectacle. Mulvey's (awkward but descriptive) "to-be-looked-at-ness" is present, but the reason for the looking is something else again.

In a citation quoted in chapter 8, Varda refers to this questioning process which is the film: "More than just Mona herself who always eludes us, who is too reserved, too closed, the film addresses 'the Mona effect' on those she came in contact with and inevitably affected. She is a catalyst, someone who forces others to react and adjust themselves in relation to her."[23] As a director, Varda is interested in questions, not answers. For feminists concerned with meanings and with films, this implies grasping the *political* power of those questions. It means seeing those questions not as limitations, which is how traditional masculine hierarchies of value understand them—conceiving of questions as "not having the answer"—but as options that allow the productive engagement in the act of questioning itself. In *Vagabond*, Varda's *Ulysses*, the "impossible portrait" reverberates with possibilities.

NOTES

1. Agnès Varda, in Barbara Quart, "Agnès Varda: A Conversation with Barbara Quart," *Film Quarterly* 40:2 (Winter 1986–87): 6.

2. Laura Mulvey, "Visual Pleasure and Narrative Cinema," *Screen* 16:3 (Autumn 1975): 18. (I have deleted Mulvey's parenthetical reference to "radical filmmakers" from this citation.)

3. *Vagabond* received the First Prize (Lion d'Or) at the Venice Film Festival and the prize given for Best Picture by the French Critics Union; Sandrine Bonnaire won the Best Actress Award (the French César) for her role as Mona. The film is distributed in the United States by International Film Exchange, Ltd., 201 West 52d St., New York, NY 10019. It is also available on videocassette.

4. Agnès Varda, "Publicité" prepared by Varda for her own French production company, Ciné-Tamaris, 1985.

5. Varda, "A Conversation," *Film Quarterly*, p. 4.

6. Ibid.

7. Ibid., p. 5.

8. Joanna Bruzdowicz was born in Warsaw in 1943 and began composing music at the age of twelve. A student of Nadia Boulanger, Olivier Messiaen, and P. Schaeffer, she has composed three operas and her works have been performed throughout the world. The quartet "La Vita" was composed for the String Quartet of Warsaw; Varda asked her to write variations on it for *Vagabond*. This information is in the Ciné-Tamaris "Publicité."

9. Varda, "Publicité."

10. Agnès Varda, "Un jour sous le ciel," *Les Cahiers du cinéma*, no. 378 (December 1985): 14.

11. Varda, "A Conversation," *Film Quarterly*, p. 7.

12. Christian Metz, *Film Language: A Semiotics of the Cinema*, trans. Michael Taylor (New York: Oxford University Press, 1974). See especially chapter 5, "Problems of Denotation in the Fiction Film," and chapter 6, "Outline of the Autonomous Segments of Jacques Rozier's film *Adieu Philippine*." Metz shows how the classic New Wave film *Adieu Philippine* possesses a rigorous and complicated narrative structure beneath the casual vitality of its random surface. My discussion of *Vagabond* in terms of the Large Syntagmatic Category has a similar intent.

13. Agnès Varda, "Mona, nomade," *Cinéma 85*, no. 322 (December 4–10, 1985): 2. This appears in a section entitled, "Varda, nomad herself."

14. Agnès Varda, in John Harkness, "Agnès Varda: Improvised Inspiration," *Now*, June 19–25, 1986.

15. Agnès Varda, in Naomi Wise, "Surface Tensions: Agnès Varda," *Berkeley Monthly* (June 1986): 16.

16. Mulvey, "Visual Pleasure," p. 17.

17. Chantal Akerman, "Interview with *Camera Obscura*," *Camera Obscura*, no. 2 (Fall 1977): 121.

18. Mulvey, "Visual Pleasure," p. 11.

19. Agnès Varda, "Agnès Varda de 5 à 7," *Cinématographe*, no. 114 (December 1985): 19.

20. Agnès Varda, in Stephen Harvey, "Agnès Varda in Her Own Good Time," *The Village Voice*, May 20, 1986, p. 64.

21. Agnès Varda, in Mary Beth Crain, "The Mother of the New Wave," *L.A. Weekly*, August 1–7, 1986, p. 33.

22. Varda, "Publicité."

23. Agnès Varda, "Press Book" for *Vagabond* (New York: International Film Exchange, 1985), p. 8,

TWELVE

Conclusion

Once the movie-crew had done its job, the result up there on the
screen was nothing less than magic: the sheer essence of beguiling
femininity. The mysterious process of moviemaking has captivated
[us] again and again. [We have] been specially charmed by the
luminescent power of Hollywood's leading ladies [who have]
insinuated themselves into the heart of America, heroines in a never-
ending let's-pretend love affair so compelling it's really not make-
believe at all.

—*Life* Magazine, Fall 1986

FROM ITS INCEPTION right through to its contemporary popular reception, the cinema has been organized in terms of a very specific representation of femininity. Yet equally pervasive, historically, has been
the attempt to challenge the contradictions posed for women by this
fundamental equation of the woman's body with the cinema-machine.
The highly conventional inscription of sexual difference in cinematic
discursive forms has implied, from the start, precise definitions and
channels for the expression of female desire. To assert this is to suggest
that any formulation of a feminist alternative must be conceived not
in terms of individuals with conscious purpose or intent, but in terms
of enunciative theories of the circulation of desire.

   This study has focused on the work of three major French women
directors whose contribution to the development of a feminist counter-
cinema is highly significant both historically (in terms of the cinema's
evolution as a form of discourse) and ideologically (in terms of the

feminist cinema's elaboration of a specific set of strategies). Traditional cinematic practice constitutes the female image as the linchpin of visual pleasure, affirming masculine dominance in its articulation of relations between author, spectator, and text. However, when the question of *female* subjectivity emerges, the unconscious processes of desire mobilized in the film-viewing situation must be re-thought. The introduction to this book suggested three ways of posing the question of feminist cinema: How can we conceptualize a "woman's desire" as it is activated in both the film-making and the film-viewing processes? How can we define the "desiring look" when the position of looking is feminine? And what are the parameters of a "female discourse" as it traverses a particular text? The intersection of all three of these areas of inquiry produces the triple articulation—viewer, author, and text—which defines the cinema while, at the same time, it inflects this constellation with the founding interrogative of sexual difference.

Another way of stating these concerns is the tripartite construction used as the working title of this book: "Women, Representation, and Cinematic Discourse." The present study has constructed a notion of feminine authorship based on an exploration and expansion of each of the terms, deriving a composite idea of authorial stance that understands each element in the complexity of its interrelation with the others. Authorship is therefore conceived as part historical phenomenon (the cultural context of social subjects, actual women in history), part desiring position (the sexually constituted processes of representation of—and by—gendered subjects, circuits of desire in the production of femininity), and part textual moment (the formal and stylistic procedures of individual texts, discursive strategies of the films themselves). And this is precisely the format of the book. In discussing the biographies of Germaine Dulac, Marie Epstein, and Agnès Varda, I have emphasized the particular importance that being a woman has had in each filmmaker's work. In tracing the historical and aesthetic context of each, I have analyzed the general national, cultural, and cinematic climate; the context chapters thus situate the films in terms of structures of representation, necessarily calling into play unconscious forces of signification. And in analyzing the specific films of all three, I have sketched the varied parameters of textual resistance to the dominant cinematic model.

In fact, this last area of emphasis brings me back to the triple question of feminist cinema, for as I stated in the introduction to this book, each woman filmmaker's work represents, in a way, an answer to one part of the question. Dulac's cinematic explorations of female subjectivity were certainly among the first attempts to *represent feminine desire,* for she turned the prevailing efforts to depict the operations of the psyche into a specific articulation of a feminine point of view. Inverting the (by then, in fact) dominant construction of the woman as object of desire into an inquiry into the feminine as the site of subjectivity, Dulac conceived of her films as illustrations of the language of the unconscious, inviting each spectator's liberated participation in the signifying process itself. Epstein, perhaps less explicit in her intent, produced works of profound consequence for theories of the apparatus, for her films can be seen as attempts to *redefine the position of cinematic looking,* to reconstitute the structures of enunciation and the gaze. Thus in her films the formative matrixes of fantasy and maternal desire are recast according to a logic which is undeniably female, the dual source of vision and desire conceived as feminine in the enunciative operations of the text. And Varda's films have continually represented efforts to *elaborate a feminine discourse* through modernist techniques of narrative and address. In her attempt to subvert the dominant masculine position—as viewer of the woman-spectacle and as controller of the narrative events—Varda has literally invented deconstructive textual strategies that rework processes of vision and narration, and in so doing she has conceived a new form of "feminine" text.

The task of defining a "female voice" in cinema has engendered the central paradox of this book, its structuring matrix, for in attempting to distinguish a viable practice of "feminist filmmaking" from those films which are simply "made by women," I have endeavored to trace the options for a textual mode of alternative cinema. The strategies suggested by the work of such feminist critics as Mary Ann Doane (a cinema that poses the complex relations between the female body and psychic/signifying processes), Teresa DeLauretis (the reorganization of cinema's structures of vision in order to define a new feminist social subject), and Laura Mulvey (a filmmaking that breaks with dominant discursive modes, its voyeuristic and fetishistic forms) are but three of the ways in which we might conceptualize "other voices," other desires which articulate the cinematic text. And these are intimately connected with—though not reducible to—the fact that there is a woman behind the camera. It is thus by this asymmetrical relation, one that implies the absolute impossibility of a simple equation between feminist filmmaking and women's cinema, that a productive definition of feminine alternatives can come about.

Such a complicated notion as "feminist" authorship can only be understood by leaving easy assumptions aside, assumptions such as intentionality, experience, and essential difference. Likewise, this notion involves rejecting the comforting binarism that contrasts the logic and order of "masculine" thought with a contradictory "feminine" otherness. What constitutes "the feminine" in any authorial voice must be grasped in terms of a complex and theoretical understanding of the production of both "femininity" and its representations. A feminist cinema implies, therefore, that there are other ways of figuring the feminine than those dictated by masculine hierarchies. At the same time, it suggests an array of possibilities for alternative aesthetics, in a move which pluralizes the simple oppositional critique of dominant cinema as a monolithic patriarchal institution. The combined preoccupations of feminist film theory—issues of sexual difference, desire, and language—suggest a way of theorizing authorship along these lines.

The central and articulating concept of enunciation provides the most productive model for theorizing feminist cinema. Founded, as it is, on the unconscious logic of signification, enunciation frames all discourse on film, from the authorial instance, through textuality, to spectatorship. And it is here that my own suggestions for feminine textuality—for positing woman as the subject of cinematic desire—can be found. The logic of enunciation—a logic that describes how the filmic vision is both organized for, and activated by, the spectator—traverses all three categories of author, viewer, and text, combining production and reception in a perpetual play of psychic and social forces. Enunciation thus offers a means of theorizing feminine subjectivity in the cinema by allowing each area its specificity, reconsidering filmmaking, film-viewing, and the text itself from the standpoint of female desire. As a mode of analysis for the systematic organization of patterns of looking, enunciation enables us to understand how a woman filmmaker negotiates the disparate visions of the text. As a means of interpreting the film-viewing process, enunciation allows us to conceptualize the possibilities for feminine spectatorship. And as a method of designating textual instances, enunciation makes visible the ways in which female desire can be said to be articulated and addressed within a particular film. And yet, this separation into areas of emphasis by no means implies the autonomy of the categories within the concept itself. It is only because of the fundamental interdependence of each of these parts that the theory of enunciation can provide such insight into the signifying operations of the cinema and, by extension, into the possibilities for representing feminine desire.

Throughout my discussions of these three French filmmakers and their work, then, I have detailed an argument that shifts its terrain from biography, through history, to textual analysis while all the while mapping the parameters of a female cinematic voice in terms of the enunciative theory just described. If the notion of a feminist counter-practice implies the articulation of another voice, it conceives of this voice as a restructuring of vision and the elaboration of alternative discursive forms. To desire differently in the cinema means speaking—and seeing—from another place. By engaging enunciation in a variety of ways, the films of Germaine Dulac, Marie Epstein, and Agnès Varda do exactly that.

Bibliography

Abel, Richard. "The Contribution of the French Literary Avant-Garde to Film
   Theory and Criticism (1907–1924)." *Cinema Journal* 14:3 (Spring 1975):
   18–40.
———. *French Cinema: The First Wave, 1915–1929*. Princeton: Princeton Uni-
   versity Press, 1984.
———. "Louis Delluc: The Critic as Cineaste." *Quarterly Review of Film Studies*
   1:2 (May 1976): 205–43.
———. "On the Threshold of French Film Theory and Criticism, 1915–1919."
   Cinema Journal 25:1 (Fall 1985): 12–33.
Adams, Parveen. "Representation and Sexuality." *m/f*, no. 1 (1978): 65–82.
Akerman, Chantal. "Interview with *Camera Obscura*." *Camera Obscura*, no. 2
   (Fall 1977): 118–21.
Andrew, Dudley. *André Bazin*. New York: Oxford University Press, 1978.
———. "Poetic Realism." In *Rediscovering French Film*, edited by Mary Lea
   Bandy, pp. 115–19. New York: Museum of Modern Art, 1983.
———. "Sound in France: The Origins of a Native School." *Yale French Studies*,
   no. 60 (1980): 94–114.
Armes, Roy. *French Cinema Since 1946*. 2 vols. Cranbury, N.J.: A. S. Barnes,
   1966, 1970.
———. *French Cinema*. New York: Oxford University Press, 1985.
L'Art Cinématographique, nos. 1–8. Paris: Alcan, 1927. Reprinted in French as
   The Literature of the Cinema. New York: Arno Press, 1970.
Artaud, Antonin. *Oeuvres complètes*, vol. 3 (Screenplays, writings about the
   cinema, letters, and interviews). Paris: Editions Gallimard, 1978.
———. *Selected Texts*. *TDR* 11:1 (Fall 1966): 166–85.
Astruc, Alexandre. "The Birth of a New Avant-Garde: *La Caméra-Stylo*." In
   The New Wave, edited by Peter Graham, pp. 17–23. Garden City, N.Y.:
   Doubleday, 1968.

Augst, Bertrand. "The Lure of Psychoanalysis in Film Theory." In *Apparatus*, edited by Theresa Cha, pp. 415–37. New York: Tanam Press, 1980.

———. "The Order of [Cinematographic] Discourse." *Discourse*, no. 1 (Fall 1979): 39–57.

Austin, L. J. *L'Univers poétique de Baudelaire*. Paris: Mercure de France, 1956.

Balakian, Anna. *The Symbolist Movement*. New York: Random House, 1967.

Bandy, Mary Lea, ed. *Rediscovering French Film*. New York: Museum of Modern Art, 1983.

Barsacq, Léon. *Caligari's Cabinet and Other Grand Illusions*. Edited and revised by Elliott Stein. Boston: New York Graphic Society, 1976.

Barthes, Roland. *Image/Music/Text*. Translated with an introduction by Stephen Heath. New York: Hill and Wang, 1978.

———. *Mythologies*. New York: Hill and Wang, 1972.

Baudelaire, Charles. *Les Fleurs du mal*. Paris: Editions Garnier Frères, 1961.

———. *Les Paradis artificiels*. Paris: Flammarion, 1966.

Baudry, Jean-Louis. "The Apparatus." *Camera Obscura*, no. 1 (Fall 1976): 97–126. Reprinted in *Apparatus*, edited by Theresa Hak Kyung Cha, pp. 40–62. New York: Tanam Press, 1980.

———. "Ideological Effects of the Basic Cinematographic Apparatus." *Film Quarterly* 28:2 (Winter 1974–75): 39–47. Reprinted in *Apparatus*, edited by Theresa Hak Kyung Cha, pp. 25–37. New York: Tanam Press, 1980.

Bazin, André. "La Politique des Auteurs." In *The New Wave*, edited by Peter Graham, pp. 137–55. Garden City, N.Y.: Doubleday, 1968.

———, et al. *La Politique des auteurs*. Paris: Champ Libre, 1972.

Bellour, Raymond. "Alternation, Segmentation, Hypnosis: Interview with Janet Bergstrom." *Camera Obscura*, nos. 3/4 (Summer 1979): 71–103.

———. *L'Analyse du film*. Paris: Editions Albatros, 1979.

———. "*The Birds*: Analysis of a Sequence." Translated from "*Les Oiseaux*: *Analyse d'une séquence*." *Cahiers du cinéma*, no. 219 (1969). Mimeograph available from the British Film Institute Educational Advisory Service.

———. "Hitchcock: The Enunciator." *Camera Obscura*, no 2. (Fall 1977): 66–91.

———. "The Obvious and the Code." *Screen* 15:4 (Winter 1974/5): 7–17.

———. "Psychosis, Neurosis, Perversion." *Camera Obscura*, nos. 3/4 (1979): 104–32.

———. "Segmenting, Analyzing." In *Genre: The Musical*, edited by Rick Altman, pp.102–33. London: Routledge and Kegan Paul, 1981.

———. "The Unattainable Text." *Screen* 16:3 (Autumn 1975): 19–27.

Bellour, Raymond, Thierry Kuntzel, and Christian Metz, eds. Special issue on "Psychanalyse et cinéma." *Communications*, no. 23 (1975).

Benoît-Lévy, Jean. *The Art of the Motion Picture*. New York: Coward-McCann, 1946.

Benveniste, Emile. *Problèmes de linguistique générale*. Paris: Editions du Seuil, 1974.

Bergstrom, Janet. "The Avant-Garde: Histories and Theories." *Screen* 19:3 (Autumn 1978): 119–27.

———. "Enunciation and Sexual Difference." *Camera Obscura*, nos. 3/4 (1979): 32–69.

———. "*Jeanne Dielman, 23 Quai du Commerce, 1080 Bruxelles* by Chantal Akerman." *Camera Obscura*, no. 2 (Fall 1977): 114–18.

Betancourt, Jeanne. *Women in Focus*. Dayton: Pflaum Publishing, 1974.

Borde, Raymond. "La France des années 30." *L'Avant-Scène du Cinéma*, no. 173 (October 1, 1976).

———. "The 'Golden Age': French Cinema of the 30s." In *Rediscovering French Film*, edited by Mary Lea Bandy, pp. 66–81. New York: Museum of Modern Art, 1983.

Bordwell, David. *French Impressionist Cinema: Film Culture, Film Theory, Film Style*. New York: Arno Press, 1980.

Bovenschen, Silvia. "Is There a Feminine Aesthetic?" *New German Critique*, no. 10 (Winter 1977): 111–37.

Brunius, Jacques B. *En Marge du cinéma français*. Paris: Editions Arcanes, Collection Ombres Blanches, 1954.

Burch, Noël. "Film's Institutional Mode of Representation and the Soviet Response." *October*, no. 11 (Winter 1979): 77–96.

Burch, Noël, and Jean-André Fieschi. "La Première vague." *Cahiers du cinéma*, no. 202 (June–July 1968): 20–24.

Les Cahiers de la cinémathèque de Toulouse 23–24 (Le Cinéma du sam'di soir). Perpignan: Cinémathèque de Toulouse, 1977.

Cahiers du cinéma, no. 54 (Christmas 1955). Special issue on American Cinema.

Cahiers du cinéma, no. 138 (December 1962). Special issue on the New Wave.

Cahiers du cinéma, no. 202 (June–July 1968). Special issue on the First Avant-Garde.

Canudo, Ricciotto. *L'Usine aux images*. Geneva: Office Centrale d'Edition, 1927.

Caughie, John, ed. *Theories of Authorship*. London: Routledge and Kegan Paul, 1981.

Cha, Theresa Hak Kyung, ed. *Apparatus* (Cinematographic Apparatus: Selected Writings). New York: Tanam Press, 1980.

Chevalley, Freddy. "Ciné-Club de Génève." *Close-Up* 6:5 (May 1930): 407–11.

Chirat, Raymond. *Catalogue des films français de long métrage: Films sonores de fiction 1929–1939*. Brussels: Cinémathèque Royale de Belgique, 1975.

Christie, Ian. "French Avant-Garde Film in the 20s: From 'Specificity' to Surrealism." In *Film as Film: Formal Experiment in Film 1910–1975*, pp. 37–45. London: Arts Council of Great Britain, 1979.

Cinémathèque de Toulouse. *Deuxième cinécure: Les Français et leur cinéma 1930–39*. Toulouse: Maison de la Culture de Créteil, 1973.

Clouzot, Claire. *Le Cinéma français depuis la nouvelle vague*. Paris: Fernand Nathan-Alliance Française, 1972.

Cook, Pam, and Claire Johnston. "The Place of Women in the Cinema of Raoul Walsh." In *Raoul Walsh*, edited by Phil Hardy, pp. 93–109. London: Edinborough Film Festival, 1974. In *Movies and Methods*, vol. 2, edited by Bill Nichols, pp. 379–87. Berkeley: University of California Press, 1985.

Copjec, Joan. "The Delirium of Clinical Perfection." *Oxford Literary Review* 8:1–2 (1986): 57–65.

———. "Flavit et Dissipati Sunt." *October*, no. 18 (Fall 1981): 21–40.

———. "*Thriller*: An Intrigue of Identification." *Ciné-tracts*, no. 11 (Fall 1980): 33–38.

Cornwell, Regina. "Maya Deren and Germaine Dulac: Activists of the Avant-Garde." *Film Library Quarterly* 5:1 (Winter 1971–2): 29–38.

Cowie, Elizabeth. "Fantasia." *m/f*, no. 9 (1984): 71–105.

———. "Strategems of Identification." *Oxford Literary Review* 8:1–2 (1986): 66–78.

———. "Woman as Sign." *m/f*, no. 1 (1978): 49–63.

———. "Women, Representation, and the Image." *Screen Education*, no. 23 (Summer 1977): 15–23.

Crain, Mary Beth. "Agnès Varda: The Mother of the New Wave." *L.A. Weekly*, August 1–7, 1986, p. 33.

DeLauretis, Teresa. *Alice Doesn't: Feminism, Semiotics, Cinema*. Bloomington: Indiana University Press, 1984.

———. "Oedipus Interruptus." *Wide Angle* 7:1–2 (1985): 34–40.

DeLauretis, Teresa, and Stephen Heath. *The Cinematic Apparatus*. London: Macmillan, 1980.

Delluc, Louis, *Drames du cinéma*. Paris: Aux Editions du Monde nouveau, 1923.

DeMiro, Ester Carla. "Personale di Germaine Dulac." *Giornate Internazionali di Cinema d'Artista*. [Florence] (December 1979).

Diacritics 5:4 (Winter 1975). Special issue on "Textual Politics: Feminist Criticism."

Dinnerstein, Dorothy. *The Mermaid and the Minotaur: Sexual Arrangements and Human Malaise*. New York: Harper and Row, 1976.

Doane, Mary Ann. "*Caught* and *Rebecca*: The Inscription of Femininity as Absence." *enclitic* 5–6:2–1 (Fall 1981/Spring 1982): 75–89.

———. *The Desire to Desire*. Bloomington: Indiana University Press, 1987.

———. "Film and the Masquerade: Theorising the Female Spectator." *Screen* 23:3–4 (September–October 1982): 74–88.

———. "Misrecognition and Identity." *Ciné-tracts*, no. 11 (Fall 1980): 25–32.

———. "The 'Woman's Film': Possession and Address." In *Re-Vision: Essays in Feminist Film Criticism*, edited by Mary Ann Doane, Patricia Mellencamp, and Linda Williams, pp. 67–82. Frederick, Md.: University Publications of America and the American Film Institute, 1984.

———. "Woman's Stake: Filming the Female Body." *October*, no. 17 (Summer 1981): 23–36.

Doane, Mary Ann, Patricia Mellencamp, and Linda Williams, eds. *Re-Vision: Essays in Feminist Film Criticism*. Frederick, Md.: University Publications of America and the American Film Institute, 1984.

Dozoretz, Wendy. "Dulac versus Artaud." *Wide Angle* 3:1 (1979): 46–53.

Dréville, Jean. "*Six et demi-onze*." *Cinégraphie*, nos. 1 (September 15, 1927); 2 (October, 15, 1927); 3 (November 15, 1927).

Dulac, Germaine. "L'art des nuances spirituelles." *Cinéa-Ciné-pour-tous*, no. 28

(January 1, 1925): 18. Reprinted in *L'Art du cinéma*, edited by Pierre Lherminier, pp. 559–60. Paris: Editions Seghers, 1960.

———. "Ayons la foi." *Le Film*, October 15, 1919, p. 46.

———. "Chez D. W. Griffith." *Cinéa*, no. 7 (June 17, 1921): 11–12.

———. "Le Cinéma d'avant-garde." In *Le Cinéma des origines à nos jours*, edited by Henri Fescourt, pp. 357–64. Paris: Editions du Cygne, 1932. Translated by Robert Lamberton in *The Avant-Garde Film: A Reader of Theory and Criticism*, edited by P. Adams Sitney, pp. 43–48. New York: New York University Press, 1978.

———. "Conférence de Mme Germaine Dulac." *Cinémagazine*, no. 51 (December 19, 1924): 516–18.

———. "Du Sentiment à la ligne." In *Schémas*, edited by Germaine Dulac, pp. 26–31. Paris: Imprimateur Gutenberg, 1927. Translated by Felicity Sparrow and Claudine Nicolson in *Film as Film: Formal Experiment in Film 1910–1975*, pp. 128–29. London: Arts Council of Great Britain, 1979.

———. "L'Essence du cinéma: L'Idée visuelle." *Les Cahiers du mois*, nos. 16–17 (1925): 57–66. Translated by Robert Lamberton in *The Avant-Garde Film: A Reader of Theory and Criticism*, edited by P. Adams Sitney, pp. 36–42. New York: New York University Press, 1978.

———. "Les Esthétiques. Les Entraves: La Cinégraphie intégrale." *L'Art cinématographique.* Vol. 2, pp. 27–50. Paris: Alcan, 1927. Translated by Stuart Liebman as "The Aesthetics, the Obstacles: Integral Cinegraphie." *Framework*, no. 19 (1982): 6–9.

———. "Les Films visuels et anti-visuels." *Le Rouge et le noir* (July 1928): 31–41. Translated by Robert Lamberton in *The Avant-Garde Film: A Reader of Theory and Criticism*, edited by P. Adams Sitney, pp. 31–35. New York: New York University Press, 1978.

———. *Germaine Dulac présente: Schémas.* Paris: Imprimateur Gutenberg, 1927.

———. "Jouer avec les bruits." *Cinéa-Ciné-pour-tous*, August 15, 1929.

———. "Mme Germaine Dulac nous parle du *Diable dans la ville*." *Cinémagazine*, no. 19 (May 9, 1924): 245–47.

———. "Mise en scène." *Le Film*, no. 87 (November 12, 1917): 7–9.

———. "*La mort du soleil* et la naissance du film." *Cinéa-Ciné-pour-tous*, no. 41 (February 17, 1922): 14–15.

———. "La Musique du silence." *Cinégraphie*, no. 5 (January 15, 1928): 77–78.

———. "Les Procédés expressifs du cinématographe." *Cinémagazine*, no. 27 (July 4, 1924): 15–18; no. 28, (July 11, 1924): 66–68; no. 29 (July 18, 1924): 89–92.

———. "*La Souriante Mme Beudet*." *Cinémagazine*, no. 6 (February 9, 1923): 239–41.

———. Unpublished manuscript. Texts collected and edited by Marie-Anne Colson-Malleville.

Durgnat, Raymond. *Nouvelle Vague: The First Decade*. Loughton, Essex: Motion Publications, 1963.

Eisenschitz, Bernard. "Histoires de l'histoire: Deux périodes du cinéma français; le muet, la génération de 58." In *Défense du cinéma français*, January 8–March 16, pp. 18–33. Paris: La Maison de la Culture de la Seine-St-Dénis, 1975.

Epardeaud, Edmond. "*L'Affiche* de Jean Epstein." *Cinéa-Ciné-pour-tous*, no. 34 (April 1, 1925): 27–28.

Epstein, Jean. *Ecrits sur le cinéma*, 2 vols. Paris: Editions Seghers, 1974, 1975.

Erens, Patricia, ed. *Sexual Strategems: The World of Women in Film*. New York: Horizon Press, 1979.

Etudes Cinématographiques, nos. 38–39, 40–42 (1965). Special issue on "Surréalisme et cinéma."

Fenichel, Otto. *The Psychoanalytic Theory of Neurosis*. New York: W. W. Norton, 1945.

Fescourt, Henri, ed. *Le Cinéma des origines à nos jours*. Paris: Editions du Cygne, 1932.

———. *La Foi et les montagnes (ou le septième art au passé)*. Paris: Paul Montel, 1959.

Fieschi, Jean-André. "Jean Epstein." In *Cinema: A Critical Dictionary*, edited by Richard Roud, pp. 328–34. London: Secker and Warburg, 1980.

Film as Film: Formal Experiment in Film 1910–1975. London: Arts Council of Great Britain, 1979.

Flitterman, Sandy. "Heart of the Avant-Garde: Some Biographical Notes on Germaine Dulac." *Women and Film*, nos. 5–6 (1974): 58–61.

———. "Montage/Discourse: Germaine Dulac's *The Smiling Mme Beudet*." *Wide Angle* 4:3 (1980): 54–59.

———. "That 'Once Upon a Time' of Childish Dreams. . ." *Ciné-tracts*, no. 13 (Spring 1981): 14–26.

———. "Woman, Desire, and The Look: Feminism and the Enunciative Apparatus in the Cinema." In *Theories of Authorship*, edited by John Caughie, pp. 242–50. London: Routledge and Kegan Paul, 1981.

———. "Women, Representation and Cinematic Discourse: The Example of the French Cinema," Ph.D. dissertation, University of California at Berkeley, 1982.

Flitterman-Lewis, Sandy. "The Image and the Spark: Dulac and Artaud Reviewed." In *Dada and Surrealist Film*, edited by Rudolf E. Kuenzli, pp. 110–27. New York: Willis Locker and Owens, 1987.

———. "'Poetry of the Unconscious': Circuits of Desire in Two Films by Germaine Dulac." In *French Cinema: Texts and Contexts*, edited by Susan Hayward and Ginette Vincendeau, pp. 00. London: Methuen, 1989.

———. "Psychoanalysis, Film, and Television." In *Channels of Discourse: Television and Contemporary Criticism*, edited by Robert C. Allen, pp. 172–210. Chapel Hill: University of North Carolina Press, 1987.

———. "To See and Not to Be: Female Subjectivity and the Law in Alfred Hitchcock's *Notorious*." *Literature and Psychology* 33:3–4 (1987): 1–17.

Flitterman-Lewis, Sandy and Judith Barry. "Textual Strategies: The Politics of Art-Making." *Visibly Female: Feminism and Art Today*, edited by Hilary Robinson, pp. 106–17. London: Camden Press, 1987.

Fofi, Geoffredo. "The Cinema of the Popular Front in France (1934–1938)." *Screen* 13:4 (Winter 1972–73): 5–57.

Ford, Charles. *Femmes cinéastes*. Paris: Denoël, 1972.

———. *Germaine Dulac. Anthologie du Cinéma*, no. 31 (January 1968): 1–48.

Foucault, Michel. "What Is an Author?" In *Language, Counter-Memory, Practice*, translated by Donald F. Bouchard and Sherry Simon. Ithaca: Cornell University Press, 1977.

Francis, Eve. *Temps héroïques*. Paris: Denoël, 1949.

Freud, Sigmund. *General Psychological Theory*. New York: Collier Books, 1963.

———. *The Interpretation of Dreams*. New York: Avon Books, 1965.

———. *Three Case Histories*. New York: Collier Books, 1963.

———. *Three Essays on the Theory of Sexuality*. New York: Avon Books, 1962.

Gledhill, Christine. "Developments in Feminist Film Criticism." In *Re-Vision: Essays in Feminist Film Criticism*, edited by Mary Anne Doane, Patricia Mellencamp, and Linda Williams, pp. 18–48. Frederick, Md.: University Publications of America and the American Film Institute, 1984, pp. 18–48.

Godard, Jean-Luc. *Godard on Godard*. Edited by Jean Narboni and Tom Milne. New York: Viking Press, 1972.

Gorbman, Claudia. "*Cleo from Five to Seven*: Music as Mirror." *Wide Angle* 4:4 (1981): 38–49.

Goudal, Jean. "Surréalisme et cinéma." *La Revue hébdomadaire* (February 1925): 343–57.

Graham, Peter, ed. *The New Wave*. London: Secker and Warburg (Cinema One), 1968.

Greene, Naomi. "Artaud and Film: A Reconsideration." *Cinema Journal* 23:4 (Summer 1984): 28–40.

Hammond, Paul, ed. *The Shadow and Its Shadow: Surrealist Writings on Cinema*. London: British Film Institute, 1978.

Hansen, Miriam. "Pleasure, Ambivalence, Identification: Valentino and Female Spectatorship." *Cinema Journal* 25:4 (Summer 1986): 6–32.

Harkness, John. "Agnès Varda: Improvised Inspiration." *Now*, June 19–25, 1986.

Harvey, Stephen. "Agnès Varda in Her Own Good Time." *The Village Voice*, May 20, 1986, p. 64.

Haskell, Molly. *From Reverence to Rape: The Treatment of Women in the Movies*. New York: Penguin, 1974.

Hayes, Carlton J. H. *France: A Nation of Patriots*. New York: Columbia University Press, 1930.

Heath, Stephen. "Difference." *Screen* 19:3 (Autumn 1978): 50–127

———. *Questions of Cinema*. London: Macmillan, 1980.

Hedges, Inez. *Language of Revolt: Dada and Surrealist Film and Literature*. Durham, N.C.: Duke University Press, 1983.

Higashi, Sumiko. *Virgins, Vamps and Flappers: The American Silent Movie Heroine.* Montreal: Eden Press, 1978.

Hillier, Jim, ed. *Cahiers du Cinéma: The 1950s, the 1960s.* 2 vols. Cambridge: Harvard University Press, 1985.

Insdorf, Annette. "Filmmaker Agnès Varda: Stimulating Discomfort." *International Herald Tribune,* June 11, 1986, p. 11.

Irigaray, Luce. *Speculum of the Other Woman.* Translated by Gillian C. Gill. Ithaca: Cornell University Press, 1985.

———. *This Sex Which Is Not One.* Translated by Catherine Porter. Ithaca: Cornell University Press, 1985.

Jeanne, René, and Charles Ford. *Histoire encyclopédique du cinéma.* Paris: R. Laffont, 1947–68.

Johnston, Claire. "Femininity and the Masquerade: *Anne of the Indies.*" In *Jacques Tourneur,* edited by Claire Johnston and Paul Willemen, pp. 36–44. London: Edinborough Film Festival, 1975.

———. "The Subject of Feminist Film Theory/Practice." *Screen* 21:2 (Summer 1980): 27–34.

———. "Toward a Feminist Film Practice: Some Theses." *Edinborough 76 Magazine* (August 1976): 50–59. In *Movies and Methods,* vol. 2, edited by Bill Nichols, pp. 315–27. Berkeley: University of California Press, 1985.

———. "Women's Cinema as Counter-Cinema." In *Notes on Women's Cinema,* edited by Claire Johnston, pp. 24–31. London: Society for Education in Film and Television, n.d. In *Movies and Methods,* vol. 1, edited by Bill Nichols. Berkeley: University of California Press, 1976.

Kaplan, E. Ann. "The Case of the Missing Mother: Maternal Issues in Vidor's *Stella Dallas.*" *Heresies,* no. 16 (1983): 81–85.

———. *Women and Film: Both Sides of the Camera.* New York: Methuen, 1983.

———. ed. *Women in Film Noir.* London: British Film Institute, 1978.

Kay, Karyn, and Gerald Peary, eds. *Women and the Cinema: A Critical Anthology.* New York: E. P. Dutton, 1977.

Kovacs, Steven. *From Enchantment to Rage: The Story of Surrealist Cinema.* Cranbury, N.J.: Associated University Presses, 1980.

Kuhn, Annette. "Women's Genres: Melodrama, Soap Opera, and Theory." *Screen* 25:1 (January–February 1984): 18–28.

———. *Women's Pictures: Feminism and Cinema.* London: Routledge and Kegan Paul, 1982.

Kuntzel, Thierry. "The Film-Work, 2." *Camera Obscura,* no. 5 (1980): 6–69.

———. "Sight, Insight, and Power: Allegory of a Cave." *Camera Obscura,* no. 6 (1980): 90–110.

Kyrou, Ado. *Le Surréalisme au cinéma.* Paris: Editions Arcanes, 1953.

Langlois, Henri. "L'Avant-garde française." *Cahiers du cinéma,* no. 202 (June–July 1968): 8–18.

Lapierre, Marcel, ed. *Anthologie du cinéma.* Paris: La Nouvelle Edition, 1946.

———. *Les Cents visages du cinéma.* Paris: Editions Bernard Grasset, 1948.

Laplanche, J., and J.B. Pontalis, "Fantasy and the Origins of Sexuality." *International Journal of Psychoanalysis* 49 (1968): 1–18.

————. *The Language of Psychoanalysis.* New York: W. W. Norton, 1973.

Leprohon, Pierre. *Histoire du cinéma.* Paris: Editions du Cerf, 1961.

————. *Jean Epstein.* Paris: Editions Seghers, 1964.

L'Herbier, Marcel. "Autour du cinématographe: Entretien avec Marcel L'Herbier par Jean-André Fieschi," *Les Cahiers du cinéma,* no. 202 (June–July 1968): 26–42.

————. *L'Intelligence du cinématographe.* Paris: Editions Correa, 1946.

Lherminier, Pierre, ed. *L'Art du cinéma.* Paris: Editions Seghers, 1960.

Lyon, Elisabeth. "The Cinema of Lol V. Stein." *Camera Obscura,* no. 6 (1980): 7–41.

MacCabe, Colin. *Godard: Images, Sounds, Politics.* Bloomington: Indiana University Press, 1980.

Mannoni, Octave. *Clefs pour l'Imaginaire ou l'Autre Scène.* Paris: Editions du Seuil, 1969.

Marie, Michel. "Les années trente." In *Défense du cinéma français,* January 8–March 16, pp. 34–44. Paris: La Maison de la Culture de la Seine-St-Denis, 1975.

————. "The Art of the Film in France Since the 'New Wave.' " Translated by Robert Ariew. *Wide Angle* 4:4 (1981): 18–25.

Mayne, Judith. "The Woman at the Keyhole: Women's Cinema and Feminist Criticism." In *Re-Vision: Essays in Feminist Film Criticism,* edited by Mary Ann Doane, Patricia Mellencamp, and Linda Williams, pp. 49–66. Frederick, Md.: University Publications of America and the American Film Institute, 1984.

Metz, Christian. "The Cinematic Apparatus as Social Institution: An Interview with Christian Metz." *Discourse,* no. 1 (Fall 1979): 6–37.

————. *Film Language: A Semiotics of the Cinema.* Translated by Michael Taylor. New York: Oxford University Press, 1974.

————. "History/Discourse: Note on Two Voyeurisms." Translated by Susan Bennett. *Edinburgh 76 Magazine,* no. 1 (1976): 21–25.

————. "The Imaginary Signifier." *Screen* 16:2 (Summer 1975): 14–76.

————. *The Imaginary Signifier: Psychoanalysis and the Cinema.* Translated by Celia Britton et al. Bloomington: Indiana University Press, 1977.

Mitchell, Juliet. *Psychoanalysis and Feminism.* New York: Vintage, 1975.

Mitchell, Juliet and Jacqueline Rose, eds. *Feminine Sexuality: Jacques Lacan and the Ecole Freudienne.* New York: W. W. Norton, 1982.

Mitry, Jean. *Le Cinéma expérimental: Histoire et perspectives.* Paris: Editions Seghers, 1974.

————. *Esthétique et psychologie du cinéma.* 2 vols. Paris: Editions Universitaires, 1963, 1965.

————. *Histoire du cinéma: Art et industrie.* 3 vols. Paris: Editions Universitaires, 1967–73.

Monaco, James. *The New Wave*. New York: Oxford University Press, 1976.

Montrelay, Michèle. *L'Ombre et le nom: Sur la fémininité*. Paris: Editions de Minuit, 1977.

Moussinac, Léon. *L'Age ingrât du cinéma*. Paris: Les Editeurs Français Réunis, 1967.

———. *Panoramique du cinéma*. Paris: Au Sans Pareil, 1929.

Mulvey, Laura. "Afterthoughts on 'Visual Pleasure and Narrative Cinema' Inspired by *Duel in the Sun*." *Framework*, nos. 15, 16, 17 (Summer 1981): 12–15.

———. "Changes." *Discourse*, no. 7 (1985): 11–30.

———. "Visual Pleasure and Narrative Cinema." *Screen* 16:3 (Autumn 1975): 6–18.

Neale, Steve. "Art Cinema as Institution." *Screen* 22:1 (1981): 11–39.

Nowell-Smith, Geoffrey. "A Note on 'History/Discourse.'" In *Theories of Authorship*, edited by John Caughie, pp. 232–41. London: Routledge and Kegan Paul, 1981.

Obliques 10–11 (1977). Special issue on Antonin Artaud.

"Pasolini-Varda-Allio-Sarris-Michelson." *Film Culture*, no. 42 (Fall 1966): 96–101.

Plaza, Monique. "'Phallomorphic' Power and the Psychology of 'Woman.'" *Feminist Issues* 1:1 (Summer 1980): 71–102.

Potamkin, Harry Alan. *The Compound Cinema*. New York: Teachers College Press, 1977.

Renoir, Jean. *My Life and My Films*. New York: Atheneum, 1974.

Rose, Jacqueline. *Sexuality in the Field of Vision*. London: Verso, 1986.

Rosen, Philip, ed. *Narrative, Apparatus, Ideology*. New York: Columbia University Press, 1986.

Rosenbaum, Jonathan. "Edinburgh Encounters: A Consumers/Producers Guide-in-Progress to Four Recent Avant-Garde Films." *Sight and Sound* 45:1 (Winter 1975–76): 18–23.

Roud, Richard. "Marker, Varda, Resnais: The Left Bank." *Sight and Sound* 32:1 (Winter 1962–63): 24–28.

Rubin, Gayle. "The Traffic in Women." In *Toward an Anthropology of Women*, edited by Rayna R. Reiter, pp. 157–210. New York: Monthly Review Press, 1975.

Sadoul, Georges. *Le Cinéma français: 1890–1962*. Paris: Flammarion, 1962.

———. *Dictionnaire des films*. Paris: Editions du Seuil, 1965.

———. *Histoire générale du cinéma*. In collaboration with Bernard Eisenschitz. 6 vols. Paris: Denoël, 1973–80.

———. "Souvenirs d'un témoin," *Etudes cinématographiques* 38/39 (1965): 9–28.

Schor, Naomi. "Female Paranoia: The Case For Psychoanalytic Feminist Criticism." *Yale French Studies*, no. 62 (1981): 204–19.

Shattuck, Roger. *The Banquet Years*. New York: Vintage, 1968.

Shivas, Mark. "*Cléo de 5 à 7* and Agnès Varda." *Movie*, no. 3 (October 1962): 33–35.

Siclier, Jacques. *Nouvelle vague?* Paris: Editions du Cerf, 1961.

Silverman, Kaja. *The Subject of Semiotics.* New York: Oxford University Press, 1983.

Sitney, P. Adams, ed. *The Avant-Garde Film: A Reader of Theory and Criticism.* New York: New York University Press, 1978.

Stam, Robert. *Reflexivity in Film and Literature from Don Quixote to Jean-Luc Godard.* Ann Arbor: UMI Press, 1985.

Steed, Judy. "Director Feels 'Close to Rebellious People.'" *The Globe and Mail,* June 10, 1986, p. D9.

Stern, Lesley. "Feminism and Cinema—Exchanges." *Screen* 20:3–4 (Winter 1979–80): 89–105.

Strauss, David. "The Rise of Anti-Americanism in France: French Intellectuals and the American Film Industry 1927–1932." *Journal of Popular Culture* 10:4 (Spring 1977): 752–59.

Truffaut, François. "Une certaine tendance du cinéma français." *Cahiers du cinéma,* no. 31 (January 1954): 15–28. In *Movies and Methods,* vol. 1, edited by Bill Nichols, pp. 224–37. Berkeley: University of California Press, 1976.

Varda, Agnès. "Agnès Varda de 5 à 7." *Cinématographe,* no. 114 (December 1985): 18–24.

———. *Cléo de 5 à 7* (scénario). Paris: Editions Gallimard, 1962.

———. "A Conversation With Barbara Quart." *Film Quarterly* 40:2 (Winter 1986–7): 3–10.

———. "Entretien avec Agnès Varda." *Cinébulles* 5:3 (1985): 4–10.

———. "Entretien avec Hubert Arnault." *Image et son: La Revue du cinéma,* no. 201 (January 1967): 40–48.

———. "Entretien avec Jean Narboni, Serge Toubiana, et Dominique Villain." *Cahiers du cinéma,* no. 276 (May 1977): 21–27.

———. "La grace laïque: Entretien avec Agnès Varda par Jean-André Fieschi et Claude Ollier." *Cahiers du cinéma,* no. 165 (April 1965): 43–51.

———. "Interview: A Personal Vision." *Passion* (June–July 1986): 20.

———. "*Lions Love*: Entretien avec André Cornand." *Image et Son: La Revue du cinéma,* no. 247 (February 1971): 96–102.

———. "Mona, nomade." *Cinéma 85,* no. 322 (December 4–10, 1985): 2–3, 11.

———. "Mother of the New Wave: An Interview with Agnès Varda by Jacqueline Levitin." *Women and Film,* nos. 5–6 (1974): 62–66.

———. "Press Book for *Vagabond*." New York: International Film Exchange, 1985.

———. "Propos sur le cinéma récueillis par Mireille Amiel." *Cinéma 75,* no. 204 (December 1975): 38–55.

———. "*Sans toit ni loi*: Publicité." Paris: Ciné-Tamaris, 1985.

———. "Entretien avec Françoise Wera." *Cinébulles* 5:3 (1985): 4–10.

———. "Un Jour sous le ciel." *Cahiers du cinéma,* no. 378 (December 1985): 11–15.

———. "The Underground River: Interview with Gordon Gow." *Films and Filming* (March 1970): 6–13.

Vernet, Marc, ed. Special issue on Christian Metz. *Ça/Cinéma*, nos. 7/8 (May 1975).

Virmaux, Alain. "Artaud and Film." *Tulane Drama Review* 11:1 (Fall 1966): 154–165.

Virmaux, Alain, and Odette Virmaux. *Les Surréalistes et le cinéma.* Paris: Editions Seghers, 1976.

Williams, Linda. *Figures of Desire: A Theory and Analysis of Surrealist Film.* Urbana: University of Illinois Press, 1981.

———. "'Something Else Besides a Mother': *Stella Dallas* and the Maternal Melodrama." *Cinema Journal* 24:1 (Fall 1984): 2–27.

Wise, Naomi, "Surface Tensions: Agnès Varda." *Berkeley Monthly* (June 1986): 16–17.

Woolf, Virginia. *The Common Reader* (1925). New York: Harcourt, Brace, Jovanovich, 1953.

Index

A Note on the Author

After receiving her Ph.D. in comparative literature from the University of California at Berkeley, Sandy Flitterman-Lewis taught at Brown University as a visiting assistant professor in the Semiotics Program. She is currently an associate professor in the English department and the Interdisciplinary Program in Cinema Studies at Rutgers University in New Brunswick, New Jersey. One of the four founding editors of *Camera Obscura: A Journal of Feminism and Film Theory* and active in its publication until 1978, she has published numerous articles on feminism, film theory, and television in such journals as *Screen, Wide Angle, Film Quarterly,* and *Literature and Psychology,* among others. Her work is anthologized in eight collections, including *Theories of Authorship, Feminist Art Criticism,* and *Channels of Discourse: Television and Contemporary Criticism.*